YO-ALH-586

CHICAGO PUBLIC LIBRARY
HAROLD WASHINGTON LIBRARY CENTER

R0033026158

REF LB   Krajewski, Robert
     2822.5   J.
     .K7
     1983   The elementary
               school
               principalship

DATE			

TION & PHILOSOPHY   FORM 125 M

The Chicago Public Library

Received   NOV 7 1983

© THE BAKER & TAYLOR CO.

THE ELEMENTARY SCHOOL PRINCIPALSHIP

LEADERSHIP FOR THE 1980s

ROBERT J. KRAJEWSKI
University of Northern Iowa

JOHN S. MARTIN
Auburn University

JOHN C. WALDEN
Auburn University

HOLT, RINEHART AND WINSTON

New York   Chicago   San Francisco   Philadelphia
Montreal   Toronto   London   Sydney
Tokyo   Mexico City   Rio de Janeiro   Madrid

Library of Congress Cataloging in Publication Data
Krajewski, Robert J.
   The elementary school principalship.

   Bibliography: p.
   Includes index.
   1. Elementary school administration—United States.
   2. Elementary school principals—United States.
   I. Martin, John S. (John Stokes), date.
   II. Walden, John C.   III. Title.
   LB2822.5.K7   1983   372.12′012′0973   82–18716
   ISBN 0-03-056746-7

Copyright © 1983 by CBS College Publishing
Address correspondence to:
383 Madison Avenue
New York, NY 10017
All rights reserved

Printed in the United States of America

Published simultaneously in Canada

3 4 5 6   038   9 8 7 6 5 4 3 2 1

CBS COLLEGE PUBLISHING

Holt, Rinehart and Winston
The Dryden Press
Saunders College Publishing

INTRODUCTION

Elementary principals are key factors in successful schools, and the degree to which they meet the challenges of the 1980s will determine the degree to which elementary schools can be effective. Rarely are there simple solutions to the many complex problems and demands inherent in the elementary principal's role. At times, the demands may seem overwhelming, the solutions difficult or impossible; and the methods that produce success in one situation may result in additional problems or perhaps even disaster in yet other situations.

To write a handbook for elementary principals in this period of change is as challenging as it is important. Statistics from the National Association of Elementary School Principals' (NAESP) study of the principalship (1978) show that almost half of today's elementary principals are under the age of 45, 13 percent are under the age of 35, less than 34 percent are over 50 years of age, and less than 5 percent are above the age of 60. About two-thirds of today's elementary principals are therefore less than 55 years of age, and further, since about half of them were not principals ten years ago, there is a desperate need for continued retraining to meet the demands of today's schools.

This book is designed to serve as a reference for principals to use in improving competence while functioning in their jobs.

The NAESP study cited above also suggests that a practical book designed for elementary principals is needed for use in preservice as well as inservice training. When asked what the main sources of their ideas for recent innovations were, principals listed in order of preference: (1) other principals and teachers, (2) professional readings, (3) local workshops, (4) outside consultants, and (5) college courses. When asked what preparation and experience they valued, both education and inservice programs ranked at the bottom of their lists. This book is also an attempt on our part to fill the apparent void in preparation and inservice that now exists.

Instructional improvement, curriculum design, student personnel administration, collective bargaining, community relations, and meeting legal problems are but a few of the elementary principal's responsibilities and challenges. Solving problems in these and other areas requires both knowledge of principles and knowledge of how to work with people, because essentially most of these problems are people problems. In solving problems, trial and error is an inappropriate strategy; rather principals must attempt to choose the best course of action from among a number of options.

Certainly no sourcebook can contain an instant readout of all principles and options for principals. But a reference that speaks to both background and method is desirable. This book is intended to serve a dual purpose. First, it is designed to provide elementary school principals with an understanding of effective professional practices. Second, it will afford elementary principals some practical methods for using existing resources within the context of an everchanging, complex job assignment. The book, therefore, also will be of value in graduate courses and inservice programs, providing informative background material for working in and improving the role of the principal.

The book is organized around basic functions of the principalship. Specific guidelines and suggestions for performing each of the tasks within the functions will be provided. Although the theoretical and research bases for the guidelines and suggestions will be noted (in order that the reader can probe the area at a deeper level), the emphasis will be primarily on practicality to help principals better serve in their role.

RJK
JSM
JCW

CONTENTS

INTRODUCTION iii

1 GETTING THE PRINCIPALSHIP IN PERSPECTIVE 1

COPING WITH CHANGING DEMANDS 1
Introduction 1
Background 2
    Suggestions for Coping 4

ASSUMING UNDREAMED-OF ROLES 6
Choosing Undreamed-of Roles 8
Job Descriptions 10
    Sample Job Description—Elementary Principal 10

COMBINING LEADERSHIP AND MANAGEMENT 13
Management 13
Administration 16
Leadership 17
Leadership Questions 18
Management and Leadership 19

THE PRINCIPAL AS THE KEY TO QUALITY 22
Things to Consider 23

THE FUTURE 25

2 MANAGING THE MANAGER 27

INTRODUCTION 28
MANAGING SELF 29
Know Yourself 29
Exercise 30
Accept Yourself 33
The Ulcer-Producer List 34
Know and Accept Others 37
Improve Yourself 37
    Example 1 37 / *Example 2* 37 / *Example 3* 37
    / *Example 4* 38

ESTABLISHING PRIORITIES 38
Priority Dimensions 39
For Whom Are Priorities Determined? 40
Creating a Positive Mindset for Establishing Priorities 41

MANAGING TIME 44
Planning 44

Organizing and Budgeting Time   45
Making the Most of Available Resources   49
Delegating Responsibilities   51

DECISION MAKING   51
IDENTIFYING INNOVATIONAL CONSTRAINTS:
A Model for School Principals   52

SELECTING AREAS FOR PROFESSIONAL DEVELOPMENT   57
CASE STUDY—THE BUSY PRINCIPAL   60

3   ORGANIZING THE SCHOOL   62

SELECTING THE TEAM   62
INTERVIEWING APPLICANTS   63
CLARIFYING ROLES   64
ORGANIZING FOR INSTRUCTION   68
MOTIVATING THE TEAM   70

4   IMPROVING INSTRUCTION   74

DEVELOPING AN EFFECTIVE PROFESSIONAL STAFF   75
Assessing Needs   76
Determining Objectives and Identifying Activities   76
Implementing the Program   76
Evaluating   77

ASSESSING INSTRUCTIONAL NEEDS   77
Rationale for Improving Instruction   77
Is the Principal an Instructional Leader?   78
Understanding Teachers and Helping Them to Understand Themselves   79

COUNSELING WITH TEACHERS   80
Proactive Practices   82
    1. Know Your Teachers   82 /   2. Praise Your Teachers   82 /
    3. Like Your Teachers   82 /   4. Get Your Teachers Involved in
    Decision-Making Activities   83 /   5. Support Your Teachers   83 /
    6. Let Your Teachers Know You Care in Every Way in Your Daily
    Actions   83 /   7. Be the Leader   83
Reactive Practices   83
    1. Listen   83 /   2. Respect Confidences   84 /   3. Advise When
    Necessary Only   84 /   4. Be Judicious   84 /   5. Discipline   84

OBSERVING IN THE CLASSROOM   85
The Teacher Self-Improvement Model   85
    Using Objective Analysis   87 /   Explaining FIAC   87 /   Video
    Taping   92 /   Combining FIAC Analysis with Video Taping   94
Self/Peer/Supervisor Ratings   95

THE CLINICAL SUPERVISION MODEL   97
Rapport   97
Preobservation Conference   99
Observation   99

Analysis and Strategy   99
Conference   99
Process Critique   100

PUTTING IT IN PERSPECTIVE   100
THE FUTURE   100

5   IMPROVING THE CURRICULUM   102

INTRODUCTION   102
ASSESSING THE NEED FOR CURRICULUM IMPROVEMENT   103
DEFINING THE TERMS   105
INFLUENCING GOALS   108
IMPROVING SUBJECT MATTER CONTENT   110
PROVIDING INSTRUCTIONAL MATERIALS   112
UTILIZING INSTRUCTIONAL TIME   113
UTILIZING HUMAN RESOURCES   113
IMPROVING TEACHING METHODS AND ACTIVITES   114
EVALUATING CURRICULUM IMPROVEMENT   114
LOOKING AHEAD   117

6   COUNSELING AND GUIDING STUDENTS   119

INTRODUCTION   119
ESTABLISHING TRUST   120
Hints for Building a Trust Relationship with Students   121
   1. Be Trustworthy   121 / *2. Listen*   121 / *3. Be Accepting*   121 / *4. Be Positive*   121 / *5. Be Fair*   121 / *6. Be Understanding*   122

COUNSELING THROUGH TEACHERS   122
Proactive Practices   123
   Establish Criteria for Assigning Students to Advisors   124 / *Effect School Schedule for Teacher–Advisor Program*   125
Reactive Practices   127

DEVELOPING A GUIDANCE PROGRAM   127
Establishing Purposes   130
Planning   131
   Planning Involves Changing   132 / *Planning Involves Communication*   134 / *Planning Involves Delineating Role Functions*   134 / *Planning Involves Decision-Making*   134 / *Planning Involves Selling of Ideas*   134
Implementing   135
Evaluating   136

INFORMING PUPILS AND PARENTS   137
LEARNING THROUGH STUDENT GOVERNMENT   138
THE FUTURE   138
CASE STUDY—HOBSON'S CHOICE   139

7 MEETING STUDENTS' SPECIAL NEEDS   141

INTRODUCTION   141
PROTECTING STUDENTS' PRIVACY   142
ELIMINATING RACISM AND SEXISM   144
ASSISTING THE HANDICAPPED   146
PROVIDING FOR THE BILINGUAL   151
FUTURE TRENDS   154
CASE STUDY—SHOULD JOEY PLAY?   155

8 REPORTING TO PARENTS   156

EVALUATING STUDENTS' PROGRESS   156
GRADING STUDENTS   158
WRITING REPORT CARDS   159
REPORTING BY CONFERENCE   162
Planning for the Conference   163
Implementing the Conference   163
Scheduling the Conference   164

CASE STUDY—PETER'S PARENTS   165

9 COMPLYING WITH THE LAW   167

IDENTIFYING THE SCHOOL'S AUTHORITY   169
PROTECTING CONSTITUTIONAL RIGHTS   170
ENFORCING ATTENDANCE   172
CLARIFYING LIABILITY OF SCHOOL PERSONNEL   173
Liability for Violation of Civil Rights   174
Liability for Pupil Injury   174
Liability for Defamation of Character   177

PADDLING PUPILS   177
PROTECTING AIDES AND INTERNS   178
SEARCHING YOUNGSTERS   179
SUSPENDING AND EXPELLING   180
CONTROLLING DEMONSTRATIONS   181
CENSORING   182
DRESSING APPROPRIATELY   182
PROVIDING PUPIL ACTIVITIES   183
TAKING FIELD TRIPS   183
STOPPING DRUG ABUSE   184
ADMINISTERING FIRST AID   185
REPORTING CHILD ABUSE   186
DEALING WITH BOMB THREATS   187
SUPPORTING YOUR LOCAL POLICE   188
DEALING WITH UNWANTED VISITORS   189
LOOKING TO THE FUTURE   189
CASE STUDY—THE ABSENT ASSISTANT PRINCIPAL   189
CASE STUDY—SURPRISE PACKAGE   191

10 GOVERNING STUDENTS   192

INTRODUCTION   192
UNDERSTANDING THE CHILD   193
REDEFINING THE FAMILY   194
INVOLVING PARENTS   196
DEVELOPING DISCIPLINE   198
PURSUING SELF-GOVERNANCE   201
FUTURE DIRECTIONS   202
CASE STUDY—LATE AGAIN   203

11 EVALUATING TEACHERS   205

INTRODUCTION   206
SPELLING OUT ASSUMPTIONS   207
ESTABLISHING THE PURPOSE   207
ESTABLISHING EVALUATOR–EVALUATEE UNDERSTANDING   208
KEEPING EVALUATION POSITIVE   208
LOOKING AT THE WHOLE PICTURE   208
CONSIDERING EMOTIONAL REACTIONS   209
SELECTING THE PROCESS   209
ESTABLISHING PRIORITIES   211
OBSERVING INSTRUCTION   211
CONCENTRATING ON JOB TARGETS   212
PROVIDING A DATA BASE   213
CONFERRING WITH THE TEACHER   213
MAKING THOSE TOUGH DECISIONS   213
EVALUATION FORMS   214
THE AUBURN (ALA.) PERSONNEL PERFORMANCE APPRAISAL SYSTEM   219
System Characteristics   219
Implementation   220
Time Schedule   221

12 PROVIDING FOR PERFORMANCE EVALUATION   230

INTRODUCTION   230
GUARDING AGAINST WRONG DECISIONS   231
DOCUMENTING FACTS   234
APPEALING PRINCIPALS' DECISIONS   235
PROVIDING DUE PROCESS   238
DEVELOPING A PERFORMANCE EVALUATION SYSTEM   239
LOOKING TO THE FUTURE   242
CASE STUDY—THE LETTER WRITER   243

13 DEVELOPING DESIRABLE COMMUNITY RELATIONS   244

INTRODUCTION   244
ESTABLISHING LINKS WITH THE COMMUNITY   245

UNDERSTANDING THE POWER STRUCTURE 248
WORKING WITH PRESSURE GROUPS 249
DEALING WITH THE NEWS MEDIA 250
DEVELOPING A COMMUNITY SCHOOL PROGRAM 252
ORGANIZING PARENTS 253
ORGANIZING A VOLUNTEER PROGRAM 255
KEYS TO DESIRABLE RELATIONSHIPS WITH THE COMMUNITY 256
THE FUTURE 258
CASE STUDY—A GRIM DELEGATION 259

14 MANAGING THE SCHOOL PLANT 261

ESTABLISHING A GOOD LEARNING ENVIRONMENT 261
DEVELOPING PRIDE IN THE SCHOOL 264
PLANNING THOROUGHLY AND CREATIVELY FOR CARE OF THE PLANT 265
PROTECTING THE CAPITAL INVESTMENT 267
PREVENTING VANDALISM 269
CONSERVING ENERGY 270
SHOWING THE SCHOOL OFF TO THE PUBLIC 271
LOOKING TO THE FUTURE 271

15 MANAGING THE MONEY 273

INTRODUCTION 273
IDENTIFYING AREAS OF ACCOUNTABILITY 274
ACCOUNTING FOR FUNDS 275
RAISING MONEY FOR THE SCHOOL 279
DEVELOPING A BUDGET 280
CUTTING COSTS WHILE MAINTAINING QUALITY 288
LEGALLY ADMINISTERING THE FUNDS 289
THE FUTURE 291

16 LIVING WITH A UNION 292

INTRODUCTION 292
A GROWING PHENOMENON 293
UNDERSTANDING THE TERRITORY 296
THE PRINCIPAL AS MANAGER 298
ADMINISTERING THE CONTRACT 299
COPING WITH A WALKOUT 301
FUTURE TRENDS 302
CASE STUDY—A SPECIAL REQUEST 303

INDEX 305

CHAPTER 1

GETTING THE PRINCIPALSHIP IN PERSPECTIVE

Coping with changing demands
Introduction
Background
Suggestions for coping

Assuming undreamed-of roles
Choosing undreamed-of roles
Job descriptions
Sample job description: elementary principal

Combining leadership and management
Management
Administration
Leadership
Leadership questions
Management and leadership

The principal as the key to quality
Things to consider

The future

This introductory chapter sets the tone for the text. In it we discuss the importance of elementary principals, examine their changing role, and suggest how principals can better use leadership and management skills in effecting their role.

COPING WITH CHANGING DEMANDS
INTRODUCTION

The elementary principalship has often been characterized as one of the most demanding, satisfying, and widely sought leadership positions in education.

Frequent and significant interaction with teachers, students, and parents provides elementary principals more professional and personal intrinsic rewards than possible at other levels of school administration. And yet, the responsibilities placed upon elementary principals are as demanding as those at other levels of administration. This characterization remains as true today in the 1980s as it was in preceding decades. Succinctly stated, the reasons are twofold: elementary principals (1) maintain a closer working relationship with teachers, students, and parents, and therefore (2) have more continuing impact with and on instructional programs, curricula, and all operational phases of the school program than does any other level of school administrators.

Since elementary principals are so closely associated with all areas of school operation, their responsibilities and demands are visible, comprehensive, and demanding. Dedicated principals accept these challenges and rise to meet the ever-increasing demands as society changes its needs and goals. Demanding as the role may be or become, elementary principals of the 1980s have a job to do, a job that is perhaps even more important than ever and one that involves the future development of young minds who will lead our nation into the twenty-first century.

BACKGROUND

Since 1928, the National Association of Elementary School Principals (NAESP) has conducted, once every ten years, a survey of the elementary school principalship. Collectively these studies reflect both the changing role and role concerns of elementary principals as influenced and determined by the changing role of the school and the changing demands of society.

In the foreword to the association's most recent study, Nellie Quander, NAESP president (1978), notes that the problems that elementary principals face are in sharp contrast to those confronted by principals just a decade ago. In the 1960s education was an expanding enterprise and federal support for education was high, fostering many new ideas in building design, in teaching techniques, and in curriculum content. That was an era of relatively good feeling, one in which administrators and teachers belonged to the same professional organization. But the picture has changed and education's (and therefore the principal's) problems include declining enrollments, reduction in staff, teacher strikes, and school closings. Elementary principals must learn to live with less: less support for educational innovation (both financial and political), less diversity within the profession (fewer women and minorities), less money available, and also less agreement among educators on all issues that face them.[1]

In any analysis of the elementary principal's role, the management function and the leadership function clearly overlap, and although leadership expectancies are always present, managerial demands seem to prevail. Many elementary principals feel they are drowning in a sea of duties. Their role expectations require

---

[1]William L. Pharis and Sally Banks Zakariya, *The Elementary School Principalship in 1978: A Research Sudy* (Arlington, Va.: National Association of Elementary School Principals, 1978), pp. xi–xii.

them to be, among other things, disciplinarians, fire drill coordinators, teachers, evaluators, curriculum supervisors, building custodians, morale builders, staff selectors, school program administrators, instructional leaders, pupil services coordinators, keepers of the keys, staff and student scheduling coordinators, team leaders, PTA leaders, managers—and yes, in some rural areas, coal carriers and furnace tenders. Most principals, however, manage to remain optimistic in the face of these multiple demanding duties and maintain their composure.

Demands are thrust upon principals from many sectors, public as well as private, each of whom consider their demands more significant than any others. Of the many duties performed by the elementary principals on a regular basis, the following ten were considered in a recent study: staff selector and orientator, instructional supervisor, public relations facilitator, pupil services coordinator, self-evaluator, curriculum supervisor, teacher evaluator, school program administrator, disciplinarian, and morale builder. The results of the study, to be reported in detail in a later section of this text, indicate that elementary principals are performing certain roles—as disciplinarian, evaluator, administrator, and public relations facilitator—more often than others, but indeed wish to perform other roles—as instructional supervisor and staff selector—more than time presently allows in their job.[2]

The 1978 NAESP study noted that principals are more highly qualified now than they were ten years ago, are less diverse as a group (more school principals are men now), are supervising smaller schools, but at the same time may be assigned more than one school. They seem to be generally more positive about their jobs, and believe that not only are students learning more than they did ten years ago, but also that they are doing just as well on basic skills—an excellent attitude for being able to cope with changing demands.

The NAESP study notes that two of the current major problems facing elementary principals are (1) managing student behavior and (2) dismissing incompetent staff. One ingredient of staff competency is managing student behavior. When teachers try to manage student behavior, the techniques that they use are important; yet mastering effective techniques is not easy. Teachers must (as principals must in working with teachers' behavior) adopt a proactive stance in managing student behavior. Through improved teaching techniques, the student behavior problem may be dissipated somewhat. Principals must therefore assume a key role in instructional improvement and staff development programs. How to develop and effect such programs will be a topic of a later chapter, as will problems of dealing with incompetent staff and managing student behavior.

The study also reveals that principals' supervision responsibilities have greatly increased in recent years. Eighty-six percent of the principals say they have primary responsibility for teacher supervision, an increase of 11 percent from only ten years ago! Another change is in the area of negotiations. Most elementary principals now work with teachers who negotiate contracts, but the percentages vary, depending on the region. Although about two-thirds of the elementary

---

[2]Robert J. Krajewski, "The Real Versus the Ideal—How Elementary Principals Perceive Their Role in Texas," *Texas Elementary Principals and Supervisors Association Journal* (May 1977), p. 13.

principals work with *teachers* who negotiate contracts, less than one-third of the principals get involved in negotiating *their own* contracts.[3]

Overall, the changing demands placed on elementary principals are varied and numerous.

- More recently we have witnessed changes brought about by the competency testing movement, the back-to-basics movement, the energy crisis, federal programs, and a number of other unexpected changes.
- Declining enrollment and reduction of central office staff (mainly supervisors and curriculum specialists) have placed greater emphasis on the principal's role as instructional and curriculum leader, but at the same time both educational and fiscal pressures are pushing the principal's role more in the direction of educational leader.
- To compound this, the increase of specialization (both subject and teacher competencies)—that filters all the way down to the elementary school—coupled with the rising power of teachers, has had a significant impact.
- The increasing daily constraints, including parental complaints, association demands, and all sorts of bandwagons, are growing and becoming more crucial, both legally and fiscally.

As we look at implications these demands present for principals' role changes in the coming years, it becomes evident that elementary principals will have more qualifications, have responsibility for more than one school, have greater responsibility in teacher supervision, be less diverse, become more sophisticated in collective bargaining, and work more effectively with such pressures as managing student behavior and dismissing incompetent staff. These, then, are but a few of the changing demands placed on the principal. They all will be discussed in later chapters. Fortunately, principals appreciate the need to cope with changing demands and seem to be taking steps to do just that.

Most research indicates that the elementary school principal has more influence on the quality of school programs than does any other single individual. However, the role demands required of the principal in order to produce a quality school program have changed significantly in recent years, and they continue to change.

Suggestions for coping

Increasingly, principals must deal with forces and events outside the school over which they may have little or no control, but that significantly affect the school's operation. In spite of the changing nature and increasing complexity of the role, there are some practical management guidelines, leadership strategies, and educationally sound administrative procedures that can contribute to elementary principals' success and, therefore, to the success of the school. We consider these guidelines as basic to effective school administration and as such they are intermediate steps to coping with changing demands.

---

[3]William L. Pharis and Sally Banks Zakariya, *op. cit.*

1. Be willing to delegate. No one person can do everything in the school well. A good way to keep abreast of things and still maintain a firm grip on the school's direction and growth is to know when and how to delegate responsibility or authority. By delegating, principals can allow themselves time to see the total school picture more clearly. If principals do not have assistants to whom authority or responsibility can be delegated, then selecting teachers who have leadership abilities and to whom authority can be delegated is a must.

2. Seek input from parents, teachers, and students. Input from significant others is both necessary and desirable. From whom input is solicited, its timing and amount(s), and the subsequent decision of how to use the input so obtained are all crucial.

3. Be effective as a manager. This statement represents a simplified description of what will be discussed in the next section of this chapter. Doing the necessary, required things and making them a matter of routine will give principals more time to do those things that promote excellence in the school.

4. Be aware of how decisions are made within the school system. Political naivety within the school system may be deadly to principals and potentially detrimental to the school program. Knowing where the power lies is not only desirable, it is crucial. Crucial too, is that principals establish their own power base from which to operate. This is to suggest that once principals know how the structure is designed operationally, it becomes easier to work within it and adjust accordingly to afford students the best possible learning program.

5. Be aware of how decisions are made within the community. The community, or geographical school boundary area, remains perhaps the most important asset elementary principals have. To use this asset for the school's benefit, principals must be aware of the community power structure and be able to work effectively within that framework.

6. Seek ways to better interpret, understand, and work through local, state, and federal guidelines in order to obtain the best possible help in improving the school program. Guideline implementation at times may be overwhelming to principals, teachers, and children. Learning to obtain and cope with program guidelines, especially those at state and federal levels, becomes a *key* to survival.

As concerned professionals, principals' attitudes will be likely to influence the attitudes of others. Principals must be careful how they relate or present change to their faculties, thus the importance of remaining objective about change. Important too is finding ways of keeping oneself on an even keel in light of all these changes. Consider, for example, that this year you will incorporate in your school federal regulations dealing with lunchrooms and various special education programs; effecting all these changes may become too time-consuming if they are taken strictly at face value. Beginning principals may be more apt to take such things at face value and simply try to survive under the pressures. But experience seems to refine our repertoires, mold us, and allow us to see changes and their results in a more realistic perspective.

Principals can become too involved in their jobs. Overinvolvement will lead to lack of effectiveness. Refrain from getting too involved with the job; when your whole life revolves around it you then face the risk of becoming dull and too narrow in thinking. Regular involvement in outside activities is necessary. If possible, interact with people other than those with whom you work; and, most definitely, while you perform the activity, try not to talk about school events or happenings. By spending out-of-school time in activities, such as church, sports, community, or cultural, principals become better able to cope with the changing demands on the job.

Elementary principals are susceptible to the administrative phenomenon called "loneliness at the top." Principals are perceived as someone special by teachers, students, and staff; this perception never really completely disappears, it comes with the job. Principals are expected to be the school leader, the person who solves the problems. Their relationships with the teachers should reflect this trust.

Every principal needs a sounding board, someone to talk to and share administrative ideas with, on a regular basis. We suggest, therefore, that principals develop a threat-free relationship with another principal, administrator, or professional person, a relationship in which you talk freely about mutual concerns and depend on each other to listen, advise, and yet reinforce each other with positive ideas. And perhaps a social support system of peers might be established (this will be discussed more fully in a later section). These, then are several methods for coping with changing demands while combatting loneliness at the top.

All of these and others play a major role or in some way affect the school operation. As principals, how do you cope with them? How can you assume the responsibilities thrust upon you by these changing demands and still operate the school in an effective manner? Here are some general guidelines:

- Try not to become unsettled by change.
- Sit down and analyze the problem(s); try using the sifters' analysis, separating the chaff from the wheat.
- Analyze the situation (considering both immediate and long-term implications) in terms of your own philosophy of education; analyze each change and study its feasibility in relation to your school situation; do not always be willing to get on a change bandwagon and do what someone says you are supposed to do.
- Have confidence in your beliefs about what you should and should not do in the school (knowing, of course, there *are* some demands and changes in the school with which you must cope).

ASSUMING UNDREAMED-OF ROLES

In the 1980s, new demands are not only creating new dimensions of the principals' role but also are requiring that present dimensions be more fully realized. In a recent issue of *National Elementary Principal,* principals who responded to the NEP's "burnout" poll note the changes they feel would enhance the elementary principal's job: more time to spend with students in the classroom, less paperwork, less federal interference, more control over the budget, and in general, more freedom to make decisions. In that same (burnout) survey 60 percent of the respondents say they definitely had positive hopes and dreams when they entered the elementary principalship—dreams they have not yet been able to realize—the first and foremost of which was time to improve curriculum and instruction. Overall, they feel that their dream of being an educator had turned into the reality of being a manager.[4]

To the question, "What is an elementary principal?," former NAESP Executive Director Bill Pharis replied, "A principal is a person infected by a national vision. Working with whatever resources . . . operating within and in spite of the constraints imposed . . . the principal is trying to make 'school equal educate.' "[5] That vision remains with today's principals, and despite what some educational writers might espouse, we believe that most elementary principals still cling to the hope that their dreams will be fulfilled—that indeed their important role in improving instruction and curriculum for children in the elementary school will be effected in this decade. Our reasons for continuing that belief are the optimism and dedication that we personally see in the principals whom we train and with whom we visit in their school surroundings, and the direct and indirect continuing reports from professors and principal colleagues throughout the country, who communicate the fact that indeed optimism among elementary principals runs high. That optimism was echoed by the respondents of the 1978 NAESP study. According to that study:

- Over half of the elementary principals have been principals for less than ten years;
- 57 percent of elementary principals say that the elementary principalship is their final career goal;
- Most elementary principals are generally positive about their job.[6]

We feel safe to assume that given such an enthusiastic working group, not only are the elementary principals of the 1980s fulfilling their dreams for the elementary principal's role, they will more than likely wish to assume even undreamed-of roles as time progresses or as they become more involved and secure in their role.

But as the NEP "burnout" poll indicates, some of the elementary principals' dreams turn out to be less than happy and in some cases may even border on being nightmares.

Consider the following vignette:

Not much different than other days. Really becoming aware of the children's home lives. William, who can't do a thing and leaves at 1:00 daily, was what I would term

[4]Sally Banks Zakariya, "Principals and Their Jobs: Candid Comments from Our Readers," *The National Elementary Principal* 58 (June 1978), pp. 57–58.
[5]William L. Pharis, "What is a Principal?" *The National Elementary Principal* 53 (May–June 1974), p. 58.
[6]William L. Pharis and Sally Banks Zakariya, *op. cit.*

momentarily insane. He never does what one asks and just gives hateful looks or laughs weirdly. Today the teacher, Mrs. McCabe, fought with him to get an orange out of his hand. The orange splattered all over the floor. To reinforce that she meant business, she started to paddle him and he ran around the room gaping and cowering along the walls as if a wild animal in danger. After the teacher's back was turned he picked up the heavy stapler to clobber her with. I asked myself if this were just a figment of my imagination. Unfortunately the answer was no.

William comes from a terrible background. His mother is in an asylum—his grandfather last week killed his third person (first being William's grandmother). Presently William lives with his father in a house of cats (parlor and all) and drugs flow freely. At school William just seems to float around and his behavior is typical of what happened today.

Recorded by an inner-city elementary principal observing a first-grade classroom, this vignette is included here to demonstrate that such realistic input should be provided in preservice and inservice training programs for principals because of its importance to the total outlook in respect to the elementary principals' role.

It is perhaps all too common for principals to be viewed in the following manner "I always thought of the principal as being the person in the office probably sitting there talking to a few people and looking around, or even counting money." Even more common is the neophyte principal explaining, "No one ever told me that I was supposed to know how to be an exterminator, chauffeur, and a repair-person. No one mentioned that I'm supposed to know how to fix everything from a small vacuum cleaner to various equipment in the boiler room. I didn't take courses on how to be a money raiser, law enforcer, and community relations expert. Neither did I expect to have to be an architect, filling out various forms on the design of buildings, and maybe even their location."

Although it may be true that neophyte principals (and some experienced principals for that matter) may become discouraged when they have to face such roles, we suggest that, with proper management, principals may reduce such roles to a minimum. In other words, if principals learn how to place job responsibilities on those persons who are supposed to perform the respective roles, such problems may be successfully solved—in most cases. Yet in reality, acceptance of job delineation is much simpler said than done.

Even if principals have their management techniques under control, there will be times it may be necessary to function in duties not anticipated on a regular basis. For example, as a custodian when the custodian cannot be found, or as a secretary when the secretary is sick or away. Reality dictates and principals must be ready to accept and face unexpected needs, calmly, in whatever form the needs appear.

CHOOSING UNDREAMED-OF ROLES

What are some of the undreamed-of (or perhaps desired) roles that elementary principals may wish to assume? We would like to list several: certainly the list is not exhaustive and readers are encouraged to add to these suggestions.

1. Visit the home of each child in the school—to better understand the problems faced by students and their parents. The principal–home relationship shows parents that principals care and are interested in the educational and personal welfare of the students.

2. Be active in teaching, at all grade levels—to refresh yourself and better understand, on a continuing basis, the problems faced by teachers in your school. Such activity will assist your keeping up-to-date on teaching methods and subject development. In addition, it will help you to better know and understand students' personal feelings, likes, and dislikes.

3. Spend more time on curriculum matters—a natural spin-off from 2. Keeping up with curriculum is arduous and time-consuming and yet is an essential task for all elementary principals. Better knowledge of the total school curriculum leads to better understanding of the school's responsibility to students and a more knowledgeable working base with teachers.

4. Find more time (theirs and yours) to spend with individual teachers, helping them improve professional competencies. Improving professional competencies begins first with attitude. Necessary to change teachers' attitude is spending time with them, getting to know them, and working with them in an effective manner.

5. Develop a more individualized teacher inservice program. When principals judiciously expand efforts on Nos. 1–4, it will be easier for them to get a better understanding of how to develop a more effective, more individualized teacher inservice program.

6. Provide an electronic data center to store demographic and evaluative information on students. This dream may already be a reality for some elementary principals, as school systems are realizing more and more the power and value of microcomputers. Instant access to individual and group student progress, if used correctly, is essential to curriculum planning, implementation and evaluation, student placement, instructional decisions, administrative decisions, and sundry other decisions. The electronic datacenter's value in enhancing the educational program, would, when the instrument is used creatively, be enormous.

7. Have the resources to provide an Individualized Education Program (IEP) for each student. One resource would be the electronic data-center, another would be the financial backing, and a third would be the space necessary within the school for material storage. The latter, though necessary, would be the least important of the resources needed for IEP implementation.

8. Have material resources available for teaching and for providing varied experiences for skill acquisition. All principals dream of having sufficient resources for teaching the curriculum; however, soaring prices of materials, lack of storage space, and lack of backing, both time and financial, for teacher inservice for using the materials seem to be major roadblocks. Teacher-made resource centers can become a reality, given proper administrative support.

9. Teach research skills to students. Use of computers, use of library, and use of

equipment in an electronic data-center are skills students should learn. These skills will enable them to view school activities from a problem-solving viewpoint.

JOB DESCRIPTIONS

Principals are expected to settle into their role and interact effectively with subordinates, peers, superordinates, students, parents, and all significant others. Seek and become acquainted with the answers to the five w's: who, what, where, when, and why. In addition, be aware of those answers for other personnel in your school (and to a large degree, in the total system).

Ask yourself

- To whom am I responsible?
- For what am I responsible? What are my duties as principal?
- Where do I fulfill my responsibilities? How should my time be appropriated to my office, classrooms, central office, and the like?
- When do I fulfill my responsibilities?
- And lastly ask *why*. To fulfill responsibilities just because someone says so or because "it has always been done that way," without at times asking *why* will not allow you to function as effectively as you might as leader.

Ask others too! Feedback from others is essential. Do not be naive about what you hear; rather, be realistic and try to put feedback into achievable goals.

If you ask yourself the five w's, where might you find the answers? Ask for a job description. A job description should include:

- Title;
- Description;
- Responsible to;
- Major duties;
- Specific duties;
- Qualifications (education, experience, skills required, knowledge, abilities);
- Fringe benefits.

Not all job descriptions contain the above-listed data. Some, however, contain even more data than listed above. Read the job desciption, study the needed data, and ask appropriate questions.

Sample job description: elementary principal

Position title: Principal of Baker School. The school is located in a metropolitan community, population 400,000, and has grades 1 through 6 with an enrollment of 450 pupils.

Responsible to: The Board of Education of the Keystone City School system along with the superintendent of schools; should work cooperatively and responsibly with any personnel staff associated with the central office in the chain of command.

Major responsibilities and key duties:

1. Learning atmosphere—Provides leadership to promote professional growth of teachers and maximum learning of pupils.
    Key duties:
    1. Observes teaching techniques and practices;
    2. Promotes cooperation and understanding among teachers, pupils, and administrators;
    3. Encourages teacher participation in professional activities and organizations;
    4. Improves the physical conditions for learning;
    5. Supports and promotes atmosphere for creative ideas and change.

2. Instruction and Curriculum—Assumes a leadership role in developing, maintaining, and improving instruction and curriculum.
    Key Duties:
    1. Provides in service programs;
    2. Provides leadership for curriculum study and instructional innovation;
    3. Assists teachers in keeping up-to-date on new instructional materials and techniques;
    4. Coordinates learning activities that utilize community resources;
    5. Cooperates with supervisory personnel on instructional improvement projects;
    6. Organizes committees to evaluate instructional material;
    7. Supports a curriculum that provides pupils with extended enrichment and learning experiences;
    8. Participates in professional organizations related to all areas of instructional improvement.

3. Administration—Assumes advisory responsibilities in the area of specialization to the school as well as central office staff.
    Key Duties:
    1. Prepares school budgets;
    2. Maintains records of all areas of responsibility;
    3. Plans and coordinates the activities of supervisors and consultants;
    4. Allocates funds for instructional materials and supplies;
    5. Carries out central office decisions;

            6   Evaluates any special projects outlined for the school for their full adequacy;
            7   Is involved in the selection and placement of teachers for the school.

4   Human Relations—Establishes and maintains effective personal relationships with faculty, pupils, community, and central office.

    Key Duties:
        1   Consults teachers about decisions in their particular teaching area;
        2   Inspires teacher confidence through sincere praise of their work;
        3   Inspires performance of all other staff members in their particular duties;
        4   Encourages parental involvement in improving learning environments and experiences dealing with the best welfare of the children;
        5   Influences school–community relations and extracurricular activities.

Qualifications:

1   Education—Has at least a master's degree in administration with advanced training and schooling.

2   Experience—Has at least four years of successful teaching (experience in an administrative capacity would be desirable).

3   Certification—Certified by the state Department of Education in the teaching and administration fields.

4   Personal Qualifications—
    1   Exhibits creativity, imagination, and leadership;
    2   Maintains self-improvement through professional growth and research;
    3   Commands respect for knowledge and ability;
    4   Works cooperatively with peers, subordinates, and superordinates;
    5   Has an optimistic outlook and sound philosophy of education.

Working conditions: Job will consist of coordinating and maintaining a staff of 25 full-time teachers, office personnel, guidance counselor, librarians, a school nurse, part-time and maintenance personnel.

Selection procedure: Apply with the personnel office of the Keystone City school system, interview with Director of Personnel and Placement. Approval and assignment made by the Superintendent and the Board of Education.

Salary: $28,000 with $2,100 annual promotion.

Fringe benefits: Along with salary there will be full medical insurance paid along with a $50,000 life insurance policy; both maintained as long as employed.

This sample job description has been included to give the reader the opportunity to view a fairly comprehensive written elementary principal's job description. Compare it with your own position and with position descriptions of other elementary principals in your area. You will, no doubt, notice some differences. And when considering undreamed-of roles, look first at present roles then those aspired; and finally those even undreamed-of roles that because of changing demands may soon be here. Think of what your ideal role would or could be as compared to what you actually do on the job.

COMBINING LEADERSHIP AND MANAGEMENT

I am trying to puncture a myth—the myth that every man does indeed want to lead and innovate. Most administrators will proclaim this as their purpose. Yet research on the behavior of administrators repeatedly gives the lie to this proclamation.[7]

— Andrew W. Halpin

What is leadership? What is management? What is their relationship to each other? Does one depend on the other? Can a person be successful in one and not the other? The answers to these and other questions concerning leadership and management as they apply to and affect the elementary principalship are important to elementary principals. This section attempts to provide straightforward, practically oriented answers to some of those questions. In it, we do not attempt to duplicate the already written excellent works on the theoretical foundations of leadership, leadership theory, and management. We will provide a bibliography of such works, however, for those readers whose interests in leadership and management are more profound than the level of explanation we provide here.

Several terms considered to be of great importance to elementary principals are: manager, leader, and administrator, and the corresponding terms management, leadership, and administration. In the next several pages, we explain these terms and their relationship to each other. We rationalize that elementary principals should be all of these—manager, leader, and administrator—and further that elementary principals *must* be all of these to be effective in coping with the changing demands of the role.

MANAGEMENT

Management is characterized, defined, and explained in many ways:

- "Planning, organizing, integrating, and measuring," a definition adopted by General Electric Company;
- A judicious use of means to accomplish an end;

[7]Andrew W. Halpin, "Escape from Leadership," *The Journal of Education,* cited in Robert G. Owens, *Organizational Behavior in Schools* (Englewood Cliffs, N.J.: Prentice-Hall, 1970), p. 118.

- Getting things done through others;
- Conducting or supervision of something.

Changing demands require changing management—in both philosophy and practice. More than ever—especially for elementary principals—management assumes a readiness and willingness to change, with the concomitant effort necessary not only to adapt to those changes but also to ferret out the "facts" and deal with the "necessary."

We define management as "working with and through people—both individually and in groups—to accomplish organizational goals." Further, we consider management to be a subset of leadership. Certainly elementary principals fit the management description and therefore management should be one of the integral components of their job. The management and leadership relationship may be depicted, for illustrative purposes, as shown in Figure 1–1. By virtue of the definition of management, and its pictorial application, management is therefore the achieving of organizational goals through leadership.

Managerial functions include planning, organizing, motivating, and controlling, and these functions remain relevent with respect to all organizations and all levels of management within the organizations. For management personnel to successfully carry out these various functions, three skills areas are necessary:

Technical skill Ability to use knowledge, methods, techniques, and equipment necessary for the performance of specific tasks acquired from experience, education, and training.

Human skill Ability and judgment in working with and through people, including an understanding of motivation and an application of effective leadership.

Conceptual skill Ability to understand the complexities of the overall organization and where one's own operation fits into the organization. This knowledge permits one to act according to the objectives of the total organization rather than only on the basis of the goals and needs of one's own immediate group.[8]

Figure 1–2, an adaptation of Robert Katz's work,[9] indicates the skills and their applications at various management levels.

In this figure, we see that elementary principals best fit at the middle management level. Skill requirements at this management level are different from those at the top management and lower management levels. Top management personnal require fewer of the technical skills than conceptual skills, whereas with supervisory management personnel, the opposite is true. At all three levels, human skills are transmitted to the workers. Our version of the adaptation reveals that elementary principals are definitely managers whose managerial tasks must be effected via interaction with people.

[8]Paul Hersey and Kenneth H. Blanchard, *Management of Organizational Behavior*, 2d ed. (Englewood Cliffs, N.J.: Prentice-Hall, 1972).
[9]*Ibid.*

FIGURE 1–1

leadership

management

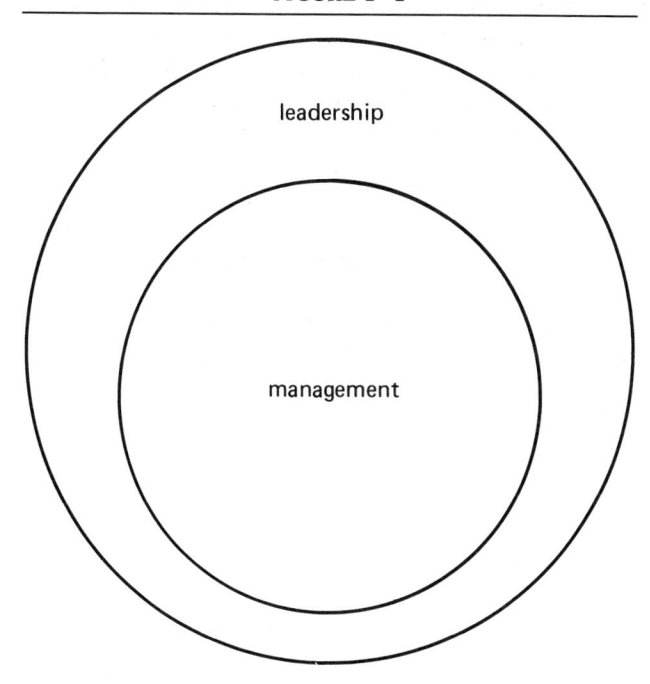

FIGURE 1–2[10]

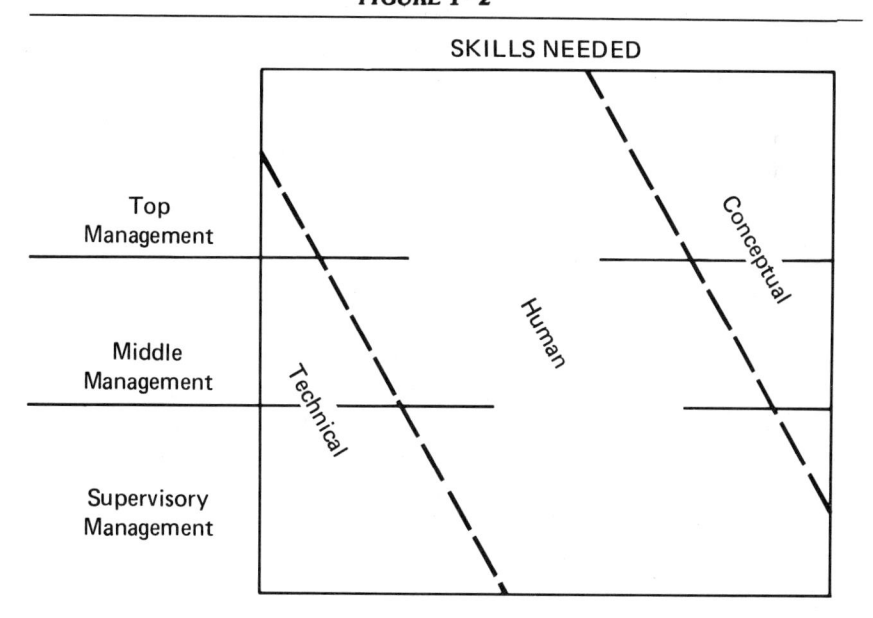

SKILLS NEEDED

Top Management

Middle Management

Supervisory Management

Technical

Human

Conceptual

[10]Picture, if you will, Figure 1–2 being placed in the management circle of Figure 1–1 and actually comprising most if not all of that circle. The geometric relationship between the circle and square is not significant, for they are merely pictorial representations, not the actual thing.

It can be theorized that principals must be effective managers before they can be effective leaders. As was mentioned, middle management requires approximately equal proportions of technical and conceptual skills. For purposes of this discussion, we will refer to these skills as a "Knowledge Base." Principals need a Knowledge Base of administrative theory, curriculum, instruction, educational psychology, pedagogy, and the like—a foundation, if you will. This foundation is necessary if principals are to solve problems proactively rather than reactively. But, as Figure 1−2 indicates, a knowledge base, though necessary, is not sufficient. Required as well is the Human Skills component (which we later refer to as rapport nurturance and we will define it and explicate its use by principals as instructional improvement leaders; for now, however, suffice it to say that the common thread required of all management levels is the human skills component). The human skills are all the more important at the middle management (principal) level because of the equal importance afforded to the conceptual and technical skill requirements.

ADMINISTRATION

Administration, as management, is defined or characterized in many ways.[11]

- A social process involving both problem solving and decision making (Halpin);
- A tool through which the fundamental objectives of the educational process may be more fully and efficiently realized (Moehlman);
- That phenomenon which coordinates the interdependent activities of individuals in achieving a common goal—the education of children (Hark et al.);
- A social process concerned with creating, maintaining, stimulating, controlling, and unifying formally and informally organized human and material energies within a unified system designed to accomplish predetermined objectives (Knezevich);
- Management—the coordination of many small tasks so as to accomplish the overall job as efficiently as possible (Taylor).

Like management, administration is subjected to changing demands and changing emphases. We consider administration to be slightly more encompassing than management. Whereas management may be considered mainly as the accomplishment of organizational objectives, administration emphasizes not only accomplishing the objectives but also relating them to each other so that there is more unity throughout the organization toward goals and their achievement.

Pictorially, then, we see administration relating to management and leadership as follows:

---

[11]These definitions are adaptations taken from "Suggested Readings," listed in this chapter.

FIGURE 1–3

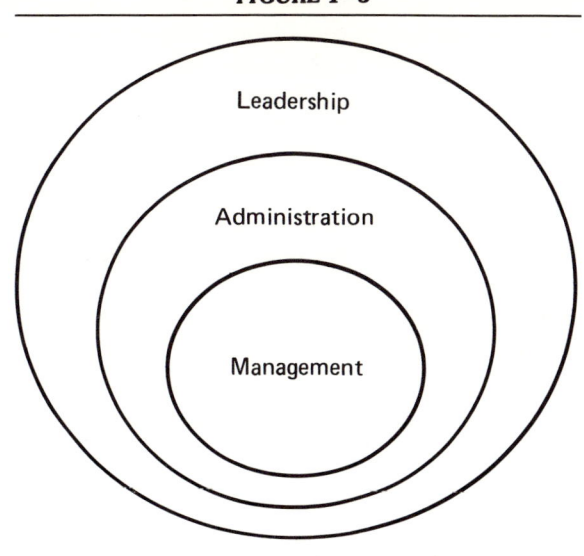

Leadership

Administration

Management

LEADERSHIP

As with management and administration, leadership is defined in many ways.[12]

- Inducing followers to act for certain goals that represent the values and the motivations—the wants and needs, the aspirations and expectations—of both leader and followers (Burns);
- Influencing the activities of an individual or a group in efforts toward goal achievement in a given situation (Hersey);
- Initiating a new structure or procedure for accomplishing an organization's goals and objectives or for changing an organization's goals or objectives (Lipham);
- Influencing people to strive willingly for group objectives (Terry).

Lipham's emphasis is on "new" and "changing" and he emphatically differentiates between administration and leadership by saying that administration uses existing procedures and structures to achieve an organizational goal or objective.

We see leadership as encompassing all of the above—and even more (see Figure 1–3). We see leadership as incorporating both self-growth and the growth of others. To accomplish these, the leader must be willing to take risks and not be afraid of occasional failure. Risk-taking almost necessitates occasional failure before it will bring about successes, change, and growth. We also see leadership as

[12]*Ibid.*

attempting to meet personnel needs that may be classified as belonging needs. This latter aspect is perhaps the most significant of the changing demands of leadership.

In past years, life seemed to be less fast paced than today. Instant communication, rationalization for the moment, "live for today and the hell with tomorrow" had not yet come into focus. The family was considered a unit; social organizations were important in most individual's repertoires, as was the church and church-related activities. A sense of belonging was felt within these units. However, today's fast paced, always-on-the-go, nonstop way of living leads us to a lifestyle in which we as individuals have fewer of our social and belonging needs met at home, in social organizations, and at church.

This leaves only one place to effect satisfaction of those social and belonging needs (as Maslow would characterize them)—at work. The work arena, however, increasingly satisfies needs for money, and perhaps esteem, the first need being extrinsic and the second being intrinsic. Sorely needed and missing is the satisfaction of those needs that have to do with belonging; and those needs require satisfying the most.

LEADERSHIP QUESTIONS

Leaders today must concentrate on trying to satisfy needs of the people who work for them—needs of acceptance by others, approval of group membership, and recognition, belonging, and social needs. Esteem or ego needs must be satisfied as well, but they take second billing to the belonging or social needs. Given today's society, the belonging needs must be satisfied and should be given top priority. (Note: We will discuss more fully the implications of satisfying belonging needs in the section on instructional leadership.)

Thus, with the specific added emphases within leadership of self-growth, growth of others, risk-taking, and meeting belonging needs, we refer then to leadership. Now we attempt to relate the explanations of management and leadership to elementary principals. How does what we have been saying affect elementary principals? Consider the following hypotheses:

Hypothesis 1: An elementary principal must be a good manager to be a good leader.

Discussion: If indeed the principal can effect management of the school so that it almost becomes routine, he or she can then afford the time necessary for leadership. One principal stated it this way: "It is very difficult for me to talk about combining leadership with management. I never really consider myself a manager but more or less a leader. If I think of myself as a leader, managing becomes easier." Translated, this means that if the principal is on top of most happenings in the school and school system, good management will be effected. Keep believing in yourself and others, care about what you are doing, and try to get others to care about what they are doing—as relates to organizational goals—and good management seems to be a natural by-product.

If we then assume that good management is a prerequisite for leadership, can we assume an "if—then" relationship? Can we assume that if one is a good manager, it then follows that one will then be a good leader? We would like to answer yes, but that answer would not hold true in all or even many cases. We now present a brief explanation of why we feel that this particular "if—then" relationship does not hold true. Management involves meeting organizational tasks or goals; it is, as we have mentioned, a subset of leadership. Leadership involves growth, of self and of followers. Management can be effected without growth of either manager or managee. Leadership requires not only growth; it also requires risk. Management requires neither. Therefore, because someone is an effective manager, we cannot automatically assume that that person is a leader. Since management is but one component of leadership, the if—then relationship does not necessarily apply. Therefore, Hypothesis 1 is rejected.

Hypothesis 2: An elementary principal must be a good leader to be a good manager.

Discussion: True, you say. Since management is a component of leadership, it naturally follows that if one is a good leader, one will be a good manager. In most cases this will be true. In some cases, however, it may not be. There are persons who are good leaders but whose management skills are less than satisfactory. If such leaders can delegate responsibility and authority so that the management is effected, then we can argue that the if—then rationale holds true. However, some cannot or will not.

Some elementary principals are not afforded the luxury of delegating for there is no one to whom they can delegate. In such cases, if the elementary principal is a good leader but not a good manager, the if—then relationship would not hold. We might add, however, that such cases are rare indeed; that if an elementary principal is a good leader, it follows that the principal is also a good manager. For if the leader takes risks, allows for self-growth and growth of others, and is effective in meeting belonging needs of managers, good management would be a natural concomitant, if not prerequisite.

Similar hypotheses may be offered using "administrator" instead of manager, but the discussion would be almost the same. We intend, instead, to concentrate on the relationship between management and leadership.

MANAGEMENT AND LEADERSHIP

The French political scientist Bertrand de Jouvenal listed the two main categories of leaders as *dux*—meaning leader—and *rex*—meaning ruler. In the *dux* category he includes the innovator type. In the *rex* category he includes the manager, or stabilizer.[13] Is it possible to distinguish the leader from manager this way? Can we distinguish between the "follow me" *dux* category and the facilitator, the *rex* category person who is sensitive to individual concerns? We ought to be able to since these two qualities are, for most people, incompatible. Yet there exist those

[13]De Jouvenal, "Special Report: Leader v. Manager," *Time* (November 8, 1976), pp. 31–49.

gifted persons who can effectively exhibit both qualities, those persons who are both managers and leaders.

De Jouvenal argues on one side of a continuum, as he states that it is difficult, if not impossible, to be both leader and manager. And his argument certainly has merit. It is indeed difficult for an individual to effectively satisfy both *rex* and *dux* requirements. Yet elementary principals are expected to fulfill the roles both of manager and of leader. Elementary principals are expected to function as manager to the entire staff in meeting organizational goals and as leader, particularly as instructional leader.

There are no easy roads to leadership, no styles guaranteed to work. Rather, one must choose the style appropriate for the situation. Consider the continuum of leadership behavior styles from that of democratic behavior to autocratic behavior.

FIGURE 1-4

DEMOCRATIC ⬅——————————————➡ AUTHORITARIAN

Which style should elementary principals use? The differences in the two styles of leader behavior are based on the assumptions the leader makes about the source of his power or authority and about human nature. The authoritarian style of leader behavior is often based on the assumption that the leader's power is derived from the position he or she occupies and that people are innately lazy and unreliable (Theory X), whereas the democratic style assumes that the leader's power is granted by the group to be led and that people can be basically self-directed and creative at work if properly motivated (Theory Y). As a result, in the authoritarian style, all policies are determined by the leader, while in the democratic style, policies are open for group discussion and decision. The style will depend on the situation.

In 604 B.C., the philosopher Lao-Tzu stated:

A leader is best
When people barely know that he exists

Not so good when people obey and acclaim him
Worse when they despise him

Fail to honor people
They fail to honor you

But of a good leader who talks little
When his work is done, his aim fulfilled

They will all say
We did this ourselves[14]

[14]Lao-Tzu, *The Book of Tao.* (ca 550 B.C.) in Witter Bynner, *The Way of Life According to Lao-Tzu* (New York: The John Day Company, 1944), pp. 34–35.

Today's elementary principals may or may not agree with Lao Tzu's statement, but the principal as instructional leader of today may well remember that his or her effectiveness is determined by how much others are stimulated to seek their own improvement, to be able to say, "We did this ourselves." Is this easy? Hardly. Can it be done? Certainly—for instructional and for other school goals as well. Troy Mills, principal of Annehurst Elementary School, Westerville, Ohio, is an excellent example of how that style works well.

If you ask Troy's teachers what they think of him as principal, they say "he's just kind of there—we don't even realize that he's the principal" (meaning that in a positive way). That's the way Troy Mills affects his teachers—the teachers simply feel that he is just there. His leadership style is one in which he is always talking to the teachers—in the lounge, in the office, and in other places as well. The teachers think of him as a colleague or friend rather than a principal. But Troy is a well-organized person and an excellent manager—and a leader too! When he talks to the teachers, he realizes all the while that he never lets his sights stray from the school goals. He does it, though, in such a manner that it is almost imperceptible to the teachers. They do not feel as though he is pressuring them. They feel, rather, that he is just talking to them. (They do not feel pressured; but Troy really does not let either them or himself lose sight of the school goals.)

Just what does Troy do to the teachers? What does he talk about? What is he up to? Well, he makes it a point to praise each teacher at least once a week. The praise may be about either professional or personal concerns. Through his continuous communication system with the teachers, he both keeps a pulse on what's happening in the school and helps satisfy the belonging needs of the teachers. Through talking to the teachers, the leader meets those belonging needs (and others as well) in individual ways. The teachers feel comfortable with him and because their belonging needs are being met, they are more likely to expend energies on accomplishing the school's goals.[15]

The approach described above works well for one principal. That principal has the management functions down to a science and thus can spend more time in leadership efforts. And although Troy's technique may work well for him and also for some other principals, it may prove to be a disaster for others. We do not suggest that every principal use this method, or even try it. What we are suggesting (by including this example), however, is that in order for a principal to be an effective leader, he or she must attempt to meet the needs of the teachers, keeping primarily in mind the goal of the organization.

In summary, leaders

- Take risks;
- Do what is necessary and sometimes risk rejection by so doing;
- Are visionary;

---

[15]"The Principal as Catalyst," an interview with Troy Mills, *Theory into Practice 18* (February 1979), pp. 21–27.

- Have a sense of timing and limits;
- Know when to press ahead, and how far;
- Promote action through motivation;
- Have open minds;
- Exhibit self-discipline;
- Point out the difficult choices and trade-offs;
- Consider long- and short-range plans;
- Listen;
- Evaluate self;
- Capitalize on strengths of self and others.

THE PRINCIPAL AS THE KEY TO QUALITY

> *The key to the educational cookie is the principal. The principal is the motivational yeast: how high the students and teachers rise to their challenge is the principal's responsibility. If some of the educational ingredients in our recipe are missing, it's the responsibility of the principal to compensate by invention or innovation or substitution or, if nothing else, by raising hell with the people who stock his pantry.*[16]
>
> — Reverend Jesse Jackson

In the decade of the 1980s, elementary principals are and should be responsible for everything that occurs at the school. And yet it seems that the persons who have the least input into determining the role are the elementary principals. In 1974, Paul Houts pleaded:

> Unless principals actively ... help add to, erase, enhance, and reshape the myriad of functions that compose their role, the principalship will indeed be rewritten and unmistakably diminished by others.[17]

Both Houts' and Jackson's pleas seem, appropriately, to put things right on the line. Perhaps today it is time for principals to raise hell.

All recent research indicates that a successful school has a successful principal. Though the 1960s and 1970s produced these research results, few, if any, support efforts have been made during that time to enhance the elementary principal's skills, at either the preservice or inservice levels.

For example, the principal is expected to be the school's instructional leader. Research indicates that most elementary principals wish to be instructional leaders and their teachers also want them to be. Yet in actuality, few principals are instructional leaders. And why? Why, as the results of most research studies

---

[16] Ed Keller, "Stocking the Principal's Pantry," *Principal* (June 1979), p. 71.
[17] Paul Houts, "The Remaking of the Principalship," *The National Elementary Principal* 53 (March–April 1974), p. 7.

indicate, do elementary principals wish to perform the role of instructional leader yet seldom function in that role at the present time? Various reasons come to the forefront: preparation programs, inservice programs, job expectations, and time constraints. Implications of time constraints will be discussed in Chapter 2; implications of job expectations will be discussed in chapters dealing with curriculum instruction; implications of preservice and inservice programs will be discussed briefly at this time.

Today there are approximately 400 institutions of higher education offering administrators' training programs. Most of the programs lead to administrative certificates or advanced degrees. Requirements for certification are established by state departments of education and training is provided by the colleges and universities. Certification requirements vary widely among the states. Overall, however, it can generally be noted that most certification programs require little or no coursework in instruction and instructional-improvement areas. Let us be more specific. In a recent edition of *Requirements for Certification,* it was noted that only 23 states offer supervision certification.[18] Of those 23, the course requirements are generalized in both administration and supervision and in only 7 of those states are minimum requirements for supervision of instruction courses stated, and of those, two or three courses constitute the number required in the certification program. We include the supervision example because of the relatedness to administration or principal certification. Because of its nature, supervision requires more courses dealing with instruction and instructional improvement than does administration. And if in supervision certification we find that courses in instruction and instructional improvement are generally not required, what therefore can be said about those requirements in administration and principal certification? It follows, logically, that instruction and instructional supervision course requirements for principal certification are practically nil.

THINGS TO CONSIDER

Principals are the key to quality in the school and must be catalysts when it comes to the quality of educational programs. When principals assume this responsibility there are always obstacles to overcome; in some cases these obstacles can be overcome easily and in other cases not only cannot they be overcome easily, they may not be overcome at all. But principals cannot give up—they must keep on trying. Principals should be able to work with teachers to ensure that a quality educational setting be provided. That requires both the knowledge and the skills of principals. The knowledge aspect indicates that principals should have a good general understanding of the educational process. In other words, *you have to know what is going on.* You have to understand the basic principles to be able to help others implement what you consider to be a good instructional program. In short, you need the conceptual skills because it becomes difficult to explain to someone else something of which you yourself have little or no understanding.

---

[18]Elizabeth A. Woellner, *Requirements for Certification,* 42d ed. (Chicago: University of Chicago Press, 1978).

The skills aspect indicates that principals should have the human skills necessary to effect implementation of a good instructional program. In other words, you have to have enough understanding of and rapport with the faculty and staff to help them develop and implement programs. In short, you need the human skills because you cannot implement programs without faculty and staff cooperation. That cooperation is more easily obtained by using effective human skills.

When discussing principals as the key to quality, several main points must be considered:

1. Teachers will only do as good a job as the principal expects them to do. One principal explained it this way: "The teachers know I have high expectations for myself and the school. They also know I have high expectations for them. All along, I communicate with them and they know that I will help them, and work with and for them. Our expectations for each other are high. The job gets done."

An old military saying is "The people will do well only what the boss checks." This translates into "Hey, I care about our mission and how we do it. I also care for everyone contributing to accomplishing the mission. I care, and I hope you care. Because I show you that I care, I am hoping that you will care more. Together we'll meet our goal."

The statement "Teachers will only do as good a job as the principal expects them to" is not meant to be an admonition for teachers, nor should it in any way be interpreted negatively toward teachers. Rather, it is meant as an administrative precept for principals: *Expect a certain quality of work from yourself and from the staff and be sure to check to see if that work is being performed to expectations.* Check and evaluate staff work in a positive manner. Teachers and others will be able to perceive your attitude as one of caring and react accordingly.

2. Elementary principals should be able to use faculty leaders to help implement programs. As a key to quality, a principal must not erroneously believe that he or she is the *only* person capable of providing certain services in the school. As we have mentioned, good leaders promote leadership within the group. Quality leadership for a specific task may not rest in the principal but rather in another staff member. As leaders, principals should take advantage of the talents and human resources that are available in the school. By drawing out leadership from faculty to implement programs, principals can better accomplish the goal of quality education. Principals, by using talents available and fostering or promoting leadership, can better accomplish the school's main role, that of instructing children and fostering their learning.

3. Elementary principals, as the key to quality, should major in the majors instead of the minors. By allowing faculty leadership potential to be realized in planning, implementing, and evaluating programs, principals better succeed in both the majors and minors of the school program and in "the major" of being the school leader, being the key to quality.

4. Elementary principals must seek advice and counsel. We all must realistically realize our capabilities, accepting ourselves for what we are while at the same time exhibiting a willingness to grow. That willingness to grow includes being willing and able to ask advice when needed. All decisions are "relatively" important and our role in reaching the right or "appropriate for the situation" decision is crucial. Knowing when to ask for advice, whom to ask for the advice, and how to

ask for it is a sign of administrative and personal growth—and, we might add, is necesssary for growth as a principal. We might even suggest that they are among the most important decisions a principal must make.

One thought to keep in mind is that some teacher(s) will be more qualified than you in a given area of expertise. Discovering that fact and subsequently making that expertise available to the school are in themselves excellent administrative skills, either not practiced or undiscovered by many principals. As far as possible use the talents of others on your staff to help reach the school's goals. Principals should not be so self-centered that they do not need others. Leadership must be a teamwork effort, drawing from the strengths of everyone to overcome the weaknesses of all.

5. Elementary principals should be willing to consider compromise on specific decisions and issues but not on principles. *Issue* can be thought of as an outcome, consequence, result, or a factor leading to a given result. *Principle* can be thought of as a foundation, rule, doctrine, or precept.

In many administrative endeavors, specific decision outcomes may be subject to interpretation or compromise. In some cases, it is necessary to subject the result to compromise before it is either feasible or desirable. On the other hand, even though the issue may be compromised, the principle behind the issue must not. In a school, for example, instruction is the foundation upon which the school is built. Compromising instruction to gain other ends would not be desirable. Principals who either compromise or consider compromising principles will not, as their staff will no doubt point out to them in some fashion, be effective.

6. Elementary principals should encourage parents' support of and participation in the school. The parental support for the school will be influenced greatly by principals. Parents are important to the school. Their attitudes towards the school, acceptance of school and staff, willingness to participate in school activities, and willingness to volunteer their assistance to school programs are all of vital concern to principals.

Principals can set the atmosphere by establishing a receptive attitude toward parents, listening to them, and working with them as part of the team. Such a total effort leads to improvement in educational processes for children. Parents can be a storehouse of support or a barrel of problems—the key could well be the principal.

THE FUTURE

We—all of us, in each of our roles—create our future by what we do today and what we allow to be done to us today, and some of us are watched more closely in our roles than are others. Anyone in the public eye, especially those who are public employees, are susceptible to this scrutiny. Elementary principals, because of their role and their close contact with students and parents, are particularly susceptible.

All too often the roles we play are not those we desire. Society, and our behavior, over the course of time, tend to identify us. Perhaps this identification is in some cases neither wanted nor justified. Nevertheless, it is there; we have it; it is ours. Simply said, we are known by what we do.

Elementary principals increasingly have a multitude of descriptors behind them. Their roles, too, have many specifications, and the preparation required for the roles is becoming more demanding. In the past fifty years, for example, the percentage of elementary principals holding an M.A. degree or higher has risen from 15 percent to over 96 percent. In just the past ten years, the percentage of elementary principals holding the sixth-year certificate has almost tripled; the same holds true for those holding the doctoral degree.[19]

A combination of factors makes the role multifaceted and complex. It is little wonder that principals sometimes seem confused over what role they are to play or which should carry the highest priority. Professional concerns and societal pressures often conflict. There are those persons, for example, who stress that elementary principals be primarily instructional leaders. Most, if not all, in that camp realize the importance of that role, but at the same time can see its place in the total picture. Recently, more voices are suggesting that the principal's role should emphasize contract management, as over two-thirds of today's elementary principals work with teachers who have a collectively negotiated contract. We do not intend at this time to explicate these factors, nor their importance to the elementary principal's role, as both will be covered in detail in later sections of this book. We do wish to point out, however, that there is a fundamental issue to be addressed—that of role demands.

If the elementary principals of the 1980s do not, through their actions and foresight, exhibit the kind of leadership they (and others) seek of themselves, they will in fact continue to have created for them a less desirable role for elementary principals; a role that some will say they deserve. Yet we believe and trust that this will not be the case. We believe that elementary principals will seize the opportunity to shape their roles—both for now and for the future. They must—for the sake of the students.

SUGGESTED READINGS

Burns, James MacGregor. *Leadership.* New York: Harper & Row, 1978.
Fiedler, Fred E. *A Theory of Leadership Effectiveness.* New York: McGraw-Hill, 1967.
Hersey, Paul, and Blanchard, Kenneth H. *Management of Organizational Behavior,* 2d ed. Englewood Cliffs, N.J.: Prentice-Hall, 1969.
Knezevich, Stephen J. *Administration of Public Education,* 3d ed.. New York: Harper & Row, 1975.
Lipham, James M., and Hoeh, James A., Jr. *The Principalship: Foundations and Functions.* New York: Harper & Row, 1974.
Owens, Robert G. *Organizational Behavior in Schools.* Englewood Cliffs, N.J.: Prentice-Hall, 1970.

---

[19]William L. Pharis and Sally Banks Zakariya, *op. cit.*

CHAPTER

2

MANAGING THE MANAGER

Introduction

Managing self
Know yourself
Exercise
Accept yourself
The ulcer-producer list
Know and accept others
Improve yourself
Example 1   Example 2   Example 3   Example 4

Establishing priorities
Priority dimensions
For whom are priorities determined?
Creating a positive mindset for establishing priorities

Managing time
Planning
Organizing and budgeting time
Making the most of available resources
Delegating responsibilities

Decision making
Identifying innovational constraints:
A model for school principals
Selecting areas for professional development
Case study—the busy principal

INTRODUCTION

No man can produce great things who is not thoroughly sincere in dealing with himself.

— James Russell Lowell

Establishing priorities for the varied expectations of the principal's role, managing time within those priorities, and selecting areas for professional development all hinge upon one's effectiveness as a manager. A must in becoming an effective manager is to first identify your own point of view, your biases and prejudices—and where they occur. In other words, have an idea of where you are going and what you believe in. Ask yourself such questions as: What are the purposes and functions of the elementary school? What should children learn? How should schools be organized? Do I concentrate on improving the quality of the elementary school program by getting the best people (employment of teachers) and by acquiring sufficient excellent instructional materials? Operational principles are generated from a philosophy: zero in on given issues to examine carefully the principles that comprise your philosophy.

In the first chapter we listed four current responsibilities of the principalship: (1) managing the students' behavior; (2) dismissing incompetent staff; (3) teacher supervision; (4) contract negotiation. Consider managing student behavior. What is your basic belief about discipline? Do you favor a proactive or reactive discipline program? Do you view managing student behavior within instructional improvement procedures or do you view it strictly as a disciplining, corrective measure? How do you view dismissing incompetent staff? How do you define incompetence? What standards do you use for deciding whether a teacher is incompetent? Do you look at the overall problem in a staff development framework or do you look at the problem as simply getting rid of those teachers who are incompetent no matter what the cost? How are your relations with teachers who you feel are incompetent or less than effective? Do you enjoy supervising and observing classroom behavior? Do you feel that teacher supervision ought to be tied in with staff development? Do you allow teachers to become involved in the teacher supervision program? Is your teacher-supervision program accompanied by instructional improvement? Do you believe in contract negotiations? Why or why not? How does what you do in contract negotiations affect your relationships with teachers throughout the year?

Few managers (including principals) ask themselves questions relating to their basic beliefs, nor do they attempt to build on these basic beliefs. Principles and beliefs about how we act and react with other people lead us to building a philosophy, and a philosophy leads to action. The intent of this chapter, then, is threefold: (1) to provide a rationale for establishing and implementing a philosophy of education, (2) to allow the readers (principals) to become more aware of how they feel about themselves and others, and (3) to allow the (principals) readers to become more conscious of the management activities they perform and the means they use to perform those activities. A philosophical awareness is necessary for everything principals do. Without first knowing what feelings and activities are important, and why they are important, priorities or policies cannot be established effectively.

MANAGING SELF

An individual's behavior depends on how he sees himself, how he sees the situations in which he is involved, and interrelationships of these two. Behavior is only a symptom, the surface manifestation of what is going on within a person.

— Arthur Combs

Managing one's own self can be thought of in the following categories:

- Know yourself;
- Accept yourself;
- Know and accept others;
- Improve yourself.

KNOW YOURSELF

What do I believe in? What do I want? How effectively do I work with other people? These are but a few of the questions to ask when you attempt to know yourself and to expose self to yourself. You can usually find the answers to such questions in your philosophy of education.

A philosophy of education is a guide to practice, a base or foundation from which you act, and your actions within all operational aspects of the school should be consistent with your philosophy. But development of an educational philosophy is seldom regarded as being important. For example, when asked if they have a written philosophy of education, teacher, supervisor, and principal inservice groups reply almost unanimously "No." And when they are assigned the task of developing a written philosophy, they frequently consider it to be a completion-type task rather than a creative and meaningful one.

Principals who do not take seriously the process of establishing a philosophy of education communicate this feeling to their teachers, and their schools therefore have little or no foundation on which to: build curriculum and instruction, establish goals and objectives for students and teachers, build student management and evaluation programs, supervise and develop staff, and allocate resources and building use. Without a philosophy, principals tend to follow one of two patterns: (1) relinquishing their leadership role and pouring energies into management minutia, with little sense of direction or purpose, or (2) becoming opportunistic and people-manipulators, building personal and professional strength by surrounding themselves with "yes" people.[1]

Patricia D. Gersin wrote an article entitled "What Is Your EP: A Test Which Identifies Your Educational Philosophy," which appeared in *Clearinghouse Magazine* in 1972. In it, she presented eleven questions, a multiple-choice format that allowed respondents to analyze their answers and determine whether their philosophy follows more the ideas of progressivism, perennialism, essentialism, or

---

[1] Orin B. Graff, Calvin M. Street, Ralph B. Kimbrough, and Archie R. Dykes, *Philosophic Theory and Practice in Educational Administration* (Belmont, Calif.: Wadsworth, 1966), pp. 10–11.

existentialism. For those readers interested in reviewing these four types of philosophies, we recommend you read this article (and other sources listed at the end of this chapter). But our intent is not for you to categorize yourself in determining your philosophy. Rather, it is to stress the importance of both *having* a philosophy and *using* it. In setting up your own philosophy of education, ask such questions as: What expectations do I hold for myself? What are my major goals and priorities today? What will they be five years hence; ten years hence? Are my expectations of self consistent with the expectations the teachers hold for me? Are my perceptions of my own behavior consistent with the perceptions of others with whom I work?

Sometimes people take philosophy for granted. When that happens, often philosophy uses them, rather than the reverse. Philosophy allows you to think about your foundations and about your outlook. Taking a look at what you believe allows you to look into the reasons for what you accept and do; it also allows you to look into the importance of your ideas and ideals. When you take these views, you can see whether or not your convictions are logical and rationally held, and you can also evaluate your beliefs or your outlook to determine if they need changing.

You must know where you are going and how you intend to get there. It is not only important just to have a philosophy, it is equally important to implement that philosophy. Also, analyze it periodically to determine if it needs revising.

EXERCISE

We have included a sample philosophy of education. Take some time to analyze it. See if you can determine how the principal who wrote it feels about such things as curriculum, goals and objectives, student discipline and motivation, and student evaluation. Then develop your *own* written philosophy.

PHILOSOPHY OF EDUCATION

Each individual is born with potential, and when developed, that potential is a marvelous thing. As principals we ought to try to give the kind and quality of education we're capable of giving to students. Far too often there is an enormous gap between what we should be doing on the one hand and, on the other, what we end up doing. The attainable ideals, the shoulds and coulds of education, are all too seldom evident in actual classroom behaviors largely because we haven't taken seriously the notion inherent in the very foundations of our government that every individual is a precious, dignified, deserving person for whom the society ought to make every opportunity available to fulfill his potential. Our obligation then is to do everything we can, given the available technology, and everything we should, given what philosophers tell us about the proper role of education, to help fulfill that potential.

Achievement is based on motivation. What we've learned about motivation suggests that individuals develop in different ways and for different reasons. It also says that some students are not motivated regardless of teacher efforts. Most of the time poor student motivation results from discouragement, failure, and the system's negative impact on self-concept and self-respect. Teachers influence students directly; principals somewhat less directly, through impact on the system and interaction with teachers and significant others. As much as we can, we (principals) seek to provide for students an atmosphere of success; and even when we challenge them—which is also healthy—we try to keep challenges within a manageable range so that students have many chances to discover that they can succeed. When they find success, they increase self-confidence not only as persons but as learners.

If you analyze this philosophy with regard to the principal's feelings toward curriculum, statements as

... enormous gap between what we know we should be doing and what we do ...
... make every opportunity available to fulfill students' potential ...
... keep challenges within a manageable range ...

might be key indicators. How do these indicators translate into action? Would this principal set up curriculum committees for specific purposes? Does this principal establish the framework within which curriculum is designed—and implemented? Do you think the principal would keep a steady watchful eye on curriculum matters? Are these curriculum comments related to instruction? If so, how?

At times job pressures cause principals to stray from implementing the philosophy they prefer. Evaluation by peers, friends, teachers, and/or a short reminder by yourself can help put you on the track once again.

Consider the following anecdote:

Bill Morrow, a supervisor, stopped by to visit Jack Townsend, an elementary principal friend. Jack was generally regarded by all as genuine, likeable, and an excellent principal who excelled in relationships with teachers. On the many occasions when Bill visited, he observed that Jack always seemed to have time to listen to teachers, empathize with them, and understand their problems. On this particular day, however, as they walked about the school, Jack seemed somewhat out of character and ill at ease in his relationships with both teachers and students. His interactions seemed strained and forced. Later, as they sat in the principal's office, Jack mentioned that he was feeling rather low today. Today, he said, was one of those days when problems seem to mount and pressures from various sides begin to close in.

"You know," he said to Bill, "I like to think of myself as an understanding person. I try to be effective in working with teachers for the improvement of instruction and betterment of the school; but recently. . . . Well, I just don't know. One day last week I asked Mrs. Peters how things were going and she replied, 'Well, Mr. Townsend, you know I really like working with my accelerated sixth-graders, but the others, well, you can't teach them anything they'll understand. Besides, judging from the attitudes they have, they wouldn't want to learn it anyway.' "

"A few days later I spoke to Mrs. Brentwood, whom I consider to be one of the mainstays of our school. She indicated that the school seems to be going downhill and with the type of students we're now getting, teaching isn't the enjoyable job it once was for her. Now, normally, Bill, these things don't bother me, but for some reason they do now. I can't figure out why and I don't know how to overcome it."

This anecdote deals with a problem described in generalities. Analyzed in more detail, we find within it problems relating to managing student behavior and teacher supervision. In this case the principal (Jack) and his supervisor friend (Bill) analyzed the situation, isolated the two problems, and then began to solve them. Bill asked Jack to analyze within his own philosophy of education and during that analysis Jack began to regain his usual positive posture and to exhibit his natural confidence and zest. The discussion included Jack's ideas on managing student behavior and teacher supervision. Such problems are perhaps common, and in this case Jack was lucky to have someone around with whom he could talk.

"That's fine," you say, "but what if I don't have an available colleague to talk over problems with in an open and free atmosphere—someone who will really listen—someone who's really a colleague?"

Well, there are several alternatives. Ask the teachers if your stated (espoused) philosophy is congruent with your implemented philosophy, either through informal conversation with them on an individual basis or through a written format administered collectively to them. Reexamine your written philosophy to check for congruence between your actions and your philosophy. You may even combine both by using teacher feedback to determine whether or not your actions are congruent with your statements of intent and policies.

Is it important to have a written philosophy of education? Yes, it is a *must*. And by all means, write it down on paper. Actually, you really do not have a philosophy until you write it down; if you do not write it down, you have less chance of evaluating it objectively and determining whether or not your "talked about" philosophy is congruent with your "working" philosophy. Do not get caught with just fleeting thoughts in your mind.

Do you want to do well at your job? Do you want to make first-rate contributions to education? Do you want to have a first-rate set of tools and a disciplined way of thinking about problems? If you do, establish a philosophy. You must possess a substantial knowledge base; but more importantly, you should have a philosophy for putting that knowledge base into action. Harold Howe said that one reason that so much of the "theory in practice" used in education is second-rate or third-rate is that a great many educators have dull tools, or no tools at all, and they are in a state of confusion because they attempt to use many tools simultaneously without having mastered any of them.[2] *Elementary principals, do not let that happen to you! Come to your job prepared with the proper tools and use your philosophy to get the show on the road. When you get into situations that hinder implementing your philosophy, give yourself sort of a slap across the side of the face, say "Thanks, I needed that," and go on to implementing once again your philosophy of education.*

John Stoops puts it this way, "The educator who turns to philosophy is not himself becoming a professional philosopher, but he is going to the field to acquire the conceptual or analytical tools and terms necessary to grip and handle with

---

[2]Harold Howe, "Education Research—The Promise and the Problem," *Education Research* (Summer 1976), pp. 2–7.

understanding the issues in his own practice, and to acquire the probes needed to examine the relationships with and among other fields."[3]

Self-awareness is a key concept for all middle managers. Know yourself in terms of philosophy, and in terms of strengths and weaknesses. It is a good idea sometimes to sit down alone and ask yourself, "Who am I? What am I?" Ask others about yourself, too. Principals who know themselves and are aware of those experiences that have contributed to their present status can interact with others more openly and professionally. Those who know themselves recognize their own strengths and weaknesses and continually strive to extend their limits and thereby improve their performance, chances for success, and effectiveness.

We believe that all elementary principals can and will be more successful if they first recognize and then capitalize on both their strengths and weaknesses. As you can see in Figure 2–1, weaknesses usually accompany strengths.

For each strength you have, there is an accompanying weakness. For example, people who are aggressive and bold sometimes appear impulsive; and people who are precise and deliberative appear slow and sometimes lacking decision-making ability. To be more effective, be aware of both characteristics and capitalize on each. Through improved self-awareness you can overcome weaknesses.

ACCEPT YOURSELF

Once you get to know yourself, accept yourself for what you are—both strengths and weaknesses. Accept yourself for the kind of person you are, the philosophy you have, and the way you work with others. And all the while, try to improve on those things you think need improving. Drucker suggests that effective managers build on

FIGURE 2–1

Strengths	*Weaknesses*
decisive	autocratic
democratic	indecisive
energetic	impulsive
flexible	lack of consistency
formal	aloof
logical	slow
trusting	vulnerable

[3]John A. Stoops, *Philosophy and Education in Western Civilization* (Danville, Ill.: Interstate Printers and Publishers, 1971), p. 2.

their strengths and on those of their colleagues. This means concentrating on those activities that they (managers and colleagues) do best.[4] If you don't accept yourself for what you are, you will find that it is most difficult for you to accept others for what they are. It will also be difficult for others to accept you. After all, if you can not accept yourself for what you are, how can you expect others to accept you? Accept yourself. Work on overcoming weaknesses by building on your strengths, and be honest with yourself.

THE ULCER-PRODUCER LIST

Try this "progress check" and see how you fare. Check "Yes" or "No" for each item as it relates to you.

YES   NO

___ ___ 1 *Work long hours.* This will do it every time. Long hours are good for you. Why take a break? You might not get your work done. Long hours—that is the solution. What else is there?

___ ___ 2 *Don't get enough rest.* Why should you? If you work long hours, you don't have time to get enough rest anyway. Rest is just for the body; your mind needs all the activity it can get so keep it busy. Your body will hold up; after all, it's been with you for quite a while. Why should it change now?

___ ___ 3 *Refuse to delegate.* Try to keep on top of everything yourself—that's the easiest way. Don't trust anyone else to do the work. After all, you know that the only way to get things done right is to do them yourself.

___ ___ 4 *Don't plan or manage your time.* Play it by ear. Plans are going to be thrown out the window anyway. There are so many things to do during the day, you can't really plan—so just take things as they come.

___ ___ 5 *Don't establish priorities.* You can't really distinguish between the majors and the minors anyway, so why bother? After all, everything is Major. Just keep after everything that you possibly can. You do the job better.

___ ___ 6 *Be satisfied with the status quo.* Why change? Don't bother. Things are going along pretty smoothly, so keep it that way. Don't rock the boat—just hang in there and be satisfied with what you have. Don't bother trying to improve your staff because there is no sense in it. They won't get that much better and they won't appreciate it either. Besides, they're probably

---

[4]Peter F. Drucker, *The Effective Executive* (New York: Harper & Row, 1967), p. 103.

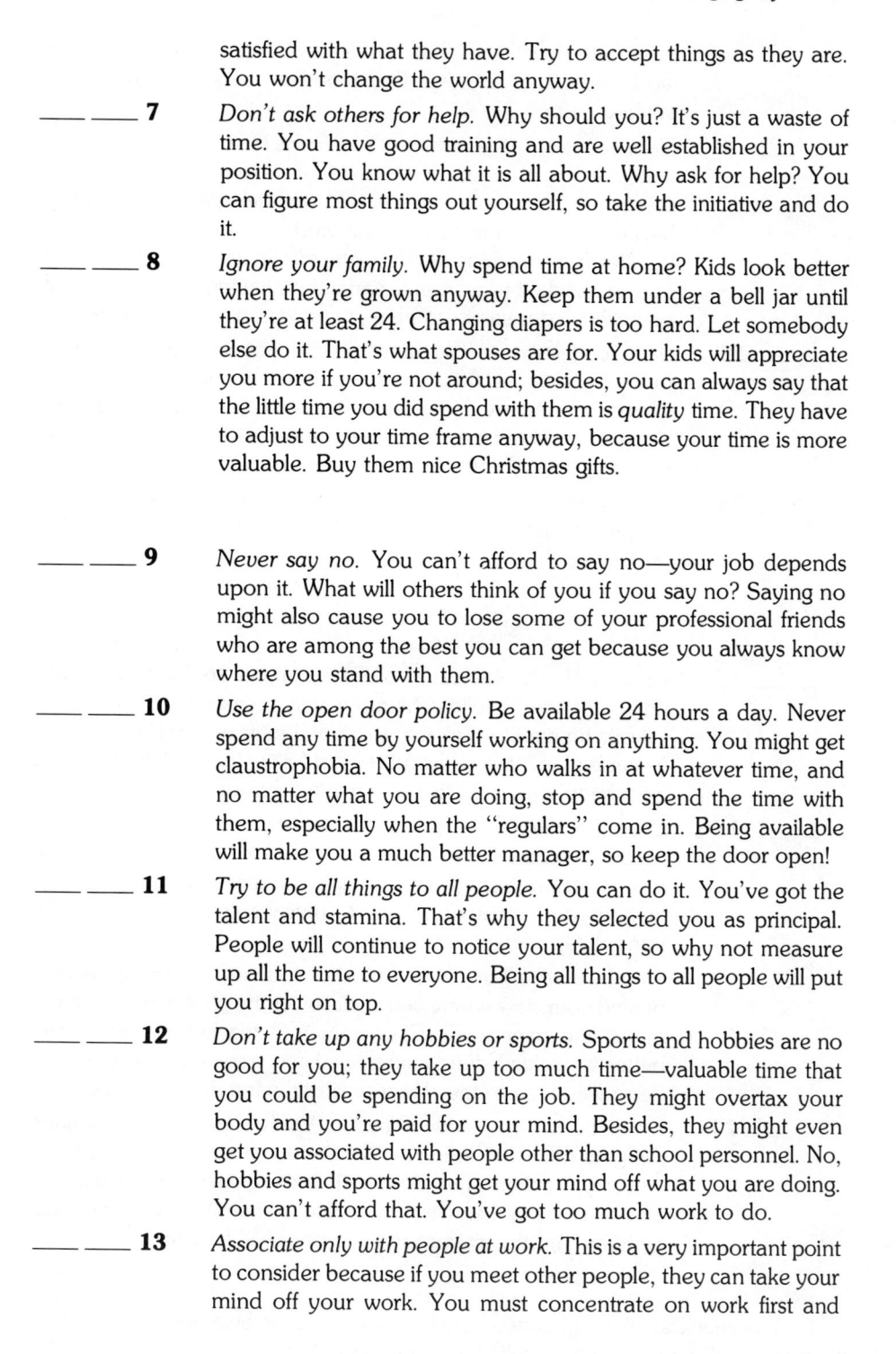

satisfied with what they have. Try to accept things as they are. You won't change the world anyway.

_____ 7   *Don't ask others for help.* Why should you? It's just a waste of time. You have good training and are well established in your position. You know what it is all about. Why ask for help? You can figure most things out yourself, so take the initiative and do it.

_____ 8   *Ignore your family.* Why spend time at home? Kids look better when they're grown anyway. Keep them under a bell jar until they're at least 24. Changing diapers is too hard. Let somebody else do it. That's what spouses are for. Your kids will appreciate you more if you're not around; besides, you can always say that the little time you did spend with them is *quality* time. They have to adjust to your time frame anyway, because your time is more valuable. Buy them nice Christmas gifts.

_____ 9   *Never say no.* You can't afford to say no—your job depends upon it. What will others think of you if you say no? Saying no might also cause you to lose some of your professional friends who are among the best you can get because you always know where you stand with them.

_____ 10 *Use the open door policy.* Be available 24 hours a day. Never spend any time by yourself working on anything. You might get claustrophobia. No matter who walks in at whatever time, and no matter what you are doing, stop and spend the time with them, especially when the "regulars" come in. Being available will make you a much better manager, so keep the door open!

_____ 11 *Try to be all things to all people.* You can do it. You've got the talent and stamina. That's why they selected you as principal. People will continue to notice your talent, so why not measure up all the time to everyone. Being all things to all people will put you right on top.

_____ 12 *Don't take up any hobbies or sports.* Sports and hobbies are no good for you; they take up too much time—valuable time that you could be spending on the job. They might overtax your body and you're paid for your mind. Besides, they might even get you associated with people other than school personnel. No, hobbies and sports might get your mind off what you are doing. You can't afford that. You've got too much work to do.

_____ 13 *Associate only with people at work.* This is a very important point to consider because if you meet other people, they can take your mind off your work. You must concentrate on work first and foremost. Your social structure is made up for you with your work associates anyway. Don't bother to go out and meet anybody else.

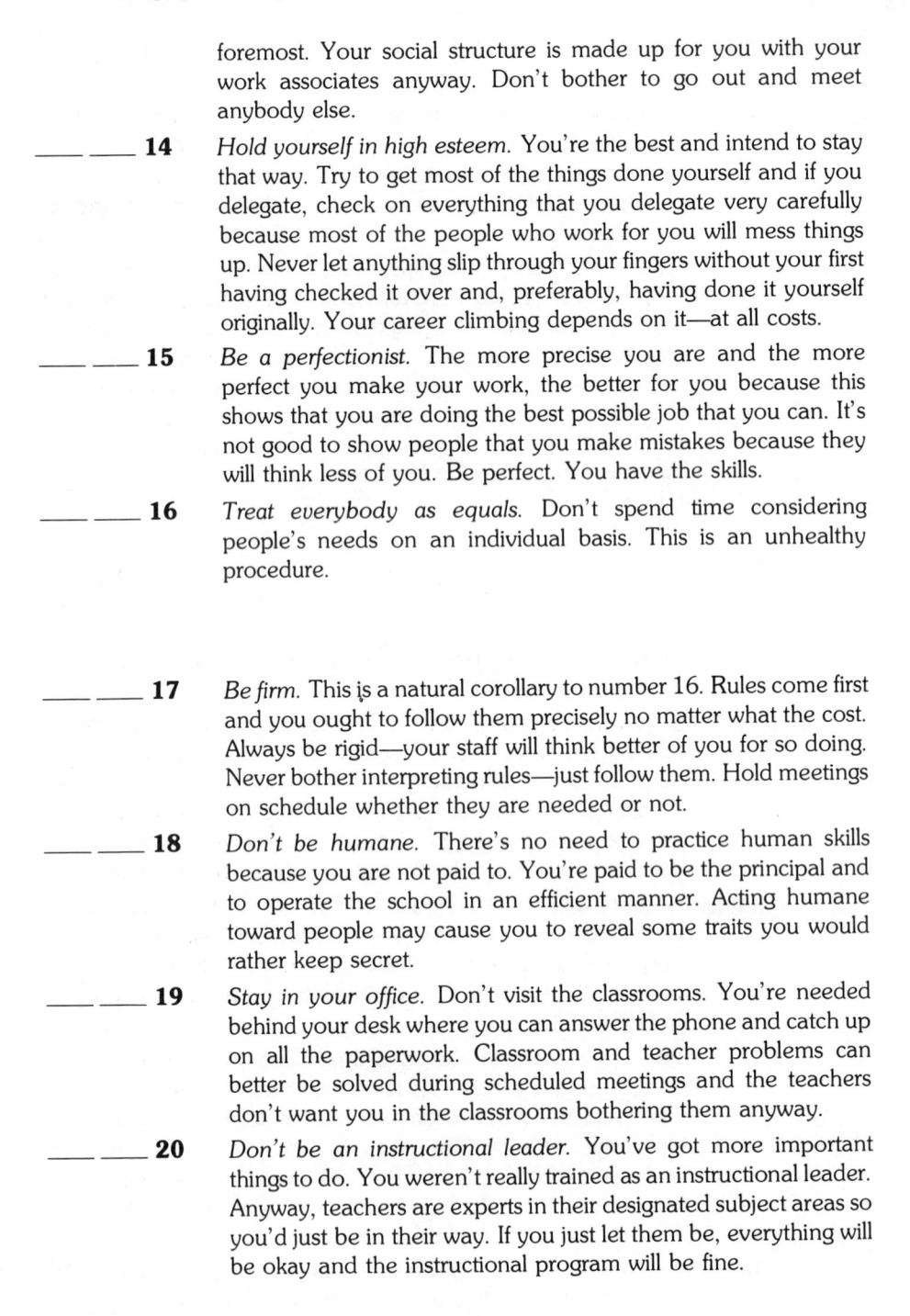

____ ____ 14 *Hold yourself in high esteem.* You're the best and intend to stay that way. Try to get most of the things done yourself and if you delegate, check on everything that you delegate very carefully because most of the people who work for you will mess things up. Never let anything slip through your fingers without your first having checked it over and, preferably, having done it yourself originally. Your career climbing depends on it—at all costs.

____ ____ 15 *Be a perfectionist.* The more precise you are and the more perfect you make your work, the better for you because this shows that you are doing the best possible job that you can. It's not good to show people that you make mistakes because they will think less of you. Be perfect. You have the skills.

____ ____ 16 *Treat everybody as equals.* Don't spend time considering people's needs on an individual basis. This is an unhealthy procedure.

____ ____ 17 *Be firm.* This is a natural corollary to number 16. Rules come first and you ought to follow them precisely no matter what the cost. Always be rigid—your staff will think better of you for so doing. Never bother interpreting rules—just follow them. Hold meetings on schedule whether they are needed or not.

____ ____ 18 *Don't be humane.* There's no need to practice human skills because you are not paid to. You're paid to be the principal and to operate the school in an efficient manner. Acting humane toward people may cause you to reveal some traits you would rather keep secret.

____ ____ 19 *Stay in your office.* Don't visit the classrooms. You're needed behind your desk where you can answer the phone and catch up on all the paperwork. Classroom and teacher problems can better be solved during scheduled meetings and the teachers don't want you in the classrooms bothering them anyway.

____ ____ 20 *Don't be an instructional leader.* You've got more important things to do. You weren't really trained as an instructional leader. Anyway, teachers are experts in their designated subject areas so you'd just be in their way. If you just let them be, everything will be okay and the instructional program will be fine.

This checklist, although tongue-in-cheek, serves as an awareness barometer. Know yourself and accept yourself. Then you're ready to . . .

KNOW AND ACCEPT OTHERS

Look at others' philosophies, their strengths and weaknesses, what they believe in, and what they want. When you do, not only will you learn to better accept others, you will also learn better what others think of you so that you can, in turn, better know and accept yourself. Knowing and accepting others is, we suggest, "the key."

For teachers to gain the students' respect, they must first respect students; in like manner, for principals to gain the teachers' respect, they must first respect the teachers. By getting to know others, by getting to accept them, by listening to what they say, their feelings and their ideas, we build respect for them and in the process, we build respect for ourselves.

IMPROVE YOURSELF

Always work toward improving yourself by building on strengths and shoring up weaknesses. Any improvement process requires practice. Don't be afraid to work on exercises that will allow you to build on strengths and reduce your weaknesses. Prepare a chart (similar to Figure 2-1) so that you can analyze both your strengths and your weaknesses. List ten strengths that you have in one column and then list the accompanying weaknesses for those strengths in the second column. Use that list to help make you stronger on the job.

Example 1

Choose your weakest quality as a principal. Select a low-risk activity in which you can practice strengthening this quality (with little or no disruption of school goals.) If, for instance, you have a problem in dealing with minute details, select a less important task to be accomplished with a colleague who is strong in working with details, and arrange a convenient meeting, whether informal, as lunch, or formal, as at the office, to begin working on it. Be sure to sit through one or more sessions of listening to and reacting to the minute details as your colleague presents them to you. At first you may feel that simply coping with listening is sufficient, and later perhaps, reacting to the details. You choose the timing and depth of your involvement. The key, however, is allowing yourself controlled practice.

Example 2

Choose one of your strongest points. For instance, if you are good in selecting personnel with potential leadership and developing them, select a colleague who might be weak in working at certain tasks and allow the colleague an opportunity to develop skills in a relatively low-risk activity you can work on together. Guide and encourage him or her (as necessary) through the activity, praise him or her effectively upon its completion, and then assist in analyzing the performance. You will reinforce one of your strong qualities, and have strengthened your colleague's skill as well.

Example 3

Select a key subordinate who has an operational style that is different from yours. Choose a high-risk activity in which you two must work closely together to see if you are flexible enough to blend your style into a compatible working relationship. At the same time you can recognize salient features of both styles and how they may or may not be effective in accomplishing the desired task. Prior to the activity you may plan questions and strategies, augment them during the operation, and analyze them after the activity is completed.

Example 4

This strategy is somewhat similar to Example 3. Choose your "checks and balance" person, the one whose style differs from yours but one who also likes to bang heads. Choose a low-risk activity and work through this activity with that person. In this case it does not matter whether the subordinate is a key subordinate. Neither will it matter if you do bang heads—in fact, it might be a good thing to do! What might result (from either Example 3 or Example 4) is a "new style," different from both beginning styles.

These are but a few examples. You can propose other strategies specifically related to managing student behavior, dismissing incompetent staff, supervising teachers, and negotiating contracts by setting up a list of strengths and weaknesses on these four specific items. In a practical manner similar to that which you have just completed, perform an analysis and strategy for those four items within your role.

The entire process of managing the manager depends on managing the manager's self. Managing that self consists of knowing yourself, accepting yourself, knowing and accepting others, and improving yourself and improving others. The proccesses involved are prerequisite to establishing priorities.

ESTABLISHING PRIORITIES

There is no shortage of time: there is only a lack of priorities.

— Peter Drucker

In the process of managing the manager, managing the self comes first; then comes establishing priorities. Establishing priorities is a practical example of how philosophy leads to doing the things we do. Philosophy allows managers to examine reasons for establishing priorities for recurrent events; it lends credence to setting up policies to take care of these events. In essence, it is basic to everything that managers do.

Elementary principals carve out their jobs in unique ways—in the leadership they espouse, in the philosophy they communicate, in the values they adhere to, and in the priorities they set. In some schools, for example, principals may choose to be primarily the instructional leader; in others, the school manager. Priorities are a hierarchy. They presume not only that some things are more important than others but also that the more important things ought to be done first. Establishing these priorities is an important yet difficult activity for all middle managers. There are so many essential tasks to perform within given time constraints that it is seldom, if ever, easy to put those tasks in a reasonable order of importance. Elementary principals in particular are well aware of this problem, for they are constantly inundated with tasks.

The demands on elementary principals' time are numerous and varied; and all too often, the necessary support bases—either administrative or fiscal—are either inadequate or unavailable. Yet the demands must be met: elementary principals have to compile seemingly endless data on a seemingly endless number of things; they are asked to do many things by various groups, each of which believes that their requests or demands are the most important. In the face of such demands, even the best-intentioned, most dedicated principals who seem to budget available time in a manageable fashion, may find that they cannot accomplish all that they would like to accomplish, and further that they cannot devote as much time as they wish to certain responsibilities. Few of them have enough time in any given school day to accomplish all the things that, according to their job description, need to be done. And thus, faced with the reality of what they are able to do within the constraints of time and support, elementary principals often end up doing those things they *value* most, are *able* to do, and feel most *comfortable* with. Some feel comfortable in the role of instructional leader; others feel comfortable in the role of building manager; still others feel comfortable in the role of "friend" of students, parents, or community leaders; and some who become less comfortable in one role will switch to another role. The point is that when elementary principals do those things in which they feel more comfortable more frequently than those things in which they feel less comfortable, this is a form of establishing priorities.

PRIORITY DIMENSIONS

There are two basic priority dimensions: sequence and importance. Sequence deals with order of arrival and how things are done. For example, many middle managers handle daily assignments on a first-come, first-served basis. Certainly there are many problems inherent in this kind of approach, but the main danger in it is that the "minors" type of activities generally outnumber the "majors." But principals can avoid the sequence trap by planning effectively. For example, all principals have to supervise teachers, visit classrooms, and interact with students. Since students and teachers are at the school only part of the day, principals can, in establishing priorities, work with those things that involve teachers and students while the teachers and students are at the school. The rest of the working day can then be set up to accomplish the other things that need to be done, but that do not necessarily involve the teachers and students.

Importance could be best placed on a continuum that is scaled from "none" to "essential." The most frequent question asked of this dimension is: What kind of contribution does this action make to the good of the organization? In any job, there are some things we have to do, whether we like them or not; importance does not matter. And most of the time, these are routine, repetitive, sequential activities. For instance, some principals may have to open the school and lock it up daily—it is an essential activity and one that maybe cannot be delegated, depending on circumstances.

A third, perhaps related, dimension of priorities is urgency, which may be shown on a continuum from "Time Not Being a Consideration" to "Time Being a Very Important Consideration." All managers have many important things to do. And when they establish priorities, they spend more time on one thing than on something else. By establishing priorities with respect to urgency, we know better what it is that is important, what kind of responses need to be made, what deadlines need to be met, and in what order. And yet urgency serves no master except time. It demands that things be done within a certain time frame. Successful principals know, however, that urgency must be balanced by both sequence and importance. Drucker notes that successful managers who seem to do so many things—and apparently, many difficult things—do only one thing at a time. Thus, they need much less time overall to do those things. They begin by asking themselves what results are expected of them, rather than with the tools or techniques of the task.[5]

FOR WHOM ARE PRIORITIES DETERMINED?

Louis Allen[6] described five action modes by which managers may determine priorities: (1) spontaneous, (2) rational, (3) centric, (4) radic, and (5) omni. The spontaneous mode is defined as intuitive action to accomplish intuitive objectives. In it, you do, more or less, what comes naturally, reacting to immediate problems and rarely, if ever, either concentrate on causes or anticipate long-term consequences of the problems. The rational mode is defined as purposeful action to accomplish predetermined objectives. In it, you think through the steps necessary to accomplish objectives. The objectives are well founded and relatively constant in terms of action. The centric mode is defined as action that gives priority to self-needs and objectives, and only secondary emphasis to group needs and objectives. It is a habit-forming survival procedure that soon becomes self-defeating because the more you act in this mode, the more your actions convince others to act in the same mode. Eventually, everyone's objectives are self-based, and the organization's objectives become lost in the shuffle. The radic mode is defined as purposeful action taken to balance concern for self-needs and objectives with concern for others' needs and objectives. In it, you show genuine concern for others' needs and objectives. This mode is not intuitive; it has to be learned. It requires both conscious effort and skill of self-discipline. The omni mode is defined as the ability to act in all the modes to meet differing situations. To successfully implement this mode, you need, as a prerequisite, both knowledge of and skills in the first four modes and must ask such questions as: Toward what goal am I establishing priorities? Who is the main focus of those priorities—myself, the school or school system, the students, or the faculty? When principals decide to establish priorities for the school system and the students using the omni mode, they can then proceed to establishing daily operational priorities. *Priorities should be set*

---

[5]*Ibid.*, pp. 24–25, 103.
[6]Louis Allen, *Professional Management: New Concepts and Proven Practices* (New York: McGraw-Hill, 1973), pp. 14–23.

preferably for the students within guidelines set forth by the school system and care must be taken by principals to communicate this to teachers and others.

CREATING A POSITIVE MINDSET FOR ESTABLISHING PRIORITIES

Technical work is closely aligned with and composed mostly of technical skills. Teachers' work is generally considered as technical work (in the managerial context). Managerial work is more closely aligned with and composed mostly of broad conceptual skills that allow one to understand an overall organization. Principals' work is generally considered as managerial work. But, realistically, principals do things that feel comfortable; and principals, like most middle managers, generally feel more comfortable in technical work. This phenomenon is explained by Louis Allen's principle of technical priority, which states that "when called upon to perform management work and technical work during the same time period, managers will tend to give first priority to technical work."[7] It infers that if principals are given a choice, they will give preference to performing technical work duties over management work duties. Since, as Allen suggests, most managers need three to seven years experience to master those managerial skills necessary for team development and effective central office staff and teacher relationships, and since many principals do not receive effective managerial skill development at either the preservice or inservice levels, Allen's principle becomes all too applicable.

Conceptual, human, and technical skills are necessary at all management levels (see Figure 1–2). As middle managers, elementary principals should employ conceptual skills in their daily assignments more often than they do technical skills. Figure 2–2, an adaptation of Allen's ideas on "management gap"—the difference between ideal and actual performance in managerial work—explains both the relationship of those skills in principals' jobs and the importance of principals' realizing that relationship in effecting management skills.[8]

The figure shows that, ideally, middle managers should devote as much as 60 to 80 percent of their time to management work and as little as 20 to 40 percent of their time to technical work. In reality, however, a management gap exists. Some managers then devote as little as 20 percent of their time to management work and the remaining 80 percent to technical work. Allen's principle of technical priority, therefore, becomes very evident. Indeed, people tend to do those things they feel most comfortable with and because of the number of demands placed upon them and the nature of those demands, a natural tendency for elementary principals is to feel comfortable in doing technical work.

It is significant that elementary principals learn to set priorities. Principals must become more comfortable in management work so they can learn to associate themselves more with management skills as required by their job description.

Here are some guidelines for establishing priorities:

1. *List your duties.* First list your duties, then arrange them in the most-important to least-important order.

[7]*Ibid.*, p. 60.
[8]*Ibid.*, p. 58.

42   Managing the manager

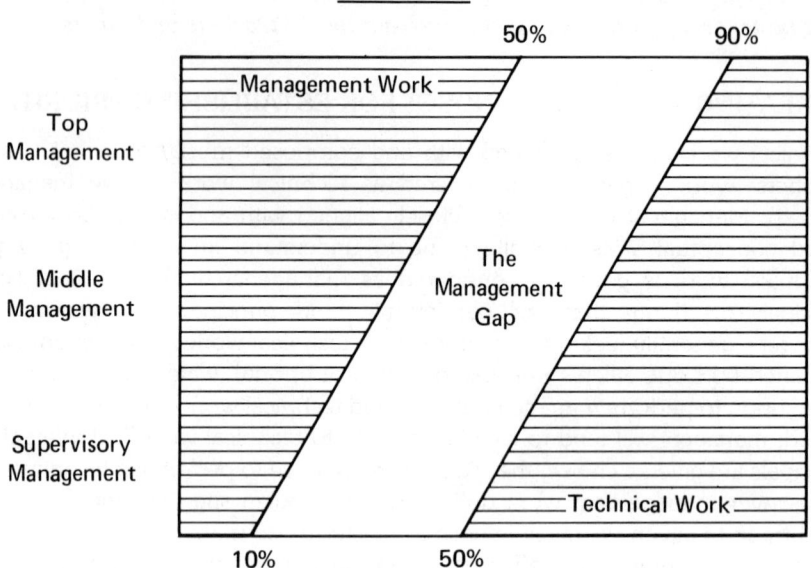

FIGURE 2-2

```
                              50%           90%
          ┌─────────Management Work─────────┐
  Top     │                  /             /│
Management│                 /             / │
          │                /             /  │
          │               /             /   │
          │              /             /    │
  Middle  │             /    The      /     │
Management│            / Management  /      │
          │           /    Gap      /       │
          │          /             /        │
          │         /             /         │
          │        /             /          │
Supervisory        /             /          │
Management│      /             /            │
          │     /             /────Technical Work────│
          └────────────────────────────────┘
         10%           50%
```

Example:

Consider a grocery shopping list. If you are on a budget (and all of us are), you wish to purchase the most nourishing food for your body at a price you can afford. Prepare a written list of those things you need and take that list to the grocery store with you. As you shop, keep a running tally on the items you buy. You know you cannot exceed a certain dollar amount for your purchases and throughout your selection process you prioritize and thus limit your purchases to the essential items.

Now apply that illustration to the elementary school. As principal, you wish to perform those role duties that will (1) promote improved learning and instruction and (2) allow you to maintain effective operation of the school. Prepare two copies—a "shopping list," so to speak—listing every possible duty that you have. Brainstorm and be as thorough as you can with this listing. On one copy, rank your "actual performance on the job" duties in the order of Most Often–Least Often. Then put that list aside for a few days.

On the second list rank on a high priority–low priority basis those things you should be doing to promote improved instruction and learning for the students, and maintain an effective operation. In other words, select those things you should be doing and put them in a "Most Often" category. Next, look at those things you consider least important and put them in the "Least Often" category.

You now have two lists—an "actual" list and a "should do" list. Compare them. Are they similar in ranking? Are the things you prioritized on your "actual" list the same (or similar to) those you listed on the "should do" list? As you compare and note the differences between the lists, ask yourself such questions as: Have I gotten into habits of doing only those things I like to do? Do I start doing something and then gradually spend more and more time at it until I neglect more important things? Do I shy away from doing things I really ought to be doing? How can I better prioritize? Brainstorm as many questions as you can think of.

Then look again at the two lists and begin to prioritize from the "Most Often" category on the "should do" list (see Figure 2–3).

Now you have a more effective method for prioritizing and finding time to set up a daily schedule in which you can do such things as

- Make and answer necessary telephone calls;
- Schedule and keep appointments;
- Find time to visit classrooms

and the like. Update your prioritizing charts as needed.

2. *Ensure that priority goals are realistic.* Priorities must be realistic. Only you know how many tasks you can accomplish and how well you can accomplish those tasks. "Should" priorities may not be attainable or realistic within your present operational framework. Suggestions for making them more realistic will be afforded below in the Managing Time section.

3. *Translate priority statements into specific, identifiable tasks.* Do this for both high-priority and low-priority duties. Not only will you learn to better perform the high-priority duties, you will also learn to eliminate the time-consuming or

FIGURE 2–3

	ACTUAL	SHOULD
High Priority	1.	1.
	2.	2.
	3.	3.
	4.	4.
Low Priority	1.	1.
	2.	2.
	3.	3.
	4.	4.

unessential low-priority duties or tasks within those duties that, over a period of time, you may have committed to habit.

4. *See only one priority task at a time through completion—reality permitting.*

MANAGING TIME

Suspect each moment for it is like a thief
Tiptoeing away with more than it brings.

— John Updike

Having established priorities, elementary principals should focus on managing time in order to carry out priority tasks. Good managers respect time, both their own and that of others. They take the time necessary to work on assignments—but no more. And they use their time judiciously (in particular, on potential time wasters as telephone calls and planned meetings in which objectives are fully reached in half the allotted time). Time-respecting managers also know that effectiveness requires a balance between work and the outside activities that refresh and enrich self.

Everyone has an equal amount of time. To make the most of it, it is essential to commit advance thought and planning.

Managing time includes

- Planning;
- Organizing and budgeting time;
- Making the most of available resources;
- Delegating responsibilities;
- Making decisions.

FIGURE 2-4

Priority	Objective(s)	Task activity	Procedure	Responsibility	Completion time
Observe lesson	Improve teaching and learning	Effect clinical supervision cycle on teacher 1. Planning conference 2. Observation 3. Analysis and strategy 4. Conference	Explain process and rationale to teacher, then arrange time schedule for four-step task	Principal	1 week

PLANNING

Establishing priorities is not only a prerequisite to effective planning, it is also an integral first step in the planning process. In planning, priorities must be established, priority objectives should be reviewed, specific tasks established to attain the objective(s), task procedures developed, task responsibilities assigned and task completion time designated. Figure 2−4 affords an example of this process.

Planning is an integral component of managing time. Ideally, middle managers ought not to have many planning problems. Why? Management work lends itself easily to categories, and planning within the categories can follow a logical, integrated pattern. In reality, middle managers do experience planning problems. Why? Well, as previously noted, middle managers tend to engage more in technical work than in managerial work, and comparatively, technical work is less easily categorized and technical planning need not be as integrated. What little planning does take place seems to be more for the urgent moment. We suggest that as managers try to become more comfortable in the management aspects of their work (as opposed to the technical aspects), their planning will, of necessity, improve.

Some planning guidelines are:

- Make notes on what you plan to do, thinking all the while that you have to both determine the value (to the students and staff) of your priorities and work on limiting your priorities and activities within them so that they may be accomplished.
- Devise a charting system (like the kind shown above) for setting priorities.
- Make goals realistic if you expect to accomplish them.
- Distinguish between individual and group-related activities so you can plan more realistically to meet all needs.
- Begin planning for a given amount of time—perhaps a year. Then, plan for a semester, then maybe a month. Work that time frame down to a week and then eventually down to a day. Although you should remain flexible, you must know what you can do within any given time frame. Your system should include those cyclical activities for which you must plan.
- Learn how to budget time.
- Allocate specific blocks of time to accomplish major projects (the majors).
- Allocate some free time for the unexpected and emergencies.
- Allocate time for creative thinking.
- Look at what you have accomplished. Compare what you are planning to what you have already achieved in order to better understand your capabilities. Such comparisons will help you limit your planned activities.

ORGANIZING AND BUDGETING TIME

According to MacKenzie, the term "time management" is actually a misnomer since time is beyond our control and it really cannot be managed. Time moves on, is irretrievable, and can be neither stretched nor shrunk. What we really mean by time management is management of ourselves with respect to time, and this basically means getting organized.

Management of time may be equated to management of self. Management of self, although a time-consuming process, is similar to a popular television commercial that advertises that its brand of television receiver is the most expensive in the United States—but darn well worth it. The same may be said of time: In the long run, getting organized is darn well worth it, for it saves us time and we usually get better results.

MacKenzie listed 15 leading time wasters encountered by middle managers.[9]

The 15 leading time wasters

1. Telephone interruptions.
2. Visitors dropping in without appointments.
3. Meetings, both scheduled and unscheduled.
4. Crisis situations for which no plans were possible.
5. Lack of objectives, priorities, and deadlines.
6. Cluttered desk and personal disorganization.
7. Involvement in routine and detail that should be delegated to others.
8. Attempting too much at once and underestimating the time it takes to do it.
9. Failure to set up clear lines of responsibility and authority.
10. Inadequate, inaccurate, or delayed information from others.
11. Indecision and procrastination.
12. Lack of or unclear communication and instruction.
13. Inability to say "No."
14. Lack of standards and progress reports that enable a principal to keep track of developments.
15. Fatigue.

Do some of these sound familiar to you? Well, everyone has time-wasting habits. All self-management involves habits. Changing of time-wasting habits requires knowing where you are now, where you want to go, how you would like to get there, and once there, how well you did throughout the process.

[9]Interview with R. Alex MacKenzie, a leading management consultant, *U.S. News and World Report* (December 3), 1973.

Controlling time wasters or changing them into time gainers is perhaps the key to time management. Some time wasters — such as lack of planning or prioritizing, attempting to do too much at one time, procrastinating, the "can't say no" syndrome, communicating poorly, lack of delegating, fighting fires (the technical work managers force upon themselves by not delegating)—are internal. Others—such as telephone interruptions, visitors, crises, and meetings—are external.

To better control time wasters, managers must first be aware of how they waste time. Perhaps the best way to make that discovery is through a weekly log. Figure 2−5 provides a possible format for a time-management weekly log.

The example, in hour blocks of time, shows what activities the manager spent time on during a given day. When preparing your time log, plan to make more frequent entries than shown in the example. Ask the secretary (if you have one) to assist you in preparing the log for a one-week period, being as specific and judicious in your logging as possible. Your log, for example, may contain many entries in say, Monday's 9−10 column, while only a few in another column.

FIGURE 2−5
Time-management weekly log[10]

Beside each hour of the day, write what you did most of that time. Then, at the end of each working day, classify your time according to this code:

#1 = Professional goal functions (curriculum planning, teacher conferences, teacher evaluation, classroom visitation)
#2 = Critical/crisis functions (vandalism, student discipline, accidents, unannounced resignations)
#3 = Maintenance functions (phone calls, cafeteria and bus duty, fire drills, enforcing dress code)
P = Personal activity

		EXAMPLE	MONDAY	TUESDAY	WEDNESDAY	THURSDAY	FRIDAY
8	#3	Open mail organize	8	8	8	8	8
9	#2	Appointment w/staff	9	9	9	9	9
10	#2	Weekend fire	10	10	10	10	10
11	#3	Answer correspondence	11	11	11	11	11
12		Lunch	12	12	12	12	12
1	#1	Called staff re: 5-yr. plan	1	1	1	1	1
2	P	Dentist	2	2	2	2	2
3	#3	Committee central office	3	3	3	3	3
4	#3	Met with parent	4	4	4	4	4

TOTALS: Count the hours you spend this week on: #1____ #2____ #3____ P____
Your goal for next week: #1____ #2____ #3____ P____

[10]Source: "The Time Management Ladder" by Michael J. Sexton and Karen Switzer, *Educational Leadership,* March 1978, Vol. 35, No. 6, p. 485.

When you have summarized your activities for the week, total the number of hours you have spent on 1, 2, 3, 4, P, as suggested by Figure 2–5, or by a coding system of your own design.

You now have a better idea of the kinds of activities you engage in during the week. And you may be rather surprised—or even shocked—at discovering the kinds of things you *do* spend time on. Now you can plan to eliminate or at least decrease time wasters. To check your improvement, you could designate your goals for the next week (see Figure 2–5), prepare another time log, and check the totals at week's end. Some principals would welcome this type of activity (the continued time log), while others would prefer a less encompassing approach. For those we suggest that after completing the initial weekly time log, you designate what you consider to be your top two-to-five time-wasting habits. Prepare a simple chart, as shown in Figure 2–6, on the left of which would be a column titled "Time-Wasting Habit." Under that column, chart those two-to-five things which you consider to be your time-wasting habits — for example, talking too long on coffee breaks, doing too many things by yourself, doing too much administrivia, or personally working on absentee charts. On the right side of this chart, write the column heading "New Habit" and between these two headings, leave space for a long column entitled "Improvement," allowing enough space for about six weeks of listings. Under this "Improvement" column, you would list those things done to establish the "New Habit." In other words, this chart will allow you to list time-wasting habits and show progress in eliminating those habits. And you can work on improving as many time-wasting habits as you wish, and in the time framework you choose. Keep in mind that time wasters can be turned into time gainers. If, for example, you have listed "telephone" as a top time waster, try to turn it into a time gainer by planning your outgoing calls, setting a limit for all calls, keeping telephone conversations brief and on target, and perhaps having the secretary better screen incoming calls. And if "visitors" (either internal or external) seem to take up too much of your time, you might consider such things as: rearrange your office furniture, meet visitors at the door, keep the "open-door"

FIGURE 2–6

Time-wasting habit	Improvement	New habit
Doing too much administrivia	Week 1: Prepare time log of all activities. Week 2: Analyze time log, compare with job description duties. Choose two administrivia items that can be delegated. Week 3: Test. Week 4: Evaluate.	Delegating

policy in proper perspective, schedule meetings on your time needs, determine items to be covered in the visit, and have your secretary screen to see if someone else can handle the problem.

The do's and don'ts of organizing and budgeting time are complex indeed—and they all point to managing self. Managing self requires more than on-the-job considerations. Time wasters such as fatigue and inability to say no are perhaps a direct result of managers' not considering the whole self in their approach to time management.

Fred Wilhelms, former Executive Director of the Association for Supervision and Curriculum Development, when reflecting upon his principal days, offered these thoughts in relation to organizing time:

> The dedicated principal who constantly works exhausting hours, taking on every job that needs to be done, may not be doing his school the service he thinks he is. For it is more important for him to build up and protect some areas of thoughtful tranquility in his life—else he has no way of creating the reserves of vision and courage that he needs in the crises. He may have to be pretty ruthless about it. It's no good waiting until the leisure and opportunities come ready-made. They won't. A man may simply have to turn his back on a lot of insistent demands—even important ones—*whether it seems as though he can, or not.*
>
> How to do it must be a purely personal matter. For one person it may be a quiet day's fishing that refills the tanks. For another it may be the quiet contemplation of good reading. Whatever works will be worth what it costs.[11]

In organizing and budgeting time, consider the whole self. You cannot be all things to all people. Plan, reduce time wasters, and the job will be easier; chances are you will do it more efficiently, too. Overall, learning what to do and what not to do and learning how to say No are key elements in all attempts at getting organized.

MAKING THE MOST OF AVAILABLE RESOURCES

Getting organized and making the most of available resources are almost impossible to differentiate. How can managers make the most of resources? One of the most important things to consider is the time log in which you make a routine check of the activities in which you are involved. By charting what you do throughout each day and during the week, you discover which things are less important (minors). You can then move to those things which are more important (majors); and learn better to use available resources.

Inherent in any role are certain responsibilities. List those things that you would like to do and compare that list to the weekly time log to determine which

---

[11]Fred T. Wilhelms, "The Delicate Art Called Supervision," *The Headmaster* (Fall 1970), p. 47.

activities you are now doing that could be better and more feasibly accomplished by other personnel—as the secretary, the teachers in leadership positions, the maintenance personnel, and in the central office—the supervisor, the coordinator, titled persons and others—as delineated in their job description. For instance, what kinds of tasks can be delegated to the school secretary—who can probably do them more efficiently than you on a regular basis? Similarly, what tasks can be transferred to a central office person who perhaps can do these things more efficiently than you because it better fits his or her job?

Consider the following principal's account of his time, as he attempts to be organized and make the most of available resources:

> As the principal and administrator of an elementary school with an enrollment of 801 children, 43 teachers and other employees, I must plan my time carefully. In order to supervise realistically, I must project and plan all activities.
>
> First, I outline and plan one month's work at a time. Then each week I revise my schedule, making any necessary changes to facilitate a smoother operation.
>
> All departments of the school are organized into teams (learning communities). Team leaders meet with me weekly to plan curriculum, solve scheduling problems, better meet student needs, plan for staff training, and air grievances, and the like. Planning is this group's main function and I must be well planned before I meet with them each week.
>
> Administrative and curriculum areas must be constantly supervised and changes occur frequently. I place "due dates" or deadlines on my calendar one week in advance to allow myself a cushion and to ensure prompt task completion. Additionally, I post or rate scheduled and unscheduled work in priority order and strive to complete the more pressing matters first. When extra-heavy work loads come up, I try to delegate tasks, if possible. This procedure eases work loads for me and ensures good training for subordinates.
>
> The most difficult thing for me is finding time to meet with teachers, students, and parents. Again, planning and scheduling is the key. I visit and work with teachers in the classroom as often as possible, and try to evaluate their teaching performance and techniques while observing students' progress. (And I also feel that this is an excellent—and perhaps the best—way to study a child who has learning or behavioral problems.) I try to schedule student and parent conferences in late afternoon after teachers have already left for the day. Open communication with teachers, parents, and students seems to be a great time-saver for me. Uninformed people cause wasted time for any principal (manager).
>
> Finally, it is necessary for me to have privacy to do correspondence, bookkeeping, budget, and unfinished reports. One Saturday is set aside a month to complete these tasks. Saturday work is especially successful since there are no interruptions.
>
> I feel the need to grow, and in order to become a better manager, the remainder of my time is spent working on my Six-Year Superintendent Certificate.

This principal seems to organize time well, tries to use available resources, and tries to delegate. Yet principals can even better use available resources such as: supervisory personnel, student council, students in other-than-student roles, community volunteers, parent volunteers, media, PTA, other outside organizations, and the like. The point is that other resources are available. Find them and use them.

DELEGATING RESPONSIBILITIES

Delegating implies sharing, and in managerial tasks, sharing requires both skill and self-discipline. Delegating is assigning work to others for which you are ultimately accountable. Delegation is a necessary component of any manager's activities. Used properly, it is a form of self-improvement. Delegating can

- Save managerial time;
- Increase subordinates' and managers' confidence and security;
- Increase efficiency and effectiveness.

Delegating requires managers to:
1. Organize and know what has to be done. Select the task(s) to be delegated. What are some tasks that might be delegated? Brainstorm a minute. Think of the times when

- You have too many routine tasks to do;
- You have specific and technical problems to solve;
- You have priorities that have been "hanging around" a long time;
- You do not have enough time;
- There is an emergency.

2. Determine whose role best fits each task to be delegated. If appropriate, assign that work to personnel within your building, or if the assignment is better fitting to the central office personnel, refer it to the appropriate person. In either case, make sure that there is enough communication between you and the personnel involved, both for the rationale of doing the job, and for understanding how to do it.

3. Provide enough support to the person(s) performing the task. Check, on a regular basis, on that person's performance progress, and if necessary, evaluate the performance.

DECISION MAKING

Managers' effectiveness is directly related to the quality of their decisions. Decision making is integral to the role of elementary principals. Some authorities even say it is the very heart of the role; still others equate it with managing. Decisions must be made in determining priorities, budgeting time, and delegating and solving problems in every area and phase of school operation. Principals are given both the authority to make those decisions and the responsibility for the results of the decisions.

To become proficient in decision making, practice is necessary. Earlier in this chapter, examples were provided to help principals improve self by overcoming weaknesses. To improve decision making, principals need similar practice, preferably in low-risk situations. Such practice, using strength areas combined with low-risk activities, will promote principals' confidence in decision making, while at the same time allowing them to further their expertise in the decision-making process.

The rationale for suggesting these practice procedures is as follows:

In many cases when principals are called upon to make decisions, they must make the decision either within a constraining time frame or within an area in which they feel less than expert, or both. Thus, principals would like to feel confident in their decision-making ability so that these variables would have little effect on them. *Practice is essential.*

Two prerequisites are necessary for decision making: the decision must be your responsibility and timing must be right for making the decision. Typical decision-making steps are:

1   Identify and define the problem on which a decision is to be made—in a realistic perspective.
2   Collect all the facts—the who, why, when, and where—from all involved personnel.
3   Develop alternative solutions.
4   Consider the consequences of each solution.
5   Choose the most appropriate solution.
6   Try it out.
7   If possible, evaluate.

The previous section dealt with time-management principles in a practical, general manner. The purpose of this section is to present a somewhat conceptual model, using time-management principles, as a principal's guide to promoting innovation and being aware of some constraints principals will encounter in such attempts.

IDENTIFYING INNOVATIONAL CONSTRAINTS: A MODEL FOR SCHOOL PRINCIPALS[12]
ROBERT J. KRAJEWSKI AND PAUL E. ZINTGRAFF

Change and innovation are key words emphasized in virtually every current reference to school administration. Either concept can be beneficial or deleterious, depending on its interpretation or application. Most educational leaders caution that change simply for change's sake is not prudent. Change is a slow process, and promoting innovation within the school is a difficult and time-consuming task. It is evident, however, that there can be neither improvement nor progress without some form of change. Consequently, school administrators at all levels must recognize and plan for needed change and innovation. A search of

---

[12]This section is taken from an article written by Robert J. Krajewski and Paul E. Zintgraff in Educational Technology *(December 1977). Reprinted with permission of the authors and* Educational Technology.

the literature produces general agreement that the school principal is the key in planning change within the school. Role responsibilities of the principal clearly substantiate this agreement. Once a plan for change has been accepted, the principal is instrumental in setting the stage for its implementation. There is no substitute for administrative leadership.

IDENTIFYING NEED

When contemplating change, the sage school principal should first recognize the need for it. Whether through a formal needs assessment, informal means, or whatever, the logical initial step is identifying the need for change. Once the need is apparent, the planning process can be initiated. The format seems simple enough: first establish objectives, then set a plan of action (who, what, when, where, why, and how) for their achievement, and finally determine an evaluation procedure. In theory, the process appears destined for success; in practice, however, this may not always be the case. The congruence of theoretical soundness and practical realities becomes lessened and sometimes voided by constraints.

CONSTRAINTS

"Constraint," according to Webster, is "the state of being held back, restricted, limited, or compelled to avoid or perform some action." Most change-oriented principals have heard such phrases as "It won't work, we've always done it this way, it's too late to try that now," and others. Some successfully overcome these negative postures and are able to innovate within their schools. Others, however, fall prey to them and thus are trapped in their efforts to change, succeeding only in maintaining the status quo, at best.

Principals are subject to innovational constraints by the school board, the administrative hierarchy, students, teachers, and school patrons, as well as by their own unwillingness to take risks. The constraints may be fiscal, legal, socio-cultural, temporal, physical, or psychological. The innovational domains within which the constraints operate are such aspects as: role expectations, organizational climate, reward system, knowledge and information, and professional skills. Constraint identification, though a necessary ingredient to effective planning (and subsequent implementation for innovation), is an arduous process, one in which principals may not have requisite skills. Yet, the constraints exist and must be identified. But how? How can the principal, within the confines of the existing daily pressures of his or her position, identify such constraints to innovation as those listed above? One answer may be self-analysis through the development and employment of a model.

A CONCEPTUAL MODEL

Figure 1 offers an example of a three-dimensional model for identification of constraints to innovation. The horizontal dimension of the model depicts various constraints: psychological, physical, temporal, socio-cultural, legal, and fiscal. The vertical dimension of the model identifies personnel who subject the principal to the above-listed constraints: teachers, students, patrons, and administrative hierarchy. The third dimension of the model contains the innovational domains within which the constraints operate: role expectations, organizational climate, reward system, knowledge and information, and professional skills. Elements of both this dimension and the horizontal dimension may vary, depending on the particular school district or school. Note that the model, as depicted, is neither all-inclusive nor absolute; rather, it is offered as a guide. The elements, as listed, may be limited or expanded. Because no one model would be applicable for all situations, we suggest that principals develop a model suitable for their purposes. It is appropriate at this time to examine functionally, through examples, some constraints identified by the model:

FIGURE 1
Model for identification of constraints to innovation

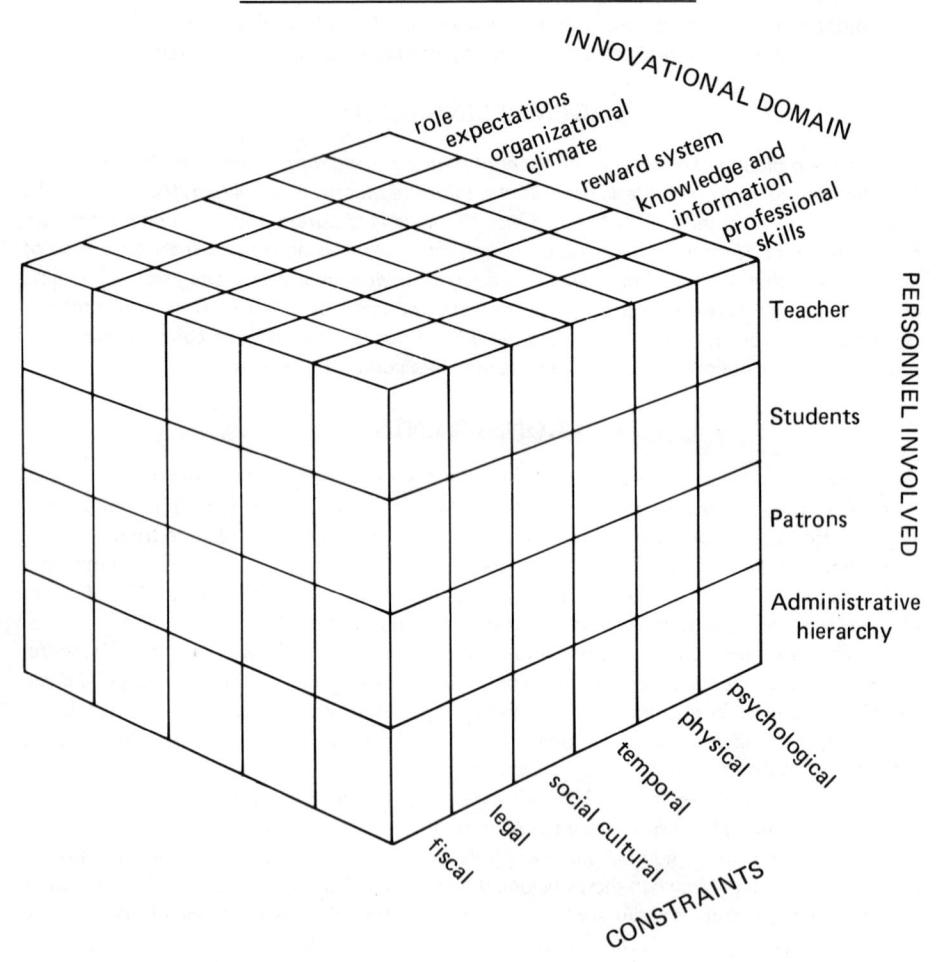

Psychological
    fear of the unknown
    inability to organize
    inability to prioritize
    inability to accept self
    lack of imagination
    lack of self-confidence
    inability to communicate
    inability to diagnose
    inability to evaluate
    tenure

Social-Cultural
    lack of self-acceptance
    fear of parental acceptance

outdated philosophies/methods
collegial acceptance
ethical boundaries
lack of understanding of students
fear of societal acceptance
meeting needs of others

Fiscal
monies available
materials needed
monies not available
teacher salary
principal salary
economic background of community
budget priority
outside funding possibilities
district money raising capacity

Temporal
school's place in societal needs
released time for teachers
daily schedule
yearly schedule
paperwork and administrivia
reputation of school district

Legal
state laws and regulations
standards of accrediting agencies
fear of tort liability
regulations imposed by school board
federal restrictions
use of federal monies

Physical
building size
space arrangement
classroom size
teacher's lounge
traffic/movement of people
climate control features
lighting of office space
efficiency of office space
lack of special-use spaces
  (nurse's office, gym, resource center, auditorium)

MODEL IMPLEMENTATION

Figure 2 affords a two-dimensional perspective of the model. In it, all cells are labeled H(igh), M(edium), or L(ow) to indicate the correlation between the constraint and the personnel group involved. In this example, the principal, upon examination, initially perceives constraint limitations in all but six of the 24 designated cells. Specifically, he or she feels secure in dealing with students and patrons in both physical and temporal constraints, with patrons in legal constraints and with students in fiscal constraints (indicated by L). More significantly, however, he or she feels least secure in dealing with all personnel in terms of both psychological and social-cultural constraints and with teachers and the administrative hierarchy in several other constraints (indicated by H). Thus, having completed the initial stage of identification of constraint correlation with personnel involved, the principal is now prepared for detailed analysis of the H cells. By so doing, he or she further refines the identification of constraints, the end result being a fairly sophisticated, logically developed list of significant constraints; and, not incidentally, a partial list of objectives with much insight into how to deal with these constraints, i.e., he or she is well on the way to dealing effectively with the constraints after the analysis is accomplished. Let us now look at two examples of detailed cell analysis.

Example 1: Teachers-psychological cell, correlation H
Relate the psychological constraints (some of which were listed earlier) to the teachers in your school. Next, brainstorm through leading questions, such as: Do the teachers accept themselves? Do they lack imagination? Can they organize, communicate, evaluate? Do they have self-confidence? Are they fearful of the unknown? Then ask the same questions of yourself in your relationship with them. Additionally, ask questions such as: How many teachers have tenure? What percentage are energetic? By listing all possibilities, you can then determine whether the H correlation in this cell is a cause for serious concern. If, for instance, the teachers are energetic and possess positive psychological characteristics, the H correlation should indicate a conduciveness to innovation and not constraint. Conversely, if the

FIGURE 2
Two-dimensional perspective of model

	PSYCHOLOGICAL	PHYSICAL	TEMPORAL	SOCIAL CULTURAL	LEGAL	FISCAL
TEACHERS	H	M	H	H	M	M
STUDENTS	H	L	L	H	MH	L
PATRONS	H	L	L	H	L	M
ADMINISTRATIVE HIERARCHY	H	H	M	H	H	H

combination of teacher characteristics and psychological constraints is not positive, then indeed the H correlation connotes high proclivity for innovational constraint.

Example 2: Administrative hierarchy-fiscal cell, correlation H
In this situation, the principal should analyze the fiscal constraints (previously listed) as they relate to upper-level administration, asking such questions as: Are they concerned about the salary of personnel involved? Do they feel that change doesn't merit a high fiscal priority? Are they convinced that outside funding is not available? Do they evaluate the background of the community as being inconsistent with the proposed change? Are too many new materials and equipment required to implement the innovation? After completing a thorough analysis of these questions, the principal can then ascertain the amount of resistance likely to be confronted if he or she attempts to implement the change. However, further analysis may indicate avenues for overcoming the constraints. For example, procurement of funds from outside sources may result in lessening constraints in other fiscal areas. The administrative hierarchy, moreover, may react positively if increases in salary and capital outlay expenses are not required. On the other hand, if none of the constraints can be changed, the possibility of successfully implementing the innovation is in jeopardy.

Essential to using the model is the analysis of all cells.

The examples noted above are but two of the cells listed as H. The principal, when analyzing each cell (particularly the H cells) becomes familiar with interactive elements of the constraints and personnel and their influence on the problem. Once the identification/analysis of the constraints is completed, the principal can then establish objectives and specify a feasible plan of action for dealing with the constraints.

CONCLUSION

The two-dimensional perspective of the model allows detailed analysis of the constraints and personnel correlation as it relates to the specific elements from the innovative domain. The actual elements of the two-dimensional model presented in Figure 2 may differ, as may the H, M, or L designations within the cells. The process of analysis within the cells, however, is a constant and remains the key for proper identifiction of innovational constraints; without it, the model is rendered useless and innovational constraint identification virtually impotent. With proper analysis, however, the principal, through use of the model, can—within the confines of his or her everyday job—effect his or her own needs assessment and thus identify innovational constraints.

SELECTING AREAS FOR PROFESSIONAL DEVELOPMENT

When you're up to your neck in trouble . . .
Try using the part that's not submerged.

— Anonymous

"Know self, accept self, and respect self, but always strive for improvement" is sage advice. All professional managers should realize that there is a continuing need to improve job performance skills, no matter what level of skills one possesses, and further that they *must* take necessary steps to improve their skills.

Various sources are available for principals' acquiring, improving, and refining skills: gathering ideas and materials from other principals and teachers, engaging in professional reading, attending state and national conferences and workshops, receiving ideas from significant others—these are but a few. Deciding which of these to pursue, and in what order to pursue them, remains, however, no easy task. Selecting areas for professional development would necessitate

- Knowing where you are and what you have;
- Conducting a needs assessment and a priorities designation within your existing reality framework;
- Effecting an action plan for acquiring and improving skills and, periodically,
- Evaluating your progress.

Know where you are and what you have

First, take stock. Determine what skills you already possess. One good method is simply to use the strengths and weaknesses chart you have already developed. From that chart, not only can you determine types of skills you now possess, you can also determine how far along the skill level chart you have progressed.

Assess your needs

Obtain feedback from others. Prepare a written questionnaire and administer it to yourself, teachers, and peers.

Armed with this feedback and given your present responsibilities and stage of development, you can prepare a needs assessment to determine which skills need refining or improving, which skills you would like to improve and why, and then determine which should be given priority. The needs assessment would not be complete if, for instance, one were to decide without any input from others, what the priorities would be (within a given needs assessment). It must have input from many, including teachers, peers, and the designated responsible administrative personnel in the school system's chain of command to whom principals are responsible.

The results of a recent study of Texas elementary principals' and teachers' perceptions of the principals' role (real and ideal) are shown in Figure 2–7.

The study revealed that:

1. Neither teachers nor principals agreed that the actual principal's role is what it should be. On the other hand, teachers and principals agreed on what the principal's role actually is and also agreed on what the principal's role ought to be and this agreement was slightly greater at the ideal level.

2. The principal's actual role in instructional improvement was viewed by principals as being mildly important and by teachers as not being too important, but they both ideally regarded it as a priority role. Principals, in fact, overwhelmingly rated it #1 ideally. Teachers ideally rated it #2.

3. The principal's role as staff selector was actually seen as not too important, but ideally both principals and teachers agreed that it deserves more importance.

4. In contrasting, both principals and teachers saw the principal's real role as

Selecting areas for professional development 59

FIGURE 2-7

	Principal real PR	Principal ideal PI	Teacher real TR	Teacher ideal TI
Instructional supervisor	4	1	7	2
School program administrator	1	4	1	1
Staff selector/orientator	9	3	8	3
Curriculum supervisor	8	2	9	4
Morale builder	5	6	6	5
Public relations facilitator	3	5	2	7
Public services coordinator	6	7	5	6
Teacher evaluator	7	8	4	8
Self-evaluator	10	9	10	10
Disciplinarian	2	10	3	9

disciplinarian as quite important, but ideally they felt it should not be important at all.

5   Both principals and teachers felt the principal's role as curriculum supervisor is not very important, but both agreed that it should be—principals more strongly than teachers.

6   Neither principals nor teachers wished to see the principal as teacher evaluator, though teachers agreed that the principals now serve this role.

7   Both teachers and principals saw the principal first as administrator; whereas teachers expected the principal to retain this priority, the principals felt more inclined toward supervision, curriculum, and staff selection.

From 2, 3, 5, and 7 it may therefore be concluded that both principals and teachers want the principal's role as instructional and curriculum supervisor to be more pronounced than it presently is, while the principal simultaneously retains the role of administrator. Of particular significance was the principals' strong conviction that they would like to see themselves first and foremost as instructional supervisors.[13]

The study was conducted specifically for needs-assessment purposes, as the intent was to find out which preparation areas should be emphasized in the university graduate preparation program. Results were distributed to elementary principal participants. A similar needs-assessment process can easily be effected by principals in their respective schools, using items specific to the principal's role, such as: instructional supervisor, curriculum supervisor, staff selector and orientor, school program administrator of materials and facilities, teacher evaluator, morale builder, public relations facilitator, pupil services coordinator, disciplinarian, and self-evaluator.

Plan action

Once you have completed needs assessment, you can begin working on an action plan for improving (designated) skills. The action plan must, of course, take place

---

[13]Robert J. Krajewski, "The Real Versus the Ideal: How Elementary Principals Perceive Their Role in Texas," *Texas Elementary Principals and Supervisors Association Journal* (May 1977), p. 13.

within the reality framework of your existing position. For instance, if travel monies are not available you cannot assume that you will have the opportunity to acquire skills by attending national conferences or workshops. If those particular skills you have deemed necessary to improve or refine are not at this time held by other principals within the school system, then again (realistically) you cannot expect to gather ideas for skill improvement from those principals. *You must design the action plan within the realities of your position and your time framework.*

Evaluate

As with any plan of action, evaluation is an important ingredient. Your plan and your progress within that plan must be objectively evaluated. Without such an objective evaluation, you cannot find out how much you have improved or, indeed, whether you have improved at all.

Any evaluation plan you decide to use must measure those things that it purports to measure. Thus, your activities must be written in such a manner that they can be objectively evaluated. The evaluation is only as good as the plan for evaluation. If you expect to get good evaluation results, you must have a good evaluation plan.

CASE STUDY—THE BUSY PRINCIPAL

The following time-management case study describes the predicament of an elementary principal who, although well-intentioned and having good ideas, never quite gets his ideas into actual pracctice due to a *time* factor—he never seems to have any.

Hinsdale Elementary School, located in the suburbs of a large Northeastern city, has an enrollment of approximately 300 students, grades K–6. Mr. Britman, the principal, is energetic, has an outgoing personality, and always seems to be on the go. He sees himself as an effective leader and has a strong interest in being a catalyst for learning. Although he visits classes frequently, his visits usually involve simply saying "Hi" to the teacher, taking a quick look around, and then dashing on his way again. When he speaks to teachers at faculty meetings or when he talks to them in his office, the hallway, or lounge, he has many good suggestions for them—in curriculum, instruction, and class projects.

As great as his ideas appear to be, however, they are seldom put into use by the teachers. In fact, over the past several years, the school has declined in student achievement scores. Teacher morale has suffered, too. What was once a highly motivated faculty now seems to be a somewhat uncommitted, demoralized group.

Buy why? Mr. Britman is talented (of that there is no doubt), dedicated (seemingly), and involved in community projects. In fact, he's just plain busy. However, something is amiss; his busyness is not producing positive, observable results.

The problem lies in the fact that Mr. Britman does not follow through with his suggestions. Perhaps this is because he does not know how to get beyond the suggestion stage. Besides, he's too busy to help. He always has something to do: paperwork, phone calls, interviews, lunchroom problems, classroom observations, and community work. He simply makes suggestions and leaves teachers on their own to initiate the suggestions and obtain results.

Although the teachers accept and welcome his suggestions, they are frustrated because their schedule provides little or no planning time and Mr. Britman offers no help.

Their frustration is compounded because they are having to assume some of Mr. Britman's responsibilities, such as lunchroom, library, reading room, activities, playground.

Recently, the central office has become concerned as they've received feedback from both community and staff concerning this problem. Indirect attempts to solve the problem were initiated at principals' meetings, yet after several months these efforts have had no impact on Mr. Britman. The superintendent then decided that more direct measures were needed and asked the assistant superintendent personally to investigate the problem.

The assistant superintendent, a mild-mannered, somewhat shy person, having a personality much less outgoing than Mr. Britman's, is considered by many to be a quite effective personnel manager. He set up an appointment with Mr. Britman for Tuesday at 8:30 A.M.

At 8:30 on Tuesday, the assistant superintendent arrives at Mr. Britman's office. The school secretary asked him to wait in Mr. Britman's office and that Mr. Britman would be there shortly. As he sat waiting he could not help but notice the untidy condition of Mr. Britman's desk and office.

As you ponder this case study, try to determine how some of the time management principles/suggestions included in this chapter might be of benefit to Mr. Britman.

SUGGESTED READINGS

Allen, Louis A. *Professional Management: New Concepts and Proven Practices.* New York: McGraw-Hill, 1973.

Association for Supervision and Curriculum Development. *Perceiving, Behaving, Becoming: A New Focus for Education.* Yearbook, Washington, D.C.: ASCD, 1962.

Bemis, Warren G., Benne, Kenneth D., Chin, Robert, and Corey, Kenneth E. *The Planning of Change,* 3d ed. New York: Holt, Rinehart and Winston, 1976.

Drucker, Peter F. *The Effective Executive.* New York: Harper & Row, 1967.

Hamachek, Don E. *Encounters with the Self.* New York: Holt, Rinehart and Winston, 1971.

Hanson, E. Mark. *Educational Administration and Organizational Behavior.* Boston: Allyn and Bacon, 1979.

Lipham, James M., and Hoeh, James A. *The Principalship: Foundations and Functions.* New York: Harper & Row 1974.

Newport, M. Gene. *The Tools of Managing: Functions, Techniques, and Skills.* Reading, Mass.: Addison-Wesley, 1972.

Powell, John, S.J. *Why Am I Afraid to Tell You Who I Am?* Niles, Ill.: Argus Communications, 1969.

CHAPTER

3

ORGANIZING THE SCHOOL

**Selecting the team
Interviewing applicants
Clarifying roles
Organizing for instruction
Motivating the team**

An organization as complex as the elementary school is only as good as the people who manage it. Elementary principals are responsible for organizing faculty and staff to effect a sound institutional program. Teachers, students, custodians, lunchroom workers, secretaries, and others all have integral roles to play. Organizing and coordinating those varied roles demands principal leadership that begins with selecting and employing a top-flight faculty and staff, proceeds with effective planning prior to implementing programs, and incorporates continual evaluation of plans, faculty, and programs.

SELECTING THE TEAM

Principals may have little or no voice in deciding which teachers are selected to staff their school. There are, generally, three ways of making that decision, depending on the size of the district and the leadership style of the superintendent or personnel director.

    1. The principal recruits, interviews, reviews credentials, and recommends teacher candidates to the superintendent for employment. In this method the principal makes all the selection decisions.

    2. The principal interviews a few qualified candidates and indicates an order of preference to the superintendent.

3. The teacher candidate is assigned without any input from the principal. In this method, the principal has no role in the selection process.

Selecting the members of a teaching team who will work well together requires professional judgement based on an objective analysis of many facts. Therefore the third selection process is probably becoming an unusual practice, except in a few large urban districts. Generally superintendents have discovered that when a principal has a voice in selecting teaching personnel the school operates with less friction, and the instructional program has a better chance of succeeding. Since the board of education must approve hiring of all employees, the methods of selecting the school team are a function of their policies. The superintendent is responsible for communicating each school's interests to the board and considers each school's operation in formulating teacher selection and recruitment policies.

Schools within a district affect one another. Personnel practices at one school may affect who is assigned or employed at other schools within the district. Usually selection procedures are facilitated through the central office, and the principal serves as a link between the school faculty and staff and the central office administration. The effectiveness of any one of the groups—the board, the central office, and the school—depends on the effectiveness of the others. Selecting the best teaching team members therefore is not solely a local school function.

The degree to which principals influence teacher selection for their school will vary from school district to school district and perhaps from school to school, but however the selection process occurs, it is of crucial importance because an instructional team (or an instuctional support team) is only as good as its weakest member. Each person has a vital role to play in the success of the school.

Whatever the selection policy or practice, the principal will have the opportunity to work with personnel assigned to the school and will have an opportunity to make recommendations regarding retention. In addition the principal is the key figure in assigning tasks and delegating responsibilities.

INTERVIEWING APPLICANTS

A personal interview can provide information to supplement, validate, and sometimes even refute information obtained from written records, references, resumés, and transcripts. If you wish to generate useful information, plan your interview strategy well in advance so the interview will not be a waste of time. Know what information you wish to seek and structure your questions and strategy to obtain that information. Use direct questions to elicit factual information and nondirective questions to determine attitudes and personality. Some general criteria for evaluating teacher applicants are:

- Performed well in school;
- Seeks professional improvement;
- Seeks responsibility;

- Is involved with people and community;
- Organizes answers logically, with insight and understanding;
- Demonstrates alertness and physical energy;
- Establishes good rapport with interviewer;
- Sells self as a capable, together person;
- Concentrates on the most pertinent skills for the position;
- Sees the interview as a two-way street;
- Is positive minded.

Throughout the interview be alert to the applicant's nonverbal behavior. The following are examples of questions you might consider using in an interview:

- Tell me about yourself.
- Why have you chosen this school district (school)?
- Do you get along well with peers? How?
- What has been your experience in similar positions?
- What strengths can you offer to this position?
- What did you especially like about your last position?
- What would you like to be doing five years from now?
- What will your family think of your assignment (career or position)?
- What do you consider to be the most important responsibilities of the principal in relation to your job?

Probably, one of most important characteristics of a teaching team member in an elementary school is the ability to work well with peers. University faculties may tolerate and even be effective when some of the members are independent workers; an elementary school, on the other hand, demands constant interaction among teachers. The ability to work with others is essential; assigning a teacher to a room with a group of pupils and leaving the activities of that group solely up to the teacher seldom exists in a successful elementary school. Cooperation and coordinating roles of faculty members will be among the greatest challenges facing the principal.

CLARIFYING ROLES

As viewed by the public, teachers, and significant others, schools are bureaucracies.[1] In some cases there are intense pressures on principals to operate schools like a business organization, a manufacturing plant, or a military unit.

---

[1]Max Abbott, "Hierarchical Impediments to Innovation in Educational Organizations," in *Organizations and Human Behavior: Focus on Schools,* F. Carver and T. Sergiovanni, Eds. (New York: McGraw Hill, 1969).

Mark Hanson describes it this way:

> Clearly, the public school has many characteristics of classical bureaucratic theory. For example, the school maintains a well-defined hierarchy of authority (teacher to principal to superintendent); power is centralized in the superintendent; rules stipulate expected and prohibited behavior (education code, district policy, school handbook); a specific division of labor exists (English teachers, history teachers, counselors, aides); positions require university diplomas and state certificates; and a precisely defined work flow is established (first to second to third grade).[2]

Principals and others who perceive the school as a bureaucracy usually fail to recognize the effects of professionalism on the processes.

Hanson views the relationship between professional and bureaucratic governance (defined as control of the decision-making process) in terms of a two-zone model of responsibility called the Interacting Spheres Model.[3] Decisions on security, allocation, boundary, and evaluation lie in the administrator's zone, whereas instructional decisions lie in the teacher's zone of responsibility. The two zones overlap when democratic decision making occurs, and when there is conflict resolution and bargaining in the school. A variation of his model is shown in Figure 3–1.

---

[2] E. Mark Hanson, *Educational Administration and Organizational Behavior* (Boston: Allyn and Bacon, 1979), pp. 113–114.
[3] *Ibid.*, p. 115.

FIGURE 3–1

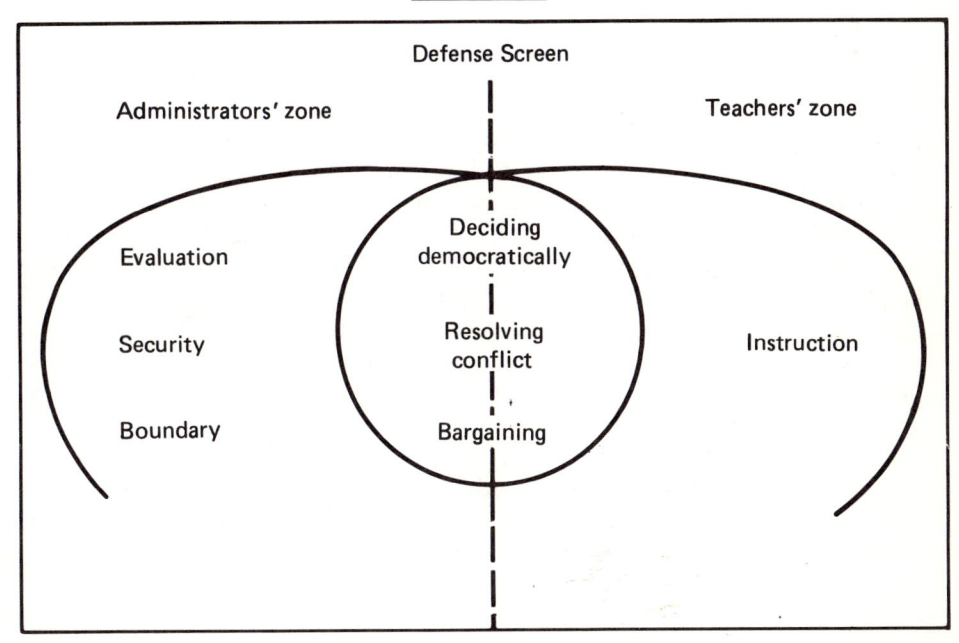

```
                        Defense Screen
                             |
   Administrators' zone      |         Teachers' zone
                             |
                      ┌──────┴──────┐
                      │   Deciding  │
         Evaluation   │democratically│
                      │             │
                      │  Resolving  │    Instruction
         Security     │  conflict   │
                      │             │
                      │  Bargaining │
         Boundary     └──────┬──────┘
                             |
                             |
```

Legitimate assumption by both principal and the teachers of necessary roles not predicted at the beginning of the school year is important, and freedom to make such decisions without creating undesirable conflict in the school is essential. Even the best-conceived written job description cannot prepare people for unforeseen task assignments. Perhaps the best a principal can do is to identify zones of decision making (as suggested by Hanson), assign specific task responsibilities when possible in terms of such zones, and make decisions about roles that may appear "out-of-bounds."

If for no other reason than that those involved will better understand what is expected of them, you can best accomplish role identification and clarification by involving those persons who will be responsible for implementing the roles. Communicate clearly so that each person knows and accepts his or her role relationship.

Prior to the first day of school principals should begin the process of role clarification and task assignment by planning the opening of the school year with the faculty and staff. The "opening of school" process can set the stage for desirable personnel relationships within an effective school program.

Principals might best initiate the preschool or role-clarification process through these stages:

1. Identify the type of decisions that need to be made and the level at which they must be made.
2. Become familar with the strengths and weaknesses of each faculty and staff member.
3. Determine task deadlines.
4. Identify resources needed.
5. Make assignments.

Throughout these stages we suggest you involve others and delegate responsibility. We also add this caution. No matter how well you initiate these stages, on the night before pupils arrive you will probably feel dissatisfied and wonder if the next day will turn out to be a total disaster. That is a natural and somewhat expected feeling, and perhaps a good feeling. It shows you care (and others will see that you care).

The role clarification and assignment process creates knowledge of the hundreds of logistic details required for organizing and coordinating the activities of many people doing many different things simultaneously. Trust in the competence of school team members. If you have planned well, clarified roles, made involved decisions, delegated with understanding, and have not attempted to usurp the "zones" of others, it will go well.

Treat teachers like professionals and provide them time to make decisions regarding their roles. For example, schedule some planning time and provide work space and facilities for teachers to plan. Making instructional aids in the lounge, at home, or while the pupils do "seat work" will decrease the teacher's effectiveness. Allow teachers to decide when *they* need to plan and leave it to them to enforce the need for cooperative use of time. Planning time is especially important to elementary teachers, who necessarily are physically active and who work in direct contact with pupils who have very short attention spans. A great variety and quantity of instructional materials and methods are required, as is almost constant supervision of the students. Teachers usually will identify the best times, methods, places, materials, and facilities for their planning if given an opportunity and a clear understanding of the limitations within which they must work.

Plan the planning carefully. A worksheet or chart like that illustrated in Figure 3–2 might be helpful. Some hypothetical tasks, people, and resources are included as illustrations.

No one wants to be assigned the unpleasant yet essential tasks. This is especially true of teachers and "nonteaching" tasks. Teachers like to eat lunch with adults, not supervise lunchrooms. They would prefer to prepare their classrooms

FIGURE 3–2 *Planning worksheet for opening school on September 7*

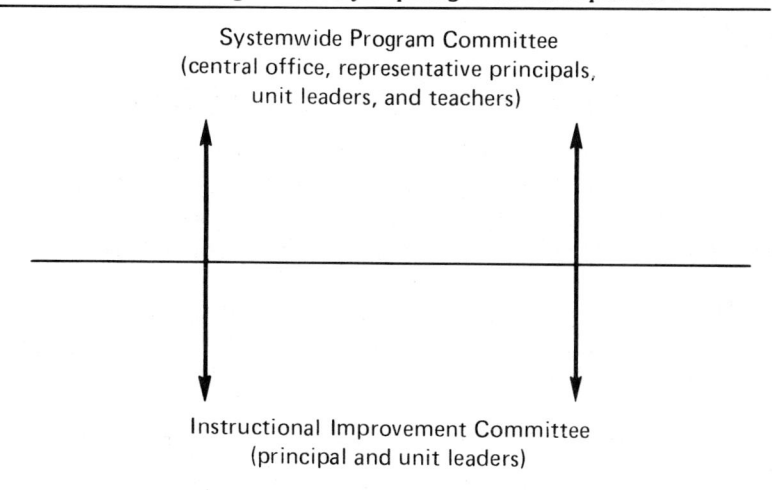

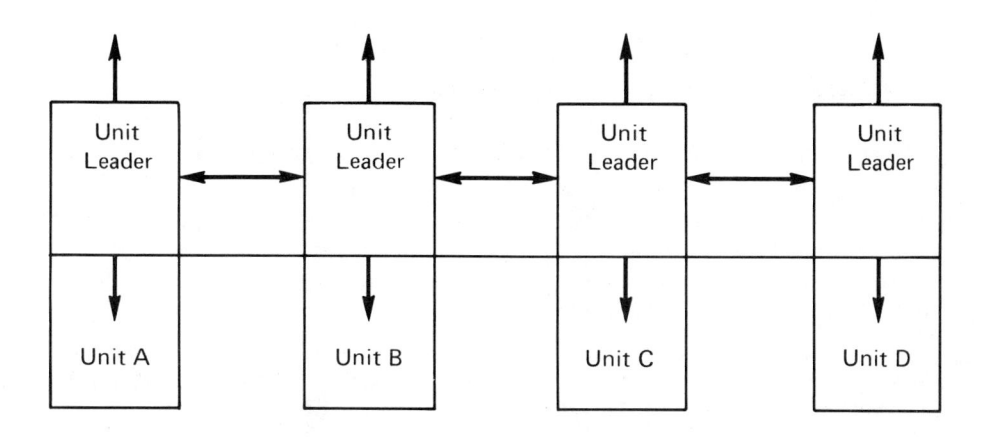

Systemwide Program Committee
(central office, representative principals, unit leaders, and teachers)

Instructional Improvement Committee
(principal and unit leaders)

Unit Leader	Unit Leader	Unit Leader	Unit Leader
Unit A	Unit B	Unit C	Unit D

for the next day and to gather materials for their own homework, not supervise bus loading.

These "necessary" duties become an unpleasant part of contract negotiations when unions are involved, and yet there are so many things that just have to be done: taking off coats, escorting children to the washroom, supervising the playground, caring for the ill, to name but a few. If such decisions are not resolved through the collective bargaining process, the principal must decide who is to do what. It is always a good idea to organize the faculty, identify what is to be done, identify limitations, and let the group decide. If, however, you wish to reserve the right to make final decisions, inform the group before they start working on the decisions that their role will be to provide advice, information, and recommendations. If the group is to make the decisions, you must be willing to abide by and enforce the decisions of the group. Do not bring a group together to make a group decision if you do not intend the group decision to prevail. Telling a group they are to make a decision "but I reserve the right to veto" is one sure way of discouraging participative decision making and lessening their trust in you.

ORGANIZING FOR INSTRUCTION

Classroom teachers are not totally free to make instructional decisions. Instructional decisions are a function of the principal's leadership and direction, other faculty's wishes and activities, group norms, physical facilities, constraints, demands, parents, pupils' characteristics and desires, subject content limitations, and other factors.

Basic assumptions made by the faculty regarding learning will help determine the organizational structure or role patterns adopted in the school.[4] Those basic assumptions might include:

1   Children are genetically different in what they can be expected to learn.
2   Growth patterns determine readiness for learning.
3   Learning can be promoted by developing a strong self-concept in children.
4   The social environment sets the limits and determines the extent of individual learning.
5   All learning is possible for all children given proper conditions.

Accepting, questioning, or rejecting the assumptions listed above are reflected in instructional personnel roles. The first assumption calls for emphasis on guiding students to accept the limitations of self and others, and for differentiating program content to accelerate movement by bright children and meet needs of slow learners who are expected to learn less. Acceptance of the readiness

---

[4]Assumptions are adapted from issues expressed by Ben M. Harris, Kenneth E. McIntryre, Vance C. Littleton, Jr., and David F. Long, *Personnel Administration in Education Leadership for Instructional Improvement* (Boston: Allyn and Bacon, 1979), pp. 51–52.

assumption results in age grouping, "prereading" experiences, and concern for physical as well as mental development. Teachers who believe in developing a strong self-concept will tend to be kind, reinforcing, and very concerned about the mainstreaming of physically or mentally handicapped pupils and the involvement of everyone in special activities. When the social environment is considered a limiting factor, emphasis is placed on heterogeneous and interracial grouping. Acceptance of the last assumption implies a variety of programs for and an emphasis on achievement by all students. These assumptions are not mutually exclusive and since they help determine instructional roles and who occupies them, principals should be conscious of where they and the faculty stand, on these and other issues. An organizational structure should be developed to help accomplish those instructional roles and objectives considered important by the faculty. If assumptions conflict, any number of problems will develop regarding organizational structure.

Organizational structure is the patterned interrelationship of roles. Sometimes the structure is informal; that is, it just occurs because people interrelate and not because they plan together. The principal's leadership style makes the difference regarding how much organizational structure is formally developed. It is doubtful that any one organizational pattern will be desirable over a long period of time. As faculty and staff change, the structure will change. A variety of class and scheduling arrangements will probably be necessary.

One of the more recent and widespread innovative attempts to improve instructional organization in elementary schools is Individually Guided Instruction (IGE), begun through efforts of Wisconsin public schools and the federally funded Wisconsin R & D Center in 1965.[5] Their efforts, as well as that of the /I/D/E/A/-sponsored "IGE Change Program," a spin-off of the orginal IGE program, continue to provide creative organizational structure frameworks for the elementary school. The IGE school is made up of learning units composed of three to five teachers. The school's Instructional Improvement Committee, a decision-making group composed of unit leaders and the principal, meets weekly to evaluate progress and plan learning programs. Communication among and between units and also between schools is the key to continuous improvement of organization for instruction; similar communications are effected in home–school–community relations. The multiunit structure alters considerably the traditional decision-making role of the principal and other personnel; studies have shown it to be effective in changing the school's organization for instruction from static to dynamic.

In IGE, students are taught by the unit team; the team is responsible for the total educational experience and the instruction afforded students assigned to the unit. The unit leader becomes a communicator, coordinator, and decision maker at both unit and school level. As noted in Figure 3–3, the unit leader is the connecting link.

There are no simple solutions for the best organization for instruction in the elementary school. Recent federal regulations have served to break traditional

---

[5]Herbert J. Klausmeier, "Individually Guided Education: 1966–1980," *Journal of Teacher Education 27* (Fall 1976), p. 199.

FIGURE 3-3
The Unit Leader: The Connecting Leader

Tasks to be done	Person(s) responsible	Expected completion time	Helpers and resources
1. Textbook processing and handout	Asst. principal	Sept. 6, 9:00 A.M.	Grade level representative, Moore, Handey, Poole, Smith, Jones
2. Welcome & orientation of new first-graders & parents	Principal, first-grade teachers	Sept. 7, 8:00 A.M.	Auditorium, name tags, student guides
3. Mother's coffee	Lunchroom manager	Sept. 7, 7:45 A.M.	Lunchroom
4. First day schedule of events	Asst. principal, principal	Sept. 4, 3:00 P.M.	Everyone

patterns (see Chapter 7, Meeting Special Students' Needs), but public concern for "back to-the-basics" probably has served to entrench the traditional, graded, self-contained classroom organization. Understanding the school's existing organizational structure, keeping an open mind, identifying assumptions and principles underlying the instructional program, and assigning staff based on the best knowledge possible of the numerous variables affecting their interaction are essential, but difficult, objectives to accomplish. Principals sometimes find to their chagrin that if they avoid or neglect these tasks, the faculty and staff will organize themselves anyhow. However, such informal organizations are usually inefficient and less effective than those that are deliberately and rationally planned.

MOTIVATING THE TEAM

Motivation of a staff by its leader has been studied, researched, and theorized. There are more unanswered questions about how best to motivate others to accomplish common goals than there are answers. As research on the subject has progressed through the years contingency theory seems to have emerged as holding the most promise for explaining the response of a staff or group to leadership styles.[6]

> Contingency theories of leadership treat contingency variables as those variables that influence the relationship between leadership styles and subordinate responses to those styles. For example, the success of a principal's style in mandating a change in classroom discipline procedures might be contingent upon the strength of the local teachers' union.[7]

[6]E. Mark Hanson, op. cit. p. 247.
[7]Ibid., p. 247.

Theories proposed by Fred Fiedler, recognized as the person responsible for contingency theories, are discussed by Hanson. "A leader has either a 'relationship-motivated' or a 'task-motivated' leadership style. Second, the three most important situational variables interacting with a leadership style are (1) leader–member relations, (2) the task structure, and (3) the formal power position. All three conditions have an impact on the degree of control of the leader."[8]

Essentially, Fiedler maintains that a person has a consistent leadership style and that situational variables interact with that style.[9] If principals are relationship-motivated they will seek support and close relations with the staff and faculty. When they acquire that support and feel secure they then pursue the esteem and admiration of superiors, and the relationship-oriented principals will strive for that esteem even if it might detract from the close interpersonal relationship they have acquired with subordinates.

The task-motivated principals obtain satisfaction from accomplishing objectives effectively and efficiently. In uncertain and anxiety-generating situations, they will emphasize structure and direction so that the task can be accomplished. When things are going well regarding task accomplishment and influence is high, task-oriented principals will relax and respond to the need for consideration of the subordinates' feelings.[10]

Unlike Fiedler, who assumes a consistent leadership style, Tannenbaum and Schmidt maintain that a leader can vary leadership style to cope with differing problematic situations. The forces a leader should consider in adopting a leadership style are (1) forces in the manager, (2) forces in subordinates, (3) forces in the situation, and (4) forces in the external environment.[11]

Fiedler's theories and those of Tannenbaum and Schmidt are mentioned here not only because they are important in explaining ways leaders relate to those whom they lead, but also to emphasize the fact that there are various opinions and a great deal of research regarding motivation. Perhaps the most acceptable notions are expressed by Hanson in terms of what he calls the management team.

> ... [T]he problems and possibilities are so complex and fast moving that one person does not have the necessary skills and expertise to effectively direct events. As such, *the chief executive steps out of a role emphasizing direct control of events and into a role where he or she plans for a management team with a mix of expertise and skills to direct the movement of events.* He also must play a major coordinating role as he works toward integrating the differentiated subsystems. Therefore, leadership can be thought of as a process by which the policies, people, and resources of an organization can be integrated into a cohesive and effective effort to accomplish goals. The process

---

[8]*Ibid.*, p. 248.

[9]Fred E. Fiedler, "Personality and Situational Determinants of Leader Behavior," in *Current Developments in the Study of Leadership,* Edwin Fleishman and James Hunt, Eds. (Carbondale, Ill.: Southern Illinois University Press, 1973).

[10]Fred E. Fiedler, "The Contingency Model—New Directions for Leadership Utilization," *Journal of Contemporary Business* (Autumn 1974).

[11]Robert Tannenbaum and Warren Schmidt, "How to Choose a Leadership Pattern," *Harvard Business Review* (March–April, 1958).

is controlled by a *management team* that works within a *planned framework* established by the chief executive.

... [T]he leadership plan calls for a delegation of authority, which the chief executive must accept if the management team is to function as intended.[12]

The team referred to on preceding pages in this chapter follows the management-team concept expressed by Hanson and promoted by many professional organizations, such as the American Association of School Administrators and the National School Board Association.

The management team is a problem-solving, program-developing, leadership unit. Ideally, the members of the team possess high performance work norms and a balanced mix of expertise and skills. The chief executive literally builds his or her management team through training and selection.[13]

Some elementary principals may not consider themselves as "chief executives." They may perceive themselves more as "head teachers" or "managers." However, those who expect dynamic leadership, motivate others, and direct an effective instructional program are chief executives. They are a link to other components of the school system, and their success or failure as chief executives will determine the success or failure of the total system.

A management team does not have to be composed of people with titles such as assistant principal, department chairperson, unit leaders, or master teacher. The team positions do not have to be formally recognized, but they must be uniformly accepted by other members of the faculty and staff. Such acceptance usually occurs when the principal announces the delegation of authority and responsibility. "I am pleased to announce that Sarah Jones has agreed to lead our efforts in developing a more effective, articulated reading program. She will be contacting you to find out how you might best assist her effort to deal effectively with one of our common concerns—the reading program."

A school-based management (or leadership) team should have a varying membership. As problems are solved the leadership will shift. Establishing the various problem-centered groups as temporary organizational structures seems to make good sense for many reasons:

1. Various faculty members will be demonstrating leadership responsibilities and will be better motivated and understanding when they know they will become a follower later.
2. The principal can make effective use of leadership strengths on the faculty.
3. A weak member of the team may be otherwise a valuable faculty member, and success is not solely determined by success as a leader.
4. Members of the faculty feel responsible and important because they are placed in positions where that is recognized by others.

[12]Hanson, *op. cit.*, p. 266.
[13]*Ibid.*

Motivating the team, then, may be accomplished in part by developing a "management" or leadership team that will share responsibility for making tough decisions, developing better instruction, and motivating others. The exact organizational patterns used to accomplish this will need to vary with characteristics of the principal and members of the faculty and staff, school district policies, problem situations, and traditions and customs of the school and community.

SUGGESTED READINGS

Abbott, Max. "Hierarchical Impediments to Innovation in Educational Organizations." In *Organizations and Human Behavior: Focus on Schools,* Fred Carver and Thomas Sergiovanni, Eds. New York: McGraw-Hill, 1969.

Barnes, Melvin W. "Administrator's Role in Humanizing the School." *National Elementary Principal 49* (February 1970), p. 38.

Gorton, Richard A. *School Administration.* Dubuque, Iowa: Wm. C. Brown, 1979. Chapter 6, "Organizing the School."

Griffiths, Daniel E., et al. *Organizing Schools for Effective Education.* Danville, Ill.: Interstate Printers, 1962.

Hanson, E. Mark. *Educational Administration and Organizational Behavior.* Boston: Allyn and Bacon, 1979.

Journal of Teacher Education 27 (Fall 1976). Washington, D.C.: American Association of Colleges for Teacher Education.

Schmuck, Richard A. *Handbook of Organization Development in Schools.* Eugene, Ore.: Center for the Advanced Study of Educational Administration, University of Oregon, 1972.

CHAPTER

4

IMPROVING INSTRUCTION

Developing an effective professional staff
Assessing needs
Determining objectives and identifying activities
Implementing the program
Evaluating

Assessing instructional needs
Rationale for improving instruction
Is the principal an instructional leader?
Understanding teachers and helping them to understand themselves

Counseling with teachers
Proactive practices
1. Know your teachers / 2. Praise your teachers / 3. Like your teachers / 4. Get your teachers involved in decision-making activities / 5. Support your teachers / 6. Let your teachers know you care in every way in your daily actions / 7. Be the leader
Reactive practices
1. Listen / 2. Respect confidences / 3. Advise when necessary only / 4. Be judicious / 5. Discipline

Observing in the classroom
The teacher self-improvement model
Using objective analysis / Explaining FIAC / Video taping / Combining FIAC analysis with video taping
Self/peer/supervisor ratings

The clinical supervision model
Rapport / Preobservation conference / Observation / Analysis and strategy / Conference / Process critique

Putting it in perspective
The future

DEVELOPING AN EFFECTIVE PROFESSIONAL STAFF

The only meaningful way of looking at education is as a life-time and life-space process in which everyone is a teacher and everyone is a student as long as they live.

— Earl S. Schaefer

Staff professional growth and development implies that a group of interrelated or interdependent elements interacts to form a collective entity in pursuit of a goal. In elementary schools, improved instruction for students is the goal and the key elements in pursuit of that goal are the teachers and the principal.

The responsibility for establishing and implementing a school-based staff-development program rests with the principal. Under the principal's leadership and direction an atmosphere of trust and mutual respect can be established. Although this kind of atmosphere will not guarantee a successful staff-development program, its absence will almost cetainly guarantee the program's failure. Principal noninterest and noninvolvement will also guarantee program failure. It is all too easy to procrastinate. Consider the following ten "principal" reasons:

1 It's too difficult and exhausting.
2 I don't have enough time or energy to fool with it.
3 My teachers won't be able to agree on anything.
4 We've already established a pretty good pattern.
5 We don't have enough expertise in our school.
6 The superintendent (or central office staff) won't support it.
7 We're not quite ready for it yet.
8 We have too many projects going now.
9 The new teachers wouldn't understand and the experienced teachers wouldn't use the suggestions anyway.
10 We've tried that sort of thing before.

Principals who reason like this cannot have an adequate understanding of staff development; neither will their school have a successful staff-development program.

The three key ingredients of staff development—identifying needs, evaluation, and responsibility—and how they relate to each other are matters of concern (and sometimes fear) to teachers. Their relationships cannot be explained or defined in an exact manner. Neither can they be constant since each situation has certain unique characteristics that must be dealt with in special ways.

Perhaps the most difficult question frequently asked about staff development (and one which causes great teacher concern) is "Is staff development tied in with evaluation?" The answer is "Yes, evaluation is a part of staff development." Evaluation *must* be tied in with staff development. In fact, there really is not any way around it. In evaluation, judgments are made about adequacy (from poor to outstanding), performance, behavior, and competence. If the standards are not met—if the performance is not at an acceptable level—you have identified a need. The need is the difference between what is and what ought to be.

Leadership for staff development can best be facilitated by the principal's clearly defining the reasons for pursuing professional staff growth and development and delineating the roles and responsibilities of principal, supervisor, and teachers. No matter how well conceived and planned a process might be, without the principal's leadership and support, it cannot hope to succeed. Realization that growth and development by self-evaluation should lead to both individual and school needs is critical and emphasis should be on achievement, self-esteem, and worthiness. With these considerations in mind, principals must proceed with the necessary leadership and direction to put the process into action.

An effective staff development process includes:

- Assessing needs;
- Determining objectives;
- Identifying activities to accomplish the objectives;
- Implementing the program;
- Evaluating.

ASSESSING NEEDS

Determine exactly what should be included in the staff-development program(s). By first finding out what the teachers already know and can do, the next logical step of determining teacher needs and what skills need improving can be more easily effected.

DETERMINING OBJECTIVES AND IDENTIFYING ACTIVITIES

From the needs list establish objectives and then prioritize to determine which skills ought to be acquired, improved, or refined. Objectives should be determined cooperatively by principal and teachers (and possibly students). If teachers do not have process input, their participation in the staff-development program will be less desirable (to them), and probably less effective. Follow the same procedures in identifying activities.

IMPLEMENTING THE PROGRAM

Staff development is a continuing process. Implementing the program requires time, patience, and support from the school-system administration. The principal is responsible for obtaining that support.

Be considerate of the teachers' time and therefore be careful to schedule programs so that teachers will feel more motivated to participate willingly and actively and learn from the various activities. Principals who arbitrarily say "No, we cannot do this" when teachers ask for innovative or creative implementation plans are (in a sense) abdicating their responsibility to the teachers, to the students, and to the system as a whole.

EVALUATING

Principals must evaluate teachers. Ask yourself "Will the evaluation be just and fair; and further, will it lead to continuous improvement of the teachers and the staff-development program?"

Involve teachers in selection of evaluation criteria and the overall staff-development program evaluation plan. Do not pull surprises on them. Make sure that evaluation criteria are fair, beneficial, and acceptable. Teacher and principal agreement on criteria must be reached.

Possible questions to ask when designing the evaluation plan are:

1. Were the professional development goals practical?
2. Were the objectives stated clearly?
3. Were the objectives carried out?
4. Was the developmental procedure adequate?
5. Did the evaluation forms serve the intended purpose?

Structure the evaluation plan with these questions in mind.

Evaluation is simply a monitoring device. It is the most difficult and, perhaps, the most valuable step in the entire professional development process. Sometimes (as discovered through evaluation) initial goals and objectives turn out not to be as feasible or valuable as originally thought. Through monitoring you will be better able to determine the feasibility and value of selected goals. You can reformulate goals and objectives when necessary.

ASSESSING INSTRUCTIONAL NEEDS
RATIONALE FOR IMPROVING INSTRUCTION

In education the return for investment is measured by the quality of the student product. A proliferation of factors, of which these are but a few samples

- The public mood as characterized by the public's unwillingness to pass bond issues during the past dozen years and by their repeated pleas for better instruction of students as evidenced by recent Gallup polls of public attitudes toward school;
- the marked increase of per-pupil costs during the past decade;
- the increase of teacher salaries during the past decade;
- the declining school enrollment;
- the decrease in student achievement;

has emphasized the concern for improving the quality of the student product.

This is an investment-conscious world. Money always seems to be a key factor in decisions, and because the public pays for schools—and it is their children who are being educated or not being educated, as the case may be—they are concerned. That concern is justified, since in most districts salaries form at least 80 percent of the total school budget. And salaries will continue to rise.

A teacher (under 30 years of age) with a current salary of just over $15,000 per academic year, and with additional fringe benefits totaling over $2,000, will, if his or her teaching career is extended to age 65, earn approximately $1.5 million (considering a 6 percent salary increase per year).[1] Thus, investment in teachers is substantial. If the school district does not make every effort to improve instruction, it is remiss, indeed, in its responsibilities to the public, to the teachers, and most important of all, to the students.

Bruce Joyce estimates that there are approximately 40,000 supervisors and about 100,000 principals (and assistant principals) who work directly or indirectly with instructional improvement, and approximately 15,000 support personnel who contribute to instructional and curriculum support in other than supervisory positions.[2] But Joyce's estimate of 150,000 is misleading. Moreover, it seems to be grossly inflated. Studies indicate that elementary principals, though they would like to be instructional leaders, seldom perform that function. Likewise, many instructional supervisors seldom see the classroom.

IS THE PRINCIPAL AN INSTRUCTIONAL LEADER?

By definition, "principal" means a person who is in a leading position or the most important member of an organization (the school). The primary function of an elementary school is to provide instruction and learning experiences for students; the principal is therefore, the instructional leader of the school.

Ben Harris says that idea is mostly a myth. He feels that principals do not devote much time to instructional (improvement) activities.[3] Consistently, literature and research seemed to support that view. In the landmark 1974 *National Elementary Principal* Chautauqua series, Harold McNally stated that principals do not exercise instructional leadership to any considerable degree, though it is widely agreed that it is their most important responsibility.[4]

In the 1978 NEP principalship update, Paul Houts said:

> We have read numerous times and have seen enough evidence to convince us that the principal is the key to the instructional program, the quality of life in the school, and the chief agent for improving teacher performance. But how well does that mesh with the realities of the situation? Not very well, we suspect. The roadblocks to educational leadership are, if anything, more formidable than ever.[5]

[1]Jerry C. Gaff, *Toward Faculty Renewal* (San Francisco: Jossey-Bass, 1976), pp. 138–139.

[2]Bruce R. Joyce et al., *ISTE Report II: Interviews, Perceptions of Professionals and Policy Makers* (Palo Alto, Calif.: Stanford Center for Research and Development in Teaching, June 1976), pp. 1–2.

[3]Ben Harris, *Supervisor Behavior in Education* (Englewood Cliffs, N.J.: Prentice-Hall, 1973), p. 142.

[4]Harold McNally, "Summing Up," *National Elementary Principal* 54 (September–October, 1974), p. 8.

[5]Paul Houts, Editorial, *The Principalship: 1978 Update* (Reston, Va.: National Association for Elementary Principals, March 1978), p. 8.

Even as recently as 1979, Robert H. Anderson felt that the nation's elementary schools could be much more effective if their principals possessed the skills, habits, and attitudes for instructional improvement.[6]

But the trend is shifting, and some healthy signs now appear that are indicative of that shift. The fifth ten-year survey of the elementary principalship notes a marked increase in principals' responsibility for supervision and instructional leadership. Principals themselves seem to be more interested in instructional leadership.[7] And this is just the beginning!

Instructional changes depend almost exclusively on principals' initiative. Even when participative leadership is practiced, teachers seldom suggest distinctly new instructional patterns for themselves. They expect the principal to assume the leadership role.

In Chapter 2 we discussed (1) managing self, (2) establishing priorities, and (3) managing time. We would hope that by now the reader will have incorporated those ideas into a self–professional growth program. We believe that such a program is a necessity for every elementary principal who expects to be an instructional leader. The basic principles of managing self, establishing priorities, and managing time, once learned by the principal, may then be taught to teachers. The foundation of the instructional improvement program then is the teachers' understanding and practicing of managing self. We would even suggest that if a teacher does not affect the principles inherent in managing self, then any subsequent efforts toward instructional improvement the principal would use with that teacher would meet with little or no success. Witherell and Erickson contend that a teacher's understanding of self is as important as his or her understanding of the child. We ought not only give teachers a set of tools for improving their instruction, we also must help them understand the teaching process and interactions as they relate to their own and to their students' development.[8]

UNDERSTANDING TEACHERS AND HELPING THEM TO UNDERSTAND THEMSELVES

Elementary teachers have little time for adult interactions. More than a decade ago, Sarason (1971) pointed out that elementary teachers' contact with children is not only different than peer contact but also has the consequence of producing loneliness.[9] Successful teachers interact well with students. A prerequisite to interacting well with students is being able to understand them. Teachers can best understand students by learning how they think and then trying to put themselves in the students' thinking framework. In simpler terms, successful third-grade teachers learn to think (and even act) like a third-grader. Consider further a

---

[6]Robert H. Anderson, *National Elementary Principal 58* (June 1979), p.44.

[7]Robert J. Krajewski, "Instructional Improvement: A Cooperative Venture," *Kappa Delta Pi Record* (December 1979), pp. 40, 44, 58.

[8]Carol S. Witherell and V. Lois Erickson, "Teacher Education as Adult Development," *Theory into Practice 17* (June 1978), pp. 229–237.

[9]Seymour B. Sarason, *The Culture of the School and the Problem of Change* (Boston: Allyn and Bacon, 1971).

successful third-grade teacher who has been teaching third grade for approximately ten years. Assume also that the teacher's social circle consists mainly of other primary or elementary teachers. In this example we see that teacher A interacts with third-grade children all day—for a number of years—and interacts mostly with other primary teachers during out-of-school hours. As principal, you are expected to interact with teacher A for managing self and improving self. But you are responsible for the instructional program of the school and thus you must not only work with teacher A but also every other teacher in the school for improving instruction. You must realize the frame of mind of each teacher and act accordingly.

Get the teachers to work together. Teacher colleagueship is perhaps the most important ally in the principal's quest for a successful instructional-improvement program. Teachers need the opportunity to

- Share and discuss what they learn;
- Share in each other's successes and failures;
- Be part of a team effort;
- Make joint decisions about the instructional improvement program.

You hold the responsibility of establishing an atmosphere and providing the guidance which encourages teachers to share with each other and grow together.

William Wayson offers these suggestions:

- Promote initiative among staff.
- Help teachers to see how their perceptions govern their behavior and the behavior of others.
- Help teachers to understand the self-fulfilling prophecies in interactions with students and with other adults.
- Treat inservice education as the most important instructional activity in the school.
- Recognize that daily life gives every school its own training program; it teaches staff "how it is done here."
- Help staff to learn from criticism and open discussion of problems.[10]

COUNSELING WITH TEACHERS

The longer I am in the business of education, the more I am convinced that the practice of good human relations is the most important aspect of the teaching–learning process.

— Dorothea Sutton

Helen B. Outlaw, on the eve of her retirement as an elementary principal, described her feelings about some of the problems facing the elementary schools:

[10] William W. Wayson, "A Tickler File for Educational Leaders," *National Elementary Principal* 53 (May–June, 1974), pp. 35–36.

To be concerned about elementary school children under pressure is to be concerned about the pressures placed on their teachers. These pressures cause overwhelming feelings of guilt. Teachers feel guilty that they are not doing their job as well as their superiors expect or as well as they themselves would like. Constant guilt feelings inevitably have a negative effect on everything a teacher does. Without hope of relief some teachers will feign support for all programs, others become upset enough to fight back in whatever way they can.[11]

Such feelings are all too common. Teachers are expected to fulfill varied role responsibilities at school. With increasing demands continually placed upon schools to update or add to an already overcrowded curriculum, while simultaneously providing sufficient learning skills in the basics, teachers feel swamped. To add to their workload, additional responsibilities of values model, parent substitute, and others which might be better served by social or religious agencies and family leadership is unrealistic and unwarranted.

Teachers frequently have responsibilities other than those incurred in their teaching roles. Some are parents, civil leaders, and the like. Such responsibilities have inherent pressures. Pressures build and when a teacher feels too many pressures, from both within and outside of school, teaching performance may be affected. This can happen to even the best teachers; when it does they may acquire self-doubts, exhibit defense mechanisms uncharacteristic of their normal behavior, interact differently with their peers and, as a result, possibly feel that their belonging needs are not being met.

With the proper blend of leadership and management skills, the principal can calm, soothe, and smooth away teachers' apprehensions and defense mechanisms. In Chapter 2, the importance of a principal having a philosophy, knowing self, accepting self, respecting self, and respecting others was discussed. The rationale used in that discussion also applies to teachers in that it is important for every teacher to have a philosophy of education, to know self, accept self, respect self—and respect others (especially students). For a teacher to have the respect of the students, the teacher must first respect the students. Most teachers do, or at least try to.

Teachers take cues from the principal. Principals serve as models—they set the tone for the school. If, for example, the principal trusts teachers, teachers will be more inclined to trust peers and students. If, on the other hand, the principal practices a spoon-feeding philosophy, combined with an authoritarian, somewhat secretive, approach to interactions with teachers, the teachers will be less likely to be trusting and sharing with each other and with their students.

A principal aptitude and attitude flashback—a sort of mini-inventory of characteristics—might be appropriate as you consider your role as teacher counselor. In such a self-brainstorming session, terms such as these may appear: thoroughness, fairness, initiative, tact, enthusiasm, emotional control, sensitivity, consistency, interest, firmness, sincerity, humbleness, consideration, respect, responsiveness, friendliness, politeness, caring, honesty, and willingness. Choose several and ask yourself how you have exhibited them recently. If you have a

---

[11]Helen B. Outlaw, *National Elementary Principal 33* (July–August, 1974), pp. 77–78.

satisfactory self-rating performance, you can probably embark on a teacher-counseling program (or session). If you do not, hold off a while, because it is not a good idea to begin counseling others when you yourself are in a temporarily less than (personally) satisfactory attitude framework.

PROACTIVE PRACTICES

1. Know your teachers

Bob Kooper was finishing his third year as a teacher at Southside Elementary School. He enjoyed his working relationships with both students and teachers but never really had what he would call a good professional relationship with Frank Barber, the principal. Nevertheless, other school relationships were very satisfactory and, thus he had mixed feelings at leaving Southside to begin work as a full-time Educational Doctorate student in math education. As he was leaving school one day, he met Frank in the hall. In the course of a brief conversation, Frank expressed his regret at Bob's leaving but wished him luck in the pursuit of the M. Ed. "Boy," Bob thought as he later reflected the conversation, "Frank should know that I already have more work toward the Ed.D. then he does. He really ought to know his teachers better."

Indeed he should. There is no excuse for the principal's not knowing the teachers. If the principal is responsible for teachers' professional growth, knowing the teachers' present educational status is a must. Know your teachers so you can garner new insights and better establish and maintain rapport.

2. Praise your teachers

I can still recall vividly a teacher observation session that took place almost ten years ago.

This particular teacher was an excellent, firm teacher. If she had any shortcoming, it would be that she did not praise the students enough. Not only did she feel that she praised students, she also felt that at times she praised them too much. In the process of reviewing her videotape and her Flanders' Interaction Analysis, she turned to me and said, "You know, I thought that I praised students almost too much, but from looking at this tape and the interaction analysis, I can now see that I don't praise my students nearly enough. This is a real shocker to me."

Some principals may be in a similar situation—feeling that they praise teachers almost too much and yet, in actuality, they probably praise teachers not nearly enough. Prepare a positive chart with a number of different praise words and phrases. Look at this chart from time to time. Pair the positives with respective teachers. Try to praise each teacher at least once each week.

3. Like your teachers

Inherent in the previous discussion of Know Yourself, Accept Yourself, Respect Yourself, is the precept "Like Yourself." If you like yourself, try also to like your teachers. The more you try to like your teachers, the more you will get to know them and the more often you will praise them.

4. Get your teachers involved in decision-making activities

Getting your teachers involved in decision-making activities allows them to have a better sense of belonging to the school, a better appreciation of peers, and probably a better appreciation of you, the principal. Involvement brings familiarity. Familiarity, if judiciously developed, will create interest and improve factors leading toward good morale.

5. Support your teachers

If a teacher has a problem with a parent or a student, afford the teacher any immediate support that you can. If a teacher needs additional inservice time, try to be as understanding as possible and be willing to approve the teacher's request for help.

6. Let your teachers know you care in every way in your daily actions

When teachers know that you care, they will have a better support base and a better base for building morale and their commitment to the school.

7. Be the leader

Teachers expect the principal to be the school leader, and they look to you for leadership. If you can not afford leadership to them, they feel frustrated. Be the leader—effect your leadership and management skills.

REACTIVE PRACTICES

Even if you are successful in using proactive practices for counseling teachers, there will still be occasions in which you must perform a reactive counseling session—actually sitting down with a teacher and discussing some problem or problem phase. Certain guidelines can be suggested for these types of counseling sessions, the first, and perhaps most important of which is:

1. Listen

In many cases teachers do not have anyone to talk to, anyone to share certain items of information they feel are important, need to talk about, and more importantly, need someone to listen to them.

When teachers are at this stage, they are not necessarily looking for advice, even though during the conference they may solicit advice from you; rather, they may simply want and need someone to listen. Teacher feedback from a session in which a principal just listens may sound like, "Boy, I really appreciated the advice that you gave me yesterday (or last week)." The principal, however, may not have given any advice; he may have just simply listened. Teachers may wish to share something with the principal or just to have someone, anyone, listen to something they feel is important. Yet they may find no one to listen. By allowing time (scheduled or otherwise) to teachers so that you can just listen to them, you are fulfilling an important responsibility. Listening can prevent some future potentially serious problems.

A recent television commercial by the Mormon Church pictures a young girl coming home very excited, wishing to share with her father something she experienced during the day. Her father is getting ready for some evening activity and does not have time to listen to her. So she runs to her mother, excitedly wanting to share with her. But her mother, too, has no time for she is preparing for something she feels is important. And so the young girl approaches her brother, wishing to share with him this important event about which she is excited. And her brother, too, is busy and cannot afford the time to listen to her. The poor little girl is next pictured on the front stairs telling this important, exciting, personal thing to the family dog. It is a sad yet often true commentary on life, but the analogy is very applicable to the school.

2. Respect confidences

There is no shorter road to destroying rapport and perhaps even school morale than to repeat things that teachers tell you in confidence.

3. Advise when necessary only

As previously noted, teachers may just want someone to listen and not really want advice. So don't give it; give advice only when it is really necessary to do so.

4. Be judicious

If a teacher is reacting emotionally in a conference, allow the teacher to release all those emotional reactions. Do not try to counter with rational explanation. After the emotional period has passed, then you can begin to discuss rational solutions to problems in a judicious manner.

5. Discipline

If you must discipline teachers, the previous four suggestions also hold true. In any type of discipline action, it is very important to get all the facts and to make an appropriate analysis of the situation prior to taking any kind of punitive action whatsoever. Find out from all parties involved exactly what has transpired, when it has taken place, and why. You may find out that a story sounds quite a bit different as you hear it from different personnel.

Teachers are usually hired because of their knowledge of subject matter and their dedication to the ideals of teaching. Granted that these are necessary factors—in fact, at times they may almost be taken for granted—their value depends upon teachers' knowledge of self and ability to communicate. It is the latter factor that causes the most concern and that must be addressed in instructional improvement programs.

Problems such as lack of awareness of what is happening in the whole classroom and not being able to perform several tasks at the same time definitely relate to teachers' knowledge of self. These in turn have a direct cause-and-effect relationship to the communication problems caused when a teacher uses a particular style or styles to excess and can not change or adjust styles to meet different situations.

OBSERVING IN THE CLASSROOM

The heart of instructional improvement is observing instruction in the classroom. We will offer two process models (with accompanying explanations) for this all-important activity:

1. The teacher self-improvement model;
2. The clinical supervision model.

THE TEACHER SELF-IMPROVEMENT MODEL

In the teacher self-improvement model, the principal and teacher list and discuss several of the teacher's instructional improvement objectives as determined from an instructional needs survey. Figure 4–1 presents an example of an instructional

FIGURE 4–1
Instructional needs survey

Area of instruction	Performance level			
	Do very well	Am usually satisfied	Am sometimes satisfied	Needs work
____ Stating objectives				
____ Planning lessons				
____ Asking questions				
____ Using student ideas				
____ Lecturing				
____ Praising students				
____ Understanding students				
____ Giving directions				
____ Making assignments understandable				
____ Evaluating student progress				

Directions: Rank order (1-10) according to your priority of concern (with 1 being your greatest concern). Place the numbers to the left of the statement in the space provided. Also indicate your present performance level.

needs survey. Ideally, both teacher and principal would like to know the teacher's present level of competence. The model (Figure 4–2) allows the teacher to compare intended objectives with present competencies in several different ways. (Note the dotted lines in the model.) The teacher may decide to check through use of a Flanders' (FIAC) analysis of a class session or a video analysis of a class session or objective student ratings or objective self-ratings—or any combination of these factors—whether the stated objectives are at a valid starting point. The dotted line thus indicates that after using one, two, three, or even four of these factors, the teacher can cycle back directly to compare objectives. If objectives need to be changed, then the principal and teacher should work together to effect changes at this time.

After objectives are restated, plan to observe a designated lesson. During the observation, you can use objective devices, such as a video recorder and an objective analysis system, to analyze the lesson and objectively record the teacher–student interaction (of course, the teacher should be aware of this decision). Use can also be made of objectively based self- and student-rating forms.

Fred Wilhelms, in a milestone ASCD publication, *Supervision in a New Key,* noted: "If I had to choose just one tool with which to take the process of teaching apart to see what makes it tick—and thereby improve the process—that tool would

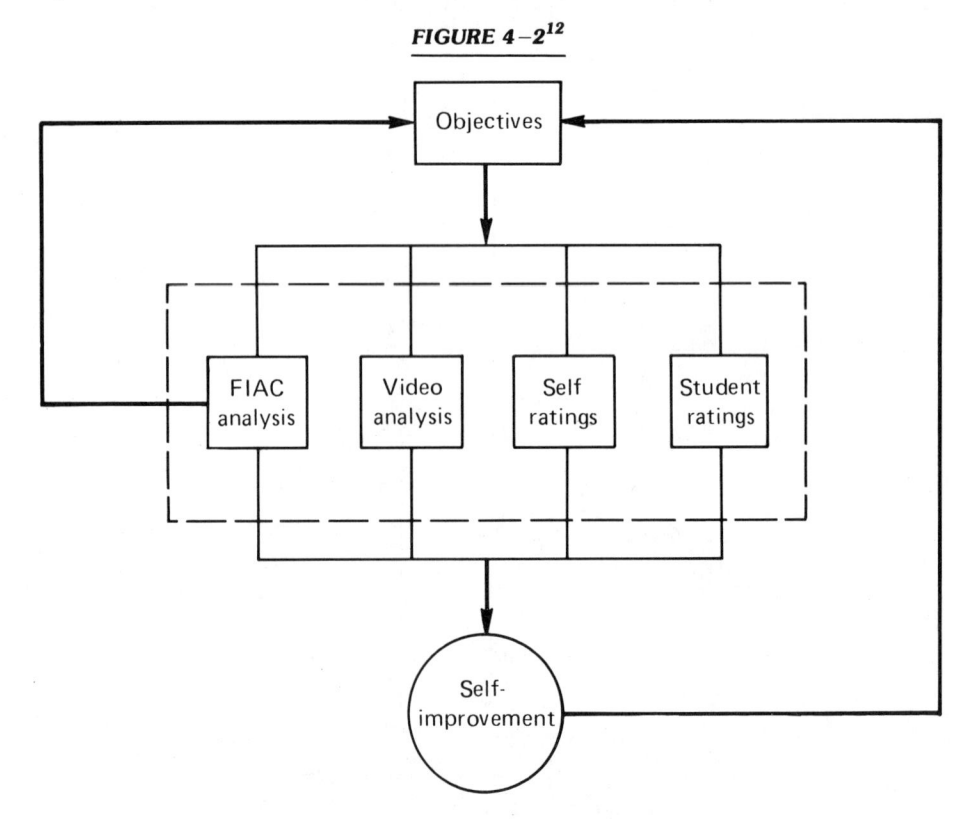

FIGURE 4–2[12]

[12]*Adapted from the* Journal of Research and Development in Education *9 (2), 1976.*

be interaction analysis." He goes on to say: "I have a hunch that administrators and teachers have hung back from using this (FIAC) and other analytical systems largely because they think it is a terribly complex and difficult process. Such fears are unjustified."[13]

Using objective analysis

There are more than 100 tested observation instruments. Their uses include teacher training, research, supervision, substitutes for tests, content for emerging education, and specifying the conditions of learning. Over 80 percent of the instruments have been used in the classroom.

Three-fourths of the instruments have affective categories and half have cognitive categories. Psychomotor, activity, content, sociological structure, and physical environment are the remaining classes of categories. Some instruments focus on one person at a time, some on two; most, however, focus on groups of three or more; some focus on the teacher, some on the pupil, but most focus on both; some focus on verbal behavior, some on nonverbal, and some on both; some require only one observer, some require three or more observers; some require audio or video tape as well. Thus, the choices of instruments are many and varied. One can even find instruments specifically designed for early childhood observation. Bales, Bellack, Blumberg, Flanders, Galloway, Hough, Hunter, Joyce, Medley, Ober, Roberson, Taba, and Withall are but a few of the more popular instruments. *Mirrors for Behavior III: An Anthology of Observation Instruments*[14] is the most comprehensive available source of information on observation instruments. It lists and describes 99 instruments in layman's terms. We suggest that you at least scan this reference to obtain a better idea of the instruments and their uses.

For classroom use, we have discovered that teachers prefer an instrument that is simple to use and interpret. They desire practical approaches and thus prefer instruments they can eventually self-administer. Of the instruments available, we feel that Flanders' Interaction Analysis Category System (FIAC) best meets the instructional-improvement program needs of both teachers and principal. It is one of the simplest to understand and use and has excellent practical classroom application. We suggest that it be used in conjunction with video tape and other objective means.

Explaining FIAC

FIAC was developed by Professor Ned Flanders, former Program Consultant for Far West Laboratory for Educational Research and Development. The system ascertains student–teacher verbal interaction in the classroom. The Flanders system is concerned with verbal behavior only, because Flanders feels that verbal behavior can be observed with higher reliability than can nonverbal behavior.

[13]Fred T. Wilhelms, *Supervision in a New Key* (Washington, D.C.: ASCD, 1973), pp. 13, 16.
[14]Anita Simon and E. Gil Boyer, Eds., *Mirrors for Behavior III: An Anthology of Observation Instruments* (Philadelphia, Pa.: Communication Materials Center in Cooperation with Research for Better Schools, 1974).

In this system of interaction analysis, the classroom verbal behavior is divided into ten categories. All teacher statements are classified in the first seven categories, as either indirect (categories 1–4) or direct (categories 5–7). Indirect teacher influence consists of four observation categories: (1) acceptance of feeling, (2) praise or encouragement, (3) acceptance of ideas, and (4) asking questions. Direct teacher influence is divided into three observation categories: (5) lecture, (6) giving directions, and (7) criticism or justification of authority. In order to make the total interaction in the classroom meaningful, the Flanders system also provides for the categorizing of student talk (categories 8–9): (8) response and (9) initiation. The last category, (10) silence or confusion, is included to account for the time spent in behavior other than that which can be classified as either teacher talk or student talk. All categories are mutually exclusive, yet totally inclusive of all verbal interaction occurring in the classroom.

Category (10) may deserve some added explanation. There are several types of silence—such as a short silence of confusion indicating that the student did not know the answer to a question or did not understand the question. An important point to note is that long silences because of student work on materials are not part of Flander's verbal interaction analysis. Also there are several types of confusion—the confusion of disorder and disruption and also the constructive type of confusion.

Operationally, every three seconds the observer records the category number of the observed interaction behavior. He records these numbers in column sequence. The tempo should be kept steady and accurate. In addition, he should note the kind of lesson being taught and its purpose.

Flanders, realizing that this system is complex, has established several ground rules for categorization. These rules, applicable to all subject areas and all grade levels, are as follows:

Rule 1: When not certain in which of two or more categories a statement belongs, choose the category that is numerically furthest from category 5.

Rule 2: If the primary tone of the teacher's behavior has been consistently direct or consistently indirect, do not shift into the opposite classification unless a clear indication of shift is given by the teacher.

Rule 3: The observer must not be overly concerned with either his own biases or the teacher's intent.

Rule 4: If more than one category occurs during the three-second interval, then all categories occurring in that interval are recorded; therefore record each change of category. If no change occurs within three seconds then repeat that category.

Rule 5: If the silence is long enough for a break in the interaction to be discernible, and if it occurs at a three-second recording time, it is recorded as (10).

An example is now given in an attempt to clarify the previous discussion and also to allow further explanation of the Flanders system.

A mathematics class, grade 8: The teacher starts off with a lecture (5's), then asks a question (4). Students think of the answer (10's). Students are called upon (6's) at random to answer the question—several do (8's); the teacher accepts their answers and clarifies them (3's), writing them on the board. The teacher puts

Observing in the classroom **89**

several correct examples on the board (5's), telling students the correct manner to do the problem (5's and 6's). The teacher asks a question (4), students give short answers (8's). Student interjected an idea of his own (9's), teacher criticizes him (7's). The teacher asks another question (4), receives short replies (8's). The teacher praised the class for attentiveness (2's), summarizes (5's), and gives an assignment (6's) which the students begin to work on. At this point the observation has ended.

The resulting list of recorded observations appears somewhat like the following:

```
        10   4   8   8   8
         )   )   )   )   )
         5   6   3   8   8
         (   (   (   (   (
         5   8   3   9   2
         )   )   )   )   )
         5   8   5   9   2
         (   (   (   (   (
         5   8   5   7   5
         )   )   )   )   )
        10   3   5   7   5
         (   (   (   (   (
         4   3   6  10   5
         )   )   )   )   )
        10   4   6  10   6
         (   (   (   (   (
        10   6   4   4   6
         )   )   )   )   )
        10   8   8   8   6
                         (
                        10
```

Note that a 10 is inserted as both the first entry (first number, left column) and the last entry (last number, right column): this is standard procedure, for we assume that each record begins and ends with silence. Entries are made in columns top to bottom and from the left column to the right.

We now pair off the numbers (first number, second number), (second number, third number), (third number, fourth number), and so on. Our first pair is (10,5), second pair is (5,5), third (5,5), fourth (5,5), fifth (5,10), sixth (10,4), seventh (4,10), etc. These ordered pairs are now tabulated in the appropriate cells of a 10 × 10 matrix with row and column heading 1–10 (see figure 4–3). These headings 1–10 correspond with the code categories previously listed.

One entry is made for each ordered pair of numbers we have listed. The first number in the pair designates the row and the second number designates the column. For example, with our first ordered pair (10,5) we look to row ten, then across to column five and make an entry, i.e., the first entry is at the intersection of

FIGURE 4-3
Sample transfer of tabulated totals from worksheet to matrix and initial analysis of totals

Interaction Matrix

	1	2	3	4	5	6	7	8	9	10	TOTAL
1											
2		1			1						2
3			2	1	1						4
4						2		2		1	5
5					7	2				1	10
6				1		3		2		1	7
7							1			1	2
8		1	2					7	1		11
9						1			1		2
10				3	1					3	7
TOTAL		2	4	5	10	7	2	11	2	7	50
COLUMN PERCENT		4%	8%	10%	20%	14%	4%	22%	4%	14%	100%

TEACHER TALK		STUDENT TALK
COLUMNS 1-7		COLUMNS 8-9
60%	.6	26%
% OF TOTAL TALK	I.D. RATIO	% OF TOTAL TALK
Columns 1-7 / Columns 1-10	Columns 1-4 / Columns 5-7	Columns 8-9 / Columns 1-10

row 10 and column 5. The seventh ordered pair (4,10) is entered in the matrix in the same manner. Look down to row 4 and across to column 10, where the entry is made. When all the entries are made we can total each of the columns 1–10 and also the overall total as can be observed in the example table. We can now proceed to analysis if such is desired.

The Flanders System of analysis allows one to analyze classroom interaction in sequence. For example, let us look at the following parts of sample matrices.

Observing in the classroom 91

	1	2	3	4	5	6	7	8	9	10
4				2	1	1		25	20	3

From the above example one might determine that the teacher asks questions well, knows the type of questions that she intends to ask, and so on. Note especially that questions are followed mostly by answers from students called upon (the 4–8 box), and by answers from students volunteering (the 4–9 box). Students evidently know the answers, as evidenced by the lack of entries in the 4–10 box.

	1	2	3	4	5	6	7	8	9	10
4	1		2	32	15	21	5	16	12	21

Note the difference in the above sequence. The teacher drags out the questions or else poses them quite unclearly (evidenced by 32 entries in the 4–4 box). The teacher also shows lack of preparation, as she has a large number of occurrences of lecture after questioning (as evidenced by 15 entries in the 4–5 box). Criticism following questions occurs as well (5 entries in the 4–7 box). Students do not understand the questions or else do not know the answers (as evidenced by the large number of entries in the 4–10 box).

The above examples show that we can, in a row analysis, determine what type of interaction we have observed in class. Looking a bit more deeply into the sequence we may be able to determine even more specifically what is happening. Considering the following example:

	1	2	3	4	5	6	7	8	9	10
4	7			7	4	2		23	19	15

	1	2	3	4	5	6	7	8	9	10
8	1	11	21	3		1		12	2	2
9	4	13	17	5		2	1		8	5
10		2	1	14	11	4		5	11	10

Initial inspection would seem to indicate that the teacher seems to be asking questions fairly well, having 23 and 19 occurrences of answers or initiations from the students. Note, however, that at the same time we find 15 occurrences of questions followed by silence. We will try to determine what this means at a later time.

Having noted from row 4 that most of the items following questions were answers from students called on or from students volunteering answers, we can now ask what occurred after these student responses.

To determine the answer to this question we have to look in the rows numbered 8 and 9. In row 8, recording responses to students called upon we note 1 occurrence of teacher accepting feeling, 11 of the teacher praising or encouraging, and 21 of the teacher using student ideas. Some answers are longer, as noted by 12 located in the 8−8 box. This can either mean that some of the questions were thinking types and required more than a simple yes−no answer or it could indicate other conclusions depending on the situation.

Looking at the 9 row we find a similar pattern, noting that after student voluntary responses we find 4 occurrences of the teacher accepting student feelings, 13 of teacher praising or encouraging, 17 of teacher accepting or using student ideas, etc.

Judging from 4, 8, and 9 rows, then, we might find that this teacher is quite indirect, praising students and using their answers in the normal course of teaching. She criticizes little and praises much, using the ideas of students where possible.

Now let us go back and pick up the 15 entries in the 4−10 box. Why are 15 instances of silence observed after a teacher asked a question? What happened after the silence? What type of interaction took place?

To answer the above questions we must now look at the ten row. Note that the ten row has some disturbing entries, particularly in the 4 and 5 columns. We note that after silence there are 14 entries in the 10−4 box. This may indicate that the teacher did not phrase her question properly and had to restate the question or repeat it. This in itself may not be too bad if it were not a regular occurrence. If it is a regular pattern then one should perhaps reexamine this teacher's questioning technique.

Similarly we note 11 instances of silence followed by lecture; another possible indicator of poorly asked or phrased questions, to be avoided if possible. The 10−8 and 10−9 boxes represent students answering after an initial period of silence, which could indicate either reticence or a pause to consider the answer carefully. The 10−10 box indicates 10 instances where the silence was of more than three seconds duration, which is not, in and of itself, alarming, but is an indicator to be questioned if too many entries occur here.

These few examples should assist you in beginning to understand the analysis process used with the matrix system.

Video taping

We suggest that you use video taping along with FIAC. Video tape and FIAC complement each other and together provide a more potent, more objective basis for observing classroom instruction.

We suggest that the video taping be done by the principal, rather than by a technician. Video tape only certain portions of the lesson, concentrating on those objectives determined by teacher and yourself. The taping should not exceed 10–12 minutes of the lesson. Short sequences of student–teacher interaction that relate to the objectives are more valuable than (and supplement better) a single 10–12 minute sequence of the lesson.

"But," you ask, "Does not the presence of the camera disrupt class?" "Can you get a normal classroom situation when you have a video tape in the class?" The answer to the first question is "It depends" and the answer to the second question, dependent on the first, is "Yes, you can."

Our answer to the first question is not an evasion of the issue. The presence of a camera and video tape unit may or may not disrupt the class. On what does it depend? The person who operates the equipment is probably more important than the equipment. In other words, how you use the equipment is the key factor. If you have good rapport with the teacher, have knowledge and skill in using effective supervisory techniques, and use the equipment effectively in the supervisory process, it is highly likely that the presence of video equipment will not disrupt the class after its initial few minutes of operation. The atmosphere quickly returns to normal.

Suggestions:

1   Before going into a class with video equipment, be sure that the teacher is willing to be taped.

2   If possible, place the equipment in a corner (or another out-of-the-way place) of the classroom quickly and preferably when students are not there. A general rule is to stay in an area where you will not have to tape toward a window—the contrast is too great for the camera. Camera and microphone placement and their use will depend on objectives of the observation. Teachers may use a lavalier mike, may carry a hand mike while moving from student to student or group to group, or may decide to place the mike in a convenient place.

3   As students come in the room, it is a good idea to pan the camera on them for a while so they get a chance to see themselves on the monitor (position it so they can see themselves). Then explain to them why you are in the class and ask them to just ignore you when the lesson begins. Also mention that only the teacher and you will view the tape. Then turn the monitor back to where only you can see it and you are ready to begin taping. This is a most valuable five-minute exercise. When the students know they will not see the tape afterward, they are less prone to "act" and class activities will be pretty normal.

4   As the students get used to the equipment, you will not need to continue showing them what they look like on the camera. The novelty quickly fades.

5   In kindergarten and first-grade classes you might experience a student or two coming over to look at the monitor during the lesson. If one does, allow him

to watch, but do not allow him to go back into the action while you are taping. If you do, chances are the "acting" will begin.

6   When you have finished taping the desired 10–12 minutes, quietly turn off the equipment. If you have prearranged with the teacher to stay in the room for the entire period, do so and continue your objective observation from your same location. If you leave the room, do so in such a manner that you will cause the least disturbance. You may, for instance, pull the equipment cords from the wall sockets and take the mike from the teacher, leaving all cords on the mobile cart so they will not distract or cause possible logistic or safety problems. Such movement on your part can be minimally disruptive and of much overall benefit (whether you remain in the classroom or leave). There is no set rule—play it by ear.

7   This type of procedure can allow you to tape from one to five teachers on any given day.

8   In an open classroom "pod" setting, position the equipment so that you can tape several teachers in sequence without having to move equipment.

Can you get a normal classroom situation when you have a video tape in the class? Yes. Students take their cue from the teacher. If the teacher is nervous, students are less apt to act in their normal patterns. If you have good rapport with the teachers, follow the suggestions as listed above and use supervision of instruction to *improve* instruction and not *evaluate* it; teachers will be relaxed enough with both you and the equipment in the class and their teaching will be (more or less) normal.

Initially, however, teachers will be at least somewhat skeptical of the entire process, either consciously or subconsciously, and until the novelty wears off, usually after the first taping, the normality of the classroom setting may not be quite as you would like. As stated, however, it will not be long, given your supervisory rapport and technique, for a class to get back to normal. The teacher will relax and few, if any, problems will remain. You may find initially that in all your attempts to get the teacher to relax, the teacher will say, "Oh, sure, I will," and then, just prior to the taping, may wish to be excused and either comb hair or put on a little more makeup. You may even find that the teacher may be dressed in a nicer suit or, if the teacher is female, she may have her hair done specifically for the occasion. One might say that this is not normal. But if the teacher cares enough, that's great! In fact, if the teacher then sees self on television and likes what he or she sees, this behavior may carry over to another day and then another day so that the teacher gets to feeling better about self and, therefore, gets to feeling better about students. So do not make it a point to say, "Oh look, you've done . . .''; just acknowledge the fact that the teacher does look nice and continue with what you are doing.

Combining FIAC analysis with video taping

It takes a while to practice and become proficient in analyzing classroom instruction using FIAC. You can perhaps practice by using an audio tape of any teacher's lesson or just by sitting in the classroom and jotting numbers down during the lesson. We suggest that you do practice enough with FIAC so that you become rather proficient in it. We also suggest that you take a clipboard with some paper into the room.

Taping should total only about 10–12 minutes (as suggested) and it ought not to be in one single episode. As you become more proficient with Flanders' and as you become more proficient with the video tape, you will have no problem in doing both at the same time. You can do a Flanders' Interaction Analysis through the whole class period and operate the video tape at the same time. Before long, you will be able to anticipate what the teacher is going to do before the teacher does it so that you will be able to capture on video tape those things the teacher is most concerned about in the stated objectives. Then the video tape becomes a much more powerful complementary factor to the Flanders' Interaction Analysis.

In using both FIAC and video taping to complement each other, you must decide how you will report to the teacher the objective information you have obtained. There is no set procedure. Yet at the same time, we do not feel comfortable in suggesting that you just play it by ear. You must know the teacher with whom you are working. At times when you are having a conference with the teacher, you may wish to show the video tape first; at other times you may wish to review and explain FIAC first, and still at other times, you may wish to use both together so that you can, during the analysis of the Flanders' Interaction Matrix, reinforce on video tape those points brought out by the matrix, and vice versa.

For the teacher to be better prepared for the conference, we suggest you give him or her your column lists of recorded FIAC numbers and let the teacher prepare the matrix. The teacher then becomes more interested in what those numbers mean and how he or she interacted with the students in accomplishing the objectives set forth for the lesson. When the teacher comes to the conference, he or she will have a pretty good understanding of the lesson interaction and can approach the conference with much more objectivity and enthusiam. Cue from the teacher by being indirect and by asking questions. Adjust your supervisory method according to the teacher's comments and feelings about the matrix.

Self/peer/supervisor ratings

The remaining parts of the instructional improvement model consist of self-rating, your rating, student rating, and perhaps even peer rating. One thing we should mention at this point is that you need not work specifically with individual teachers in this process. You may decide (when you are comfortable with the process) to allow other teachers to participate in this process as well, so that peers observe each other and give each other healthy input and analysis of each other's teaching. Any rating sheets you might decide to use should be objective and their use should be clearly understood by teachers and rater. The rating sheet will be used specifically for improvement of instruction and not for evaluation purposes.

There are many such instruments. One example is the *Stanford Teacher Competence Appraisal Guide* (see Figure 11–4). It is comprehensive and easy to administer. Depending on the wording, it can be used as a student rating sheet as well. For primary grades you can use a student rating sheet consisting (see Figure 4–4) of the Smiling Face, the Neutral Face, and the Unhappy Face choices. This type of rating form is excellent.

Use of these rating forms should be decided upon prior to actual observation

FIGURE 4-4

My teacher looks like

How my teacher feels when I ask for help

What I would like my teacher to look like

My teacher feels this way about me

and so on.

of the classroom teaching. Together with the Flanders' Interaction Analysis and the video taping, they provide an objective description of the teaching as seen through the eyes of the camera, the students, you, the teacher, peers, and an objective analysis device. Using these devices to help improve instruction, you will, therefore, allow the teacher to reach in some measure the next step of the model, which is self-improvement. Note that the model, as depicted, is cyclical. It never ends. How often you decide to use this model will depend upon individual circumstances. You may wish, for example, to use this model fully with each teacher in your school once a year, twice a year, or maybe even three times a year. Probably the full model, given the constraints of time, should see maximum use three times a year. The partial model may be used more frequently. For instance, it would not be too difficult for teachers to eventually become proficient enough to do a Flanders' Interaction Analysis on their own classroom, simply by putting a small audio recorder in their class, taping the lesson, and then just completing a Flanders' Interaction Matrix. The teacher may then, alone or in conference with you, discuss progress toward objectives.

THE CLINICAL SUPERVISION MODEL

The *Dictionary of Education* defines supervision as: All efforts of designated school officials directed toward providing leadership to teachers and other educational workers in the improvement of instruction.[15] The supervisor's role has three basic components: administration, curriculum, and instruction.

Instructional supervision is a subset of supervision. It consists of those activities performed by school personnel for improving instruction by changing teacher behavior. Clinical supervision is that phase of instructional supervision that focuses primarily on face-to-face interaction between supervisor (principal) and teacher in either direct or indirect analysis of the teaching act. Figure 4–5 depicts the relation between supervision, instructional supervision, and clinical supervision.

Clinical supervision can be implemented through steps, as depicted by the model in Figure 4–6.

Rapport

By definition, "rapport" means a harmonious relationship, especially one of mutual trust; and "nurturance" means to nourish, promoting development or growth. To be effective, elementary principals implementing clinical supervision must command both a knowledge of instructional theory and skill in its practical application with teachers. Throughout the implementation, *rapport* is vital. The very nature of the clinical supervision process produces some sort of (conscious or subconscious) anxiety feeling within teachers. Perhaps the anxiety can never be totally eliminated, but if the elementary principal builds rapport throughout the process, it can be minimized or at least lessened. This is why rapport is mentioned in the model as being a key element throughout the entire process. Rapport must be worked on continually.

[15]Carter V. Good, Ed., *Dictionary of Education,* 2d ed. (New York: McGraw Hill, 1959), p. 539.

FIGURE 4–5[16]

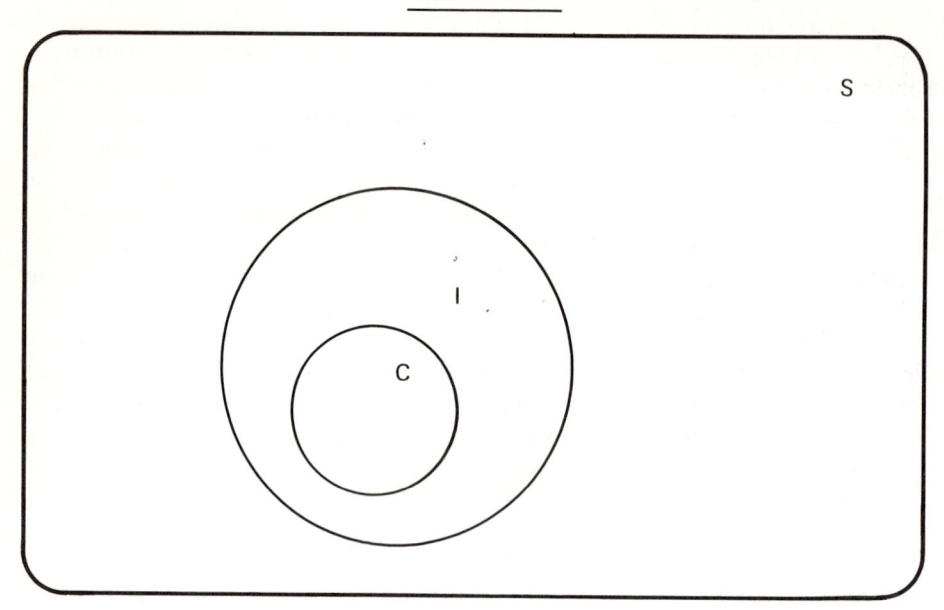

```
S = all of supervision
I = instructional supervision
C = clinical supervision
```

FIGURE 4–6

Clinical Supervision Model	
Preobservation	R
	A
Observation	P
	P
Analysis and strategy	O
	R
Conference	T
Process critique	

[16]Adapted from Robert Goldhammer, Robert H. Anderson, and Robert J. Krajewski, Clinical Supervision: Special Methods for the Supervision of Teachers, 2d ed. New York: Holt, Rinehart and Winston, 1980, p. 21.

Preobservation conference

During the preobservation conference, supervisor and teacher agreement is on: lesson objectives, observation methods and logistics, and other observation concerns. Also, any desirable changes can be initiated at this time. The preobservation conference allows you and the teacher a chance to discuss these things in a cordial and relaxed atmosphere.

Most observation planning, therefore, should be done together during this period. We would assume that only minimal further planning need be done prior to actual observing in the classroom.

Observation

When you observe in the classroom, do so from an objective viewpoint. Preobservation planning will be carried out in the observation. As suggested from the previous mode, you could or should probably use a video tape and some sort of objective analysis system if agreed upon by both you and the teacher. Focus only on those items that you and the teacher have previously agreed upon. Where you are to sit in the classroom, how long you remain, what instrument(s) you use for observation, and when and how you leave the classroom if the lesson is still going on should all have been decided upon in the preobservation conference. In observation you simply carry out those plans.

Analysis and strategy

This step is perhaps one of the most important in the entire process. In analysis you review all the information pertinent to the teacher's lesson and assess that information in terms of the teacher's intentions and repertoire. Once the analysis has been completed, you need to then develop a supervisory strategy to present the information to the teacher. Decide on the role you intend to play, in the conference, how much information you will present to the teacher, the manner this information should be presented, and also whether you intend to effect maximum teacher change in a minimum amount of time or some change this time and perhaps some change later.

As in any strategy for improving instruction, you should concentrate on working with the teachers' strengths, if possible, and deal with the behavior exhibited by the teacher. Most important is to try to decide how the conference should be opened and perhaps have several alternative strategies prepared for opening the conference.

Conference

The conference provides feedback to the teacher on those elements you have observed regarding both the teacher's intended objectives for the lesson and the carrying out of those lesson objectives. The conference serves as a basis for improving the teaching of future lessons. Your conference technique is the key to success or failure.

Too many mistakes have been made by principals who are either too forceful or too dominant in the supervision conference. We suggest, if possible, that you be indirect. Try to elicit teacher comments objectively. It is important to know how the teacher feels about the lesson and whether or not his or her objectives were met. One procedure might be to begin with a showing of a portion of the video tape, without any comment whatsoever and then let the teacher take the lead in discussing it. Another strategy might be to begin with showing the teacher the Flanders' matrix and perhaps discussing one or two points from the matrix or even asking the teacher what the teacher's impression was about the lesson based upon FIAC. Both methods (and there are others) will allow the teacher to have input into the conference and will also allow you to have better insight into how the teacher feels about the lesson and, therefore, be able to guide the conference based upon the teacher's feelings.

Process critique

The process critique is the supervisor's self-evaluation. In it the supervisor asks the teacher how he or she felt the process was conducted, what the teacher got out of it, and how the principal can improve his or her affecting the process itself.

PUTTING IT IN PERSPECTIVE

Recently, Patricia Novotney, an elementary principal in Irvine, California, suggested that elementary principals who are instructional leaders have four traits in common. They

1 Believe that instruction is important;
2 Analyze their own commitment;
3 Act;
4 Persist, no matter what.[17]

These four traits are the meat of what we have been discussing in this chapter. If, indeed, you believe that instruction is central to the purpose of the elementary school, you will find time to promote better instruction in your school. Further, you will analyze your own commitment to the instructional improvement program and will no doubt perform those activities that will effect instructional improvement. In other words, you will find time to counsel with teachers proactively, to assess instructional needs, and to observe in the classroom by using models similar to those as depicted in this chapter.

THE FUTURE

The 1980s are already being characterized as the decade of inservice and staff development. That the elementary schools continue the quest for instructional

---

[17]Patricia B. Novotney, "Principal as an Instructional Leader," *Educational Leadership* (March 1979), pp. 405, 406.

improvement is most desirable and important. Rather than jumping on a bandwagon, principals should

- Extend their present commitment to improving instruction and
- Through their own professional growth and skill development for instructional improvement, work with teachers in improving instruction.

Given the principles of time management and the principles of knowing self (as discussed in Chapter 2) and allowing oneself time to become proficient in a form of interaction analysis such as FIAC, becoming more supervisory-oriented and more skillful in supervision techniques, and learning how to operate video tape equipment, any elementary principal cannot help but improve instruction in the school.

Involving teachers in meaningful activities, creating new mechanisms for sharing our decision-making authority, and providing varied opportunities for teachers' instructional development are necessary. Principals, you are charged with this assignment. Can you do it? We think you can. We know you must. We hope you will.

SUGGESTED READINGS

Goldhammer, Robert, Anderson, Robert H., and Krajewski, Robert J. *Clinical Supervision: Special Methods for the Supervision of Teachers,* 2d ed. New York: Holt, Rinehart and Winston, 1980.

Educational Leadership 37 (February 1980). Alexandria, Va.: Association for Supervision and Curriculum Development. Theme: Supervision as Staff Development.

Flanders, Ned A. *Analyzing Teaching Behavior.* Reading, Mass.: Addison-Wesley, 1970.

Havelock, Ronald G. *The Change Agent's Guide to Innovation in Education.* Englewood Cliffs, N.J.: Educational Technology Publications, 1973.

Journal of Research and Development in Education 9 (Winter 1976). Athens: University of Georgia. Theme: Clinical Supervision.

Perceiving, Behaving, Becoming: A New Focus for Education, Yearbook. Washington, D.C.: Association for Supervision and Curriculum Development, 1962.

Simon, Anita, and Boyer, E. Gil, Eds. *Mirrors for Behavior III: An Anthology of Observation Instruments.* Philadelphia, Pa.: Communication Materials Center in Cooperation with Research for Better Schools, 1974.

Theory into Practice 18 (February 1979). Columbus: The Ohio State University. Theme: The Role of the Principal as Instructional Leader.

Wilhelms, Fred T. *Supervision in a New Key.* Washington, D.C.; Association for Supervision and Curriculum Development, 1973.

CHAPTER

5

IMPROVING THE CURRICULUM

Introduction
Assessing the need for curriculum improvement
Defining the terms
Influencing goals
Improving subject matter content
Providing instructional materials
Utilizing instructional time
Utilizing human resources
Improving teaching methods and activities
Evaluating curriculum improvement
Looking ahead

Elementary principals directly influence operational factors impacting on what children are taught in the school. Their ever-increasing (and changing) curriculum responsibilities, immense as they might seem, are further compounded by the impreciseness of the term "curriculum" and lack of agreement concerning methods of improving curriculum. This chapter presents a practical and somewhat unusual approach to elementary school curriculum improvement. It addresses principals' concerns over vagueness of defining terms and identifying improvement through the topics discussed in the chapter.

INTRODUCTION

Throughout this text, we place emphasis on the leadership role of the school principal rather than on the manager role, because we assume that the principal influences what children learn in school and can facilitate the teaching process as an instructional leader. Improving the curriculum is a constant challenge and responsibility requiring the exercise of leadership skills to assist teachers in making decisions about what they expect pupils to learn at school, as well as to support and facilitate the teaching act, for curriculum improvement ultimately takes place in the classroom.[1]

Many forces, both within and outside the school, have a great influence on classroom curriculum decisions, not the least of which are legally mandated requirements stating the subject areas to be taught. Local boards of education set requirements; state boards of education recommend scope and sequence; and state legislatures may even establish laws requiring pupils to demonstrate their competency in knowledge of subject matter. In addition, outside pressure groups sometimes demand that pupils either learn, or perhaps not be exposed to, certain content. Principals cannot ignore these forces. Decisions have to be made if the school is to operate effectively and efficiently, and in the final analysis what children are taught in the elementary school—or in any school—depends on numbers of factors within the principal's span of control.

There are many difficult curriculum decisions to be made, and we believe the principal has a responsibility to influence positively those decisions by leading the process of curriculum improvement. Improvement, by definition, implies a change for the better, thus the principal who leads the process of improvement influences change—for the better. There are no specific prescriptions or simple lists of do's and don't's to follow for curriculum improvement. However, there are some guidelines that may prove helpful, and they are presented in this chapter. Throughout the presentation we hint that leadership in curriculum improvement may be more of art than science; indeed, that supposition was a major force in the evolution of this chapter.

ASSESSING THE NEED FOR CURRICULUM IMPROVEMENT

First, we assume that the curriculum can always be improved; knowledge increases in geometric proportions every day. Teachers simply cannot teach everything, and to keep abreast in any one subject matter area is a nearly impossible task. And yet teachers have a responsibility to try their best, for somewhere in the mass of facts, skills, and attitudes available are those that are considered important enough to teach.

There has to be some stability, some point at which the teacher can start the continuing learning process, and some way to exercise judgments about how well pupils learn what the school intended them to learn. The improvement process requires not only an assessment of what exists as a curriculum, but also a knowledge of what changes in the curriculum will constitute improvement. If, for a given school, a judgment is made that a curriculum change will not be for the better, it is prudent to stick with the present program. Schools are bombarded with forces to change what they expect children to learn, and all too frequently curriculum-improvement proposals are adopted and implemented without a valid assessment of the real need for improvement. The only valid criterion for determining whether

[1]See Daniel and Laurel Tanner, *Curriculum Development*, 2d ed. (New York: Macmillan, 1980), Chapter 15, "Curriculum Improvement: Role of the Supervisor."

a curricular change results in improvement is whether the change better enables the school to achieve its currently defined educational goals.[2]

> Goals may be stated in broad terms (pupils will become good citizens), or they may be stated specifically and behaviorally (the seventh-grade student will be able to identify four reference books).[3]

Most schools have curriculum goals, even though in some cases they may be poorly defined. Identifying goals is the first step in curriculum improvement, and that is no easy task. Once curriculum goals have been objectively identified, the next step is to evaluate the goals themselves. The following questions summarize some of the more important considerations.

1 Are the goals clearly stated and understood by the faculty?
2 Are the goals appropriate for the school in terms of what is known about the pupils, the community, and legal requirements?
3 Are the goals realistic in terms of the means and resources available to the school?
4 What is the priority order of the goals in terms of their importance?

Answers to the first three questions will probably range somewhere between "definitely not" and "definitely yes." Priorities will probably range from "relatively unimportant" to "extremely important." Existing identified goals may be listed, and faculty, parents, and pupils involved in making that list can offer their opinions by responding to some type of scaled instrument.

It is important to realize that this first step in need assessment is determining what goals currently exist and not how well the school achieves each.

When current curriculum goals are identified and defined, the next step—that of determining what goals to retain and what additional goals are worthy of pursuit—may be implemented. There are at least two dimensions to what "should be": (1) those goals that are needed and (2) those goals that are desired by specific groups or by individuals. It may be desirable for all children to learn to swim, for example, but like all desires, this has to be considered realistically. The school cannot do all that seems desirable to everyone. The process of making curriculum decisions is important, as is the determination of who is to be involved in that process. Usually the acceptance or rejection of goals is a community affair and involves establishment of goal priorities by group consensus. In many cases schools probably have attempted to do too much by succumbing to wishes or even demands of well-meaning interest groups.[4]

In determining goals, someone usually makes a strong argument for omitting goals that cannot be evaluated by some quantitative means. Should this argument

---

[2]Richard A. Gorton, *School Administration* (Dubuque, Iowa: William C. Brown, 1976), pp. 235–239.

[3]Arden D. Grolelueschen and Dennis D. Gooler, "Evaluation in Curriculum Development," in *Curriculum Handbook,* Louis Rubin, Ed. (Boston: Allyn and Bacon, 1977), p. 151.

[4]For an excellent discussion of this problem, see John I. Goodlad, *What Schools Are For,* a publication of the Phi Delta Kappa Educational Foundation, 1979.

be accepted, almost all affective learning goals would have to be omitted. For example, faculty, parents, and others may consider patriotism an important instructional outcome. Measuring patriotism skills may not be possible within the school's curricular and instructional framework.

Quantitative measurement is not always appropriate as a major criterion for making judgment about validity of educational goals; patriotism is but one example.

There are policies, regulations, and laws that require additions or limitations to the curriculum. But even then there are many alternatives if the curriculum is considered in terms of educational goals rather than only subject matter content or discipline areas. Not only does the goal approach to curriculum improvement make it possible to identify and use performance indicators for evaluating how well the goal has been achieved, it also allows subject matter content to be considered as a means for achieving a goal rather than simply as an end product. Thus the schools can include goals that require extra-curricular activities which are extremely important to pupils and the life of the school. They can also include certain activities and functions sometimes considered "support" rather than curriculum. For example, there are educational goals that might appropriately be pursued through the school lunch program. If the lunch program is used for the purpose of teaching something, it might be placed on the "needed" list and receive a high priority.

As principal, you should provide the leadership in assessing the school's current curriculum and in developing realistic curriculum goals in some priority order. These should be stated, communicated, and considered as a basis for making judgments about the effectiveness of the total school program. The planning process should be carefully designed, and those goals resulting from the process that are not being pursued then become a starting point for improvement.

Another basis for improvement results from curriculum evaluation or employing ways and means for accomplishing better those curriculum goals that have been adopted. Criteria for evaluating the curriculum are prevalent in the literature,[5] and some guidelines are included in this chapter.

Curriculum improvement involves much more than improving subject-matter content. It will involve all those factors that have influence on what is taught in schools, and children learn from how we teach and how we perform our daily activities in the school. When considered operationally, curriculum improvement involves those factors common to every school program. It is a continuous process and involves not only assessing and identifying curriculum goals, but also effective use of other factors that have a direct influence on what is taught and learned in the school. A clear definition of what is meant by the term "curriculum" should now be developed. One concept of the term is described in the next section of this chapter.

DEFINING THE TERMS

The first step needed to influence anything consciously is to identify it, and curriculum is difficult to identify because it is not one "thing." It results from the continuous interaction of a number of "things." Consequently there are well over a

---

[5]For example, see Tanner and Tanner, op. cit.

hundred definitions of the term "curriculum" in the literature. Different people have different conceptions of the meaning of the term, and since curriculum is an abstraction and not a "thing," each definition is probably correct. The definitions are the personal property of the individual in whose mind they occur, and even sharing the concept does little to help the school principal know what to change or what to control to produce curriculum improvement. The principal can only manage or control things and influence to some degree the behavior of people. Concepts are the personal property of the individual conceptualizing.

The term "curriculum" is so ambiguous that it requires some definition if it is to be considered operationally. Certainly, educational goals compose one component, but as principal, you have a responsibility for helping to control other factors that may serve to improve the curriculum. Perhaps Craig Wilson's concept that "curriculum is a planned set of human encounters thought to maximize learning,"[6] comes close to fitting an operational definition. Fenwick English speaks of the curriculum as "the school system's major vehicle to achieve some economy of scale in the acquisition and use of its resources. It is the linkage between teaching and learning from the system's perspective."[7] If these concepts are accepted, the major problem principals face in curriculum improvement is how to influence positively the interaction of a number of components in the school program that contribute to desired pupil learning: It is only through facilitating desirable alteration of one or more of those components that the curriculum can be improved. We will consider those factors common to all educational programs that are subject to some control by teachers and administrators.

The terms "cake" and "curriculum" are analogous and most people would agree that they understand what is meant by each of the terms. And yet, both cake and curriculum exist in many forms. There are chocolate cakes, birthday cakes, upside-down cakes, and fruitcakes. There are elementary curricula, science curricula, special-education curricula, and sex-education curricula. Descriptors noting the general content and the purpose for the use of both cake and curriculum provide a somewhat more specific concept than just the terms themselves.

Both cake and curriculum are created by combining several ingredients and stimulating their interaction to produce results having characteristics unlike any one of the ingredients; both can be altered as a whole when any one ingredient is altered or omitted. In preparing cakes, specific recipes are used so that it will not be due just to chance that a desired cake is produced. In preparing curriculum, curriculum design is better than randomness or chance that desired learning will occur.[8] Both cake and curriculum can produce reasonably predictable consequences when consumed or applied. However, application of curriculum is the complicated and complex process of teaching and there is no guarantee that what pupils learn is that they are taught.

---

[6]L. Craig Wilson, *The Open Access Curriculum* (Boston: Allyn and Bacon, 1971), p. 64.

[7]Fenwick W. English, "Management Practice as a Key to Curriculum Leadership," *Educational Leadership* (March 1979), p. 409.

[8]*Ibid.*

Most cakes are made by a recipe that stipulates controlled measuring of identified ingredients. A dozen, a hundred, or a thousand cakes can be replicated one after another from the same recipe under the same controlled conditions, and the results will be almost identical. This is not the case with curriculum, since neither the ingredients nor the conditions that go into producing a curriculum can be controlled precisely. Yet elementary principals are accountable (and held partially responsible) for the results produced by the curriculum. Principals therefore should take an active role in improving the curriculum through improving as much as possible the components that go into making it.

Deciding about the desirability of a cake is much easier than determining the desirability of curriculum. In the first place, a cake is obviously what it appears to be. It is either plain or with frosting; either it has nuts or it does not. The results of its eating can usually be anticipated and its desirability judged accordingly. But a curriculum is not necessarily what it appears to be. An espoused curriculum may differ considerably from the practiced curriculum. "There are two kinds of curriculum in the schools—the one in the curriculum guide and the one in the classroom when the teacher shuts the door. They are not always the same."[9] In the final analysis, the teacher in the classroom is the determinant of the curriculum.

It follows, then, that if elementary principals are to improve the curriculum, they must assume an active decision-making role regarding the nature of its ingredients, facilitate the creation and maintenance of desirable conditions in which the ingredients will interact, and in other ways assist the classroom teachers in producing desired pupil learning.

Seven major curriculum factors are influenced by principals and classroom teachers. They are:

1   Curriculum goals;
2   Subject matter content used to achieve the goals;
3   Instructional materials and equipment;
4   Time for learning;
5   The physical environment in which learning occurs;
6   Human resources used for the instructional process;
7   Instructional methods and activities used by the teachers.

Curriculum improvement can be achieved through implementation of strategies leading to the utilization of the seven controllable factors listed above. Principals do not have total control over any one factor, but can influence each of them to some degree by working with other people who also have a direct influence: pupils, teachers, other members of the school staff, parents, and others who significantly affect one or more of the factors.

[9]*Ibid.*

INFLUENCING GOALS

Educators are sometimes embarrassed if they cannot quickly respond to questions regarding the intentions of the school. Minimum competencies, exit examinations, behavioral objectives, accountability, and quantification are but a few of the terms that produce feelings of guilt and apprehension among principals and teachers. Critics of the schools maintain that educators cannot define the goals of education because if they did, then they would have to admit that they do not know how to reach them. They accuse principals, teachers, boards of education, and responsible others of not accepting goals because they do not reflect the consensus of all concerned. The problem is complex and frustrating.

> For a public school curriculum to have more clarity than the larger society's vision of its destiny often seems to require either a miracle of insight or the determined imposition of parochial administrative bias. Yet, curriculum theorists and practitioners alike must continually strive for an educative design that nudges the culture's enduring values into a positive and viable position, invites a continuing re-examination of their relevance, and sponsors a safe sanctuary of debate for completing alternatives—even those that appear irresponsible, dangerous, or alien.[10]

Defining the goals is an essential process, however, and there are some broad areas of general agreement. For example, there is little or no disagreement that the elementary school should teach pupils how to read, write, and understand arithmetic. However, there may be great disagreement regarding what they should read, how they should write, and what the scope of arithmetic should be.

Some argue that curriculum goals should not be predetermined because to decide what is to be learned stifles initiative, creativity, and natural curiosity. Certainly there is nothing more detrimental to the active pursuit of knowledge than the boring search for preconceived answers to predetermined questions. However, assuming that the ends of education are limited to the acquisition of known facts underestimates the intelligence of learners and their teachers. We all know of pupils who learn regardless of the kind of teachers they have and of teachers who cause learning regardless of the kinds of pupils they teach.

The fact is, schools have little choice about whether or not to attempt to define what is to be taught if public support is to be maintained. It is not unreasonable to expect principals and teachers to state what educational goals they are trying to achieve.

For principals, identification of educational goals and learning objectives exists when there is faculty agreement regarding what curriculum should be taught to pupils attending the school. The faculty could be wrong regarding the desirability of what should be taught or the appropriateness of the subject matter content, but that is not the major problem principals face; reaching consensus is, and the first step in reaching consensus about anything is to define it.

Establish written curriculum goals for the school and share them with all

---

[10]Wilson, op. cit., p. 55.

concerned. Putting goals and objectives in writing to provide something to work from is an excellent beginning strategy. In its initial stages, goal identification is simply an academic exercise, so do not try to make it anything else. Later, as the curriculum is shaped, the academic exercise begins to take on real significance.

A goal is an intention. A curriculum goal statement answers the question, "What do we (the faculty and others) intend for pupils to learn at school?" This general question may be considered in various ways. For example, "What do we intend for pupils to learn about mathematics?" or "What do we intend for pupils to learn about working with others?" or "What do we intend to teach pupils about themselves?" The questions may be derived in general faculty meetings, by a representative committee, a group of parents, teachers, and pupils, or by any number of methods. Written answers to the questions regarding intended outcomes for learning and teaching become curriculum goal statements.

Be more concerned about the statements' meanings rather than their precise wording. Ask whoever is involved in the process to discuss the meaning of statements and then determine if the statements communicate the same idea to all who read them. There are numerous books and even individualized learning packets that can help a group write goals and objectives. One pitfall to avoid is the tendency for semantics and proper construction to become ends rather than means for communicating concepts.

Eliminate ambiguous or controversial goal statements. Retain all statements, and set the ambiguous or controversial ones aside during the initial stages of determining goals. This may mean you set aside almost all of the initial statements. That is all right, because all involved should feel that they agree. Concentrate on agreements and not disagreements. Of course, some goals are more important than others, or may appear to represent more urgent needs. Priority determination is a later step in the process, however. First identify what everyone can agree with. Once a few major goals are determined, you can go from there. You may wish to consult the goal-identification process developed by Phi Delta Kappa. Contact your local chapter.

Retain goal statements that everybody agrees with or at least has little objection to. Fenwick English states:

> While a heterogeneous society does indeed possess conflicting goals for its institutions, there are also areas of broad agreement. Ten years of the Gallup Polls in education reveal a rather remarkable record of public consensus about what the school should do and be . . . . in times of program and organizational retrenchment, job security and internal system politics have often clouded a rational discussion by educators about the outcomes of education. . . .
>
> The continuing dodge into ambiguity by some educators merely exacerbates the problem public education is now encountering with maintaining a modicum of public confidence.[11]

Organize school faculty, staff, and parents to examine, discuss, and reach

---

[11]English, *op. cit.*, p. 410.

consensus on statements of goals and objectives. Guide the organization through formation to functioning status. Throughout, you may wish to be an active member. Whatever you decide, principals should initiate and guide the process of examining goals; and because even the best of goals and objectives are rendered useless unless they are achieved, take care to:

1   Keep the number of educational goals to a minimum.
2   Establish priorities.
3   Set a realistic target date for achieving each goal.

Goals serve as a basis for measuring educational results, so be sure to specify indicators for each goal. If quantitative measures are important, determine what the quantities should be. Possible affective outcomes such as love, loyalty, and humor may be easily observed or indicated but difficult to quantify.

There are many resources for improving goal-writing skills. When modifiers or ways to indicate achievement of a goal are added, a goal statement becomes an objective. For example, if the curriculum goal is to incorporate the teaching of reading skills as a part of the instruction of all subject matter content by the end of the school year, there are several possible indicators of achievement. Teachers could write lesson plans for teaching reading skills with other subjects, or the principal may observe instruction on reading skills in the classroom as other content is being taught. A cardinal rule is never to abandon a good intention just because it cannot be stated well or you cannot determine how to measure it. There are many resources for helping improve goal-writing skills.

Stay within the framework of policies and laws governing your school. Principals have responsibility to lead others in determining goals within the framework of laws and policies governing the operation of the school and to assist teachers in their tasks of identifying and defining instructional objectives. Above all, make the goals and objectives known to everyone who is interested.

Lead, don't push. Principals positively influence the curriculum when they lead the process of goal definition, not when they impose their own ideas regarding what should be taught. Express your ideas, but allow those directly concerned to join you in the decision-making process. With involvement, good identification takes longer, but the result will be far better if many people are involved in making the decisions.

IMPROVING SUBJECT MATTER CONTENT

The quantity of subject matter content available for transmission to others continues to increase in geometric proportions. Just consider how much is known today compared to only five years ago. Selection of appropriate subject matter to use in helping achieve identified learning objectives for pupils becomes increasingly difficult. Learning objectives classified under United States History, for example, might call for subject matter dealing with social and political issues of a period, great events, influential people, wars, development of technology, evolution of labor unions, religious movements, or many other topics. Each of them includes a veritable mountain of subject matter. Content must be carefully selected in terms of goals and the learning characteristics of the pupils for whom it is intended.

How do you choose? On what basis should the decision be made? Principals can and do directly affect those decisions and consequently affect curriculum through influencing the nature of subject matter content. The better the decision, the better the curriculum. So the major problem principals have regarding this component of the curriculum is how to facilitate the selection of appropriate subject matter by teachers who use it in the instruction of identified pupils.

Subject matter content used to achieve the educational goals of the school should be identified primarily by the classroom teachers, and principals should facilitate and guide that process. Principals may make decisions about whether or not a class can go on a field trip, whether wall maps should be ordered rather than globes. Most of these kinds of decisions result from requests from teachers and involve methods or instructional materials that deal with specific subject matter content. Sometimes principals find that they do not have the information and the understanding to make a proper decision. In fact, it would be wiser for principals to develop means for teachers to make such decisions rather than assume that responsibility.

Curriculum can be improved when the process for deciding about subject matter content is improved. Two major factors are involved in improving the decision process:

1 Improved information regarding learning styles, problems, and assets of pupils;
2 Improved data regarding appropriateness of content for achieving educational goals.

Principals should allow teachers to assist in making decisions regarding subject matter content. Select or appoint a representative teacher from each grouping of students or subject matter area (for example, a representative from each grade and each program area such as language arts, mathematics, performing arts, and physical science). Assign this schoolwide group responsibility for making decisions when one or more designated areas of the school would be affected by the decision. This type of decision-making structure has proved very effective in some elementary schools; yours perhaps is one of them. It is a good, practical organization for any type of elementary school. There is a proviso, however. If teachers in your school are highly unionized and are in formal collective bargaining, they can only make themselves heard through their union representative. Under such conditions, principals' actions are usually controlled by terms of the negotiated union contract. The principals (and maybe the teachers) have little to say about the process of participatory decision making. Decisions are made at the bargaining table.

Schools usually have more data available regarding the learning modes and problems of pupils than can be effectively accumulated and used. If this is not the case in your school, ask for help in establishing simple but effective pupil learning inventories and profiles. Many are available.

PROVIDING INSTRUCTIONAL MATERIALS

Instructional materials and equipment are too often the major determinant of content to be taught. Textbooks, for example, dictate content, methods, sequence, goals and objectives, and evaluation measures. Publishers sell more books when teachers and principals make fewer decisions about curriculum matters. Also, state departments of education and state boards of education often establish "approved lists" and criteria to use in selection of materials for purchase with state funds. In some instances, restrictions have almost amounted to censorship and courts have been called on to make judgments about use or restriction of materials. Perhaps the most famous was the "Scopes Trial" in Tennessee regarding the teaching of evolution.

A quick and effective way for principals to improve curriculum is to improve the selection process of instructional aids, materials, and equipment.

Curriculum is improved when principals:

1   Facilitate development of criteria to be used in selection of appropriate materials and equipment for teaching.
2   Ensure that materials are properly stored and classified in terms of their intended use.
3   Check to see that materials are properly used.
4   Get materials to the classroom teachers when they are needed.

Every board of education should have a policy regarding criteria for selection of instructional materials. Improving the selection process is impossible unless:

1   Teachers and principals can evaluate materials and equipment available.
2   Teachers and principals can write the specifications for materials or manufacture their own.

Principals should work with appropriate central office personnel to identify ways and means of obtaining effective instructional materials at the best price.

Good teachers probably never have enough instructional materials and equipment to satisfy their demands. There always seem to be some pupils that "need something else." Principals directly influence curriculum by facilitating the provision and utilization of instructional materials needed by the pupils. Hopefully, the school district makes it possible for teachers to write specifications needed in materials and equipment, seeks to find materials and equipment meeting the specifications, and purchases them at the lowest possible price.

UTILIZING INSTRUCTIONAL TIME

Organize the staff and faculty to develop schoolwide schedules built around shared resources. When to schedule lunch period, when to use equipment, or when to call a school assembly are decisions that should be made on the basis of as much information regarding planned teaching activities as possible. A schoolwide, representative group of faculty will probably make a better decision than the principal can make alone. Among other things, consider:

1. What schedules are necessary to prevent conflicts regarding utilization of materials, equipment, and space?
2. What are those characteristics of pupils that should be taken into account in scheduling learning activities?
3. Who should coordinate use of commonly used space and materials?
4. What should be the policy regarding study trips, and use of outside resource people?
5. What is the best homework policy?
6. How can board of education policies regarding school year calender, beginning of school day, tardiness, absence, and so on be improved?

Keep instructional time inviolate. Interruption of instruction by blaring announcements or messages (no matter how important) indicates a disregard by the principal of what is occurring in the classroom. A scheduled time of announcements is preferable. All other interruptions should be eliminated.

Principals and teachers should also ask themselves what they are teaching when they make staying after school or extra work a punishment. What do they teach pupils to value?

UTILIZING HUMAN RESOURCES

Pupils, teachers, teacher aides, parents, consultants, and custodians are human resources that may be used to improve the curriculum. They should be involved in not only teaching a preconceived body of content, but also in expanding the scope of the school's curriculum.

Develop criteria for effectively utilizing parents, community volunteers, resource personnel, and aides. Each of the groups may assist regularly in the school and should have their roles and expectations clearly identified. Representatives of the groups, along with classroom teachers, can assist in formulating descriptions of their tasks. Principals should lead in this process. Consistency in expectations and enforcement of standards for work in the school will improve public relations and provide a valuable dimension to the curriculum. Effective use of human resources must involve consideration of character and personality as well as knowledge. Desirable adult models are needed in most elementary schools.

Use pupils as a resource. In some situations pupils can do more to help other pupils learn than can their teachers. Usually pupils assist most by communicating concepts and facts. Also some pupils will learn better if they know they are to assist in teaching others; hopefully, they become more conscious of themselves as learners and develop a concern for others.

Consider everyone in the school as a potential source of knowledge because that is what they are. When professional school personnel plan for and utilize human resources in the teaching—learning process in school, these resources become part of the curriculum. Care should be taken to select and utilize them accordingly.

IMPROVING TEACHING METHODS AND ACTIVITIES

The supervisory role of principals is the most common means used to assist teachers in improving teaching methods and learning activities. Assuming that improvement will occur most when teachers rationally employ a variety of methods appropriate to the content and learning styles of pupils, principals should faciliate opportunities for teachers to learn about new methods and how to employ more effectively the tried and true.

Organize the school day and make teacher assignments to allow for instructional planning by classroom teachers. Assist teachers in grouping activities that will be appropriate and will enhance rather than interfere with other learning. Discuss with them what their methods might teach and what they might convey to students through their personality.

Provide professional development opportunities for teachers to improve teaching skills and discover improved teaching methods. Why not take over a teacher's classroom responsibility for a few hours and let the teacher visit another school or another classroom? Ask teachers to report on some promising practices they are using that seem successful. These and other strategies will make it possible for good teachers to keep current information regarding successful practices. The point to remember is that principals must make professional growth opportunities available if they are to occur without undue difficulty. Teachers will use different methods if they perceive them as appropriate to the pupils and the subject matter they are teaching. By facilitating the acquisition and implementation of effective methods, principals improve what is learned and teach professional development by example.

EVALUATING CURRICULUM IMPROVEMENT

The thesis of this chapter is that principals improve curriculum through proper management of those components that make up the curriculum: goals, subject matter content, instructional materials, time, physical environment, human resources, and teaching methods and activities. The curriculum results from the interaction of these components with the learners, and the nature and quantity of that interaction can be planned.

The determination of how closely students do approximate what is expected of them is the first step in evaluation. However, the following assumptions might prove helpful in developing both formative and substantive evaluations.

1. Judgments about the adequacy of a curriculum can only be made with validity in terms of identified goals of the curriculum.
2. Indicators may be both processes and products and are evidences of behaviors—not the behaviors themselves.
3. Effectiveness of principals' roles in curriculum development and improvement results from the degree to which principals facilitate the interaction of people directly responsible for affecting learning of pupils.
4. Curriculum improvement can always be indicated but not always measured.
5. Principals have responsibility for curriculum improvement and, therefore, should expect to be evaluated in terms of how well or how much improvement occurs.

Evaluation is a process of making judgments about the adequacy or desirabilty of a curriculum. The extent to which it influences curriculum improvement will depend in large measure on how effectively the principal as curriculum leader can utilize what is found through evaluation to improve one or more of the factors influencing the curriculum. David Pratt has identified eight functions of evaluation as it relates to learner achievement. They are summarized as follows:

1. To inform learners of their attainment;
2. To diagnose areas of strengths and weaknesses of individual pupils;
3. To guide decisions about academic and career futures of pupils;
4. To inform interrelated agencies of student competence;
5. To provide feedback into the instructional system;
6. To provide an operational target for the learner;
7. To serve as a basis for licensing candidates for a profession or occupation;
8. To promote minimal educational equality.[12]

Evaluation in terms of performance criteria is applicable to pupils and teachers.

> Objectives identify desirable states in the learner, most of which are private and unnoticeable. The function of performance criteria is to specify actions on the part of the subject that will allow valid inferences that such states have come about.

---

[12]For a discussion of each of these functions, see David Pratt, *Curriculum Design and Development* (New York: Harcourt Brace Jovanovich, 1980), pp. 195–200.

The term performance criterion is related to the larger concept of what is known as criterion-referenced measurement. In a brief, but significant article published in 1963, Glaser used the term criterion standard in making the distinction between criterion-referenced and norm-referenced measures. Criterion-referenced measures evaluate the student's achievement against a fixed standard of performance; norm-referenced measures evaluate the student's achievement relative to that of his or her peers.[13]

When making judgments about the adequacy of the curriculum, different criteria might be used. You will need to establish your own, but the following gives some idea of the type of general criteria that might be considered. More specific criteria may be established by reviewing the preceding discussion regarding factors influencing the curriculum.

1. Are educational goals and objectives of the school identified, clearly stated, and prioritized?
2. Do the subjects taught relate directly to instructional objectives of the school and help promote their attainment?
3. Does the subject matter content meet the needs of all pupils?
4. Does the school teach those subjects expected by the community it serves?
5. Is the curriculum within the legal and regulatory framework of school district policy?
6. Does the content of the curriculum provide for the learning of attitudes, values, knowledge, and skills?
7. Are instructional methods and subject matter content appropriate for the interests, abilities, and developmental levels of pupils?
8. Are learning objectives established for pupils by teachers clearly stated and consistent with school goals?
9. Do pupils adequately learn what is taught?
10. Is subject matter articulated between grade levels, correlated among subjects, and comprehensive in scope?
11. Are time periods during the school day adequate to provide for teacher planning?
12. Are time schedules consistent with development levels of pupils?
13. Does the physical environment contribute to effective learning?
14. Are instructional materials adequate and available when needed?
15. Is effective use made of available human resources from within and outside the school?

The above criteria do not include all you and the faculty and staff will wish to consider in evaluating your curriculum but are presented only as examples of what

[13]*Ibid.*

you may consider. Evaluation should be an ongoing process. Therefore, do not attempt to evaluate all of the identified curriculum factors simultaneously.

A major need, along with the criteria used, is evidence to indicate that the school's goals have been met; usually evidence is in the form of a process or a product. For example, if a school goal is to develop criterion-referenced tests, the written test is a product. If the goal is to develop more effective teaching methods, the demonstration of those methods by teachers is process evidence. When you add conditions and acceptable evidence as part of a goal statement, you have created an objective.

LOOKING AHEAD

Curriculum has been presented in this chapter as a number of controllable factors that have an effect on teaching and learning: school goals, subject matter content, teaching methods, instructional materials and equipment, time employed in instruction, human resources, and evaluation. There are no simple answers to how principals might best improve curriculum, but there is evidence that public and professional expectations for accountability for what is done in the school will increase. It is important that the total school staff identify those factors over which they exercise some control, and decide together what the school intends to accomplish and the most practical and realistic means for achieving those goals.

Currently there are many curriculum issues that have become public concerns. The issue regarding teaching about creation has again become a matter for the courts to decide. Equal educational opportunity, private versus public education, testing, teacher competence, administrative competence, and minimum standards for student competency are but a few of the topics that indicate a vast array of public and professional concerns.

Perhaps it can be safely said without fear of much contradiction that principals administer more for compliance with directives, court orders, and public pressures than they do to lead the school in a controlled process of curriculum improvement. Perhaps successful curriculum improvement will, in the long run, relieve some of the outside pressures. Perhaps professional educators, vitally concerned about what children learn, can once again regain control of the curriculum. The key to curriculum improvement is the school principal and there is little indication that in the future the responsibility for leading the process of curriculum improvement will lie elsewhere.

SUGGESTED READINGS

Association for Supervision and Curriculum Development. *Curriculum Leaders: Improving Their Influence.* Washington, D.C., 1976.
Beauchamp, George A. *Curriculum Theory,* 3d ed. Wilmette, Ill.: The Kagg Press, 1975.

Goodlad, John I. *What Schools Are For.* Los Angeles: Phi Delta Kappa Foundation, University of California, 1979.

Marks, Sir James R., Stoops, Emory, and King-Stoops, Joyce. *Handbook of Educational Supervision: A Guide for the Practitioners*, 2d ed. Boston: Allyn and Bacon, 1978.

Molnar, Alex, and John A. Zahouk, eds. *Curriculum Theory.* Washington, D.C.: Association for Supervision and Curriculum Development, 1977.

Smith, Vernon, and George A. Gallup. *What the People Think About Their Schools: Gallup's Findings.* Fastback 94. Bloomington, Ind.: Phi Delta Kappa Foundation, 1977.

Tankard, George G., Jr. *Curriculum Improvement: An Administrator's Guide.* West Nyack, N.Y.: Parker Publishing Company, Inc., 1974.

Tanner, Daniel, and Laurel N. *Curriculum Development, Theory into Practice*, 2d ed. New York: Macmillan, 1980.

Wilson, Craig. *The Open Access Curriculum.* Boston: Allyn and Bacon, 1971.

CHAPTER

6

COUNSELING AND GUIDING STUDENTS

Introduction

Establishing trust
Hints for building a trust relationship with students
1. Be trustworthy / 2. Listen / 3. Be accepting / 4. Be positive / 5. Be fair /
6. Be understanding

Counseling through teachers
Proactive practices
Establish criteria for assigning students to advisors
Effect school schedule for teacher–advisor program
Reactive practices

Developing a guidance program
Establishing purposes
Planning
Planning involves changing / Planning involves communication / Planning involves
delineating role functions / Planning involves decision making / Planning involves
selling of ideas
Implementing
Evaluating

Informing pupils and parents
Learning through student government
The future
Case study—Hobson's choice

INTRODUCTION

The elementary school is a link between family and society. It is the first place other than the family where children learn to socialize with each other on a sustained, formal basis. By the time children enter school their behavior has been conditioned by parents, peers, and nonpeer society (through observation, interaction, and television). And although school tries to use constructively the influence of their peers and family in designing and organizing effective learning programs, most students soon discover that there are differences between school and their other experiences. They learn that the expectations of home, peers, and school do not always agree. Some things they do at school are not acceptable behavior at home; similarly, some of the things they do at home are not acceptable behavior at school.

Is there an effective way to organize school experiences to constructively use the encompassing influences of family, peers, and society? Our conscience tells us we had better find a way or at least search for a way.

Students can react to school experiences in one of four ways: they can (1) be receptive and enthusiastic, (2) be passive, (3) rebel, or (4) drop out. All our efforts must be focused on keeping them receptive and enthusiastic. Thus the educational and social environment we afford them must be one that meets their needs. When students ask questions, we must be ready to answer or to lead them to an answer; when they excel, we must reward them; when they need us, we must be available. In short, students are the reason we are in elementary schools. They are our responsibility. They expect us to help guide them through learning experiences, to share with them our knowledge, and to share in the ups and downs of their growth throughout the elementary school years. We must accept that responsibility with each child.

ESTABLISHING TRUST

Children learn initially by trial and error. They learn to develop their basic muscles, learn what they can do with their fingers and toes, and then their arms and legs. They also learn by constant observation of what happens when they do certain things and by how others react to their behavior. They learn that their physical behavior affects their social behavior. And by this process of physical and social trial and error, children discover who will listen to them, love them, and play with them. Most important, they discover who they can and cannot trust. This learning process begins at home with family and then with peers.

School presents a formal, structured social environment to which children are not accustomed. When children get to the elementary school, we stifle somewhat their trial-and-error practices, by not allowing them the errors, the trials, and the observations to see what happens when they do something. Some, perhaps most, of the children become confused at the signals they receive (or are not allowed to receive) from us. And so their method for determining trust is rendered, for the most part, ineffective. We ought to provide them, as principals and teachers, more sophisticated and mature methods for establishing trust while at the same time teach them to function well within the school setting.

Establishing trust is an interactive process. Establishing trust involves taking risks and building close relationships. Trust equates with confidence and belief; it means relying on another's truthfulness or accuracy of information; and it means commitment. Little happens in any relationship until people trust each other. Trust reduces the fear involved in accepting and supporting. Students try to establish trust with teachers. They try to learn which teachers they can trust and how to go about establishing that trust.

But students find that establishing trust can be a slow and painful process. The risks of being rejected, of being ridiculed are sometimes all-too-apparent to them as they either directly or indirectly feel the effects of the risk taking—from their peers, sometimes from relatives or loved ones, and sometimes from principals and teachers. Some never learn to establish trust, either because they are afraid to or because we do not afford them the opportunity to do so.

Teachers and principals ought to establish trust with students. To do so they must learn and continually improve trust-building actions and attitudes. Unless teachers and principals are able to earn the trust of students, they will be unable to fulfill the commitment of providing students the best learning situation possible.

HINTS FOR BUILDING A TRUST RELATIONSHIP WITH STUDENTS

1. Be trustworthy

The key to establishing trust is being trustworthy. Warmth, openness, and sincerity are musts. Show genuine acceptance and support for students (but not necessarily for their behavior if it is inappropriate). Be sure that your verbal and nonverbal behavior are congruent. Students get to know you by how you react to them. By demonstrating acceptance and support of students, you will help reduce or eliminate their fear—of school, of you, and maybe even of themselves.

2. Listen

We have a long history of not listening to children. Far too often we follow the old saying "Children should be seen and not heard." Acceptance of others depends on acceptance of self. Students' self-acceptance is built on self-awareness. All trust is built on some degree of self-disclosure. Being receptive to self-disclosure is a prerequisite to openness. When students self-disclose, they are asking for your support. Listen to students. Allow them to tell you about themselves. Listen! Listen! Listen!

3. Be accepting

It is important to accept and respect students for who they are. Though you should help students grow, do not impose your own values on them. Respect and accept them and their values.

4. Be positive

Every student does something right, so, when you can, give rewards for good behavior. A simple pat on the back may be in itself a reward if good teacher–pupil or principal–pupil rapport exists. Think positive. If self-fulfilling prophesies occur, it is best that they occur in a positive thinking atmosphere.

5. Be fair

Students must feel (and be shown) that you are fair and that you are honest and genuine. They need the opportunity to tell their part of whatever (problem) has occurred. And you must be willing to listen. When a student has been sent to the office for inappropriate behavior, the problem may have stemmed from something that has been happening for some time prior to the actual misbehavior witnessed by the teacher. This is where counseling comes into play and this is a key behavioral incident in which trust can be established or destroyed.

6. Be understanding

Students need to feel listened to. They need the opportunity to tell someone about those things leading up to an observed situation. All students need to feel there is enough worth about them for us to check into what they tell us. And they need to feel that someone understands that they were angry or frustrated when they misbehaved. A good technique to use to help students feel understood and to clarify their feelings is a mirroring statement or question. Example: "Sally tore my paper, and I just tore hers!" "How did you feel when Sally tore your paper?" or "So, you were angry (or mad) when Sally tore your paper?"

If a student's behavior is inappropriate and he or she does not tell the truth about it—consistently—then you must show the student that there is reason for not trusting him or her. Students deserve the courtesy of your checking out their story and the opportunity to see that you will follow up on what they said and not automatically distrust them.

COUNSELING THROUGH TEACHERS

Many students find it difficult to adapt to the elementary school. There exist wide differences in students' backgrounds, values, expectations, and needs. In attempting to bring these differences into a single focus, the school places constraints on students. Necessary as they may be, these constraints are the source of problems or potential problems for all students. Some students, through help from a combination of sources, are able to cope well with the problems. Most students, however, do not receive adequate help and need some sort of counseling assistance in the schools. Indeed, at one time or another all students need counseling help.

Teachers' job descriptions list both the different roles teachers must assume and the kinds of activities they need to perform in those roles. Students' needs are the determinants of those roles. Elementary-school-age children's needs are varied—love, acceptance, and a sense of "being" in a multidirectional, omnidemanding emerging lifestyle—and at different times they need or expect teachers to be father figures, mother figures, models of appropriate adult behavior, social counselors, and academic counselors to help them satisfy those varied needs. And in each of these expected roles, teachers must be in a trust relationship with students if they expect to be effective. Further, they must willingly accept these roles if they expect to be effective teachers.

Good teaching *is* good guidance. Good teaching creates a climate for learning and fosters personal mental health for both students and teachers in their respective roles. The essence of counseling is helping students to assume responsibility for their own behavior. Teachers can best initiate such counseling by looking at the whole student, in relation to the student's learning development. And thus development of the whole child is enhanced through providing a good climate for learning. This climate of learning begins in the classroom.

Boy and Pine feel that the following conditions facilitate a good learning climate:

1   Student involvement and activity;
2   Internalization of ideas;
3   Personalization, promotion of difference, and confrontation;
4   Right to make mistakes;
5   Tolerance for ambiguity;
6   Promotion of self-evaluation;
7   Openness of self;
8   Trust in self through an atmosphere of respect and acceptance.[1]

We advocate all these conditions and feel that the last two—openness of self and trust in self through an atmosphere of respect and acceptance—are the keys to teachers' establishing trust with students and counseling them. In addition, we feel that the best counseling program to be initiated by teachers is a proactive one. Certainly, some teacher efforts can be expended in reactive counseling, and reality demands that reactive counseling be sometimes resorted to, since it is impossible to prevent all problems from occurring. Once problems have occurred, the teacher must deal with them to maintain an effective learning climate. But we feel that more emphasis on proactive counseling of students by teachers is necessary. Such counseling may be of a group or an individual nature or a combination of both. Regardless of the plan(s) chosen, there must be some time allotted during the school day for teachers to implement the plan(s).

PROACTIVE PRACTICES

Many students' problems are socially based. Many students' learning problems therefore are caused by a lack of ability to adjust to social groups and norms. Teachers should sit down with students individually or in groups to help them work through social problems—before the problems become serious. Principals should allow teachers necessary time during the school day to counsel students.

Elementary principals have several options to deliver proactive counseling:

1   The "hit or miss" approach;
2   The elementary counselor;
3   Cooperative approach: counselor–teacher–pupil.

---

[1] A.V. Boy and G. J. Pine, *Expanding the Self: Personal Growth for Teachers* (Dubuque, Iowa: William C. Brown, 1971), pp. 114–118.

The first choice, though too-often prominent, is, for effective schools, really no choice at all. The second choice is realistically not viable for at least two reasons: (1) many elementary schools still do not have counselors, and (2) in schools with counselors, the student-to-counselor ratio is too high to be generally effective. (Note that a latter part of this chapter deals with this problem.) This leaves the third choice—not simply by the process of elimination, but because it is a feasible and cooperative one that draws on the individual strengths and skills of all faculty persons and pairs them with pupils who need such skills. The following sections will describe the teacher's role in such an approach.

Each student should have a teacher advisor with whom he or she can learn to build a trust relationship. Ohlsen suggests that the following nine children's needs can be met in such a program:

1. Physical needs (health, diet, balance of rest and activity);
2. Understanding physical and emotional changes;
3. Self-acceptance;
4. Acceptance, love, and understanding from others;
5. Recognition from others;
6. Understanding of responsibilities to others;
7. Development of independence;
8. Management of fear and guilt feelings;
9. Ability to face reality.[2]

The concept of pairing students with teacher-advisors is an important part of the counseling program in the elementary school. In fact the development of the teacher-advisor program is one of the first and basic organizational changes the elementary school must make when implementing a counseling program. The principal sets the tone for the relationship between the teacher and student by making clear to the staff the importance of the advisor relationship. The advisor concept should be built into the school day and time should be scheduled for both individual and group conferences. Transition to such a program will not take place overnight and the principal must offer support, encouragement, and leadership during this transition. If this concept is implemented properly, many students' potential problems will have been averted.

Establish criteria for assigning students to advisors

It is important that a student has an advisor with whom he or she can feel comfortable in building a trust relationship. Thus it would be to the students' benefit to have available information about teachers who might be appropriate as advisors for them. Make available to students a teacher directory that would include teachers' biographical information, hobbies, likes, and dislikes (those which would

---

[2]Merle M. Ohlsen, *Guidance Services in the Modern School,* 2d ed. (New York: Harcourt Brace Jovanovich, 1974), pp. 58–70.

be of interest to students). Each student would then identify several teachers whom he or she would like to have as an advisor. The advisor for each student may then be selected in either of two ways: (1) the principal makes the decision or (2) the team makes the decision. The latter method is more desirable. It presumes that, first of all, the school operates under a team concept and that the team members will have a better working knowledge of students assigned to them than will the principal.

If nonteaching school professional personnel are included in the advisor system, the advisor–advisee ratio will be more advantageous to the students. The principal may decide to participate in this program. Naturally there are pros and cons for such involvement. We suggest you decide whether to participate or not based on the circumstances in your particular school situation. Within the team a primary advisor and secondary advisor are assigned to each student so that if for some reason the primary advisor is not available, the student will have someone to go to. Throughout the selection process, it is important as well to follow guidelines suggested for racial makeup of teams and advisor.

The advisor-selection process may be effected once each year, on a total or partial basis. If a complete advisor turnover is desirable each year, then the total selection process should be implemented. If, on the other hand, it is deemed more desirable or appropriate for advisory teams to remain with their advisee students during the students' entire career at the school, then advisor-selection decisions need be effected only for the group of students new to the school each year. A third alternative would be to assign students who were grouped with one team last year to a new team this year—intact. In either the complete turnover plan or the continuation plan(s), advisor selection for new students coming in during the ongoing school year may proceed as normal.

Effect school schedule for teacher–advisor program

Within the limits of reality, the teacher-advisor counseling system should be individualized in the sense that instruction should be individualized. Implied in the concept of individualized instruction is that different kinds of instruction are employed to meet the students' needs, to include small group, large group, one-on-one peer pairing, and independent study. Similarly, the counseling program should include advising in small groups, in large groups, one-on-one peer pairing, and independent work.

As previously noted, good teaching is good guidance. Good teachers therefore carefully manage their time, abilities, and energies to effect—in some small way—proactive guidance practices in their classes. Yet to expect teachers to implement a guidance program for students without proper administrative support and direction is neither desirable nor feasible; indeed, such procedure would simply amount to abdication of administrative responsibilities.

The teacher-advisor program should be designed to operate during normal school hours, and adequate support should be given to teachers throughout its planning and implementation. The advisor concept must not be viewed by teachers as just another duty added to their already busy schedule. For any innovative program, especially one such as this, teachers need support from the principal, and lots of it. We will not prescribe a specific schedule for the advising program via the diagram method. Instead we suggest that any schedule used within your school be flexible, realistic, and workable, and determined, for the most part, by the teachers' and students' schedules. Its flexibility will depend on the number of early student arrivals each school day, the number of late departures each day—both depending on the bus schedule—team designation during the day, and whatever scheduling can be agreed upon by principal, team, and individual teacher personnel (and counselor, if the school has one).

Suggestions:

1. If a prescribed time for meeting with individual advisees is desirable each day, teachers should probably meet with two to three students each day and spend approximately 15 minutes with each. If a teacher is responsible for 20–24 advisees, he or she can meet individually with each one about once every two weeks. Individual advising time for each teacher would be from 30 to 45 minutes per day per teacher. Group advising may be effected once each week for a prescribed amount of time. Similar plans are advocated by the IGE proponents. Principals who wish to study such plans are advised to look at materials designed by either /I/D/E/A/ or the Wisconsin-based IGE personnel. Principals familiar with either plan may wish to adopt a similar plan. It is suggested that both early-arriving students and late-departing students be scheduled for individual advising at those respective times.

2. If a prescribed time for meeting with individual students is not necessarily desirable each day, then a hybrid of the first plan may be considered. Further, it may be desirable to use Plan 1 at the beginning of the year, perhaps at specific times within the year, and then again at the end of the year.

3. Since it may be assumed that good teaching allows time for individual counseling time during the day—both within the teaching interaction and in designated advising sessions—it may be more desirable to allow for flexible scheduling and prescribed scheduling during the day—for a half an hour or so, depending on the felt need—for individual advising. One student may need the entire half hour on a given day. The teacher should be allowed to make that decision. Other forms of counseling may be going on concomitantly.

4. Teams may decide to individualize the program each half or quarter year, on a prescribed schedule. Each team within the school may decide to use their own schedule. One team may, for instance, decide that group counseling is more important than individual counseling and design their strategy to incorporate that philosophy. Another may decide that individual counseling will be their foundation. Still another may feel that peer design is the key.

Other possibilities may be suggested. The point is that whatever plan is chosen, it should be the one that best meets the needs of the students within the available time framework of the teachers. The principal's responsibility is to provide the leadership necessary to plan, develop, implement, and evaluate the program. If a guidance person or an assistant principal can help, that's great; if either or both can effect the various stages of the program, that's great too. The principal is still responsible for providing the leadership, however.

REACTIVE PRACTICES

Most reactive counseling effected by teachers will be at the request of the principal, guidance person, or perhaps even by the parent. On the one hand, reactive counseling may suggest failure; on the other, it may be a natural consequent of the very behavior we ought to expect of children as they learn how to establish trust and how to accept responsibility for their actions. We prefer the latter suggestion, for in reactive counseling teachers have an excellent opportunity to help students build a trusting relationship. Teachers effecting reactive counseling should adhere to those hints given earlier for building a trust relationship with students. Similarly, principals may reflect back to suggestions in Chapter 4 for reactive practices in counseling teachers, for those principles—listening, advising only when necessary, being judicious, and disciplining—are easily adaptable to the teacher's work with children.

A (student) candidate for reactive counseling may be in a less than trusting, less than accepting mood—both of him or herself and of others. By listening, teachers can help build a student's self-acceptance and concomitantly build a foundation for establishing trust. Most of all a student needs to feel that someone understands why he or she acted in a given manner (which precipitated the reactive counseling session). If he is given the opportunity to tell that, he will be better able to accept the fact that he needs to change his way of handling particular poblems.

In such a relationship, teachers should take care to

- Give alternatives, not answers.
- Give descriptions, not judgments.
- Build a trust relationship slowly.
- Give attention to students' feelings.
- Be conscious of timing.
- Keep suggestions on a "need to know" basis.

Since reactive counseling will be limited to specific students, teacher advisors need not develop as extensive a plan as that required in proactive counseling. The quality of the plan must, however, be equally impressive. Time to effect the plan is also necessary. In addition, some reactive counseling may be better effected in a setting in which only the student and the advisor are present. Time within the school day should be provided for such student conferences. Parent conferences may also be necessary. At times, a joint student–parent conference may be desirable.

DEVELOPING A GUIDANCE PROGRAM

The origin of guidance in the schools can be traced to the turn of the century, when Frank Parsons (the father of guidance) initiated the first significant development in vocational guidance because he felt that eighth-graders were not ready to make

128 Counseling and guiding students

career decisions. The earliest significant involvement in elementary schools can be traced to Boston, where, in 1909, a "counselor-teacher" was appointed for each elementary school and high school. From then until midcentury, guidance people did not make a significant impact on the elementary school, for in the early 1950s the number of elementary guidance personnel had grown to only 700. But the 1960s proved to be a significant time for growth, and by 1970 the number of guidance people in the elementary school had grown to over 7000. But the figures seem somewhat clouded. Stafford Metz of the National Clearinghouse for Educational Statistics, HEW, reported that 66,000 public school counselors were employed in the spring of 1970.[3] If that were true, there would have been approximately 20,000 elementary guidance personnel at that time. Later figures are equally confusing. Myrick and Moni reported that in 1976 there were about 11,000 counselors in the elementary schools, an average of about one counselor per six elementary schools.[4] But Shertzer and Stone (1980) noted that data from Lewis' 1978–1979 *Occupational Outlook Handbook* estimated that in 1978, only 10,000 counselors were in the elementary schools.[5] Though an official estimated number is not presently available, the total number of school guidance counselors appears to be increasing. We will assume, then, that between 11,000 and 15,000 (or more) counselors are now employed in the public elementary schools. We hope that your school has a guidance counselor or has budgeted for such a position to assist your efforts to provide an effective guidance program for the students.

The federal government has had the most influence on this rapid expansion of elementary school guidance services through the passage of legislation such as the George-Barden Act in 1946, which provided for salaries of guidance personnel; the National Defense Education Act (NDEA), Titles V-A and V-B, in 1958, probably the most significant piece of legislation ever for guidance; the Vocational Act in 1963, with subsequent amendments in 1968; and the Elementary and Secondary Education Act (ESEA) in 1965. Consolidation of federal support in the early 1970s caused, however, a lessening of support for guidance programs—the effects of which can be observed in the reduction in the rate of growth of elementary guidance persons, as earlier reported. But in 1974 the American Personnel and Guidance Association began efforts to reaffirm federal support and succeeded in gaining passage of P.L. 94-482, Title III, part D(1976), in which the federal government is asked to cooperate with states to support counseling and guidance in the elementary schools. The APGA efforts continue. Other legislation has been passed at both federal and state levels.

Aggressive state legislation in states such as Florida, Hawaii, Oklahoma, North Carolina, Tennessee, and Wisconsin is helping to provide the needed

---

[3] Stafford Metz et al., *Counselors in Public Schools, Spring 1970* (Washington, D.C.: Government Printing Office, 1973), p. 1.

[4] Robert D. Myrick and Linda Moni, "A Status Report of Elementary School Counseling," *Elementary School Guidance and Counseling* 10 (March 1976), pp. 156–164.

[5] Bruce Shertzer and Shelly C. Stone, *Fundamentals of Counseling*, 3d ed. (Boston: Houghton Mifflin), p. 34. Source based on data reported in 1978–1979 *Occupational Outlook Handbook* and estimates by Charles Lewis, executive vice-president, American Personnel and Guidance Association.

support for guidance services. In 1976, the state of Virginia passed the first state counselor licensure law; others are following in that pattern. Helpful too, are the accreditation agencies. In Florida, for example, elementary schools cannot be accredited unless they have a guidance person assigned to the school. But these efforts are not enough. The counselor–student ratios are still too high. In Georgia, for example, the state department reports that in 1979–1980, 215 elementary counselors were employed. They serve less than 18 percent of the elementary schools in Georgia. The counselor-to-student ratio in Georgia's elementary schools is 1:3,362.[6] Ratios in other states range from 1:450 to 1:13,000. In Georgia alone 1,100 more elementary counselors are needed. So although the states are pushing forward to build better guidance programs, much still needs to be done.

And much can be done by the principal. Aggressive action by principals is necessary for guidance services to become a better functioning part of the elementary school program. The previous information was included to alert you to the problem, and to give you preliminary information with which to base your efforts. More specific information follows.

State education agencies normally have guidance and personnel professional staff members who provide a link to the federal agency if your school or school system does not have guidance personnel at the elementary level. We suggest that you contact through your school system, the state education department and inquire from the guidance personnel how you might be able to get money from either state or federal sources to provide guidance personnel for the elementary school. The state education department will have the various federal statutes affecting school counselors in which funds are authorized and will be able to assist you in determining how to go about trying to obtain funds for obtaining guidance personnel. This would be an important first step in establishing a guidance program if you do not already have a guidance person trying to find the location of monies or support from state and federal agencies for development of your program. Even if you cannot at this time obtain grants from one of the various programs, you might be able to obtain direction from the program to see where in the future you might be able to obtain them. In addition, as you initiate programs, structure them to comply with the guidelines for role positions for the guidance personnel and for the duties thereof so that you can better fit into one of the categories from the federal or state programs.

There are five basic federal statutes that might be of interest in your efforts.

1 P.L. 93-380 of the Education Amendments of 1974.
2 P.L. 94-482 of the Education Amendments of 1976.
3 P.L. 95-93, Youth Employment and Demonstration Projects Act of 1977.
4 P.L. 95-208, The Career Education Incentive Act.
5 P.L. 94-142, Education of the Handicapped Act.

[6]Adapted from Georgia State Department handouts on guidance and counseling programs in the state.

ESTABLISHING PURPOSES

Most principals and teachers would certainly agree that youngsters growing up today face many more pressures and problems then they themselves did when they were growing up; instant communication—so often coupled with instant logic, with little or no thought or concern for long-range consequences—drug and alcohol abuse; the fast pace of living and the mobility of society; the high divorce rates; the declining influence of church and social organizations, and even the family; crime and delinquency; high social and communicable disease rates coupled with earlier social expectations, and many others.

Research shows that about 50 percent of a child's intellectual development occurs between conception and age 4, 30 percent between ages 4 and 8, and 20 percent between ages 8 and 17, and that children establish lifelong behavioral patterns during the ages 6 through 10.[7] The elementary years are thus the most critical in developing a sense of values, a sense of understanding self and others, and a sense of success. Learning to make decisions, to cope with and solve problems, to follow directions, and to begin to learn to make plans are some of the life skills that need to be developed during this crucial time. Never has the demand for guidance services in the elementary schools been greater. But we have not convinced boards of education. We have not gathered data to show them how great the need is. We have not stressed to them that some children by the first grade have deep-seated emotional problems and improper role modeling from which to learn, and that some have, by the time they have reached 6 years of age, ideas about telling the truth and about physical aggression that are completely at variance with the normal expected patterns. And for these reasons and others, many boards of education and superintendents pay only lip service to the idea that the formative years (elementary school) of a child's education are the most important. Any study of the facilities, services provided, and so on, at various levels of education shows that elementary schools always have the least. There exist few counselors, little planning time, and little exploratory equipment. Teachers in elementary education must plan for reading, language, spelling, math, social studies, science, writing, physical education (most often), and possibly other subjects and activities. In many cases they have little or no designated planning time. Secondary teachers, in contrast, have fewer preparations and usually are provided a planning period; department heads usually have two planning periods daily.

Given such constraints, it is unfair to expect elementary teachers to assume the major role of the guidance program. Principals should, if they do not already have a guidance person in their elementary school, present a unified school staff plea to administration, school board, and community for such a person to be included in the school budget.

There exist yet today varied approaches to guidance. It is seen as vocational, a series of supplemental services, a clinical process, a racket, an adjustment process, counseling, problem solving, developmental, or any combination of these. Whatever definition or approach viewpoint one chooses, however, the basic purposes of

---

[7]Robert D. Myrick, "The Practice of Counselng in the Elementary School," in *The Status of Guidance and Counseling in the Nation's Schools: A Series of Issue Papers* (Washington, D.C.: APGA, 1979), p. 47.

the guidance (and counseling) program in the elementary school are twofold: to assist students to

- Better understand themselves;
- Realize their potentialities more fully.

PLANNING

Mitchell and Gysbers say that a systematic and comprehensive guidance program is based upon and is shaped by eight assumptions.[8]

1 The program is student-centered, based on student needs and desired outcomes;
2 All students are beneficiaries of the program;
3 The program is consistently implemented across student populations;
4 The program is articulated throughout the student's enrollment;
5 The program is developmental;
6 The emphasis is on enabling students to participate in their own development;
7 Interventions are growth and development oriented rather than problem oriented;
8 The counselor is accountable for the outcome of program implementation.

To establish any program, planning, implementing, and evaluating are musts. Setting objectives that fit the existing school philosophy serves not only to establish direction but also to assess needs to be addressed in the program's direction as well. Depending on present practices, implementation may be relatively easy; on the other hand it may involve relearning and changing practices to accommodate the proposed program objectives. Evaluating the entire administrative process ought to be the most important element of the program, as evaluation gives credence to both program objectives and their implementation.

Every elementary school has (or ought to have) a philosophy of operation. This philosophy determines the nature and extent of the guidance program, its services, boundaries and course(s) of action, and relationship to other programs offered within the school. Planning begins with a study of the philosophy, followed by or concomitant with learning what the functions of the counselor are and then meshing the two into a workable situation for your school.

In 1966, a joint committee of the Association for Counselor Education and Supervision (ACES) and the American School Counselor Association (ASCA) defined the elementary counselor's role as consisting of three functions:[9]

1. *Counseling* of students on an individual or group basis to help them gain

---

[8]Anita Mitchell and Norman C. Gysbers, "Comprehensive School Guidance Programs," in *The Status of Guidance and Counseling in the Nation's Schools: A Series of Issue Papers* (Washington, D.C.: APGA, 1979), pp. 27–28.

[9]Jeanette A. Brown. Adapted from ideas in *Organizing and Evaluating School Guidance Services: Why, What and How* (Belmont, Calif.: Wadsworth, 1977), pp. 9–10.

better self-concept and self-understanding, learn more effectively, and develop essential life skills.

2. *Consulting* with parents, teachers, and significant others (such as medical specialists, diagnosticians, special education personnel, social workers, psychologists, and visiting teachers) to assist students by such activities as: identifying and placing exceptional children or children with special needs, fostering a positive school climate, interpreting test data, planning appropriate curricula, and inservice training.

3. *Coordinating* the organized efforts of both school and community for students as learners, to include working with parents, teachers, volunteers, pupil personnel, community personnel, and others in implementing classroom and other guidance activities, parent conferences, volunteer programs, and all other activities that contribute to the total effort in the child's behalf, striving for efficiency and trying to eliminate duplicating, potentially wasteful efforts.

Planning involves changing

Planning involves teachers and other key personnel with whom the guidance person will be working. Note from the outset that changes will be necessary in the operational schedule of school for any meaningful guidance program to be implemented. And if you expect to plan without the input of students and parents, you might be doomed to failure.[10] Needless to say, the guidance person cannot shoulder all the responsibility. The principal must afford the support, must instill the attitude for wholesome change acceptance and must call on self-strength professionally for helping to make and to adjust to the necessary changes the guidance program will bring about. Changes may be painful—for you, for the teachers, and even for the students. To make them seem less painful, it would be advisable for the planning group to evaluate the effects of possible changes so that they will be better prepared to make changes and anticipate their consequences.

PARENT/TEACHER OPINIONNAIRE

Our proposed guidance program will soon become a reality.

One of the major objectives, and a very necessary part in planning and designing the guidance program, is involvement of parents and teachers.

Please take the time to present your ideas for services to be included in the guidance program.

I. For students

		Yes	No
a	each student should have a teacher advisor	_____	_____

Place a check in the appropriate blank(s)

[10] See the following Parent/Teacher Opinionnaire.

b	Guidance activities provided	Indiv.	Small Group	Entire Classroom
	self-understanding	_____	_____	_____
	self-acceptance	_____	_____	_____
	self-discipline	_____	_____	_____
	self-confidence	_____	_____	_____
	decision making	_____	_____	_____
	problem solving	_____	_____	_____
	attitudes and values	_____	_____	_____
	study skills	_____	_____	_____
	group cooperation	_____	_____	_____
	management of fear	_____	_____	_____
	development of independence	_____	_____	_____
	ability to face reality	_____	_____	_____
	career development	_____	_____	_____
	planning	_____	_____	_____
	family life	_____	_____	_____

II. For teachers

	Yes	No
teachers should serve as an advisor to students	_____	_____
teachers should be integral part of guidance program	_____	_____
teachers should effect classroom guidance	_____	_____
counselor should effect teacher discussion groups	_____	_____
teachers should be involved in team planning for guidance	_____	_____

III. For parents

	Yes	No
parents should be an integral part of the guidance program	_____	_____
parents should receive individual visits from teachers or counselors	_____	_____
parents should receive training sessions	_____	_____

	Yes	No
performance level expectations for their children	_____	_____
teacher–child relationships	_____	_____
school expectations for their child	_____	_____
classroom guidance activities	_____	_____
career-education efforts	_____	_____
placement of children with special needs	_____	_____

Planning involves communication

Planning involves representatives of all groups who will work with the guidance person. Under the overall supervision of the principal and the working supervision of the guidance person, planning should be carefully articulated and carried out. It should not be rushed, and within reason, should be effected through consensus. Communication is essential in every phase of the guidance program, but especially so in the planning stage.

Planning involves delineating role functions

Earlier in this chapter we noted that one of the teacher's roles should be that of advisor to students. The counselor, as consultant and coordinator, helps teachers to plan and implement the teacher-advisor role, first by suggesting how to initiate individual and group advising and later by affording teacher inservice for both the advising and counseling role. The counselor also plans with other school (district), parent, and community personnel for implementation of the program and inservice needs.

Planning involves decision making

The school philosophy determines the guidance objectives for various services to be offered by staff members and others in the total guidance program. These objectives form the basis for the program boundaries, links with other programs, and plans of action that result in fulfillment of the plans. Careful decisions must be made as to which plans should be effected and which objectives should be carried out within the reality of the situation. Constraints of time, personnel, and money will mean that only certain objectives and plans can be implemented. Decisions should be made by planning groups if possible and communicated to all affected personnel, including students.

Planning involves selling of ideas

We have previously discussed the importance of rapport between the principal and teachers in the instructional program. The same principles apply in the guidance program. Whatever process is used by the guidance personnel, throughout that process—the planning implementation and evaluation—rapport between the guidance person and all other involved persons is essential. Just as the principal observing in the class is threatening to teachers, so will the guidance person be threatening to teachers and perhaps others as well.

Teachers have to understand (and the counselor must inform them):

- What can and cannot be done through counseling;
- What the guidance person can and cannot do.

The point is that often programs fail because of unrealistic expectations. Proper communication by the counselors is essential.

With an excellent knowledge base and rapport with personnel when implementing the program, threats to persons will be lessened and even eliminated. The nature of the guidance services, however, produces tensions, and thus threat with some personnel is never eliminated, no matter how effective the rapport efforts by the guidance person.

IMPLEMENTING

Care must be taken to include all three functions of the counselor's role in implementing the guidance program. Helpful would be a weekly planning chart for scheduling consultation, classroom guidance, staff meetings, inservice, facilitation time, flexible time, individual and group counseling, team planning, and coordinating efforts. Weekly schedules are prioritizing facilitators and effect organization for the guidance person in fulfilling the varied role functions. Keat suggests that preschool time be spent on facilitative and miscellaneous matters as well as with group work with teachers. He suggests that the lunch hour is an excellent time for making contacts with adults and other pupil personnel workers. After-school hours and evening hours are typically devoted to work with adults as well.[11]

Myrick suggests that top priority be given to consultation with teachers (about 30 percent), followed by flexible time, individual and group counseling, classroom guidance, and parent consultation.[12] He also suggests that parent counseling, both individual and group, be scheduled sometimes at night to free the day schedule for other activities.

Weekly schedules will vary, and will necessitate adjustments during the week. But scheduling promotes efficiency and productivity. Others feel more confident and willing to participate in the guidance program if they feel the guidance person is organized and works through a schedule. See the following copy of a counselor's weekly schedule (Figure 6–1).

A guidance council should be established, if possible. It should have representatives from various groups but membership should be kept to a workable number, perhaps no more than ten persons. Its function could include coordinating, policy making, or consultative matters. There is no set rule, but consideration should be given to the type of school and the manner in which the philosophy of the school is implemented. Some schools may be comfortable with a guidance council serving in the role of establishing policies, making recommendations, and

---

[11] Donald B. Keat, *Fundamentals of Child Counseling* (Boston: Houghton Mifflin, 1974), pp. 269–270.

[12] Robert D. Myrick, "The Practice of Counseling in the Elementary School," in *The Status of Guidance and Counseling in the Nation's Schools: A Series of Issue Papers* (Washington, D.C.: APGA, 1979), p. 51.

FIGURE 6-1
Counselor Weekly Schedule

	Monday	Tuesday	Wednesday	Thursday	Friday
8:00	Teacher consultation	Facilitation	Community contacts for home visitation	Teacher consultation	Parent consultation
8:30	Group 1: understanding self	Individual 3		Flexible	
9:00	On call	Flexible	Team 6 teacher consultation	Classroom visitation	Flexible
9:30	Individual 1	Group 2: sharing		Parent consultation	
10:00	Team 3 teacher consultation	Classroom guidance	Individual 2	Team 1 teacher consultation	Teacher consultation
10:30		Team 2 teacher consultation	Flexible; classroom guidance		Test interpretation
11:00	Classroom guidance			Group 5: responsibility	Flexible
11:30	Individual 2	Lunch	Lunch	Lunch	Lunch: Rotary
12:00	Lunch	Flexible	Individual 1	Classroom guidance	
12:30	Group 3: emotions	Classroom guidance	Flexible	Flexible	Classroom guidance
1:00	Team 2 teacher consultation	Group 4: rules	Classroom guidance	Teacher consultation	Individual 4
1:30		On call	Team 4 teacher consultation	On call	Group 3:
2:00	Meeting principal	Facilitative		Team K teacher consultation	Flexible
2:30	Parent consultation	Team 5 teacher consultation	Teacher inservice advisor concept		Parent consultation
3:00				Student Advisory Committee	
3:30					

assisting in program evaluation. Other schools may feel more comfortable with the council serving as a coordinating group. Still others may feel comfortable with the council serving only in a consultative capacity. Program implementation should include a guidance council. Its function should be the decision of the school principal and staff.

Any implementation should have a modification and adjustment valve. Feedback from various constituents, including the guidance council, should make it possible to keep a running account on program effectiveness and thus to make changes as deemed necessary for improvement.

EVALUATING

Evaluating is an ongoing process and should be integral to every phase of the guidance program. An evaluation design should be selected in the planning stage, as should the evaluation instruments, data-collection procedures, monitoring system, data analysis, strategy procedures and final analysis reporting. Reports should be given periodically by the evaluation committee to the designated person or group, be it the principal, the guidance council, or a committee so designated. Evaluation should be communicated to all constituencies of the school guidance program, to include all workers and students. Only with an excellent evaluation program design can the intended objectives of the guidance program be realized.

INFORMING PUPILS AND PARENTS

Even though student and parent groups have been included in the planning, implementing, and evaluating stages of the guidance program, it is necessary to disseminate information about the program to pupil and parents. Informing pupils may best be effected informally. The guidance person should make himself or herself available to the students. Listen to the students. Talk to them when possible. Let them know that you are available and that you are concerned about them. If students feel that the guidance person is interested in and concerned with them, they will feel more inclined to accept the program. If they feel they can talk to the guidance person freely and about the problems that concern them, the rapport we discussed as being important will soon be effected and the program will have started on the road to successful implementation. Communication with students is the key and they must feel that the guidance person has a sincere interest in them.

Parents can be informed in several ways or combinations of ways. Handbooks, handouts, PTA or PTO meetings, and newspaper articles are but a few of the suggested avenues. Whatever object of communication is appropriate, *use it*. The counselor might give talks to local community service clubs. Parents should be informed of services on a first-hand basis. If that necessitates working with some parents individually, then do it. If you need the student's consent to talk with the parent, then get it. If a student would like you to talk with the parent about the program because he or she feels unable to talk to the parent, then avail yourself of that opportunity as well. Whatever communicative device will work, use it. Your reputation will depend to a great deal on the communication you effect with the parents and the rapport you manage to effect with them. One of the best things you can effect is a good reputation. Work on it through communication with parents about the guidance program. A good communication network will work wonders. If you gain rapport with one parent, the word will spread. Your reputation will be affected by the manner in which you communicate the program to parents. And the communication must be a continual effort. You might think you have communicated, but sometimes a spot check will prove otherwise. An illustrative example comes readily to mind. Several years ago, parents were asked what they thought of the open classroom concept, as one of the questions on the functioning of a middle school which was in its third year of operation. The administration thought they had effected a pretty good information program for the parents during the first two years of the middle school program, but admittedly did not concentrate on the communicative aspects during the third year. They were shocked to read some of the answers the parents gave concerning the open classroom question—such as "It's OK when it's not raining" or "I'm afraid my child will catch a cold." Communication—continual communication of program objectives and happenings—is essential. For further ideas on communication with the public, the reader is referred to Chapter 13, Developing Desirable Community Relations.

LEARNING THROUGH STUDENT GOVERNMENT

To many principals in the elementary school, a student government or student council is a no-no. Yet as noted, children are growing up faster today and are expected to do things at earlier ages than previously. Children are really capable of far more than we might want to give them credit for. And, let us not forget, the guidance program means changes and sometimes changes hurt—even principals. We all do what we feel comfortable with, and many of us do not feel comfortable with having students making decisions about what will be happening in the elementary school. If a student government is too big a leap, then consider a student advisory committee.[13] Let the committee work with the guidance person and teachers, and perhaps suggest that they use parent advisors for their committee. Aspects of the guidance program may be discussed and improved through the work of such a committee. Elementary school is not too early to let students be involved in a meaningful way in those things that affect them. And certainly the guidance program affects them. Allow them to have input as a group into every stage of the program—its planning, implementation, and evaluation. The program will be better for it and the very principles we wish to instill in students' behavior will have been learned in a practical manner.

THE FUTURE

Elementary counselors are change agents—a necessary, viable, growing force in elementary schools. However important their role, they serve best as members of a team. But in order for a guidance team to function well, it needs leadership and stability. "Soft-money" counselors cannot provide the time it takes to develop and implement a long-range guidance plan. Neither can they demonstate the necessary and desired leadership for building a firm foundation for the guidance program if they are not offered job security.

The guidance program cannot exist without the principal's uncompromising support. Principals are the key to a successful guidance program. Thus, their support of the guidance position in the regular school budget (rather than a portion of a federal grant) and support of the guidance person in establishing and implementing the guidance program is vital.

As counselors become better established in the elementary schools, their leadership will emerge and their roles will change and grow. That is important for the school; it is crucial for the students.

[13]Jeanette A. Brown. Adapted from ideas in *Organizing and Evaluating School Guidance Services: Why, What and How* (Belmont, Calif.: Wadsworth, 1977), pp. 64–67.

CASE STUDY— HOBSON'S CHOICE

"Hobson's choice"—the choice of taking either the thing offered or nothing—is, according to the *American College Dictionary,* traced to Thomas Hobson of Cambridge, England (1544–1631), who rented horses and obliged each customer to take in his turn the horse nearest the stable door or none at all. In this case study, Peter Hobson has a choice, either to change his pattern of thinking toward the role of counselor or to continue in his mode of operation to which he has grown accustomed.

Peter Hobson has been principal of Holloway Street Elementary School for the past 14 years. Holloway Street is a three-story (and basement) inner-city school, in a city with a population of approximately 140,000. The school is located in a section of the city that at one time had housed the affluent, but today houses minority and migrant families. The once majestic houses now show signs of age and poor maintenance. The school population has changed from all-white to all-minority, and now with court-ordered busing, the white–minority, ratio is 1:4.

A branch of the state university frequently sends students to Holloway Street for their intern teaching experience and Peter Hobson is quite supportive of the program. He knows well and has a good working relationship with the elementary education faculty who place and supervise the interns.

Holloway has 500 students. Through the acquisition of federal monies, the school district has been able to place a full-time counselor at Holloway, due in part to Peter Hobson's efforts. But Peter sees the counselor role as that of disciplinarian and will not allow the counselor to establish a guidance program. Working with individual students referred by teachers for discipline reasons is the only role the counselor serves.

Shirley Cornett, the elementary education professor, for whom Peter has great respect and with whom he has an excellent working relationship, dropped by his office today. She explained to Peter that she required her interns to keep a log of their intern experiences—as an integral part of their intern experience. She reviews the log once every two weeks when she visits the respective interns. Pat Bush has been a first-grade intern at Holloway for four and a half weeks. Shirley asked Peter to read the entry Pat made for yesterday morning's reading lesson (for which she was in an observer, not a teacher role). It reads as follows:

> Not much different than other days. Really becoming aware of the children's home lives. William, who can't do a thing literally and leaves at 1:00 daily, was what I would term momentarily insane. He never does what one asks and just gives hateful looks or laughs weirdly. Today the teacher, Mrs. McCabe, fought with him to get an orange out of his hand. The orange splattered all over the floor. To reinforce that she meant business, she started to paddle him—he ran around the room gaping and cowering along the walls (as if a wild animal in danger). After the teacher's back was turned he picked up the heavy stapler to clobber her with—I stood there the whole time feeling this was just a figment of my warped imagination.
>
> William comes from a terrible background. His mother is in an asylum—his grandfather last week killed his third person (first being William's grandmother). Presently William lives with his father in a house of cats (parlor and all) and drugs are loosely around. I've wondered why no one does anything for this child at home or at school. He just floats around and was only approached this one ungodly time. Details about each of the thirty students could fill this notebook, but having experienced today my heart goes out to this neglected human, William.

"Peter," she said, "I know you feel that the counselor should work only with discipline referrals, but you really ought to consider changing your conception of the counselor's role. This is only one example, of course, but it clearly points to the need of someone's being able to work with a student in a counseling capacity, with the parent, perhaps a community agency referral, and maybe even with the teacher in a counseling capacity. Can you afford some help?"

Peter was dismayed. Both the content of the intern's log and Shirley's plea were unexpected; but perhaps both were blessings in disguise. Maybe he did need to reassess the guidance role. But could he accept the change that might occur? "How shall I begin?" he asked himself.

SUGGESTED READINGS

Baker, S. B. *School Counselor's Handbook: A Guide for Professional Growth and Development.* Boston: Allyn and Bacon, 1981.

Ballast, Daniel L., and Shoemaker, Ronald L. *Guidance Program Development.* Springfield, Ill.: Charles C. Thomas, 1978.

Epstein, J., Ed. *Portraits of Great Teachers.* New York: Basic Books, 1981.

Gysbers, Norman C., and Moore, Earl J. *Improving Guidance Programs.* Englewood Cliffs, N.J.: Prentice-Hall, 1981.

Millman, H.L., Schaefer, C.E., and Cohen, J.J. *Therapies for School Behavioral Problems.* San Francisco, Calif.: Jossey-Bass, 1980.

Muro, James J., and Dinkmeyer, Don C. *Counseling in the Elementary and Middle Schools.* Dubuque, Iowa.: William C. Brown, 1977.

Winters, K., and Feiber, M. *The Teacher's Copebook: How to End the Year Better than You Started.* Belmont, Calif.: Pitman Learning Inc., 1980.

CHAPTER

7

MEETING STUDENTS' SPECIAL NEEDS

Introduction
Protecting students' privacy
Eliminating racism and sexism
Assisting the handicapped
Providing for the bilingual
Future trends
Case study—Should Joey play?

In a sense every student is special and has unique needs. At the same time there are some identifiable needs that at a given point in time may be characterized as essentials for all or large portions of the school population. This chapter is addressed to several of those needs.

INTRODUCTION

Since the close of World War II there has been a dramatic acceleration in the recognition that every human being has worth, dignity, and rights that government may not violate. Society has taken notice that large segments of the population have been excluded from the mainstream of society because of their race, religion, ethnic background, sex, or physical handicap. Society has also recognized that governmental agencies have become huge repositories of information about citizens and that such information, if improperly used, can cause great harm to innocent people. As a result, a series of federal laws has been enacted in recent years for the purposes of guaranteeing youngsters' rights and of meeting some of the special needs of students. Some of the requirements of these laws are discussed in this chapter.

PROTECTING STUDENTS' PRIVACY

During the course of a youngster's career in school, a great deal of information about the student and his or her family is acquired by the school. Some of that information could, in some instances, be damaging to the youngster if it were to be disseminated to the wrong parties. School personnel have long recognized that fact and over the years have for the most part dealt with confidential information in a professional manner. However, in recognition of the potential for misuse of information regarding individual students, Congress enacted in 1974 what has been called The Family Educational Rights and Privacy Act.[1] The Act is also known as the Buckley-Pell Amendment.

The act has two principal features. First, the law requires that schools must provide students' parents access to official records directly related to their children and an opportunity to challenge such records on the grounds that they are inaccurate, misleading, or otherwise inappropriate. Second, the law provides that schools must obtain the written consent of parents before releasing personally identifiable data about students to third parties. There are a few specific exceptions to this latter requirement and they will be noted below.

Rights under the law are given to parents of students under 18 years of age. Rights are given to students if they are 18, provided, however, that if they are dependents as defined by the Internal Revenue Code, parents continue to have the right of access to their (students') records.

In general, all records maintained by a school relative to a student must be available for inspection by the parent or student (if the latter is 18 years of age). There are important exceptions to this rule. The law does not require that parents have access to student records maintained by school personnel that are retained by the individual and are not disclosed to any other person. Thus, a counselor or principal, who may be working with a student over a period of time, can maintain the confidentiality of notes regarding the student provided that the contents are not disclosed to any other individual. A second exception is that records of a law enforcement unit of an educational agency or institution are not open to parental inspection if such records are maintained apart from other student records and are used solely for law enforcement purposes. All other records must be made available to parents upon request.

It is incumbent upon school districts to inform all personnel of pertinent requirements of the law. Parents must also be informed. The law mandates that parents be notified annually of their rights under the law. School districts must also provide for the need to effectively notify parents who have been identified as having a primary or home language other than English. Notification of parents can be accomplished by handbooks, letters, or bulletins sent to parents at the beginning of each school year.

Student records should be kept in a place where security can be maintained. Only personnel who have a legitimate, professional interest in a student's record should have access to it. When a request is made by a third party for data regarding

---

[1] 20 U.S.C. 1232(g); 45 C.F.R. Part 99 (1976). Final rules for implementing the Act were published in the *Federal Register, 41* (118), June 17, 1976, pp. 24662–24675.

a student, the school may not release the information without the written consent of the parents. The consent must be signed and dated by the parent and include: (1) specification of the records to be disclosed, (2) the purpose or purposes of the disclosure, and (3) the party to whom the disclosure may be made. The school must maintain a record of all requests for information regarding a student as well as all disclosures of information. The record does not have to include disclosures of information to parents or to school personnel who have been determined to have legitimate educational interests in the record.

In certain instances students' records may be released without the consent of parents. These would include:

1   Releasing of records to other school personnel who have a legitimate reason to see the records;
2   Sending a student's records to a school to which the youngster is transferring, provided the sending school has previously notified parents that it is the school's policy to comply with such requests;
3   Providing student data to organizations conducting studies for the purpose of developing, validating, or administering predictive tests, administering student aid programs, and improving instruction, provided that the studies are conducted in such a manner that will not permit the personal identification of students and parents and the information is destroyed when no longer needed for the purposes of the study;
4   Providing information to accrediting organizations for accrediting purposes; and
5   Disclosing information in compliance with a judicial order, provided that the school makes a reasonable effort to notify the parent in advance.

The law also permits disclosure of "directory information" relating to a student without obtaining parental consent if: (1) parents are notified of the information the school is classifying as "directory"; and (2) the parent has the opportunity of refusing to permit the designation of any or all of the categories of information with respect to the student as directory information. In other words, parents must be informed as to what is "directory information" and have the opportunity of telling the school that any or all of the information may not be released. "Directory information" includes data such as the student's name, address, telephone number, birthdate, participation in activities, dates of attendance, awards received, and other similar information.

Student records should be reviewed periodically and purged of irrelevant or erroneous information. In addition, teachers should be advised to place no written comments in a student's folder unless (1) the comment can be supported with factual data; and (2) the comment is clearly made for the purpose of assisting other professionals and parents in planning for the student's educational progress. Judgmental statements should be avoided.

If a parent asks to inspect his or her child's records, the school is obligated to produce the records and to explain and interpret them. (A school may presume that either parent has authority to inspect unless the school has been provided with evidence that there is a legally binding instrument that provides to the contrary.)

The school has 45 days, by law, to respond to a parent's request, but for a school to delay opening a student's records to a parent for such a lengthy period of time probably would cause public relations problems.

As noted earlier, parents may challenge their students' records if parents believe the records contain misleading or inaccurate information. The law does not contemplate parents' challenging factual data—grades, for example. That is, a parent can challenge the accuracy of reporting a grade, but could not dispute the grade itself.

The Family Educational Rights and Privacy Act of 1974 has focused attention on protecting students' privacy. However, the act has not been unduly burdensome to principals, except, perhaps, in its record-keeping aspects. Most school principals were already acutely conscious of professional obligations to protect information regarding students and to disclose it only to those persons who had a legitimate interest in it. In a sense, then, the Buckley-Pell Amendment only confirmed good practice.

ELIMINATING RACISM AND SEXISM

Two of the strongest movements in America in recent decades have been the drives to eliminate racism and sexism throughout society. The public schools have been focal points for both movements. It is beyond the scope of this volume to document the long and arduous struggle to eliminate prejudice from society and from its public institutions. A combination of extremely hard work on the part of many people, federal and state laws, and court decisions have brought about progress in both areas. America's conscience has been awakened. At the same time the struggle is not yet over. Prejudices still abound and schools, like all other social institutions, have their role to play in combatting them.

Schools cannot alone eliminate prejudice in society. Principals alone cannot change the hearts and minds of all persons whose lives they touch. However, principals and their staffs can, through sensitive and honest efforts, establish a climate in their schools in which prejudice cannot grow.

A first step in establishing a climate in which racism, for example, is not tolerated is to recognize that racism still exists. Having done so, the principal then is in a position to be sensitive to its manifestations in speech and behavior. It is incumbent upon the principal to assist staff and students in recognizing when they may have exhibited, either deliberately or unthinkingly, prejudicial behavior. Such behavior cannot be tolerated within a school, and the principal must be alert to it and be prepared to cope with it. Counseling with individual faculty may be required. Small groups of faculty and students might also be utilized to develop programs to bring about better understanding among racial groups. One elementary school, for example, organized a "Problem Fighters" group that met with the principal to discuss racial problems and to propose solutions for them.[2] Other

---

[2]Pepperell Elementary School, Opelika, Alabama. The group was organized by the Principal, Dr. Martha Bailey.

schools have sought opportunities to place students with different backgrounds in situations where they can work together and, thus, grow to appreciate each other as persons.

Much can be done through the curriculum to combat various forms of prejudice. Through art, music, the language arts, and social studies, the contributions of various cultures and ethnic groups to the growth of America can be highlighted. There is an abundance of materials. The Association for Supervision and Curriculum Development (ASCD) is one source for such materials. Several examples are:

1   *Ethnic Modification of the Curriculum,* 1970;
2   *Education for an Open Society,* The 1974 ASCD *Yearbook;*
3   *Eliminating Ethnic Bias in Instructional Materials: Comment and Bibliography,* 1974;
4   *Global Studies: Problems and Promises for Elementary Teachers,* 1976;
5   *Multicultural Education: Commitments, Issues, and Applications,* 1977.

The point is that through the leadership of the principal such materials can be employed to help students see themselves and their follow students in positive ways; thus to enhance understanding between and among groups.

Sexism is another form of prejudice. Originally the term "sexism" meant prejudice against females, but today the term implies prejudice against either gender. Title IX of the Education Amendments of 1972 was enacted by Congress for the purpose of eliminating sex discrimination.[3] Regulations implementing the act became effective July 21, 1975. Elementary schools were to be in full compliance with the act by July 21, 1976.

By 1976 each school district was to have:

1   Conducted a self-evaluation of its practices in order to eliminate practices that were discriminatory.
2   Adopted and published a grievance procedure to resolve student and employee complaints.
3   Appointed a Title IX coordinator.
4   Notified the public of its policies with respect to Title IX.

Title IX deals with sex discrimination in curricular offerings, student services, extracurricular activities, athletics, and employment practices and policies.

In general, schools may not sponsor or support clubs or organizations whose membership is limited to a single sex. Certain organizations were exempted from this provision of the act. Among these organizations were the YMCA, YWCA, Girl Scouts, Boy Scouts, and Camp Fire Girls.

All courses in the curriculum are to be open to all students. Sex cannot be

---

[3] 20 U.S.C. 1681.

used to exclude a student from a course. An exception is instruction in sex education. Girls and boys may be separated for instruction when human sexuality is the focus of discussion. Instruction in voice or chorus may not be designated as being for one sex or the other. Instruction may be limited to certain vocal ranges or qualities, however, which may result in classes of one or of predominantly one sex. Physical education classes may not be conducted separately on the basis of sex. However, students may be grouped by ability, as assessed by objective standards, within physical education classes.

Counseling services may not differentiate on the basis of sex in terms of: (1) career or course guidance offered and (2) tests or other materials used for appraising or evaluating students.

Title IX also prohibits establishing different standards of conduct for girls and boys, including rules for appearance. Discipline may not vary on the basis of sex.

Because of the potential for violating the First Amendment to the U.S. Constitution, textbooks and curricular materials were excluded from regulation under Title IX. However, states and local school districts were encouraged by the U.S. Department of Health, Education and Welfare to eliminate vestiges of sex discrimination in curricular materials.

In dealing with racism, sexism, and other forms of prejudice, the principal might consider inservice education programs designed to:

1   Sensitize one to one's own prejudices;
2   Develop techniques to enable each person to overcome discriminatory behaviors;
3   Provide assistance in developing curricular materials that are nondiscriminatory;
4   Encourage staff to learn more about all cultures' contributions to American society.

ASSISTING THE HANDICAPPED

Enactment of Section 504 of The Rehabilitation Act of 1973 and The Education for All Handicapped Children Act of 1975 (P.L. 94-142) culminated a long struggle to obtain for handicapped children those rights to a public education that previously had been available only to the nonhandicapped. The two acts may be viewed as another example of congressional recognition that discrimination against another segment of society must be ended. The two pieces of legislation, like the Civil Rights Act of 1964, were preceded by a number of state and federal court decisions that had begun to lay the foundation for establishing that all children, including exceptional children, are entitled to an appropriate education at public expense.

The rights of handicapped children to a public education stem from the Fourteenth Amendment to the U.S. Constitution. As pointed out in *Brown v. Board of Education*,[4] the landmark case dealing with racial segregation in public schools,

[4]*Brown v. Board of Education*, 347 U.S. 483 (1954).

where a state has undertaken to provide public education, the state must provide education to all on equal terms. That basic constitutional assumption was successfully used to challenge the exclusion of the handicapped from public schools in two landmark federal cases. In *Pennsylvania Association for Retarded Children* v. *Commonwealth of Pennsylvania*,[5] the court ruled that it was the state's responsibility to place each mentally retarded child in a free, public program of education and training appropriate to the child's capacity. The court also stated that placement in a regular public school class was preferable to placement in any other type of program. In *Mills* v. *Board of Education*,[6] the court held that children with all types of handicaps were not being provided an opportunity for education and that their exclusion from public school was a denial of due process of law. Thus, Section 504 and P.L. 94-142 were natural outgrowths of court decisions dealing with the civil rights of children in general and of the handicapped in particular.

Regulations for implementing Section 504 and P.L. 94-142 were issued by the Department of Health, Education and Welfare in 1977. In general, the regulations:

1 Prohibit discrimination against qualified handicapped persons in all aspects of school district employment solely on the basis of handicap.

2 Require that facilities, programs, and activities of a school district be accessible, usable, and open to handicapped persons.

3 Require that a free appropriate education be provided for each handicapped child, including nonacademic and extracurricular activities and services.

4 Incorporate full due-process rights for children and parents into referral, evaluation, and placement procedures.

5 Require an individualized education program for every handicapped child.

6 Require regular review of each child's program.

7 Require that the placement of a handicapped child be in the least-restrictive environment.

8 Require that testing and evaluation materials and procedures used for the purposes of evaluation and placement of handicapped children must be selected and administered so as to not be racially and culturally discriminatory.[7]

Principals bear a heavy responsibility for implementing legislation providing for the education of handicapped children. The central office may establish policies and provide special assistance to schools in one form or another, but the burden of effecting the policies and of making certain that handicapped children receive all the rights to which they are entitled, legally and morally, will be borne largely by school principals. Principals, then, must be cognizant of the various aspects of the law and communicate them to their staffs.

[5]*P.A.R.C.* v. *Commonwealth of Pennsylvania*, 334 F. Supp. 1257 (E.D. Pa. 1971).
[6]*Mills* v. *Board of Education*, 348 F. Supp. 866 (D.D.C. 1972).
[7]Adapted in part from William H. Roe and Thelbert L. Drake, *The Principalship*, 2d ed. (New York: Macmillan, 1980), p. 207.

Handicapped children and their parents are entitled to full due-process rights in referral, evaluation, and placement procedures. These due-process rights and considerations become effective ". . . at the moment a pupil is suspected of educational problems that may require behavioral evaluation beyond the observations that any classroom teacher makes of all pupils assigned to the room."[8] Before any diagnostic procedures can be undertaken, the child's parents must be informed in writing and the parents must give written consent for a preplacement evaluation. The notice must be written in understandable language, or in the native language of the parents, unless it is clearly not feasible to do so, in which case it may be transmitted orally.[9] In some instances it may be necessary for the school district to employ the services of an interpreter to assist in communicating with parents.

A variety of personnel may be involved in developing diagnostic data. Once those data have been gathered, a conference must be scheduled to include all personnel participating in the evaluation, an administrator of special education representing the superintendent's office, the student's teacher, the parent, and, if appropriate, the student. Although the law does not mandate the principal's participation in the conference, in most instances the principal probably will play some role in it. The purpose of the conference is to determine whether the student should be placed in special education or has a need for special services. An individualized education program is to be formulated for the student. The parent must give written approval of the child's placement and of the plan before either can be implemented.

Should parents disagree with the recommendations made in the conference, the evaluations of their child, or later change their minds regarding placement of their youngster, they are entitled to a hearing before an impartial hearing officer if the differences of opinion cannot be resolved within the school district. Parental rights include:

1 The right to written and timely notice of the place and time of the hearing;
2 The right to review all information and records the school has compiled on their child;
3 The right to obtain an independent evaluation at the expense of the school;
4 The right to be represented by counsel;
5 The right to bring witnesses;
6 The right to present evidence;
7 The right to cross-examine witnesses;
8 The right to a complete written report of the hearing proceedings and findings;
9 The right to appeal the decision.[10]

[8]*Ibid.*, p. 209.
[9]*Ibid.*, p. 210.
[10]*Ibid.*, p. 211.

Parents can stop the placement of their child at any of several steps in the process. It is possible that parents, reacting emotionally, will refuse to recognize that their child requires special assistance. The principal and the school district then will have to confront the problem of dealing with a very difficult situation. Roe and Drake suggest that the school district would have a "... moral obligation to initiate further hearings on behalf of the child," even to the point of pressing charges under child-neglect laws.[11]

The Individualized Education Program (IEP) is an integral part of the process of providing for the education of handicapped children. The IEP must be in written form and signed by all participants in the evaluation conference. The content of the IEP includes:

1   A statement of the child's present levels of education performance;
2   A statement of the annual goals;
3   A statement of the short-term instructional objectives;
4   A statement of the specific special education and related services to be provided to the child;
5   A description of the extent to which the child will be able to participate in regular educational programs;
6   Projected dates for initiation of services and the anticipated duration of the services;
7   Appropriate objective criteria, and evaluation procedures and schedules for determining, on at least an annual basis, whether the short-term objectives are being achieved.[12]

Each student's IEP must be reviewed at least annually. A conference must be held to include all personnel working with the student, the parent and, if appropriate, the child. Objective and subjective data can be used to evaluate the student's progress. This conference also can serve to formulate the student's IEP for the next year.

The intent of P.L. 94-142 is that handicapped children, to the maximum extent appropriate, be educated with children who are not handicapped, and that special classes, separate schooling, or other removal of handicapped children from the regular educational environment occurs only when the nature or severity of the handicap is such that education in regular classes with the use of supplementary aids and services cannot be achieved satisfactorily. Out of that statement from P.L. 94-142 have come the concepts of "mainstreaming" and "least restrictive alternative" in terms of placing the student.

There is little question that honest disagreements will arise among professional personnel and parents regarding services required for a youngster and the extent to which the child should be placed in a regular classroom. Parents are entitled by law to challenge recommendations by school officials on both counts.

[11]*Ibid.*, p. 213.
[12]*Ibid.*, pp. 213–214.

The law in this area is being developed on a case-by-case basis. Each child's case is unique, so understandably it is exceedingly difficult to generalize from the case law thus far developed. It is clear, however, that courts are holding to the concept that the handicapped child must be educated in regular classes unless there is a *compelling* educational justification for placement elsewhere.[13] This means that the regular classroom must be given first consideration in every case of placing a handicapped youngster. It also is clear that courts will require that school districts provide a variety of special services and equipment to assist handicapped children.

The principal's role in providing appropriate educational services for handicapped youngsters is a crucial one. The principal must be knowledgeable about the law and be able to provide information to teachers about legal requirements. The principal also needs to be aware of services available to assist teachers in planning for educational needs of the handicapped. A list of services would include resources both within and outside the school system. The list should include names of specialists and agencies that can supply assistance to the handicapped. There are a number of agencies, both governmental and nongovernmental, that have resources for helping handicapped students. Services range from counseling to providing interpreters to purchasing equipment. The number of agencies available will vary somewhat from community to community, but the following types of agencies and institutions could be contacted in order to determine what resources might be made available: service clubs, United Fund agencies and local, state, and federal agencies for mental health, rehabilitation services, aid for dependent children, and so forth. Colleges and universities with special education programs also can be used as resources for seeking assistance for handicapped youngsters. The point is that in attempting to provide services to students, the school district's search should be as broad as possible.

It is essential, too, that principals take the leadership in working with the school district's special-education consultants to provide inservice programs for regular classroom teachers. When P.L. 94-142 became effective, most "regular classroom teachers" were unprepared to work with handicapped children. This is fully understandable and is not a criticism of teachers. Teachers who had no previous experience with handicapped youngsters were expected to provide instruction for those students and at the same time carry on their regular instructional program for their nonhandicapped students. In some cases teachers' problems have been minimal. In other instances teachers have had a very difficult time.

Staff development programs and activities are required that focus on the needs of regular classroom teachers as they attempt to serve handicapped students. Suggestions for such programs and activities include:[14]

---

[13]In *Hairston v. Drosick,* 423 F. Supp. 180 (S.D. W.Va. 1976), the court held that a child whose condition included incontinence of the bowels was entitled to placement in a regular classroom.

[14]Adapted from Philip H. Mann, "Training Teachers to Work with the Handicapped," *The National Elementary Principal, 58* (1), 1978, pp. 14–20.

1. Providing opportunities for special-education teachers and regular classroom teachers to work together in planning programs and discussing problems and concerns;
2. Giving teachers the opportunity to observe other schools' programs with established linkages between regular and special educators so that teachers may select programs that are appropriate for their own situation;
3. Helping teachers understand the roles of all personnel in providing for handicapped students;
4. Requesting that regular teachers provide a list of their own inservice needs in this area and then planning programs to meet those needs;
5. Providing assistance to teachers in developing skills in "managing the learning environment," which becomes more and more difficult as teachers try to meet more and more individual needs of students;
6. Arranging for meetings of parents of handicapped children and teachers to exchange ideas and information and to discuss mutual concerns. (Principals and teachers should also seek opportunities to inform parents of nonhandicapped children of the school's programs for the handicapped and to work with those parents in dispelling myths about handicapped students.);
7. Arranging for teachers to attend workshops and university courses dealing with the handicapped.

Principals also can assist teachers by providing psychological support for their efforts and by being sensitive to the teachers' problems. Principals can make certain that curriculum consultants and specialists provide the kind of information and services that teachers require. All personnel working with classroom teachers need to be reminded of the practicalities of the classroom and be urged by the principal to support teachers accordingly. The goal of providing the best possible instruction for all students cannot be achieved otherwise. The principal's leadership role in this area, then, is crucial.

PROVIDING FOR THE BILINGUAL

Lau v. *Nichols*[15] might be described as the genesis for the current bilingual education movement; the recognition of another group of school children who have special needs. In *Lau* the U.S. Supreme Court held that students whose native language was Chinese, not English, were entitled to special assistance by the school in learning English. Without such help, the court pointed out, the students would be severely handicapped in making progress in school. The court did not specify the kind of assistance that would be required. It did make clear that the purpose of the instruction should be to help the students learn English.

[15]*Lau* v. *Nichols*, 414 U.S. 563 (1974).

It would be difficult to find a school district that does not have some students who come from homes in which the predominant language is not English. Certainly these youngsters may have difficulties coping with instruction that is provided only in English.

Moreover, the problem may not be confined only to students whose native language is not English. In 1979 a federal district court judge ruled that a school district must give special attention to students in its schools who spoke English.[16] The court upheld the plaintiffs' contentions that the school district failed to take the children's spoken dialect into account and failed to teach them to read standard English. The court mandated inservice education programs for teachers to sensitize teachers to the problems of children who spoke black English. This was in addition to the special help required for the students themselves. One of the principal problems in assisting black English-speaking students is overcoming teachers' negative attitudes toward such students. Studies have shown that when the negative perceptions of teachers have been changed, these students do better in school.[17]

This court decision has prompted some people to suggest that schools will need to provide special assistance to all students who speak "nonmainstream" English. The bilingual education movement may therefore have even broader implications for schools in the future.

An obvious first step in providing for bilingual students is identifying them. Teachers can be of assistance in noting students in their classes who come from homes in which English is a second language. Teacher identification alone, however, is not sufficient. Too many errors can be made if children are identified in a superficial manner. Testing is required to determine each youngster's dominant language and to determine the child's skills in English and the child's native language. Tests vary in sophistication and cost of administration. With the assistance of curriculum specialists, appropriate tests should be selected to complete the identification process.[18]

The identification process should assist the school in determining the number of students who need assistance and the languages that are spoken in the home. The process also should assist in assessing the needs of individual youngsters. Some children may be coping very well with learning standard English. Others may not. The kinds of problems and the numbers of students involved need to be carefully determined.

A next step is to establish goals and objectives for the bilingual education program. Without clear direction, the program will be handicapped from the start. It is clear from the *Lau* decision, the thrust of federal efforts in this area, and the

---

[16]*Martin Luther King, Jr., Elementary School Children v. Ann Arbor School District*, 473 F. Supp. 1371 (E.D. Mich. 1979).

[17]Sharon Kossack, "District Court's Ruling on Nonstandard Dialects Needs Cautious Interpretation," *Phi Delta Kappan 61* (9) 1980, p. 618.

[18]For a discussion of the strengths and weaknesses of various tests, see Perry A. Zirkel, "The Why's and Ways of Testing Bilinguality before Teaching Bilingually," *The Elementary School Journal 76* (6) 1976, pp. 323–330.

thinking of experts in the field, that the major purpose of bilingual education is "... instruction designed to enable them [bilingual children], while using their native language, to achieve competence in the English language."[19] The ultimate goal, then, of a bilingual education program is for students to become competent in English. At the same time the bilinguality of students should be encouraged and students' appreciation for their cultural heritage should be enhanced.

Some people expect bilingual students to achieve complete mastery and literacy in two languages. Equilingualism in people is rare and is impractical as an objective for a bilingual education program. Children simply will not have equal opportunities to learn two languages.[20] It is more practical to conceptualize bilingualism as a broad continuum of listening and speaking skills in two languages.[21] A youngster may have "domains" in which one language or the other is dominant. For example, a child may be Spanish dominant at home; English dominant at school.[22]

Another step in planning a bilingual education program is to identify resources.[23] Title VII Resource Centers located around the nation can be tapped for ideas and materials. The Centers were established as a result of Title VII of the Elementary and Secondary Education Act, often called the "Bilingual Education Act."[24] Two other sources are:

Center for Applied Linguistics
1611 North Kent Street
Arlington, Virginia 22207

Teachers of English to Speakers of Other Languages
(TESOL)
455 Nevils
Georgetown University
Washington, D.C. 20057

Selecting personnel for the program is another task. Persons are required who can speak the languages to which the children are accustomed and at the same time assist children in learning English. This is a difficult task and may call for the employment of not only certified personnel but also aides and volunteers.

The school has a dual problem in providing instruction for bilingual students. The first problem is helping students make reasonable progress in school. This almost certainly will require that some instruction be given in the native language. The second problem is to assist students in learning standard English. The ultimate goal is to preserve the bilinguality of the student, no easy task.

[19] 45 C.F.R. 123.01 (1979).
[20] Zirkel, *op. cit.*, p. 324.
[21] *Ibid.*
[22] *Ibid.*, pp. 324–325.
[23] A list of resources is given in Karen Joseph Shender, "Bilingual Ed: How Un-American Can You Get?" *Learning* 5 (2) 1977, pp. 32–41.
[24] 20 U.S.C. 880(6).

The current bilingual education movement, reborn after *Lau,* is still growing and developing.[25] Its proponents are still divided on some issues and resources are still being developed. However, it is a movement that will touch virtually every school in the next decade.

FUTURE TRENDS

During the next decade individuals and groups will continue to press for recognition of their civil rights and for programs to satisfy their unique needs. Schools will continue to be required to provide special programs and services to meet those needs.

At least three major problems face schools in their efforts to deal effectively with students' special needs. Two of the problems, in the areas of personnel and financing, already are creating pressures on school districts. The third problem, that of the potential reaction of parents of so-called normal children, may be just over the horizon.

Enacting legislation and seeking court decisions requiring schools to establish programs for the handicapped and the bilingual is one thing. Having personnel to develop and implement specialized programs is another. There is, and there will continue to be, a shortage of specialized personnel properly prepared to work with some groups of youngsters who have specific instructional requirements. Furthermore, as new needs are identified, additional specialized personnel will be necessary. In addition, "regular" teachers will continue to require assistance in managing instruction for classrooms that will contain students with a broader and broader range of needs. Principals will have to call upon all of their leadership skills and creativity in order to seek out support services for their schools and to provide necessary inservice programs for their staffs.

Educational financing already has reached the crisis stage. Inflation and demands for additional services have outstripped growth in funds available for education. Indeed, there will be less federal money and, in many states, less money in general, to support education in the next several years. There is no question that the public and legislative bodies confront some hard choices in determining how the education dollar will be spent. Schools will not be able to provide every service expected by every individual or group. Neither time nor money will permit it. Some programs simply must be modified or discontinued unless appropriations for education are increased dramatically in the near future. It is unlikely that this will occur. Therefore, the next decade will witness intense lobbying and jockeying for position by special interest groups as they attempt to maintain their programs. Only the future will reveal who will be most successful.

As special services for students proliferate it can be expected that parents of so-called "normal" children will begin to demand some of the same kinds of services for their youngsters. The IEP is an integral part of P.L. 94-142. Will parents

---

[25]Bilingual/bicultural programs were prevalent in certain areas of the United States prior to World War I. Zirkel, *op. cit.,* p. 323.

of nonhandicapped children begin to pressure for individualized educational programs for their children? Will these parents also begin to demand the same kind of evaluation of their child's progress as is required for the handicapped student? These are only two small examples of what may lie in the future. A crystal ball is not required to forecast that as more specialized services are offered in the school there will be increasing numbers of parents who will be bringing pressure on legislatures and courts to secure those services for their children.

CASE STUDY— SHOULD JOEY PLAY?

Fifth-grader Joey Sims is one of the most popular and active boys at Dean Road Elementary School. Unfortunately Joey was severely injured in an automobile accident when he was eight years of age. As a result, Joey lost the sight in his right eye and suffered a slight loss of vision in his left eye as well. Despite his handicap, Joey has made good progress in school, including active participation in most physical education activities.

Joey's favorite sport is soccer, which he plays well. During a soccer instruction session one afternoon in a physical education class, Joey is struck in the head rather severely by a kicked ball. The teacher, knowing Joey's condition, is upset by the incident. He confers with the principal and they decide that in order to protect Joey, they should restrict him from any activity which could result in potential damage to his left eye.

Joey, understandably, is heartbroken. He appeals to his parents. His parents appeal to the principal, requesting that Joey be allowed to participate freely in soccer and similar types of activities.

How should the principal respond? Is there a way Joey can play and be protected from further injury? Is there a way the school can protect itself from liability if Joey is permitted to play and is injured?

SUGGESTED READINGS

Barbacovi, Don R., and Clelland, Richard W. *Public Law 94-142: Special Education in Transition.* Arlington, Va.: American Association of School Administrators, undated.

Pottker, Janice, and Fiskel, Andrew, Eds. *Sex Bias in the Schools: The Research Evidence.* Cranbury, N.J.: Fairleigh Dickenson University Press, 1977.

Roe, William H., and Drake, Thelbert L. *The Principalship.* New York: Macmillan, 1980.

Shender, Karen Joseph. "Bilingual Ed: How Un-American Can You Get?" *Learning* 5 (2), 1977, pp. 32–41.

Zirkel, Perry A. "The Why's and Ways of Testing Bilinguality before Teaching Bilingually." *The Elementary School Journal* 76 (6), 1976, pp. 323–330.

CHAPTER

8

REPORTING TO PARENTS

Evaluating students' progress
Grading students
Writing report cards
Reporting by conference
Planning for the conference
Implementing the conference
Scheduling the conference

Case study—Peter's parents

Reporting to parents should be a continuous process. It helps set the stage for a positive communication link between school and home; it also helps parents to know better what is happening in the school and where their child fits in. When parents are informed of the school's objectives and the progress their children are making toward those objectives, the school is much more likely to receive parental cooperation and thus can better promote the development of each student. Reporting to parents therefore is vital to the success of the school. Whatever means or combination of means is used in reporting to parents—report card, individual parent conferences, team conferences, open house, school newsletter, notes on students' work brought home, radio, newspaper or television—it is essential that an open, two-way line of communication be used.

This chapter is designed to address problems inherent in reporting students' progress to parents.

EVALUATING STUDENTS' PROGRESS

Evaluation techniques are varied and numerous. Selection of the technique(s) to use is directly linked with the marking and reporting systems to be used. Evaluation may be positive to the student's growth if the techniques chosen are appropriate for the student, for the student's progress, and for the school's accomplishment of objectives; further, the techniques must provide data to describe growth toward accomplishment of the objectives. Since growth of children occurs in many ways and since each child has some individual characteristics unlike those of other children, it seems appropriate to argue for diversity of evaluation techniques within any given school and perhaps even within any one given classroom within the school. Some possible evaluation techniques are:

1. Teacher-made subject tests. The tests should be used as learning experiences for both teacher and student in determining the amount of content understanding the student possesses, and for level placement of students in the tested areas. Tests can be formative or summative.

2. Achievement tests in specific subject areas, used for comparison with students in other schools. The tests may be used at the beginning or at the end of the school year. Specific, not composite, scores, should be used for diagnostic purposes.

   Standardized tests should not be used to place students in special classes. The National Research Committee (1982) said it could not justify using test scores to remove a child from a regular class "unless there is a reasonable expectation" that special aid will be more effective. Ability tests have limitations and thus should be balanced with other sources of information. Tests are limited since they are not responsive to individual styles, stamina, or stress; nor do they measure inherent qualities; further, they predict performance reasonably well for the first year and become increasingly unreliable as time passes. In spite of the emphasis on test limitations, the committee noted that ability tests are important predictive tools if they are carefully developed and validated and if users can interpret them.[1]

3. Commercial, nonsubject-matter tests, used to help identify students' interests, establish general group characteristics, and help students know selves better. These tests are most useful for planning group lessons and activities within the classroom.

4. Dated record of individual student writing assignments, and creative work samples kept in a file folder labeled with a child's name. Formative folder content analysis may be useful in discovering student interests, strengths, weaknesses, and improvements. This is an excellent means for parents to see what type of work their child does.

5. Dated record of observation of students' behavior for such things as use of time, work and play habits, peer relationships, health status, and reading habits. Observations should be made for specific purposes, and if possible should be made with systematic observation instruments.

6. Reading bibliography and word list, used to indicate understanding and interest level, and to provide interaction level—student to teacher.

---

[1] "Standardized Testing Fair, but Overused, Study Says," *Education USA*, February 8, 1982, pp. 182 and 189, taken from the report "Ability Tests: Uses, Consequences, and Controversies" published by National Academy Press.

7 Free-response writing samples used to test creative thinking skills as well as general communication skills, feelings, beliefs, and understandings.

All evaluation depends on evidence. Teachers must be able to document objective, observable data about students, both formal and informal. Evaluation should be as comprehensive as possible so that grades may be fair, expressive, and motivate students' improvement. The above-listed examples point out the varied types of evaluative techniques available. Teachers should use those techniques that fit their objectives, facilities, and overall situation.

GRADING STUDENTS

A grade is an alphabetical or a numerical symbol or mark that indicates the degree to which intended outcomes have been achieved.[2] It is the logical next step in the evaluation process.

The type of grades or marks students receive depends on the reporting system used. Grading and reporting are so closely interrelated that it is impossible to discuss one without taking into account the implications it has on the other. Grades are given to communicate. They communicate to students how well they are progressing in relation to both their own goals and other students. They communicate to teachers how well students are progressing in relation to the school and teacher goals, both individually and as a group. And they communicate to parents how well their child is progressing both in relation to self and to others. Grades are just symbols on paper but they have different interpretations emotionally for all three concerned groups. And all three groups are concerned.

With these thoughts in mind, let us now review types of grading commonly used in elementary schools.

1. Norm-referenced grading, comparing a student's achievement with that of a norm group, usually the rest of the class or several classes, by rank ordering and then by assigning a letter grade. There are three methods:

a normal curve
b pass–fail
c standard score

But norm-referenced grading only ranks students. It says little, if anything, about the student's actual achievement. It is simply a *relative* grade.

2. Criterion-referenced grading, comparing a student's performance to prespecified criteria. The standards are absolute and thus specific information about the student's achievement can be provided. Sometimes letter grades are given, sometimes percentage grades are given, and sometimes a class ranking is given. The grade is determined by the number of objectives the student reaches.

[2]L.R. Gay, *Educational Evaluation and Measurement: Competencies for Analysis and Application* (Columbus, Ohio: Charles E. Merrill, 1980), p. 510.

3. Percentage grading, averaging test scores and converting them to a percentage. The actual percentage may be reported or the letter-grade equivalent may be used. This method, however, tells neither how a student compares with the rest of the group, nor actually how the student achieved in relation to specified criteria.

4. Future-referenced, measuring a student's performance in relation to learning potential or amount of improvement. Its reliability for the time periods in question (over which improvement is measured or predicted) does not lead to a highly dependable source of grading. This method seems popular as a supplementary method for grading.

Which type(s) of grading should be used? It depends. All four types have merits and shortcomings. Perhaps multiple grading is desirable and the reports to parents can include some or all of: (1) letter grades, (2) written description of performance, (3) number grades (such as 1, 2, 3, 4, 5), (4) percentage grades, and (5) pass—fail (satisfactory, unsatisfactory) reports. By using multiple reporting systems, teachers can better communicate to parents their child's performance and overcome disadvantages inherent in using the grading methods individually.

WRITING REPORT CARDS

Students need to be informed of their progress in school and indeed they have the right to be informed of their progress. Most teachers can successfully evaluate their students' work and academic progress, but meet with less success when they try to report evaluations in acceptable language and format. It seems that no matter what the method of evaluating and reporting used, someone will always object. Furthermore there is no perfect report card, one that

- Is simple;
- Is easy to fill out;
- Tells what needs to be told about student progress;
- Tells it in a way that is understood and accepted by all parents.

A primary concern in reporting to parents is *What do the parents need to know?* and also perhaps, what do the parents have a right to know? Parents need to know that their child, and not the subject matter being taught, is the focus of the school curriculum, the focal point around which most of the decisions about the school are and will be made. They need to know that the school is interested in the student's knowing the why as well as the what, and that the why is as important, and in some cases, even more important than the what. Communication of this basic notion will better equip teachers to help parents understand that seeing a purpose in learning provides better motivation for children than does any external motivation device. Parents also need to know that evaluation of their child's progress goes far beyond test scores and grades, for no matter how accurate the test score and how nearly accurate the grade (by whatever grading means), they cannot give the whole picture. Perhaps nothing can give the whole picture, so that ideal may never be reached, but with a professional concentration on making the grading and reporting system better and coupling it with parent conferences and other communication of the child's progress to parents on a continuing basis, grading and reporting will take on a more beneficial meaning, for the student, the parent, and the school. All will benefit and grow.

Principles for developing a grading and reporting system:

1. Assess the needs of the users. Determine what grading and reporting should accomplish.
2. Explore the grading and reporting system of other schools.
3. Work cooperatively with users throughout the development.
4. Base the system on specific objectives.
5. Provide both practical and diagnostic capabilities.

All grading and reporting practices should be adjusted to the local situation. Most often, some type of letter grades are given. But, while a mark of B may be considered average for students in one community, it may be considered an above-average mark in another. And within any school system, the same kind of disparity may exist. Perhaps in a given elementary school (maybe even yours) the grading will differ significantly from its neighbors. It is necessary, therefore, for all teachers within the school to be oriented to accept and practice the same grading philosophy and method of operation. Teacher inservice training is essential.

Report cards vary from a simple letter grade for individual subjects, to comprehensive and complex computer printouts of the student's progress.

Figure 8–1 gives an example of a report card that is somewhat simplistic, yet offers both a letter (S,U) grade and teacher comments.

The example in Figure 8–2 is somewhat more comprehensive, as it specifies objectives within a subject area (Language Arts). Other subjects on the report card, as appropriate, should also contain measurable objectives. This type of report card may have as the achievement and work-habit indicators, (1) letter grades, (2) number grades, (3) percentage grades, or (4) verbal indicators, such as "outstanding," "satisfactory," "unsatisfactory," or, as shown, the continuum "always"–"never."

Report cards can also be written, as in a letter format. Although such reports may be desired by some parents, their use should be approached with caution as they are difficult to prepare, are time consuming, and may be subjected to misinterpretation. If a written report is used, these suggestions may help:

1. Write in nontechnical, easily understood terms.
2. Be informative.
3. Be brief, direct, and personal.
4. Assume a positive tone.
5. Avoid generalizations.
6. Be able to support statements with evidence (if called upon).

FIGURE 8-1

SUBJECT	Unsatisfactory	Satisfactory	COMMENTS
Progress Report — Name _____ Date _____ Grade _____ Teacher _____			
READING			
LANGUAGE			
SPELLING			
WRITING			
SOCIAL STUDIES			
MATH			
SCIENCE/ HEALTH			
PHYSICAL EDUCATION			

FIGURE 8-2

PROGRESS REPORT

Language arts	Always	Most of time	Some of time	Seldom	Never	Language arts work habits	Always	Most of time	Some of time	Seldom	Never	Comments
Reads with understanding						Listens attentively						
Reads independently						Uses time well						
Shows increasing vocabulary						Follows directions						
Applies oral communication skills						Shows initiative						
Uses grammatical skills correctly						Cooperates with others						
Writes legibly						Maintains interest						
Expresses written ideas well						Completes assignments on time						
Applies spelling skills												

7 Write in grammatically correct, complete sentences.

8 Indicate provisions made to meet special needs of the student.

9 Point out ways parents can help (when desired).[3]

Regardless of the type of report card to be used, objectivity and practicality[4] remain the main issues of concern.

REPORTING BY CONFERENCE

Everyone can benefit from a parent–teacher conference; teachers learn to understand both parents and students better and thus can more effectively provide for the student's needs; parents learn more about how their child learns and how they can assist in the learning process; and, most importantly, the child benefits from the parent–teacher communication efforts through a better planned, more effective learning program.

The parent–teacher conference should be an integral part of the reporting

---

[3]Adapted from George I. Thomas and Joseph Crescimbeni, *Individualizing Instruction in the Elementary School* (New York: Random House, 1967), p. 148.

[4]Robert F. Mager, *Preparing Instructional Objectives* (Palo Alto, Calif.: Fearon Publishers, 1962).

system. It is an excellent supplement to report cards and therefore should be conducted periodically to help report a student's progress.

PLANNING FOR THE CONFERENCE

Effective conferences, like effective lessons, require teacher preparation. And preparing for conferences is very similar to preparing for lessons. A conference plan should include listing the conference objective(s), tentatively organizing the sequence of events, choosing the strategy (or strategies) to be used, knowing the material to be covered (and having it readily available for viewing during the conference), listing the key questions, anticipating parent questions, and providing the proper rapport to facilitate the conference. If desirable, the student may also help to plan the conference.

Parent planning, by providing a list of things that might help the teacher better understand their child, and by listing things they wish to find out from the teacher about their child and his or her progress relative to the teacher's and school's objectives, is also desirable.

IMPLEMENTING THE CONFERENCE

Parents may be informed of the conference time and place by either a written notice or telephone call or both. Written notices should come directly from the teacher; parent verification is necessary. Telephone notices can come directly from the teacher or from the school secretary (with instructions from the teacher). Since a telephone call is more personal, it is the preferred method of setting the stage for the conference.

Each parent conference should include three stages: the opening, the transition, and the closing. In the opening of the conference, the teacher should strive to establish rapport and then nurture it during the remaining stages. Start by letting parents know you like children and specifically their child. Do it in a friendly, casual atmosphere. Throughout the conference, and especially in the opening, be positive; and be sure to use language that parents can understand. It might be a good idea to confer in the child's classroom—but do not sit behind your desk, and be sure to have adult-size chairs and tables for the conference.

If the conference takes place in the classroom, the parent can easily visualize the daily activities as they are explained. Also, if the child is present during the conference, he or she can assist in explaining the activities and his or her way of participation in them.

The transition stage is designed for sharing information about the child's progress. Identify and describe the child's strong points, but also remember to be honest and sincere and objective in pointing out where improvement can be made. Temper the honest with tact. Ask yourself "Is there a *need to know?*" and "How best can these points be addressed?" Prior strategy planning is essential. Ask parents for their suggestions as to how both you and they might assist the child in needed improvement areas, then together develop a plan. As you discuss the child's progress, be specific about standards and how the child performs according to those standards. Whenever you can, give examples of the child's performance. Keep the child's work folder handy and use it appropriately.

Throughout the conference, and especially in the transition stage, try to relate to the whole child—the academic, the work habits, attitude, and social skills—and make suggestions and plans accordingly.

The closing is designed for summarizing the child's progress and planning a course of action for maintaining or improving upon the progress. Input from parents is desirable; overall, however, it is the *teacher's* responsibility to design (and implement) a positive plan of action. Positiveness is the keynote.

Before leaving the conference, both teacher and parents should be aware of and accept their responsibilities in the progress improvement plan.

Thus far, we have listed a lot of do's for the conference. Perhaps just as important is a list of don't's.

1. Don't put the parent on the defensive about anything.
2. Don't talk about other children or compare this child with other children. It is unprofessional.
3. Don't talk about other teachers to the parents unless the remarks are of a complimentary nature.
4. Don't belittle the administration or make derogatory remarks about the school district.
5. Don't argue with the parent.
6. Don't try to outtalk a parent.
7. Don't interrupt the parent to make your own point.
8. Don't go too far with a parent who is not ready and able to understand your purpose.
9. Don't ask parents questions that might be embarrassing to them. Only information pertinent to the child's welfare is important. Questions asked out of mere curiosity are unforgivable.
10. After the conference, don't repeat any confidential information the parent may volunteer. It is most unprofessional and can be very damaging to the parent and the child.[5]

We have suggested that the student may play a role in planning and implementing conferences. Some teachers may feel comfortable with this procedure while others may not. The principal may wish to suggest a standard school procedure for this all-important activity.

SCHEDULING THE CONFERENCE

In scheduling conferences, teachers should allow adequate preparation time. Ideally, each student's parent should have a conference with the teacher as soon

---

[5]V. Bailand and R. Strong, "Parent-Teacher Conferences," in Norman E. Gronlund, *Measurement and Evaluation in Teaching*, 3d ed. (New York: Macmillan, 1976), p. 533.

after receiving a report card as possible. This goal can be achieved in part by first holding a group conference and then scheduling individual conferences over a two-to-three month period. When implemented twice each year, such conference scheduling can effectively supplement the report card system.

CASE STUDY—PETER'S PARENTS

Mary Clements teaches second grade in a rather well-to-do suburban area (Flosswood) located outside a major city. Many Flosswood residents work in the city and commute daily by train. Keeping up with the Jones' is a favorite community activity.

Tomorrow's conference is with Peter Christopher's parents, and Mary seems concerned about it. Peter's parents are perfectionists; they want Peter to excel. Peter is an active boy, well developed and taller than most of his classmates. His arithmetic skills are above average and he does superior work in reading and language arts. He also is quite creative and loves music. He is lacking in interpersonal skills however. Peter is disrespectful toward adults and very aggressive and negative with other children at school.

Mary has spoken to Peter's mother on several occasions concerning his attitude toward others but has met with little success. His mother seems to feel that the problem lies with the teacher and not with Peter. "Peter," she said, "never exhibited this type of behavior in first grade, and we never have seen him act this way at home. I am sure his father wishes to discuss this situation with you." Yet Peter's mother's perception of reality, it seems, is somewhat distorted. Jennifer Graves, the first-grade teacher who taught Peter, had similar problems. Both parents seemed to ignore the problem, or at least play it down. "He'll grow out of it," they said.

In planning the conference, Mary thought she might begin (the conference) by pointing out to Peter's parents his growth in skills

- In reading, by showing his reading records;
- In language arts, by showing examples of his writing vocabulary, his dictionary skills, and his creative story-writing ability;
- In arithmetic, by showing his addition assignments.

She would then point out, using examples noted in her observance of Peter's behavior, group-adjustment skills deficiencies. She also would ask his parents to assist her in planning a program to help Peter grow in the use of group interaction skills. One of her ideas was to try to draw Peter out of his shell. Most of the time he wanted to work alone and rarely shared with others. He also seemed to be afraid of failure. She hoped to convince his parents to support and encourage his schoolwork and also to allow Peter to participate in activities that would lead him to sharing with others. "Above all," she thought to herself, "I've got to establish rapport with Peter's parents at the beginning of the conference." And so she planned to be cordial, casual, and supportive in her opening comments.

When Peter's parents arrived for the conference, Mary was anxious but ready. As she began her rapport-establishing technique, Peter's father interjected and said, "Mrs. Clements, my wife and I feel you are not doing a very good job at all with Peter. We are seriously thinking of requesting that he be placed in the other second-grade classroom." What should Mary's reaction be? How would you handle the situation?

SUGGESTED READINGS

Armstrong, David G., Denton, Jon J., and Savage, Tom V., Jr. *Instructional Skills Handbook.* Englewood Cliffs, N.J.: Educational Technology Publications, 1978.

Brandt, Ronald S., Ed. *Partners: Parents and Schools.* Alexandria, Va.: The Association for Supervision and Curriculum Development, 1979.

Hoover, Kenneth H., and Hollingsworth, Paul M. *A Handbook for Elementary School Teachers.* Boston: Allyn and Bacon, 1978.

Rutherford, Robert B., Jr., and Edgar, Eugene. *Teachers and Parents: A Guide to Interaction and Cooperation.* Boston: Allyn and Bacon, 1979.

Schroder, William B., Ed. *Measuring Achievement: Progress Over a Decade.* San Francisco, Calif.: Jossey-Bass, 1980.

CHAPTER

9

COMPLYING WITH THE LAW

Identifying the school's authority
Protecting constitutional rights
Enforcing attendance
Clarifying liability of school personnel
Liability for violation of civil rights
Liability for pupil injury
Liability for defamation of character

Paddling pupils
Protecting aides and interns
Searching youngsters
Suspending and expelling
Controlling demonstrations
Censoring
Dressing appropriately
Providing pupil activities
Taking field trips
Stopping drug abuse
Administering first aid
Reporting child abuse
Dealing with bomb threats
Supporting your local police
Dealing with unwanted visitors
Looking to the future
Casy study—the absent assistant principal
Case study—surprise package

The focus of this chapter is on the legal rights of students and the authority of the school. In recent years principals have undoubtedly felt beset by the courts. Students and parents have rushed to the courts, seemingly over any trivial rule, and, more often than not, emerged victorious. Sometimes principals have spent as much time with their lawyers as they have with their teachers. Although secondary school principals' problems have been more severe than those of their colleagues in the elementary school, legal problems have not been confined to high schools. The landmark *Tinker* case,[1] it will be recalled, involved an elementary-school youngster as well as secondary-school pupils.

The high-water mark for litigation between pupils and schools, especially cases involving discipline, occurred in the 1960s and early 1970s. In the last several years there have been fewer court cases. Furthermore, more of the cases have been decided in favor of the schools. Several reasons have been advanced for this shift in court decisions regarding public schools. First, the 1960s were marked by the Viet Nam War and Watergate and a general reaction against authority throughout society. Schools were challenged, as were virtually every other institution of government. The general mood of society has changed since that period and people appear to be less politically active then they were a few years ago. Thus, there are fewer attacks on the authority of the school.

A second reason advanced for the decrease in the number of lawsuits regarding pupil discipline is that the courts have become more conservative. Unquestionably, the judiciary has become less willing to entertain lawsuits of a trivial nature. Courts in recent years have begun, more and more often, to raise the question: Does the rule that the plaintiff questions truly involve a constitutional right? Courts in general appear to be shifting toward a position that gives more credibility to school authorities' judgment. The more conservative mood of the courts is perhaps a reflection of the times. As Finley Peter Dunne, the author of the political philosophy of "Mr. Dooley," observed many years ago, "No matter whether th'Constitution follows th'flag or not, th'supreme court follows th'illiction returns."[2] Changes in the political climate of the nation frequently are reflected in court opinions.

A third reason for the decline in litigation over pupil discipline is that most of the major issues concerning the school's authority over pupils have probably been resolved. Lawsuits in this area in the 1980s will deal with specific situations based on principles developed earlier. There is no question that the decade before 1980 saw many of the major questions revolving around the schools and pupils decided. These questions will be noted later in this chapter.

Fourth, and finally, perhaps the major reason there are fewer court challenges to the school's authority is that school principals have become more cognizant of the law as it applies to school rules. Burned sufficiently, a person usually avoids dropping a match near a can of of gasoline. School officials in general, and school principals specifically, have questioned their own rules. They have carefully examined dress codes, haircut rules, regulations concerning suspension, and a host of other rules, for the purpose of determining whether or not the regulations really are essential to the functioning of the school and, thus, can pass

---

[1]*Tinker v. Des Moines Independent Community School District*, 393 U.S. 503 (Iowa, 1969).
[2]Finley Peter Dunne, *The Supreme Court's Decisions*, as quoted in John Bartlett, *Familiar Quotations*, 13th ed. (Boston: Little, Brown, 1955), p. 834a.

constitutional muster. In other words, principals themselves, concerned not only about lawsuits but also acutely conscious of the effect rules have upon pupils, have taken the lead in eliminating many of the potential sources of legal problems. Rules that are not necessary have been eliminated. Rules that are necessary have been refined, clarified, and explained to children and their parents. Principals, in general, no longer are so vulnerable as the high-school principal, who several years ago, in a dispute over a dress code, stated: "I apply the dress code as I see it. We don't define the term dungarees as what it is."[3]

That the courts, both state and federal, have had a profound effect on methods of student discipline is almost axiomatic. That in recent years there has been a gradual yet discernible trend in the courts toward opinions favorable to school officials is apparent, also. One of the major reasons for this trend is that many of the most significant issues regarding student rights have been largely resolved in the courts. These issues, as well as those that yet appear to be unresolved, will be discussed below.

IDENTIFYING THE SCHOOL'S AUTHORITY

No court, state or federal, has ever questioned that schools have the legal authority to govern pupils. There have been questions about specific rules and about methods of student control, but the basic authority of school officials to maintain order and to accomplish the mission of the school remains intact.

Schools have the necessary authority, indeed the responsibility, to establish and enforce rules for students in order that the educational purposes of the school can be achieved. Where it can be established that certain rules are necessary—for example, pupils may not smoke in school because such may be injurious to their health—then a court certainly will support school personnel.

Schools also have the responsibility to set out regulations for student governance not only for the accomplishment of the school's mission, but also to protect youngsters entrusted to their care. A school would be remiss, for example, if there was a drug abuse problem in the school and school officials did nothing about it. It is possible that a lawsuit could be maintained alleging that the principal and teachers were negligent in their responsibility toward the children in their care. In a lawsuit involving drugs, a court spoke directly to that point, stating that school authorities, in view of the "distinct relationship" between them and their students and the right of parents to expect that certain safeguards will be taken, have a duty to protect children entrusted to their care.[4]

School personnel, thus, stand *in loco parentis* to pupils. *In loco parentis* means "in place of the parent." This concept does not mean that the school has carte blanche with respect to youngsters, nor does it imply that principals and teachers have every right that parents enjoy regarding their children. It does mean that while children are at school, or under the school's direction, principals and

---

[3]*Bannister v. Paradis,* 316 F. Supp. 185 at 186 (1970).
[4]*People v. Jackson,* 319 N.Y.S. 2d 731 (N.Y., 1971).

teachers have the authority normally accorded parents for governing youngsters. It also means that schools have a responsibility to protect children given into their care. This last point can hardly be overemphasized. Parents, sometimes unwillingly, comply with compulsory attendance statutes and send their children to school. By doing so, parents surrender to the school some of the parents' fundamental authority over their youngsters to school officials, specifically in educational matters. However, as school personnel accept this authority, they also accept the responsibility of protecting and caring for those children during the time the pupils are entrusted to them. This is a heavy, but not awesome, responsibility.

PROTECTING CONSTITUTIONAL RIGHTS

It was in 1969 that Mr. Justice Fortas, writing for the majority of the U.S. Supreme Court in *Tinker* v. *Des Moines,* stated that students and teachers do not shed their constitutional rights "at the schoolhouse gate."[5] The *Tinker* case, often characterized as the "armband case," caused shockwaves throughout the school administration community. (It was not the first, nor the last shockwave. Others were to follow.) In *Tinker,* the High Court ruled on the issue of pupils wearing black armbands at school in protest of the Viet Nam War. In the absence of disruptive conduct on the part of the student, the Court ruled, the student, like his or her adult counterpart, was entitled to the guarantees of citizenship protected by the U.S. Constitution. In this case the students' behavior was protected by the First Amendment, which guarantees all citizens the right of freedom of speech. Wearing an armband in opposition to the conflict in Southeast Asia was "symbolic speech" and, thus, came under the protection of the First Amendment.

Tinker v. *Des Moines* has been characterized as a landmark case in public education. It has been cited often in subsequent cases dealing with students' constitutional rights. The essential meaning of *Tinker* is that all American citizens, including those citizens who are of school age, are entitled to the rights guaranteed by the U.S. Constitution. In no way does this court case, or any other for that matter, indicate that school officials may not control conduct that is disruptive or that threatens to thwart the school in the pursuit of its mission. *Tinker* does suggest, however, that school personnel must tread lightly when they approach constitutionally protected areas and be able to justify any intrusion into rights guaranteed by the Constitution.

Court decisions concerning constitutional rights of pupils should not be interpreted as meaning that school-aged children enjoy precisely the same rights as do adult citizens. It is difficult for courts, and certainly for laypersons, to draw distinctions between constitutional rights of adults and of children. There are many gray areas. Sometimes the only answer that can be given lies in a specific factual situation. For example, while adults may read virtually anything they wish, it is clear that parents, and schools, can protect youngsters from certain kinds of reading material (or literature, if you will). Less clear are questions revolving around

[5]*Tinker, supra.*

freedom of speech, for example, when pupils are involved in protests against societal or school rules. Suffice to say that elementary-school principals must recognize that pupils of all ages do enjoy the protection of the Constitution and that where a school rule might intrude among those rights, the principal should be prepared to present a valid rationale for the rule.

"Due process of law" has been a part of education language for so long that the phrase is almost a cliché. Principals have been heard to say that a student has been "due processed." It is safe to assume that when administrators speak of due process of law in this sense, they are talking about procedural due process of law. Procedural due process is a vital aspect of law, but it is only one aspect. Another facet is substantive due process. Both are basic to an understanding of pupils' rights.

Substantive due process of law involves the subject matter of a rule or regulation. A child may challenge in court a school rule that the pupil believes infringes upon a right guaranteed by the Constitution. *Tinker* is an example of such a case. In examining such a case, a court may follow this process: First, this question is asked: Does the rule infringe upon a basic constitutional right, for example, freedom of speech? If the court answers this question in the negative, then the case can be laid to rest. There is no case. However, if the answer is affirmative, then another question must be raised: If a constitutional right is abridged in some manner, on what basis can the school justify restricting pupils' behavior in this area? To put it in another way, is the rule necessary in order that the school's educational mission can be fulfilled? These are critical questions for the school principal. Whenever a school gives consideration to establishing a rule governing students' conduct, the school must give serious thought to the questions of whether or not the rule is necessary to the functioning of the school (or to the classroom) and whether or not the rule violates a constitutional right.

Procedural due process of law refers to the means of enforcing rules and regulations. Fundamentally, due process, in this sense, means "fair play." Procedural due process of law, contrary to popular notion, is not a static concept. The procedure required varies with the situation. The process required by law changes with the nature of the offense and the severity of the penalty that might be imposed. Expulsion of a student from school, which is a severe punishment, requires a relatively elaborate procedure. A mild punishment for a minor offense does not. For example, assume that a school has a rule prohibiting smoking by pupils. (Such a rule could be justified on health grounds.) If a principal saw a youngster violating the rule, it would not be necessary to conduct an elaborate hearing, complete with lawyers, to impose a reasonable penalty for violating the rule.

The essential question in procedural due process of law cases is: Has the youngster been treated fairly? Another set of questions a court might ask—and a principal should ask—is: Did the pupil know that his or her behavior would violate a school rule? Did the student have the opportunity of presenting his or her side of the case when accused of violating the rule? In reaching a decision in the case, did the principal make the decision based on the evidence presented? A "hearing," then, may be informal or formal, depending on the nature of the case and the severity of the penalty.

School principals must be cognizant of the fact that students, like teachers and principals, are U.S. citizens. As such, young people enjoy the protection of the Constitution. However, school rules, based on evidence that the rules are necessary to the functioning of the school and enforced fairly and consistently, will stand a test in court.

ENFORCING ATTENDANCE

All states have compulsory attendance laws. While such laws often have been challenged in the courts, they just as frequently have been upheld. The interest of the state in general in having an educated citizenry usually has been sufficient for a court to uphold a compulsory attendance statute. More recently, courts have begun to take the position, also, that children have a fundamental right to an education. Thus, compulsory attendance laws, which circumscribe basic parental rights, can be justified on more than one ground.

Principals, through supervisors of attendance, are responsible for enforcing their state's compulsory attendance laws. Principals need to know at what ages children are included in the law and what exceptions there may be to the law. They need to be certain that proper attendance records are maintained and the local procedures that should be followed if a youngster is absent without proper cause.

Every state provides for some exceptions to compulsory attendance.[6] Generally, these exceptions include: (1) mental, emotional, or physical disability (45 states),[7] (2) lack of transportation (16 states), (3) employment required to support dependents (23 states), (4) attendance at a nonpublic school (24 states),[8] (5) private tutor (14 states), (6) completion of a minimal educational program, usually high school (29 states), and "other" reasons, approved by specific officials (20 states).

Student absenteeism appears to be a major problem for school administrators. In a survey conducted in 1979, some 52 percent of administrators reported that more than 5 percent of enrolled students are absent on an "average" day. Of the respondents to the survey 47 percent stated that absentee rates ranged from 6 percent to 10 percent.[9] Urban school districts and states with changing school populations appear to have a growing problem with student absenteeism, and it is expected that the problem will worsen for all school districts.[10] Indeed, the problem may even be worse than reported in that in some urban areas student absenteeism is much more severe.

---

[6] Kern Alexander and K. Forbis Jordan, *Legal Aspects of Educational Choice: Compulsory Attendance and Student Assignment* (Topeka, Kan.: National Organization of Legal Problems of Education, 1973), pp. 66–67.

[7] Such provisions do not negate federal and state laws requiring education of handicapped children.

[8] The right of parents to send their children to private schools was sustained in *Pierce v. Society of Sisters*, 268 U.S. 510 (1925).

[9] *The School Administrator* 36 (8), p. 1.

[10] *Ibid.*, p. 8.

Solutions to the problem of student absenteeism are not easy to find. There are no simple solutions, since there are a variety of sources for the problem. Answers to the problem fall into two categories: long-range and short-range.

Respondents to the survey cited curriculum as a major factor affecting attendance. Therefore, a school with an absentee problem might well look to curriculum improvement as one of the long-range solutions to its problem. Higher attendance rates were reported where teachers provided individualized attention, used open-ended questions, and were responsive to pupils.[11] All of these suggest that instructional methodology may affect to some degree students' attitudes toward school and, thus their attendance patterns. Teacher and staff attitude and teacher quality also were mentioned as factors in school attendance. Instructional methodologies and personnel attitudes cannot be changed overnight. Therefore, where such changes are indicated, time is required.

More immediate steps can be taken to deal with the problem. These include the following:

1. Analyze pupils' attendance records. High absenteeism may occur on certain days, during particular periods of the year, among certain groups of youngsters, and so on. Specific classes or teachers may have higher absentee rates than others. In short, a first step is to attempt to determine the extent of the problem. Accurate analysis of absenteeism data may suggest solutions to the problem.
2. Develop clear, concise policies regarding attendance. Make certain that there is a rationale for policies; that the reasons for policies can be understood by any person who reads them.
3. Clearly communicate such policies to students, to teachers, and, most of all, to parents. It is important that parents, for example, understand the policies and the reasons for them. Parents must believe that attendance policies are for the benefit of their youngsters.
4. Once policies are announced, enforce them. This does not mean blind adherence to rules, but it does mean that policies cannot be effective if the school is not consistent in following them.

In summary, principals are responsible for enforcing state attendance laws. Policies should be developed that clearly communicate attendance regulations. A step in the solution of any attendance problem is to analyze the pattern of absenteeism.

CLARIFYING LIABILITY OF SCHOOL PERSONNEL

Three aspects of liability that are of particular importance to principals and teachers are discussed in this section. The first is a school official's liability for damages under

[11]*Ibid.*, pp. 1, 8.

Section 1983 of the Civil Rights Act of 1871. The second aspect is liability for damages arising from injuries to pupils and lawsuits alleging negligence on the part of a teacher or principal. The third area discussed is liability for defamation of character.

LIABILITY FOR VIOLATION OF CIVIL RIGHTS

Section 1983 of the Civil Rights Act of 1871 was enacted originally by Congress to prevent racial discrimination. Briefly, the act provides that any person acting on behalf of government who deprives a citizen of his civil rights may be liable for damages. School principals serve state agencies. Therefore, they fall within the purview of the act. Section 1983 has been used in a number of school-related court cases, but the most well known case is *Wood v. Strickland*,[12] decided in 1975 by the U.S. Supreme Court.

One of the issues in the *Strickland* case was the procedure used by the board of education in suspending youngsters from school. The Court, in upholding a lower court's decision, ruled that the students' rights to due process of law had been violated. Furthermore, and of critical importance to school principals, the Court held that school officials are not immune from liability for monetary damages if they know or *reasonably should have known* that the action they took would violate a pupil's constitutional rights. The Court stated further that officials could be liable if their action was taken with the malicious intent to deprive a pupil of constitutional rights. The Court went on to point out that monetary damages would be appropriate only if school administrators acted maliciously or with such disregard of a pupil's clearly established constitutional rights that the administrators' behavior could not reasonably be characterized as good faith.

Despite the fears by school people, *Wood v. Strickland* did not result in a flood of lawsuits against schools. Few judgments have been returned against principals. Nevertheless, this case makes it clear that the principal should be aware of rights guaranteed students by the Constitution. To be aware is the first step in guarding against violation of those rights.

LIABILITY FOR PUPIL INJURY

A second area of potential liability is tort liability. A tort is a civil wrong; an act that results in injury to another person. School personnel are legally responsible for their actions that result in injury to students. The injury may be to the pupil's person or to his or her reputation (defamation of character).

A great many legal actions against school personnel are initiated every year. It should be noted, however, that in the large majority of cases, the lawsuits are resolved in favor of the schools. Accidents, pure accidents, do happen, and courts are cognizant of that fact. Principals need not be unduly apprehensive about injuries occurring to pupils. This does not suggest that they, or teachers, should be careless regarding youngsters' safety. It does suggest that if a child is hurt, a school employee will not necessarily be held responsible in a court of law.

---

[12]*Wood v. Strickland*, 420 U.S. 308 (1975).

The legal test of a tortious act is: (1) a legal duty of one person to another, (2) a breach of that duty, and (3) a causal link between the breach and the injury to the person.

Principals should advise their faculty that a teacher owes youngsters in his care protection from injury, either to person or to reputation. The state, through its compulsory attendance laws, requires children to attend school. During the time youngsters are at school, teachers, and principals for that matter, bear a significant responsibility for the children's well-being.

A breach of duty may be an action that leads to an injury or it may be a failure to act. For example, a teacher could be held liable for a student's injury by placing the pupil in a situation that could result in injury or by failing to act when the teacher observed that the youngster was entering into a dangerous situation. It is the principal's responsibility to make certain that teachers are aware of their responsibilities toward children and the potential for being held liable.

In order for a school employee to be held accountable for a pupil injury, it must first be established that an injury has occurred. If a student has a broken leg, it is clear that the child has been hurt. Mental distress, where it is alleged that something a teacher or principal has said or written has injured a student, is significantly more difficult to establish. A few cases have been brought against teachers charging damage to a child's mental health, but it would be rare that a teacher would be held liable.

Finally, in order for a person to be held liable, it must be shown that whatever the person did or did not do was the cause of the injury to the child. Again, accidents do happen and it must be demonstrated to a court's satisfaction that whatever happened to the student was not an accident, but was, indeed, the result of the behavior of the person charged.

There are several points that principals should bear in mind in order to protect themselves, and teachers, from suit.

The degree of supervision to which students are entitled is related to the youngster's age. Obviously, the younger the child, the more a teacher is responsible for protecting the child from harm. A 6-year-old needs more protection and supervision than a 12-year-old.

Supervision is a key point in tort cases. In such cases, the question always asked is: Was the child "properly" supervised? There is no single answer to the question because the degree of supervision required is related to specific situations. A classroom is different than a playground. Principals should be aware of areas and activities that are potentially dangerous and act accordingly. Pupils should be supervised from the time they arrive at school to their departure. This may mean assigning personnel to playground duty before and after school, in addition to times during the regular school day.

Teachers whose responsibilities include the operation of equipment and the use of potentially dangerous chemicals or who supervise pupils engaged in physical activities have special responsibilities. Three key points should be noted: (1) Equipment should be kept in proper repair. Not only may unsafe equipment be dangerous for students, but teachers or principals permitting its use could be held responsible should a youngster be injured. (2) Before using any equipment or engaging in any physical activity that could result in injury, children must be instructed in how to use the equipment or how to participate in the activity or game. (3) Where safety rules are required, all students should be informed of the rules and the rules must be consistently enforced. The principal's responsibilities regarding these points are clear. The principal must inform teachers of their responsibilities. In addition, the principal must make certain that teachers exercise proper supervision and do not utilize equipment that may be faulty.

To illustrate the foregoing, a physical education teacher was held liable for permitting two boys to engage in boxing, where one boy was injured, when the boys had not received instruction in boxing. In another case, a girl was seriously injured when struck by a truck while she was running across a driveway between a gymnasium and an athletic field. The school's defense was that it was the girl's fault because she had violated the school's rule forbidding running across the driveway. The court held the school liable when the court determined that teachers rarely invoked the rule and to ignore it was commonplace.[13] Finally, a case originating in Washington illustrates several of the points mentioned above. In this case children had rigged a teeterboard across a playground swing. A youngster was injured when he fell from the board and his parents sued the teacher, alleging inadequate supervision. The court held for the parents and stated:

> If the teacher knew it [that the pupils used the teeterboard as they did], it was negligence to permit it, and if she did not know it, it was negligence not to have observed it.[14]

The best protection against suits alleging tortious conduct is, of course, anticipating potential problems and taking steps to avoid them. However, as every school administrator soon learns, no one is perfect. Some school employee (perhaps even the principal) will make an error and a child will be injured. Or a parent will sue despite the evidence that the injury resulted from the child's misconduct. School personnel should therefore protect themselves from lawsuits by securing appropriate insurance, especially in those states where the school district cannot be sued or where local policy precludes the board of education from assuming the costs of an adverse judgment.

The attitude of school districts with respect to suits for tort liability varies widely across the United States. In some states, a school district may be sued. In others it may not. In still other states, a school district may, or is required by law to, assume the financial burden if an employee is sued for a tort. It is incumbent upon school principals to know the law in his or her state and advise teachers regarding it. In addition, it is wise for school personnel to have insurance to protect themselves if they are not otherwise covered by their local boards of education. Insurance may be secured individually or, more commonly, through membership in a professional organization. Before securing insurance a person should check the coverage and the cost carefully.

---

[13]For a discussion of this point, see John C. Walden, "Contributory Negligence," *National Elementary Principal* 54 (2), (1974), pp. 86–87.

[14]*Bruenu v. North Yakima School District No. 7,* 172 P. 2d 569 (Washington, 1968).

LIABILITY FOR DEFAMATION OF CHARACTER

In addition to being held accountable for a physical injury to a student, it is possible for a teacher or principal to be held liable for defamation of character (slander or libel) where damage is done to a pupil's reputation as a result of something the teacher or principal said or wrote. Few suits have been brought in this area and fewer still have resulted in a judgment being awarded.

Nevertheless, school personnel should be certain that whatever they say or write about a pupil is factual and is communicated to the proper person, that is, to the student's parents or to teachers who have a legitimate professional interest in the information. It is possible that school personnel can render professional judgments about pupils and not be held liable, even if the judgment is wrong. However, the principal or teacher should be prepared to provide a basis for that judgment if demanded.

Because a person claims that his or her reputation has been damaged does not necessarily mean that a court will award damage. In order to sustain a defamation of character case, the following points must be established: (1) a false statement has been published or communicated, (2) the statement brought hatred, disgrace, ridicule, contempt, or in some way diminished a person, and (3) damage resulted from the statement.[15]

The keys to providing information about youngsters are: (1) information is provided only to those persons who have a legitimate right to it, (2) the information is true or the person releasing it believes it to be factual, (3) the teacher or principal is acting in his or her professional capacity at the time the information is released, and (4) the principal or teacher is attempting, through providing the information, to assist the pupil—in other words, is acting in the best interests of the child.

For example, if a principal should have evidence that a youngster is involved in drugs, it would be quite proper to inform the child's parents. The parents might not wish to hear the news, but the principal would be on solid ground in that he or she would be informing a proper party, acting on the basis of factual data and in the administrator's professional capacity, and is acting in the best interests of the child so that the youngster might be assisted.

Similarly, where parents have provided written permission for the release of certain information about their child, the principal should not be apprehensive about doing so.

PADDLING PUPILS

Since the inception of schools the paddle has been used as one means to discipline pupils. It is used in today's schools, although much less frequently than in previous years. Parents and educators disagree among themselves regarding the merits of corporal punishment, but with the exception of one or two states, it is permissible

---

[15]Kern Alexander, Ray Corns, Walter McConn, *Public School Law* (St. Paul, Minn.: West, 1969), p. 325.

by law. In a 1977 case the U.S. Supreme Court upheld the use of corporal punishment in the schools.[16] It had been alleged that the use of corporal punishment violated the Eighth Amendment to the U.S. Constitution, which prohibits the use of "cruel and unusual punishment." The Court held that the Eighth Amendment applies to criminal cases and not to school discipline cases. The Court also pointed out that if school personnel misuse corporal punishment, they can be sued for tort. Therefore, if one chooses to use physical punishment on a youngster, one should be cautioned that there always is a risk of physical injury to a pupil and the possibility of a resulting lawsuit. Furthermore, such punishment should never be administered in anger, nor in any manner in which malice can be inferred.[17]

The wisdom, morality, or efficacy of paddling a child can be debated. However, if a school determines that paddling is a means of disciplining that should be employed, then the following points should be noted:

1   A policy statement should be developed regarding corporal punishment so that students, teachers, and parents will know that it may be used and under what conditions.
2   Corporal punishment should be used only as a "last resort."
3   Youngsters (and their parents) should know what offenses might result in paddling.
4   It should be clear who may and who may not administer a paddle.
5   No one should paddle a youngster without an adult witness.
6   Corporal punishment should never be administered publicly.
7   Whenever corporal punishment is administered the principal should maintain a private, written record of the event, to include: the name of the child, who administered it, the witness, and for what reason the punishment was undertaken.

Finally, schools may use corporal punishment only in accordance with school district policies and state law. Local school policies must not be in violation of higher authority. Indeed, a few school personnel have lost their jobs because they paddled youngsters in violation of school board regulations.

PROTECTING AIDES AND INTERNS

Many schools assume the responsibility of preparing future teachers by accepting student teachers or interns. In addition, the use of teacher aides and volunteers has become widespread in recent years in elementary schools. Since virtually none of

---

[16]*Ingraham v. Wright*, 430 U.S. 651 (1977).
[17]For further discussion of this issue, see John C. Walden, "On Expulsion and Corporal Punishment," NAESP *Spectator*, (1975 October), 14–15, and "Dismissal and Corporal Punishment," NAESP *Spectator*, (1975 December), 6–7.

these persons possesses a professional certificate, questions have been raised about the school's liability should an intern's or aide's behavior result in injury to a pupil.

There is little law in this area. There are few court cases and even fewer states that have applicable statutes.[18] The principal seeking answers to questions about liability in this area must look to general principles of law, rather than to specific statutes for guidance.

First, anyone, be that a principal, teacher, student teacher, or parent volunteer, can be held liable for his or her negligent acts. Thus, it is possible for a student teacher, for example, to be held accountable for an act of negligence. Second, and very importantly, an aide or student teacher may be left in charge of students provided that: (1) in the professional judgment of the supervising professional the aide or student is capable of assuming that responsibility, (2) the situation is such that the nonprofessional can reasonably be expected to cope with it, and (3) the student or aide has been properly instructed on how to deal with various situations that might occur.

This last point is particularly important for school principals, at whose feet ultimate responsibility may lie. "Instruction" is the key word. There should be no fear on the part of principals in using aides, for example, to supervise pupils provided that those aides have been given proper instruction in their duties and responsibilities. This does not mean that a semester-long course in controlling students is required. It does mean that principals should make certain that noncertificated personnel be given direction in such matters as what to do in certain situations, who to call upon for assistance, how first aid may be obtained, potential danger spots, and so forth. In short, the principal should not permit any person to supervise youngsters who does not have a clear conception of what he or she may or may not do under certain circumstances.

SEARCHING YOUNGSTERS

Occasionally principals are confronted with the question of whether or not to search a student or the pupil's desk or locker. The decision is never an easy one, because educators almost instinctively find searching students to be repugnant. There also is the potential for legal problems when one searches a person. Nevertheless, there always is the possibility that a principal will have to decide whether a search is warranted. More and more principals have faced this problem recently, not only because of thefts in the school, but also because pupils have brought weapons and drugs onto school premises. As pointed out earlier in this chapter, school officials have an obligation to protect children in their care. That obligation includes protecting youngsters from those who bring potentially harmful items to school.

The Fourth Amendment to the Constitution and its applicability to schools has been the issue in a number of search cases. The Fourth Amendment prohibits "unreasonable searches" and provides that searches may be made only "upon probable cause." As interpreted by most courts, the rigid standards required of law

---

[18]See John C. Walden, "Paraprofessional Personnel and the Law," *National Elementary Principal 51* (5), (1972), pp. 100–102.

enforcement officials by the amendment are not required of school officials. For example, the courts require only that school personnel have "reasonable" cause to search, a less strict standard than "probable" cause. It is expected that principals, for example, will exercise judgment in determining if a pupil is harboring unsafe or illegal materials and if it is necessary to conduct a search. The principal must exercise judgment on the reliability of his or her information and the necessity that a search be instituted to obtain the item in question.

It should be emphasized that searches by police require a stricter adherence to Fourth Amendment mandates. If a police officer initiates a search, a warrant is required. If a school officer initiates a search, a warrant is not required. A word of caution is in order on this point. A principal should never permit himself or herself to be placed in the position of acting on behalf of law enforcement officials in searching a youngster. That is, to search a locker, desk, or child at the request of a police officer probably would void the search as being violative of the pupil's constitutional rights.

Assuming that a school official, acting reasonably, conducts a search and finds illegal materials, the majority of courts have held that the materials can be turned over to the authorities. In several such cases, youngsters were successfully prosecuted in court on the basis of evidence found in a school search.

In order to protect themselves from possible litigation over searches, principals would be well advised to follow these guidelines:

1   Make certain that students and parents know the kinds of materials that are prohibited at school.
2   Indicate clearly to students that desks and lockers are subject to search under specified conditions.
3   Conduct a search only if convinced it is necessary and it is on the basis of reliable information.
4   Avoid random searches, so-called fishing expeditions.
5   Searches should be conducted as privately as possible.
6   When searching a student's desk or locker, have the student present, if possible. In addition, have an adult witness.
7   Try to avoid searching the person. If such is necessary, have the pupil empty pockets.

School officials, then, in order to protect youngsters and acting under the doctrine of *in loco parentis,* may conduct searches at schools provided they exercise judgment and have reasonable cause to do so.

SUSPENDING AND EXPELLING

Pupils whose conduct interferes with the operation of the school may legally be suspended or expelled from school. Some people question the utility of exclusion from school as a means of pupil control. Nevertheless, suspension and expulsion are viable in terms of the law.

Suspension is temporary exclusion from school for a short period of time and is normally the prerogative of the principal, acting in accordance with state statutes. Expulsion is a longer period of exclusion, sometimes for a semester or more. Only a board of education may expel a student.

Whenever a student is excluded from school there is always a question regarding the pupil's rights to due process of law. *Goss v. Lopez* is a recent landmark case in this area.[19] In this case the Supreme Court stated that no student may be excluded from school without fundamental due process of law. The Court did not prescribe rigid procedures. The Court did state that the student must be notified of the charges against him or her and be given the opportunity of a hearing. He or she must be given the opportunity to present his or her side of the story.

Earlier in this chapter, due process of law, both substantive and procedural, was discussed. The point was made that procedural due process of law is based on the concept of fairness. This is the point made by the Court in *Goss v. Lopez*. In suspension cases, the principal must make certain that the student knows why he or she is being suspended and be given the opportunity to defend himself or herself against any charges. The "hearing" may be conducted in the principal's office and may be informal in nature. Suspension from school is an administrative decision. It is not a criminal case. All the requirements of such cases, including lawyers, are not necessary. The essential point, again, is that the principal has followed a process that has been evenhanded, fundamentally fair, to the student.

Expulsion from school, which is the prerogative of the board, necessitates a more elaborate procedure than does a suspension for a few days. Again, however, a ". . . court-like atmosphere does not have to govern a disciplinary hearing."[20]

CONTROLLING DEMONSTRATIONS

The number of student demonstrations has declined since the early 1970s, and even then, secondary schools, rather than elementary schools, were the primary targets of disruptive conduct.

Schools are established for the purpose of educating young people. In order to carry out this purpose certain standards of order must be maintained. For example, it is hardly possible to conduct a reading class if outside the classroom persons are conducting a noisy demonstration. No one, pupil or outsider alike, has the constitutional right to organize an assembly anywhere at any time or to disrupt a school in its pursuits of its educational mission. Schools have the right to control student assemblies in order that the school is not disrupted. Therefore, the principal should not be reluctant to develop policy statements concerning demonstrations and nonschool-sponsored assemblies of pupils. The school can insist that:

1   The assembly or demonstration take place at such time and in such a place that it will not disturb the normal operation of the school.

---

[19]*Goss v. Lopez*, 419 U.S. 565 (Ohio, 1975).
[20]H.C. Hudgins, Jr. and Richard S. Vacca, *Law and Education: Contemporary Issues and Court Decisions* (Charlottesville, Va.: Michie, 1979), p. 240.

2 The assembly or demonstration be related to the interests of the pupils.
3 The assembly or demonstration does not cause damage to persons or property.

The First Amendment to the U.S. Constitution guarantees the right of people to *peaceably assemble.* At the same time courts have pointed out that an orderly system of administration of the schools must be maintained.[21] Principals are responsible for so doing.

CENSORING

As with demonstrations, secondary schools, significantly more often than elementary schools, have been the target of student editors. Problems have resulted from both on- and off-campus publications. More than one principal has had his or her gorge rise at something printed in a student-edited newspaper or magazine.

It is clear from a number of court decisions that the student press, both at school and off the campus, enjoys the protection of the First Amendment. A school cannot, without justification, censor a student newspaper. This applies whether or not the publication is school sponsored. It also is clear that the age of students is a criterion courts will use in deciding what may be prohibited from being published. The maturity of the youngster is a key point in such cases. For example, in a case originating in New York, the U.S. Court of Appeals for the Second Circuit held that school officials could deny publication where they reasonably could show that the publication could be emotionally damaging to immature youths.[22] This was a high school case which dealt with a student publication that planned to survey the sexual attitudes of students. The court upheld the school in prohibiting distribution of the questionnaire, at least to ninth- and tenth-grade students. The importance of this case for elementary schools is that such schools can, given a rational argument, prohibit certain forms of publication to elementary-school pupils. A persuasive argument can be made that certain subjects and specific words are not appropriate for children of elementary-school age. In taking such a position the principal is not attempting to impose a set of values or morals upon pupils. The principal is simply recognizing that children are obligated to attend school and that the school has a responsibility to protect youngsters in its charge from materials to which parents might reasonably object and to which children should not be exposed until their judgment has reached a certain level of maturity.

DRESSING APPROPRIATELY

Dress codes for pupils were a source of abundant litigation in the 1960s. A rather large volume could be published on haircut and other types of such cases. No

---

[21] See, for example, *Passel v. Ft. Worth,* 429 S.W. 2d 917 (Texas 1968).
[22] *Trachtman v. Anker,* 426 F. Supp. 198 (S.D. N.Y., 1977), aff'd 563 F. 2d. 512 (2d Cir., 1977). Supreme Court *review denied,* 435 U.S. 925 (1978). See also John C. Walden, "The Student Press," *National Elementary Principal 53* (3), (1974), pp. 69–71.

longer is this the case. One reason is that many schools decided that codes of dress for pupils were not worth the effort and abandoned them. Another reason is that school officials, having read the pertinent court decisions on the issue, took a second—and third—look at their regulations concerning pupil dress and held onto only those rules that clearly were necessary to the effective functioning of the school. Finally, a third reason is that principals and teachers turned to youngsters and parents in developing dress codes.

Courts have not determined that dress codes, per se, are unlawful. Courts have only asked the question: Why? Thus, where school personnel have been able to answer the "Why?" question in terms of the school's functioning, the rule (or rules) regulating pupil dress has been upheld by the court. It is difficult for a principal to explain why a child must wear his or her hair at a certain length or why a girl must wear a dress instead of pants. It is not difficult to provide a reason that pupils should wear shoes or attend school fully clothed.

Principals also have found it helpful to involve teachers, students, and parents in the process of formulating dress codes. What is appropriate for dress in school does vary from locale to locale. Courts so recognize. Therefore, courts, when a dress code has been at issue, have been supportive of codes that have been developed from a broad base. This does not mean that a majority can impose its will on a minority if a constitutional right is involved, but this would be rare, indeed, in the case of a dress code.

Principals, then, where dress regulations are in effect, should be prepared to answer the question of "Why?" if a specific rule is challenged. In addition, the likelihood of a dress code surviving a test in court will be enhanced if the policies are developed by those who will be most affected by them. In a real sense, students will be regulating themselves.

PROVIDING PUPIL ACTIVITIES

Given recent developments in case law and statutes enacted by Congress, it is almost axiomatic to state that all activities sponsored by the school must be open to all students on a nondiscriminatory basis. Simply put, this means that no club, group, affair, class, or any other activity may be denied a pupil on the basis of sex, race, color, religion, or ethnic origin.

This does not mean that standards, which are nondiscriminatory in the sense noted above, cannot be used in permitting students to participate in activities. It makes no sense, for example, to recognize scholarship if grades are not a criterion. One cannot reward good attendance if absenteeism is not noted. Nor can one have a soccer team if there can be no differentiation among those persons who can play and those who cannot. If the basis is such that everyone who is *capable* is able to do so, then a court is not likely to uphold a case against the school.

TAKING FIELD TRIPS

Field trips have been an integral part of the elementary school's curriculum for many years. Children have been taken to zoos, fire departments, museums, dairies, courts, and a variety of other locations too numerous to list. So long as those visits have been a part of the instructional program there has been little or no reason to question them. There is, however, the question of the school's liability if a pupil is injured on a field trip.

Schools frequently use permission slips, liability waivers, or release forms before taking youngsters on a trip. Such forms are useful in informing parents, but they cannot waive the school's responsibility for caring for the children.[23] Because a parent signs such a form, he or she may be more reluctant to file suit if his child is injured, but a release form cannot in itself preclude a lawsuit. Hudgins and Vacca report only one known instance in which a court disallowed a claim because a person signed a liability waiver.[24]

Principals, then, should make certain that pupils are well supervised on field trips. Parent volunteers may be used in such a capacity, but they should be under the direction of a certified employee and be given instruction on what children may and may not do on the trip. The host for the students (museum, zoo, and so on) has some responsibilities for the protection of its guests, also, but the school ought not to depend upon the host to absolve the school of its responsibilities.

STOPPING DRUG ABUSE

Once largely confined to high-school-age students, the use of a variety of forms of drugs has spread into elementary schools as well. More and more children of elementary school age have become exposed to alcohol, tobacco, marijuana, and other controlled substances.

Schools have a responsibility to recognize when a problem exists and to initiate such steps as may be practicable to cope with it. A first step is for the principal to understand appropriate state laws that deal with drugs. Every state has statutes in this area and the principal should be cognizant of the law and how it may be applied to schools and to school-aged youth.

A second step is to develop, preferably at the school district level, policies regarding drugs in the schools. Such policies should be clear on such points as: (1) what substances are prohibited at school and at school-sponsored events, (2) what disciplinary measures will be taken against pupils who violate the policies, and (3) under what conditions information will be relayed to law enforcement officials.

Policies should be distributed to students, parents, and teachers and they should be specific. References to state law should be made where appropriate. It is suggested that policies state:

1   A definition of "drugs";
2   That drugs are prohibited at school or at any school-sponsored activity;
3   That parents will be notified of their child's violation of the policy;

---

[23]Hudgins and Vacca, *op. cit.*, p. 87.
[24]*Ibid.*, p. 88.

4   That law enforcement officials will be notified of violations of state and federal laws;
5   The specific penalties the school will impose for various violations of the policy.

Schools have a legal responsibility, beyond the task of educating children about the dangers of drugs, to protect children from drugs. Schools cannot do the job alone, of course. Drugs are available to children from a variety of sources. Nevertheless, schools must make an effort to control the problem insofar as they are able within the confines of the school. Therefore, clear policies must be developed and enforced. To do less is to invite criticism and possible legal action for failure to do so.

A final word of warning for the principal is in order. The principal would be well advised to not make judgments that other authorities should make. Law enforcement officials and juvenile officers are in a much better position to determine what should be done when a youngster is discovered possessing, using, or distributing a controlled substance. The principal who attempts to make such judgments, deciding whether to report to authorities or not, is opening himself or herself not only to criticism but also to potential legal problems. It is far better to determine in advance under what conditions reports will be made to police, adopt such a policy, and then follow it. Certainly a number of people can assist in developing a policy on reporting to authorities. Once a policy is adopted, however, the principal should follow it and not attempt to play the role of judge.

ADMINISTERING FIRST AID

Since educators stand in loco parentis to pupils, they are obligated to administer first aid when necessary. Teachers and principals should not go beyond emergency care, however. Educators are not physicians and should not attempt medical treatment. To do so is to invite adverse legal action.

It would be well if every educator were trained in at least the basics of first aid. Few teachers and principals have been trained or certified, however. In view of this, principals might be well advised to secure such training for themselves and encourage their faculties to do so. No one can anticipate when an emergency will occur, and then it is too late to secure preparation in advance.

In anticipation of possible emergencies, principals should formulate procedures to deal with them. The procedures should be in written form and widely distributed. It is too late to develop a plan when a serious accident occurs. A plan to deal with serious accidents would include:

1   A form signed by the parent stating who should be contacted in the event the youngster is involved in an accident (this form should be in the school's office and every effort should be made to secure one for each pupil);
2   A list of school personnel who are qualified to offer emergency first aid measures;

3 The agencies, such as ambulance, fire department, and police, who should be called in the event a parent cannot respond to the emergency or if the situation is so serious that authorities should be called at once. (This list should be in priority order and include telephone numbers, what to say, and so on);

4 The procedure for notifying parents if an ambulance, police, or other agency is called;

5 The procedure for preparing a written record of the incident.

The school's first responsibility is to the child. It is incumbent upon school personnel to respond to any emergency involving a pupil. School personnel may not act as doctors, but they are required to behave responsibly and to administer such first aid treatment as may be necessary before competent medical assistance can be secured. Procedures for dealing with emergencies must be established in advance. A school without such procedures is inviting disaster to a child, and a lawsuit.

REPORTING CHILD ABUSE

In recent years child abuse has grown into one of America's largest social problems. No one is certain how many children are physically assaulted by their parents each year. In response to this problem, all 50 states and the District of Columbia have enacted legislation. There has been a steady trend in legislation broadening the class of conditions that are reportable.[25] Four principal classes of reportable conditions now appear in state statutes. They are:

1 *Nonaccidental physical injury.* This is currently reportable in all 50 states and the District of Columbia. Most laws include bruises, burns, and broken bones in this category.

2 *Neglect.* Most generally defined as failure to provide the necessities of life—food, clothing, shelter, and medical treatment. It is reportable in all states but Indiana, Maryland, and Wisconsin.

3 *Sexual molestation.* This is rarely defined, but is reportable in 40 states and the District of Columbia.

4 *Emotional or mental injury.* This element is often described as a secondary effect. A report must be made if it is believed the child has suffered emotional distress or mental injury as a result of abuse or neglect. Some 37 states and the District of Columbia require reporting in this area.[26]

In addition to the trend noted above, another trend has been to enlarge the group of persons *required* to make child abuse reports. By 1977, 42 states required

---

[25]*Trends in Child Protection Laws—1977.* Educational Commission of the States (Denver, Colorado: The Commission, 1978), p. 3.
[26]*Ibid.*

teachers or other school personnel to make such reports (all states except New Jersey, Oklahoma, Rhode Island, Tennessee, Texas, Utah, Vermont, and Wyoming).[27] And in a number of states penalties can be imposed on persons who have a duty to report suspected cases of child abuse but who fail to do so. Persons who do report cases of child abuse in good faith are protected from civil and criminal actions based on those reports.[28]

Clearly school personnel have both moral and legal obligations to report suspected cases of child abuse. Principals should inform teachers of their obligations under the law of their state and establish, through working with local authorities, a reporting procedure. Principals also could consider inviting authorities to provide a program for teachers in which information could be provided on how to recognize when a child may be suffering from maltreatment.

DEALING WITH BOMB THREATS

While most bomb threats are without foundation, none can be ignored, and the principal must act to protect the safety of students and faculty. Each school district should have a uniform procedure for dealing with such cases. The procedures should be formulated with the advice of local police and fire departments and with the telephone company.

When a telephone threat is received the person receiving the call should obtain as much information as possible from the caller regarding the bomb and its location. The individual receiving the call also should be alert to obtaining information about the caller. A checklist for a person receiving such a call might include the following:

1. Location of bomb;
2. Type of explosive;
3. Appearance of bomb;
4. Time it will explode;
5. Whether caller is adolescent or adult;
6. Approximate age of caller;
7. Exact words used by caller;
8. Date and time of call;
9. Sex of caller;
10. Any background noises on caller's end of the line;
11. Type of speech used by caller, for example, slow, rapid, accented, excited, soft, loud, and so on.

[27]*Ibid.*, p. 6, 18–19.
[28]*Ibid.*, p. 9.

Any information obtained should be retained for making a written report for authorities.

Procedures should be established for the following:

1   Notifying authorities;
2   Notifying faculty and staff without alarming pupils;
3   Making the decision to evacuate the school;
4   Evacuation of the school.

SUPPORTING YOUR LOCAL POLICE

More and more often, it appears, educators and law enforcement agencies are in contact. It is therefore important that schools and juvenile authorities plan together so that each understands the other's responsibilities and authority.

In order for schools to have more effective communication with the local police department and juvenile courts, it would be well if a district-level administrator, or a principal, had the responsibility of serving as a liaison with the police. The person so designated would be better able to deal with the police and the courts on school matters after he or she understands the systems and knows the proper personnel to contact.

It is also suggested that the schools take the initiative and request the appointment of a liaison person from the police department for the schools. This person can work with each school to develop procedures for dealing with law enforcement problems within the schools.

Police in the schools are not necessarily an indication of trouble or disruption. Police can enter the school upon invitation of school authorities for a variety of reasons. Police also may enter a school if they possess evidence of a crime having been committed or if they have a warrant for arrest or search. Interrogation of pupils by police should take place privately within the school and in the presence of the principal or his or her representative. Parents or guardians should be informed and should be present. Law enforcement officials will know the proper procedures to be followed when interrogating juveniles and the legal rights to which youngsters are entitled.

Should a principal come into possession of an item that might later be used in a criminal proceeding, the principal should be careful that his or her actions will not interfere with a later attempt to introduce the evidence into trial. The item should be kept in the custody and under the sole control, if possible, of the person who discovered it. All items should be marked with the initials of the person who obtained them as well as the date on which possession was taken. Suspected narcotics, for example, could be placed in an envelope, sealed, and then the envelope marked as noted. A property tag could be placed on other, bulkier items and marked accordingly. Items should be kept in a locked desk or closet until turned over to police.

It is important that sound school–police–court relationships be maintained and it is critical that each understands the role and responsibilities of each other. Principals should not attempt to act as police officers; neither should law enforcement officials attempt to make educational decisions.

DEALING WITH UNWANTED VISITORS

Sometimes schools have problems with unauthorized persons on school premises. Schools have a duty to protect students and staff from any danger that might result from trespassers.

In recent years state laws and local ordinances have been enacted to deal with this problem. Such laws, carefully written, have been upheld by the courts. A principal having a trespasser problem might seek to have a local ordinance enacted to provide support for action he or she might be required to take.

Notices also might be posted about the school directing visitors to the school office before attempting to visit classrooms, staff, or students. If a person refuses to leave the school after being asked, or is loitering about the school, then the principal should not hesitate to call police.

LOOKING TO THE FUTURE

In the areas discussed in this chapter the law is relatively clear. In the 1980s there might be some adjustments on some fine points of law, but the basic principles are not likely to change. That young people of all ages enjoy the protection of the U.S. Constitution is well settled in law. That children's rights differ from those of adults is also clear. There are some gray areas between youth and adult, but that will always be so.

It also is clear from the court decisions of the last two decades that school authorities have not lost their basic authority to administer the schools. They have been required to provide justification for rules and regulations, but where they have been able to do so the courts have not disturbed their judgment.

CASE STUDY—THE ABSENT ASSISTANT PRINCIPAL

The majority of pupils at Third Street Elementary School are transported by bus, and each afternoon at the close of school Principal Marian Hockman stations herself at the bus loading area. (See Figure 9-1.) On a rotating basis a teacher is stationed near an exit on Elm Street where a number of children generally leave the school to begin their walk home. The Assistant Principal, Peter Rossi, is assigned to the playground where a small number of children use a rear exit from the building, cross the playground, and leave the school through a gate on Fourth Street. Since a relatively few children exit the school across the playground and Rossi often has business at the close of the school day, he often is late to his duty.

On the day in question, however, Rossi is on time and is on the playground watching

FIGURE 9-1

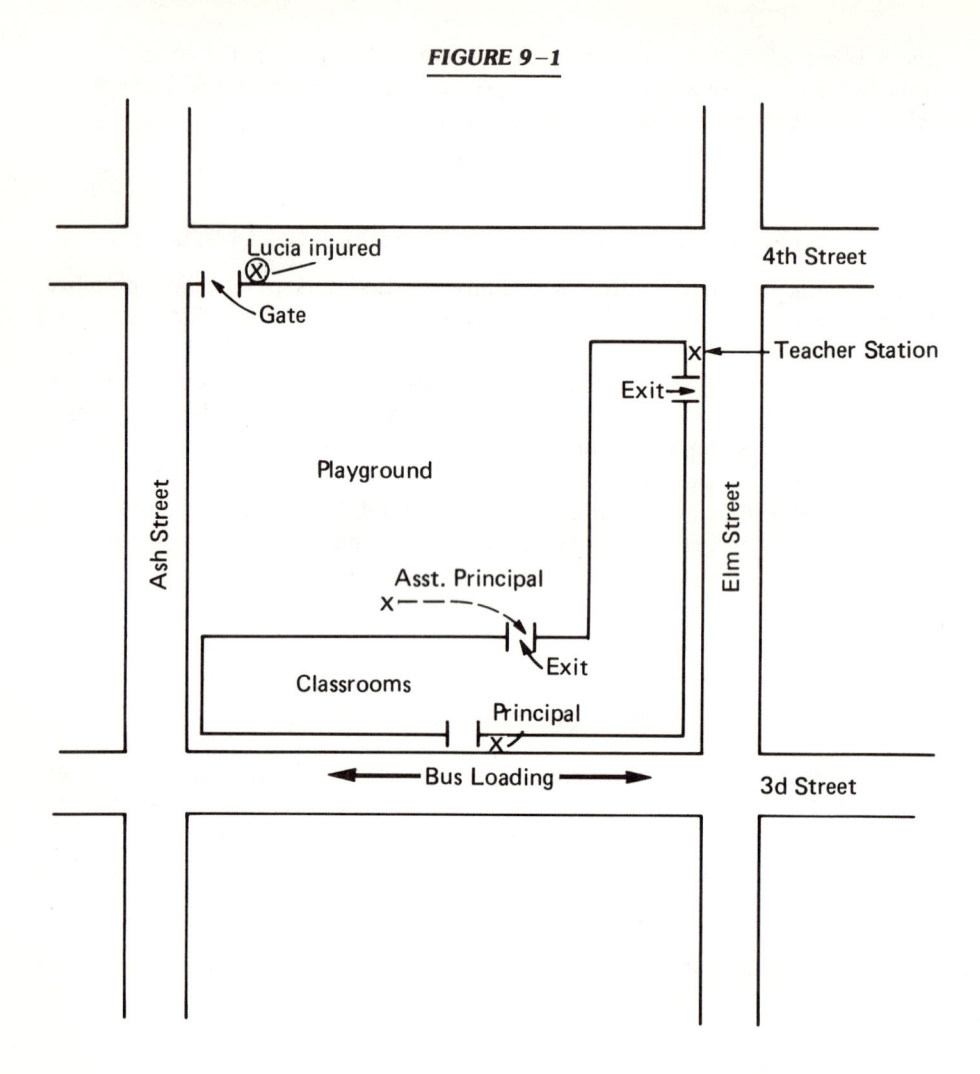

[Diagram showing a school playground bounded by Ash Street (west), 4th Street (north), Elm Street (east), and 3d Street (south). Features labeled: "Lucia injured" (marked X near gate on 4th Street), Gate, Teacher Station (marked X on Elm Street side), Exit (east side), Playground, Asst. Principal (marked X with dashed line to Exit), Classrooms, Exit, Principal (marked X), Bus Loading (along 3d Street).]

children crossing the playground when a teacher calls to him from the classroom exit to the playground. The teacher calls, "Mr. Rossi! I need to see you right away!"

Immediately Rossi leaves the playground and enters the building. At about the same time Lucia Wilcox and some other fourth-grade youngsters are approaching the gate to Fourth Street. They are tossing a ball back and forth to each other. Someone throws the ball to Lucia who fumbles it through the gate and into Fourth Street. She turns and runs after it, directly into the path of a car. She is struck by the automobile and suffers a broken leg and arm.

Peter Rossi, finding that the "emergency" was not an emergency, returns to the playground just in time to see a crowd gathering around the injured Lucia.

Subsequently, Lucia's parents sue Peter Rossi, alleging negligence on his part for leaving the children unsupervised.

1   What do you believe will be the outcome of the case? Why?

2   What conditions dictate which areas should be supervised?
3   Should children have been permitted to leave the school on Fourth Street?

CASE STUDY—SURPRISE PACKAGE

Kirk Allen, a sixth-grade student at Henry Elementary School, has enjoyed some notoriety among his fellow pupils since his older brother was arrested at high school on a charge of selling marijuana. Some teachers at Henry had wondered earlier if Kirk had been involved in drug distribution among the "more mature" students at Henry. Nothing concrete had ever developed from those suspicions, however.

A few days after the arrest, Kirk and two other boys were observed placing a package in a locker of one of the boys. The teacher who witnessed the incident reported that "The boys acted guilty about something. They kept looking around to see if anyone saw them. They didn't see me."

The principal, Jay Means, sent for the student whose locker was in question and asked what was placed in his locker. The boy refused to say. Then the principal asked the boy to open his locker for inspection. Again the boy refused. Mr. Means then ordered the boy to remain in his office while he (Mr. Means) went to the locker. The principal opened the locker, took out the package, and examined the contents. The package contained magazines and photographs of women and men in sexual poses. Mr. Means took the materials to his office and confronted the student, reminding the boy that school rules prohibited such material from being brought to school.

The boy argued that the principal had no right either to open his locker or to punish him for the magazines and pictures. "You were looking for something else anyway," the boy charged. "You have no right to do anything about the pictures. Besides, there's nothing wrong with them."

1   What, if any, of the student's legal rights were violated?
2   Can the pupil be punished?
3   How would you have dealt with the situation?

SUGGESTED READINGS

Hudgins, H.C., Jr., and Vacca, Richard S. *Law and Education.* Charlottesville, Va.: Michie, 1979.
Peterson, Leroy J., Rossmiller, Richard A., and Volz, Marlin. *The Law and Public School Operation,* 2d ed. New York: Harper & Row, 1978.
The Yearbook of School Law Published annually by the National Organization of Legal Problems of Education, Topeka, Kansas.
Zirkel, Perry A., Ed. *A Digest of Supreme Court Decisions Affecting Education.* Bloomington, Ind.: Phi Delta Kappa, 1978.

The National Organization of Legal Problems of Education (5401 South West 7th Avenue, Topeka, Kansas 66606) is an excellent resource in law for school administrators. The organization publishes numerous monographs on specific legal problems and issues, a bimonthly review of state and federal court decisions, a monthly newsletter, and the *NOLPE School Law Journal.*

CHAPTER

10

GOVERNING STUDENTS

Introduction
Understanding the child
Redefining the family
Involving parents
Developing discipline
Pursuing self-governance
Future directions
Case study—late again

INTRODUCTION

Governing students, pupil control, or school discipline—call it what you will—is a topic that has drawn considerable attention in the literature. Teachers worry about it, especially first-year teachers; and parents, according to the polls, constantly express concern about the state of discipline in the public schools. It is a subject, then, that elementary-school principals may not ignore. Principals have the responsibility of establishing a climate in which a student-governance system can be developed that will facilitate the achievement of the school's educational mission.

The courts (see Chapter 9) have provided a framework for developing a student-governance system. The framework is based solidly on the U.S. Constitution and requires that any system of governance be compatible with democratic principles; that is, recognize that all citizens, regardless of their ages or stations in life, have certain guaranteed rights.

The school's task is to provide a setting in which young people can learn. Since learning rarely occurs amidst chaos, this implies some sort of order. Order can be accomplished through various means, including methods that are absolutely autocratic. However, in a democratic society autocratic means of control not only are incompatible with the basic tenets of society, they are also unlikely to succeed.

Persons accustomed to an open society are not likely to respond favorably to dictatorial methods. The school, therefore, while seeking to establish an orderly society within its confines, must do so by democratic means. Only through such methods can the next generation begin to understand democracy.

The school's problem is compounded by the fact that it does not deal with adults who have years and years of experience and understanding. The school's clients are young and their experiences are limited—often very limited. In dealing with children in developing a student-governance system, one of the first requirements for the elementary-school principal is to understand the world in which students live.

UNDERSTANDING THE CHILD

"Children come to the elementary school from various backgrounds and experiences. They will have a variety of needs and desires; some common, many different. They will exhibit a potpourri of sizes, shapes, and hues. They are, in a sense, the givens in the elementary school."[1] The school's task is to understand these "givens"; to shape the school's programs, including the governance program, in terms of children's needs (not necessarily their preferences) in order that the students can emerge from the school better equipped to meet future challenges.

Schools must deal with students both collectively and individually. As females and males, blacks and whites, 6-year olds and 11-year olds, students come to the school as members of groups, thus sharing some common characteristics. It is fundamental that teachers and principals know what natural groupings of students exist in their schools. Various groups—religious, ethnic, racial, age—have certain common characteristics and value systems. Much is known about the commonalities that exist within various groups. Principals and teachers need to understand them in order to deal effectively with different groups of children. In no sense does this mean that students are not individuals. One must guard against falling into the trap of making judgments about persons primarily on the basis of their group membership. To do so is both unwise and immoral. Nevertheless, educators should be aware of the variety of student groupings within their schools because such can make a difference in understanding children's needs. A first step, then, is to identify the student population.

As emphasized above, students are, above all, individuals. They come from rich and poor families, from loving families and from no families at all. They have their own secret hopes, ambitions, and fears; they have strengths and, because they are human, they have weaknesses as well. Principals must insist that teachers know their students. One cannot deal effectively with students in developing a system of governance if one does not understand his or her clients. To know students as individuals is to guard against stereotyping. All too often educators fall victim to

---

[1] Edward T. Ladd (with John C. Walden), *Students' Rights and Discipline* (Arlington, Va.: National Association of Elementary School Principals, 1975), p. 69.

developing mind sets about youngsters. As one writer put it, "Stereotypes are not challenged in our educational system; they are nourished."[2] Every effort must be made to know and understand students as individual human beings.

To know children as individuals provides a shield against misuse of information and research regarding children as members of groups. While it may be true that inner-city black youngsters *generally* may feel this way or that way about certain aspects of life, the same may not be true of 9-year-old Yvonne. It is imperative that teachers and principals understand this point and be guided accordingly. To know children as individuals also provides a basis for understanding and evaluating research into the life of the child. For example, most people assume that children from "broken homes" will have problems with learning and social adjustment. Such may or may not be the case. A report of research conducted among lower-middle and middle-class elementary-school children in Michigan stated that there were "no significant differences in self-concept, mathematics and reading achievement, immaturity, withdrawal, or peer relations of children from divorced and intact families."[3] In another study, it was reported that children viewed their parents' separation and divorce as extraordinarily stressful. There also was evidence that some children's behavior in school was noticeably affected by the dissolution of their parents' marriage.[4] Although these are only two studies, their results point up the fact that educators constantly need to examine and reexamine the assumptions they make about children. They also emphasize the point that not every child reacts the same way to every situation. Finally, these studies of the impact of the family on the child raise one of the most critical issues of all when one is attempting to understand the world of the child. It is the family itself.

REDEFINING THE FAMILY

There have been profound changes in American family life in the past several decades. These changes are important to an understanding of the elementary-school student's world.

That the American family has grown smaller over time is well known to everyone. The decline in the birthrate, 50 percent between 1800 and 1970, certainly is a major factor in families becoming smaller. However, this is only part of the story. In the past, and into the early portion of the twentieth century, many American households contained relatives and nonrelatives.[5] Studies show that in Rhode Island in 1875 almost a quarter of all families contained nonrelatives. These

---

[2]William W. Wayson and Gay Sue Pinnell, "Educating the Inner-City Child," *National Elementary Principal* 56 (5), 1977, p. 21.

[3]Janice M. Hammond, "A Comparison of Elementary Children from Divorced and Intact Families," *Phi Delta Kappan* 61 (3), 1979, p. 219.

[4]Joan B. Kelly and Judith S. Wallerstein, "Children of Divorce," *National Elementary Principal* 59 (1), 1979, pp. 51–58.

[5]Much of the following analysis of the American family is drawn from an excellent article by Maureen A. Mahoney, "The American Family: Centuries and Decades of Change," *National Elementary Principal* 55 (5), 1976, pp. 6–10.

were servants, boarders, and lodgers. Even as late as 1920 it is estimated that as high as 20 percent of U.S. families had boarders.[6] Two phenomena have occurred that have had a powerful effect on the child's world. One has been the decline in size of the nuclear family and the other has been the virtual disappearance of adults, other than the mother and father, from the household. In pointing out that nonrelatives in the household probably were role models, friends, and confidants to children, Mahoney suggests that the critical transition in American family life has been the elimination of nonrelatives from American households.[7]

There is a tendency, then, for American families to be small, with perhaps two children, born close together. Because families have fewer children, it is more likely that a "generation gap" between parents and children will develop. In the past older brothers and sisters bridged that gap. In connection with this point, it might be noted that the concept of adolescence as a time of crisis did not exist until the last two decades of the nineteenth century. Fewer children in the family means that "transition through the various stages of the life cycle becomes more difficult when there are no siblings to serve as role models. . . ."[8] Thus, the American child has begun to grow up in a world where there are fewer role models and in which it appears that a generation gap must inevitably develop between the child and parent.

At the same time that structural changes in the family have been occurring, the child's role in the family has undergone significant change as well. In earlier times children were productive members of the family and of society. No one wants to return to the days when children were mercilessly exploited by parents and industrialists, but it is a fact that over time children have become separated from the workaday life of the larger society.[9] They may no longer have meaningful household chores or be responsible for the care of younger siblings. They no longer spend significant portions of their time working outside their home. In turn, their parents' jobs are often remote from the child's world, and the child grows up with little understanding of the everyday life of society.

Three additional developments in American family life that impact on youngsters should be mentioned. First, the majority of mothers of school-age children now work. Second, the trend toward one-parent families continues. One-parent families, of course, may result from one of several causes: divorce, death of one parent, the decision to rear a child where there has been no marriage, and so forth. By the end of the 1970s, almost 20 percent of school-age children came from one-parent families.[10] (It might be added that the illegitimate birth rate has increased steadily in recent years. In 1960 the rate was 45 per 1000 births. By the late 1970s it was 130 per 1000.[11]) Third, parents are no longer playing the significant roles they once had in the education of their children.

[6]*Ibid.*, p. 8.
[7]*Ibid.*, p. 7.
[8]*Ibid.*, pp. 8–9.
[9]Sarane Spence Boocock, "Today's Childhood—A Unique Condition," *Today's Education* 68 (1), 1979, p. 51.
[10]Mahoney, *op. cit.*, p. 9.
[11]*Ibid.*

The combination of working mothers and one-parent families simply means that adults are in the home fewer and fewer hours. When adults are present, they are tired from a long day of commuting and work. They are not able to assume the educational responsibilities parents once assumed for their children. This does not mean that parents are more irresponsible than in previous years. It does mean that today's parents have less time to devote to their children than did previous generations of parents.

Schools cannot be expected to bear the full responsibility for educating the young. However, apparently that is precisely what is being expected today. The changing nature of American family life has gone unnoticed in many quarters. Some parents' apparent distress with the job schools are doing may be the result of their not understanding the role parents previously played in educating their children. In the past parents found the time to reinforce what their youngsters were learning in school. Today parents rarely can find the time to work with their children. Cultural values, Mahoney points out, cannot be transmitted en masse to a classroom of 30 students.[12] Parents, single or otherwise, have a responsibility in this area. That responsibility, from all indications, is not being fulfilled as it once was.

Children no longer have an opportunity to discover what will be expected of them as working adults or as parents.[13] In some other nations, Sweden, for example, girls and boys "from the elementary school years on have classes in sex education, home maintenance, child care, and the dynamics of family life. By contrast, U.S. elementary schools offer little practical education in subjects relevant to family life."[14]

Children, then, come to the elementary school somewhat as sailors adrift on the sea, without anchors and without clear direction. In a true sense they are isolated from the real world. Without role models, without parents who can provide them with precious time, their cultural void is filled with television and their peers. Elementary-school principals and teachers must understand the increasing importance of peer influence and the medium of television in the development of students.

INVOLVING PARENTS

With the foregoing in mind, what can schools do to involve parents in their children's learning and to bring the school closer to the home? Although the family has undergone significant, even radical, changes in the past several decades, there are few people who are willing to predict its demise. The family will endure in some form. It remains for the school to take the initiative in reaching out to the family. If the school waits for the initiative to come from the other direction, it may be waiting until it is too late.

Dorothy Rich, director of the Home and School Institute, has a number of

---

[12]*Ibid.*, p. 10.
[13]Boocock, *op. cit.*, p. 52.
[14]*Ibid.*

suggestions for principals who wish to develop better linkages between the school and the family. Among her suggestions are the following:

1. Designate an underused or unused classroom as a family room in the school. Invite parents to use the room while visiting the school. Employ older children as babysitters so mothers can leave small children while they are observing classrooms.
2. Establish a toy and book lending library. Make certain the library is open at some time when working mothers can visit it.
3. Organize make-it-and-take-it workshops, designed to help parents make inexpensive learning materials for use at home with their children.
4. Have neighborhood meetings in homes of students, with the principal attending, to discuss school programs, provide advice to parents, and answer questions.
5. Ask parents to construct learning centers for classrooms.
6. Encourage parents to "have coffee with the principal" at school on a periodic basis.[15]

The suggestions given above are only for illustrative purposes. Principals interested in these types of activities can develop additional activities of a similar nature. The basic idea is to bring the school closer to the home and to involve parents more in the learning process.

Extending the concept of school–home involvement further, Zakariya has described a number of programs in which schools are providing services to families in their areas.[16] Whereas Rich's suggestions dealt principally with involving parents in school-related programs, Zakariya has focused on outreach activities of schools. Such programs obviously must be tailored to the needs of the community, and each involves not only a great deal of time and effort but also the involvement of agencies other than the school. Some schools provide parents with referral services, assisting parents to locate the proper agencies for help, whether it be health care, welfare, legal aid, or similar services. Other schools have developed health centers, first aid classes for parents, day-care centers, workshops on child development, and so on. The development of such programs would depend upon the willingness and ability of the school to reach out into the community it serves.

Finally, in accommodating the growing number of one-parent families, Parker Damon makes these suggestions for principals:

1. Set up one inservice workshop each year to discuss problems of separation and loss in families.

[15] Dorothy Rich, "A Letter to Principals," *National Elementary Principal* 55 (5), 1976, pp. 71–77. The Home and School Institute is located at Trinity College, Washington, D.C. 20017. One of the Institute's publications is *101 Activities for Building More Effective School–Community Involvement*.

[16] Sally Banks Zakariya, "What Schools Are Doing for Families," *National Elementary Principal* 55 (6), 1976, pp. 59–61.

2. Make professional help available to families and teachers by redirecting or expanding existing services.
3. Try to keep track of the children involved in separation, divorce, and remarriage. Assign a mentor to those children.
4. Be careful about both direct and indirect discrimination against children in these situations.
5. Hold "parent activities," not "father and mother activities."
6. Schedule conferences and meetings at times that are convenient to these parents.
7. Provide teachers with opportunities to share information from one year to the next.[17]

DEVELOPING DISCIPLINE

The principal, more than any other single person, has the responsibility for the development and implementation of the student-governance program in the school. This does not mean that the principal has the sole responsibility, but it does mean that the principal must exercise the initiative. The principal must be certain that all personnel understand their responsibilities in the total program. The principal must see to it that norms for behavior are defined in such a manner that they are clear to everyone. It is the principal's responsibility to work with the faculty and students in order to assure that appropriate disciplinary or governance policies and procedures are developed and implemented. Finally, it falls to the principal more than anyone else to interpret governance practices to the community.[18]

Fundamental to developing a sound program of student governance are the following: (1) deciding what behavior may and may not be permitted in school; (2) deciding the roles various persons are to play in the governance process; and (3) assisting teachers to develop effective classroom control measures.

A student-governance program cannot be successful if there is constant uncertainty regarding rules of behavior. It is basic, then, that attention be given to defining the kinds of behavior that will be permitted.[19] This applies to student behavior, but not exclusively. School personnel need to consider their relationships with and behavior toward students, also. It is important to reach agreement on the kinds of behavior expected of students. It is equally important for teachers and principals to determine what to expect of themselves as professionals.

The principal must take the leadership in working with teachers, students, and even parents in establishing the framework for the governance program. Long hours of work may be expected, and the outcomes will vary fom setting to setting

---

[17]Adapted from "Ten Tips for Principals," in Parker Damon, "When the Family Comes Apart: What Schools Can Do," *National Elementary Principal 59* (1), 1980, p. 71.

[18]For additional discussion of the principal's responsibility in this area, see Ladd, *op. cit.*, pp. 39–43.

[19]*Ibid.*, pp. 21–22.

because expectations regarding student behavior obviously will vary somewhat among communities. Fundamental legal requirements and constitutional rights will not be different, but there will be specific differences in community expectations of children. The point is that principals have the obligation of sitting down with the aforementioned groups for the purpose of establishing fundamental principles of behavior expected of all students and of all professional personnel. This will require meetings with various groups of people, but it is the critical first step in developing a sound governance program. Without agreement on expectations of behavior, there will be uncertainty and misunderstanding.

Principals also must take the initiative with teachers in determining for what aspects of discipline each should bear responsibility. In a school the principal generally is the "court of last resort." If teachers send every problem to the principal, then the principal's ability to solve discipline problems is inevitably diluted. Moreover, a successful student-governance program cannot be administered in the principal's office. Everyone, including teachers and students, has a role to play in the governance program. The principal has the responsibility of working with the faculty in deciding what problems should be handled in the classroom and what problems should be dealt with in the principal's office. There always will be unusual circumstances and exceptions to basic policies, and principals ought not to be rigid in this regard. However, there should be a clear understanding among all teachers regarding their responsibilities with respect to student discipline. If teachers or principals abrogate their responsibilities, then problems will result.

It is critical, therefore, that upon establishing basic rules of behavior, a second step be taken, that of determining who is to do what under what circumstances. Without building the framework for discipline in terms of fundamentals, inevitably there will be ambiguities and misunderstandings, translated into headaches for the principal.

In developing a sound program of student discipline, one of the principal's major tasks is to assist classroom teachers, particularly the inexperienced, with their problems in the classroom. If classroom problems can be resolved, then it is much more likely that the school's problems can be resolved as well.

Perhaps the first thing teachers need to understand is "that there is no single 'best' method of dealing with discipline in the classroom."[20] Children come from different backgrounds and experiences, and discipline methods must be tailored somewhat to the uniqueness of students. In addition, in order for teachers to make good techniques of discipline work, they must practice them. There are no instant cures or panaceas that will solve all classroom discipline problems.

Library bookshelves are filled with volumes on student discipline, testifying to interest in the subject over time. For beginning teachers, one suggestion a principal can make is for the new teacher to do some reading on the subject in order to gather a perspective as well as to obtain some practical ideas. Other suggestions for principals to use in assisting new teachers might include the following:

---

[20]Frederic H. Jones, "The Gentle Art of Classroom Discipline," *National Elementary Principal* 58 (4), 1979, p. 28.

1. Be patient. Resist the temptation to change new teachers' practices immediately.
2. If a teacher is having a problem with discipline, let her or him know—gently—that there is a problem and you know it.
3. Open up frequent opportunities for informal talks about their problems—perhaps over coffee.
4. Be supportive and sympathetic, not reproachful. Let them know everyone can have a failure.
5. Invite beginning teachers to use you as a resource, to call you in, or to send children to you.
6. Try to avoid telling the new teacher what to do. Instead, suggest several alternatives.
7. Do what you can to keep experienced teachers from putting pressure on the beginner.
8. Arrange for the new teacher to visit the classes of, or to team teach with, other teachers who might help.
9. Provide specific suggestions whenever possible.[21]

While new teachers may have some unique problems regarding classroom behavior, all teachers (and principals) probably need to be reminded of some basic principles of good classroom discipline. Some of these are:[22]

1. Have a few rational rules. Be certain they are clear to students.
2. Be consistent in enforcing rules.
3. Do not punish a group for the actions of one student, or of a few students.
4. Be alert to the possibilities for disruptive conduct. If a youngster seems to be behaving differently from normal, try to act before a real problem develops.
5. Make certain that directions are clear to students. Often discipline problems arise when instructions regarding classroom routine are unclear.
6. If a disruption begins, move to stop it at once. By failing to respond, or by responding slowly, the teacher modifies the rules.
7. Reward positive behavior.
8. Never issue an ultimatum unless you are prepared to carry it out.
9. Remain calm. Losing one's temper can only exacerbate a situation.
10. Never be afraid to apologize to a student if you punish him or her unjustly. Apologizing for an error is a sign of strength, not of weakness.

[21] Adapted from Ladd, *op. cit.*, pp. 51–52.
[22] Adapted from Ladd, *op. cit.*, pp. 46–54; Jones, *op. cit.*, pp. 28–29; and Richard M. Mallory, "The Teacher Who Disciplines Least," *Today's Education* 68 (2), 1979, pp. 23–26.

Finally, keep records on students who are behavior problems. The records should reflect what happened, when it happened, who was involved, and what was done about it.[23] Such records can reveal patterns of behavior that can be helpful in attempting to assist a particular student who is having problems. In addition, if it is necessary to impose a severe penalty on a youngster, records maintained by the teacher and principal can support the action.

PURSUING SELF-GOVERNANCE

In many, if not most, books and articles on school discipline, teachers and principals are urged to involve students in the governance process. As Ladd has suggested, the prerequisites of education for citizenship include giving the growing student increasing freedom and an increasing share in decision making.[24] The majority of educators would agree that experience is a prerequisite for learning and that if students are to begin to understand what democratic self-government means, they must learn how to participate intelligently in that process.

While cognitively principals and teachers might support the idea that students should be granted more and more freedom to determine their own rules, educators generally are not too confident about putting the idea into practice. There are several reasons why this is so. First, there is a feeling that students often are not ready to handle a great deal of freedom and that freedom might become license. Second, there often are fears that community reaction to a school that is largely student-governed will be negative. Third, most principals and teachers are uncertain of where to begin in involving students in self-governance.

It should be recognized at the outset that there are risks attached to transferring some adult authority to students. Inexperience will lead to mistakes. Inevitably there will be occasions, at least in the early stages, where students will use their new freedom in ways that principals and teachers consider unwise, even obnoxious. If students have never had the opportunity to govern themselves, they almost certainly will make some errors in judgment. (It might be helpful for principals and teachers to remember that even experienced educators make mistakes occasionally on these same matters.) If a school genuinely wishes to pursue the goal of self-governance, then this risk should be noted at the very beginning and the school should be prepared to face it.

Community reaction to student self-governance, especially where judgmental errors are made, can be negative. Principals have the responsibility of interpreting to parents the goals of the program and of responding to questions and criticism. Teachers, too, have a role to play in this regard because many parents' questions will be directed to their child's teachers. The school's faculty should be prepared to deal with such questions.

[23]Mallory, op. cit., p. 25.
[24]Ladd, op. cit., p. 11.

If a school commits itself to the goal of student self-governance, there are several guidelines that should be followed in order to minimize adverse reaction and to enhance chances for success. These guidelines are:

1. The principal and teachers should have a commitment to the program. This may take a number of meetings of the staff, but unless people understand the goals of the program and its risks and are committed to it, the program is not likely to succeed.

2. Agreement must be reached among the faculty as to what authority is to be given to students and what authority is to be retained by adults. This is an important step and every effort should be made to communicate clearly to everyone precisely which responsibilities are being placed in students' hands and which are not.

3. Parents need to be informed, perhaps through PTA and other types of meetings, about the program and its details.

4. Consideration should be given to the level of maturity of students and their previous experience with self-governance in determining how much responsibility students may be granted initially.

5. It probably is best to grant students responsibility in increments rather than to provide too much at the beginning.

6. Once agreement has been reached on transfer of responsibility to students, the students must be permitted to exercise it. The program cannot work if students are not really given responsibility and authority.

7. The principal must take the leadership in monitoring the program, in evaluating its progress. This will require regular meetings with teachers, students, parents, and combinations thereof. Through careful monitoring, many problems can be solved when they are small and before they grow to such proportions as to threaten the success of the entire program.

FUTURE DIRECTIONS

Self-governance, which is the ideal of a democratic society, should be a goal for students. For a school to pursue this goal, it is necessary first to understand the child's world and the societal changes that are impacting on youngsters. One of the critical changes in American society is the radical shift in the structure of the family. Children are becoming increasingly isolated from the adult world. The school must bear a responsibility for attempting to bridge the gap between the child and life. One of the ways to do so is provide a structure where students, through self-governance, can learn the nature of freedom.

CASE STUDY—LATE AGAIN[25]

For the third consecutive day Jack is late to Edie Chalmers' class following lunch. The school's rule is that students who are late to class should report to the principal's office before being admitted to class. On the two previous occasions Jack has slipped quietly into his seat and Edie, giving him a frown to indicate her displeasure with his tardiness, has proceeded with the class without further comment.

On this occasion, however, Jack stomps into class, drops his books onto his desk with a bang, and says loudly, "Well, late again!"

There are some giggles and laughter in the fifth-grade classroom and Edie, striving to hold her temper, says to Jack, "That will be enough, Jack. I don't care for your being late."

An impish grin on his face, Jack replies, "So?" More laughter from the audience.

"*That* will be enough, Jack!" Edie says sharply. "You go to the office!"

Jack shrugs, gets up, and slowly, maddeningly slow to Edie, exits the classroom.

Ten minutes later Jack returns to Edie's classroom, an "admit slip" in his hand. The slip, signed by the principal, indicates that Jack has been tardy on one occasion and therefore will not be penalized for the first offense.

"But this is the third time you've been tardy, Jack," Edie says. "Why didn't you tell Mr. Foster?"

"He didn't ask. Besides, you only sent me to the office once. The first two don't count."

"We'll see about that," retorts Edie.

As principal, how would you counsel Edie?

Should the first two tardies "count"?

Should Mr. Foster have inquired of Jack if he had been tardy before? Would this have cast doubt on Edie's performance?

How could Edie have avoided a confrontation with Jack?

Should Edie have ignored the first two tardies?

SUGGESTED READINGS

Boocock, Sarane Spence. "Today's Childhood—A Unique Condition," *Today's Education* 68 (1), 1979, pp. 50–53.

Canter, Lee. "Taking Charge of Student Behavior," *National Elementary Principal* 58 (4), 1979, pp. 33–41.

Jones, Frederic H. "The Gentle Art of Classroom Discipline," *National Elementary Principal* 58 (4), 1979, pp. 26–32.

Kohurt, Sylvester, Jr., and Range, Dale G. *Classroom Discipline: Case Studies and Viewpoints.* Washington, D.C.: National Education Association, 1979.

Ladd, Edward T. (with John C. Walden). *Students' Rights and Discipline.* Arlington, Va.: National Association of Elementary School Principals, 1975.

Mahoney, Maureen A. "The American Family: Centuries and Decades of Change," *National Elementary Principal* 55 (5), 1976, pp. 6–10.

---

[25] From an idea suggested by Mallory, *op. cit.*, p. 23.

Mallory, Richard M. "The Teacher Who Disciplines Least," *Today's Education 68* (2), 1979, pp. 23–26.

Rich, Dorothy. "A Letter to Principals," *National Elementary Principal 55* (5), 1976, pp. 71–77.

Zakariya, Sally Banks. "What Schools are Doing for Families," *National Elementary Principal 55* (6), 1976, pp. 59–61.

CHAPTER

11

EVALUATING TEACHERS

Introduction
Spelling out assumptions
Establishing the purpose
Establishing evaluator–evaluatee understanding
Keeping evaluation positive
Looking at the whole picture
Considering emotional reactions
Selecting the process
Establishing priorities
Observing instruction
Concentrating on job targets
Providing a data base
Conferring with the teacher
Making those tough decisions
Evaluation forms
The Auburn (Ala.) personnel performance appraisal system
System characteristics
Implementation
Time schedule

In Chapter 4 we noted that (1) staff evaluation is integral to staff development, (2) in evaluation, judgments are made about adequacy of job performance, interpersonal behavior, and professional competence, and (3) staff development needs are identified when performance standards are not met. We begin this chapter with both an affirmation of those ideas and the assumption that evaluation is a positive term and is used constructively toward positive ends—staff growth and improvement of instruction.

INTRODUCTION

As early as 1900, formal teacher evaluation was used in schools. In Wisconsin, in 1910, E. C. Elliott proposed a teacher "merit plan" containing specific and general items that were given weighted values. The teacher's merit was determined by the totaled values.[1] Today evaluation systems vary widely in number and purpose. Some of the more common approaches are: formal and informal observations of the teacher by supervisors, principals, or peers; ratings by these respective groups; MBO-type approaches one or more times per year; scores on specific exams such as the National Teacher Examination and Teacher Perceiver Interview or on locally developed practical or theoretical exercises; personality inventories (Minnesota Multiphasic Personality Inventory and Minnesota Teacher Attitude Inventory); students' standardized test scores (gains) measured in varied ways and at varied times during the year; inservice sessions with the principal and curriculum director to establish goals for merit pay, salary increments, rehiring, dismissal, or promotion; checklist rating forms listing characteristics of good teaching used by a supervisor to arrive at an overall rating; performance of a teacher's students on year-end standardized tests and comparison with national norms; judgment of teaching deduced from SAT, PSAT, or CEEB scores; clinical supervision goal setting and implementing on a one-to-one basis; performance of a teacher's students on standardized tests at the entering and leaving level; performance of a teacher's students on year-end standardized tests and comparison with students of another teacher of the same grade or subject.

Donald Haefele critiqued twelve evaluation approaches in a recent *Phi Delta Kappan* article and presented research to help point out the serious disadvantages within each. He concluded that of those available, the most favorable (and the most demanding in time and effort) is the goal-setting approach because it is the only one with a mutual trust basis.[2] We highly recommend this article.

No matter which approach to evaluation is used, it has both strengths and weaknesses. Furthermore, no matter how the evaluation is used, it invites some kind of controversy. Some feel, for example, that indicators of good teaching remain at best a matter of personal opinion and are not substantiated by research results. Thus they claim that one cannot objectively say just what it is that the effective teacher is or does. Others say that it is unfair to evaluate *teachers;* rather, they believe that the act of *teaching* should be evaluated.

No single evaluation approach fits the needs of all schools or school districts. Those to be affected by it must participate in its design and implementation.

There are three fundamental methods of evaluating:

1 Evaluation based on research. This method usually proves to be too nebulous; in addition, it is too difficult to establish or to get evaluation norms.

---

[1] A.C. Boyce, *Methods of Measuring Teachers' Efficiency,* Fourteenth Yearbook, National Society for the Study of Education (Chicago: University of Chicago Press, 1915).
[2] Donald L. Haefele, "How to Evaluate the Teacher—Let Me Count the Ways," *Phi Delta Kappan* (January, 1980), pp. 349–352.

2 Evaluation based on opinion. This method would be all right to use except for the fact that we do not teach people well enough how to form opinions, opinions that are based on logic and syllogistic reasoning.

3 Evaluation based on policy. This method consists of establishing policy and then checking to see if the activities performed are consistent with the goals and philosophy inherent in the established policy.

We chose to use the third method in our discussion of teacher evaluation. In essence, it is the goal setting approach advocated by Haefele.

SPELLING OUT ASSUMPTIONS

Principals should assume several things prior to even thinking about evaluation of teachers:

1 Teachers feel that they are competent and are doing their jobs reasonably well.

2 The principal is the key to the evaluation effort.

3 Everyone profits from evaluation—teachers, students, and principal. The principal can learn better how to improve instruction and can learn much about the curriculum, the teacher, and the students.

4 Evaluation can be a positive process.

Try to make evaluation fair, objective, and relevant to the purposes of the school. The evaluation program must be tailored to the school and staff needs. Keep evaluation positive.

ESTABLISHING THE PURPOSE

Evaluation has multiple purposes—and some conflict with others—but it is generally agreed that evaluation is a cooperative, continuing process designed to improve the quality of instruction. A more formal statement of the purpose might read: Evaluation is a means of determining teacher competency based on performance.

No matter how good the teaching, there will always be a need for improvement. Establish objectives within this need. Objectives are observable, and they identify indicators. For example, if a teacher is working on improving reading skills with individual students, you can easily identify this process activity. And if the teacher is to be making materials, you can observe whether, in this product activity, the teacher actually did or did not make the materials. The point is whether we observe process or product, objectives are almost always observable. Strive to make objectives job-related and connected with instructional improvement.

ESTABLISHING EVALUATOR–EVALUATEE UNDERSTANDING

Do not surprise teachers. It is the principal's responsibility to establish role understanding and differentiation. In any role differentiation, there are zones of responsibility: the principal is responsible for A, B, C, D, and E; the teacher is responsible for D, E, F, G, and H. There will be some necessary overlap and problems do occur in these overlap zones.

Since both principal and teachers share the responsibility for instructional improvement, teachers and principals must be comfortable with each other; hopefully, neither will surprise each other. Evaluator–evaluatee understanding is crucial to the entire evaluation process. The evaluation format should be understood and accepted by both principal and teachers. For example, try to let the teacher know when you will be in the classroom to check on job targets.

Teachers need to know that the principal will be making professional judgments during the principal–teacher conference, and how frequently these judgments will be made. Teachers also should be aware that these judgments will be used for planning and for determining their progress on job targets. New teachers will probably feel threatened by evaluation. Principals should be reassuring to them and do everything possible to remedy threatening situations, thus establishing rapport.

KEEPING EVALUATION POSITIVE

Support and facilitate the evaluation process. If improvement is not forthcoming, sometimes it is the principal who flunks out, not the teacher. Decide beforehand—jointly between yourself and the teacher—those things that the teacher must do to improve teaching performance. In the pre-evaluative session, come up with some sort of agreement (or contract if you will) and document it. Then, throughout the process, support and facilitate the procedure. Both principal and teacher share responsibility for evaluation being looked at positively. Improvement of teaching performance is dramatically enhanced when the teacher is significantly involved in the entire process. And when the emphasis is on performance and the intent of the process is to improve rather than prove, a climate of confidence and positiveness will prevail. Within this climate, both teacher and principal can better achieve their roles and reach higher levels of effectiveness. Searching for strengths instead of weaknesses is perhaps the most important single advice to keeping evaluation positive. Do not forget it! Also, do not forget that process is more important than the instrument used. Instruments are only vehicles to accomplish the task. Use the instruments; do not let them use you.

LOOKING AT THE WHOLE PICTURE

Evaluation need not be a lockstep process. Every teacher must be evaluated. But do not think of evaluation simply as an exercise in filling out forms. It is much more than that. Evaluation may include those things necessary for improving instruction that may not be considered by some to be job-related, but for which the school has responsibility. For example, does your school make it possible for teachers to obtain advanced studies and degrees through, perhaps, release time or provision of tuition?

The district probably has evaluation guidelines that must be followed. Consult them. Teacher unions may have some say in how and how often teachers will be evaluated. It so, consult their guidelines too.

A major problem in many evaluation instruments is that they rely on evaluation of personality factors. However, evaluation must be directly tied to performance. The question is how to do it. Personality traits that are tied in with the teacher's performance must be considered only in the way they relate to the job. For example, a teacher's dress and neatness may be related to performance. Teachers serve as models for the students. It may be suggested that how one dresses indicates how one feels about self and others, and that teachers should dress appropriately for the job that needs to be done. Dress and appearance either enhance job performance or they interfere with the job. Decisions for evaluating dress and neatness should be made if dress or neatness are considered appropriate for the instructional activities to be accomplished. Another example would be the respect that teachers show for students and for each other. If it is appropriate to include it in the evaluation process, do so. A third example would be that of the teacher's scholarly appearance. If factors have some bearing on the instruction and affect students' learning, then they should be considered in evaluation.

CONSIDERING EMOTIONAL REACTIONS

Evaluation always has emotion tied to it. Teachers will probably be somewhat skeptical of evaluation; some even fear it. The teachers' fear can be partially alleviated through explanation and understanding of the evaluation process. If possible, allow teachers to help determine those things that determine their evaluation. When you plan together, chances are better that emotion will be little or no factor in the evaluation process. Deciding together takes the unknown out of evaluation. The principal's consistency and ability to look at evaluation as instructional improvement will further increase the chances of emotion playing little, if any, part in the evaluation process.

Teachers need support; they need reassurance. They need to know that you are going to expect them to keep on job targets; they need to know those job targets; they need to know the overall school goals. Inform them. When you set job targets, do it cooperatively.

SELECTING THE PROCESS

Inservice activities are usually designed to improve the teaching competency levels, as determined by the evaluation process. The evaluation process should:

- Be continual;
- Include mutually agreed-upon performance objectives and job targets, with projected completion dates;
- Include communication and understanding between principal and teacher in every phase;
- Include classroom observation;
- Include documentation to support ratings, whether they be satisfactory or not.

There are many items that may be added to the "include" list in any evaluation process. Rather than put them in narrative form, we have chosen to provide a Teacher Evaluation Process Checklist, which we hope will assist in the process of evaluating teachers. This checklist should be adapted as necessary for your individual situation.

Teacher Evaluation Process Checklist

Assessing needs: *Date Completed*

1. Review current research on evaluation. _____
2. Review other school systems' evaluation procedures. _____
3. Review own school system's evaluation procedures. _____
4. Analyze own school system's evaluation purposes and effectiveness. _____

Planning:

1. Present rationale and need to central office. _____
2. Organize planning committee. _____
3. Determine planning committee responsibilities. _____
4. Establish communication plan. _____
5. Analyze teacher job description. _____
6. Determine evaluation *what*. _____
7. Determine evaluation *who* and *when* (tenured vs. nontenured). _____
8. Determine evaluation methods (rating scales, performance comparisons, student achievement—video tape, objective analysis, simulation, microteaching). _____
9. Determine evaluation procedures (preconference, observation, postconference). _____
10. Organize evaluation records system. _____

11   Determine evaluators (self, peers, students, lay persons, consultants, supervisor and principal, central office staff).

12   Provide evaluator and evaluatee inservice.

Implementing:

1   Operationalize plans with each teacher:
    a   cooperatively establish job targets;
    b   clarify roles;
    c   set individual action plan.
2   Allow for feedback.
3   Provide for necessary process change.

Evaluating:

1   Collect and analyze process data.
2   Make implementation change decisions.
3   Effect continual evaluation monitoring process.

ESTABLISHING PRIORITIES

Cooperatively with the teacher, select only two or three growth targets—for the more targets selected, the more evaluation becomes simply an exercise to perform and not a method of improving. List the targets, set a time period for the progress, and keep priorities as objective as possible.

Examples:

1. The school is in the process of implementing a new reading program. What might teacher A do to improve her instructional delivery as she attempts to adjust to the new program? Specify targets.

2. The target focus is individualized instruction. What specific things should the teacher plan to do to improve individualized instruction in her class? Specify target(s).

In large schools, it becomes more difficult to work with every teacher individually as often as you would like. If your school is organized by grade levels, or departments, allow teachers to work in small groups to determine individual job targets. Teachers appreciate input for developing and implementing their evaluation and professional growth program. Also establish priorities on whom to evaluate first.

OBSERVING INSTRUCTION

It is necessary to observe the teachers' instruction often; but it is not necessary that every observation be used in the evaluation plan. How often principals observe for evaluation, what is observed, and how it is documented should be predetermined jointly with teachers. Some teachers may wish to be observed often as part of their professional growth plan (see Chapter 4), but not as part of their evaluation plan. They may wish to be evaluated on somewhat different observation criteria. Potential problems may arise if such dilemmas cannot be resolved through proper communication. We suggest that you work within the school system and school guidelines in making decisions regarding such dilemmas. Remember that guidelines are like road maps; usually there are several alternate roads to a destination.

When you observe, do it:

- Objectively;
- Systematically;
- Professionally;
- Thoroughly;

and observe those things on which you and the teachers have agreed. Use objective instrument aids (interaction analysis, video and audio tape, rating scales or checklists) when appropriate, desired, and mutually agreed upon.

William Gephart cautions:

> The state mandates to evaluate teaching have created a search for observation schedules, rating scales or checklists. Many of them exist but educators should be cautious in implementing evaluation of teaching using a rating form developed by someone else. Research on teaching effectiveness does not prescribe the set of items that should be used in measuring the quality of teaching. There are a very small number of items that consistently correlate with student growth. Few of us would agree to accept those research validated items as a complete picture of teaching. Some of us would add "concern for the individual" as a characteristic of good teaching. Research data will not support or reject that item. Some of us would add "the way the teacher is dressed." Again research is inconclusive. Items such as these are things we value and we would include them or exclude them on the basis of our values.[3]

Be judicious in the use of any instrument. Again we caution: Use the instrument, do not let it use you.

CONCENTRATING ON JOB TARGETS

Always spell out job targets for the teachers. Work on developing and improving your self-confidence in making professional judgments based on accurate data from preestablished goals. A knowledge base for designing objectives is necessary.

Determine how successfully teachers have met job targets. Do not purpose-

---

[3]William J. Gephart, "Structuring Observation for Evaluating Teaching in Your School," *Practical Applications of Research,* Newsletter of Phi Delta Kappa's Center on Evaluation, Development, and Research 2 (3) (Bloomington, Ind., 1980), pp. 1–2.

fully avoid making professional judgments. However use them effectively, fairly, objectively, and consistently. If job targets are not met, try to remedy the situation. Document, and if improvement is not forthcoming, make an administrative decision.

PROVIDING A DATA BASE

Evaluation of instruction is but one component of teacher evaluation. All evaluation efforts must have a firm data base. The data base is best obtained through formative techniques (evaluate throughout the year) to arrive at a summative decision (at conclusion of process). Data should be obtained on all elements of the agreed-upon teacher job targets for evaluation. Data should be systematically collected. Strive for objectivity. Use data-gathering tools that are objectively based. Set your schedule (p. 211) accordingly.

CONFERRING WITH THE TEACHER

Evaluation conferences may be classified as: (1) pre, (2) during, and (3) post. A "pre" conference sets the stage at the beginning of the school year. Its main purpose is to set a framework, to establish the objectives, tone, and parameters for the evaluation effort. Principal and teacher cooperatively determine the what, when, why, how, and where of evaluation. This evaluation plan should be documented and adhered to throughout the evaluation process. If changes in the plan are deemed desirable or necessary during the process, they can be effected, but only upon mutual approval.

The "during" (formative) conferences serve as a barometer of improvement. They allow both teacher and principal to view the teacher's progress and help determine where efforts need to be focused. Keep them objectively based, but seize the opportunity to praise teachers' improvement efforts.

In the "post" (summative) conference, all objective data are shared with the teacher. This might include principal, self, peer, and student evaluations, where appropriate. Review carefully the evaluation objectives, growth targets, and then discuss the teacher's progress in achieving those targets. Document the progress (or nonprogress) made and thoroughly discuss implications of the results. Give the teacher a copy of the results. The postconference serves many purposes. Though classified as summative, it is also formative for a several-year growth plan. In addition, the latter part of it can be thought of as a "pre" conference since the results obtained can be the basis of decisions for determining future growth targets.

MAKING THOSE TOUGH DECISIONS

An evaluation plan should include: clearly defined program objectives; provisions for involving teachers in developing and revising program; clearly delineated procedures and explanations; schedules; and provisions for follow-up and assistance to the teacher. From evaluation results obtained, you may decide to change a teacher's assignment—grade level, subject, or student group—in an effort to improve instruction. If possible, make that decision cooperatively with the teacher, after careful and thorough analysis of the situation. The principal should be responsible for seeing that assistance is provided to the teacher from appropriate sources.

Finally, it may be the case that the only method of improving instruction in a given situation is to terminate the teacher. Some teachers are going to fail, and the principal must face the difficult task of recommending dismissal. When this happens, facts will be demanded. Principals must be cognizant of teachers' needs for documentation related to personnel appraisal, and a good system provides for such. A termination decision requires thorough documentation and valid reasoning. The reader is directed to Chapter 12.

EVALUATION FORMS

Teacher evaluation formats vary in length, content, and degree of complexity. Response dimensions are varied and range from a simple check to yes–no, to does–does not meet minimum standards, to a numerical Likert scale, to a narrative scale (unsatisfactory–super outstanding) to full narrative. Combinations of the above are also used. Attempts to simplify the evaluation process often reduce the teacher's instructional performance, in all its complexity, to merely numbers on a sheet of paper. Sample content categorization descriptors include:

1 performance, responsibilities, personal qualifications (El Paso, Texas);

2 classroom management, pupil–teacher relationships, professional attitude and conduct, preparation and planning, knowledge of subject matter, public relations, techniques of instruction, pupil adjustment, pupil evaluation, personal (Vestavia Hills, Alabama);

3 personal qualities, teaching qualities, professional qualities (Pleasant Valley, Iowa);

4 professional preparedness and growth, planning, principles of teaching-learning, organization and control, logistics and physical environment, use of resources, evaluation, organizational responsibilities, other (Portland, Oregon);

5 instructional skills, classroom environment, professional attitude and commitment, personal attributes (Lyndhurst, Ohio).

Figure 11–1 is an example of one teacher evaluation instrument used by elementary principals. It is comprehensive in nature and includes space for suggested improvement areas.

Figure 11–2 is an example of a teacher evaluation instrument used for either self or peer evaluation. It is less comprehensive than the example given in Figure

FIGURE 11−1
Teacher evaluation form (Example A)

The purpose of this evaluation is to provide an objective means of measuring teacher competency. Although evaluative materials will be confidential, inservice plans for instructional improvement will be based on results obtained from evaluation efforts.

GENERAL INFORMATION

Name _____ School _____

Years of service in district _____ Grade or subject area _____

Date of conference _____

I (evaluatee) have been evaluated, have discussed the evaluation results with the evaluator, and am in general agreement with both results and suggestions for improvement.

Comments: _____
_____
_____

                                        Evaluatee _____

                                        Date _____

I (evaluator) have performed the enclosed evaluation with the evaluatee, have discussed the results with the evaluatee, and have made the following suggestions for improvement:

Planning Skills:

    (1) _____
    (2) _____
    (3) _____

Teaching skills:

    (1) _____
    (2) _____
    (3) _____

Professional attitude:

    (1) _____
    (2) _____
    (3) _____

Personal characteristics:

    (1) _____
    (2) _____
    (3) _____

Other:
_____
_____
_____
_____
_____

Evaluator _____

Date _____

Directions: Please rate each of the following as (5) superior, (4) strong, (3) average, (2) fair, or (1) poor. Comment where appropriate.

A PLANNING SKILLS:

1	Develops long-range goals	5 4 3 2 1
2	Prepares weekly and daily plans	5 4 3 2 1
3	Includes objectives, key questions, reinforcement strategies in lesson plans	5 4 3 2 1
4	Is creative and flexible	5 4 3 2 1
5	Plans for needs of individual students	5 4 3 2 1
6	Knows subject matter well	5 4 3 2 1

B TEACHING SKILLS:

1	Adapts plans to meet each situation	5 4 3 2 1
2	Provides for individual differences	5 4 3 2 1
3	Uses basic skills effectively	5 4 3 2 1
4	Objectively evaluates students' progress	5 4 3 2 1
5	Asks questions well	5 4 3 2 1
6	Praises students	5 4 3 2 1
7	Encourages students	5 4 3 2 1
8	Implements innovative techniques	5 4 3 2 1
9	Encourages student self-discipline	5 4 3 2 1
10	Provides a challenging and facilitative atmosphere	5 4 3 2 1
11	Exhibits effective speech patterns	5 4 3 2 1
12	Provides effective time on task	5 4 3 2 1
13	Maintains student rapport	5 4 3 2 1

C PROFESSIONAL ATTITUDE:

1	Works well with peers	5 4 3 2 1
2	Assumes responsibility	5 4 3 2 1
3	Reacts well to constructive criticism	5 4 3 2 1
4	Seeks professional growth	5 4 3 2 1
5	Keeps excellent records	5 4 3 2 1
6	Is punctual	5 4 3 2 1
7	Attends required meetings	5 4 3 2 1
8	Is willing to adapt as necessary	5 4 3 2 1
9	Keeps abreast of curriculum and instruction	5 4 3 2 1
10	Observes professional ethics	5 4 3 2 1
11	Demonstrates pride in work	5 4 3 2 1

	12	Exhibits continuing interest in students	5 4 3 2 1
	13	Encourages parent interest	5 4 3 2 1
D		PERSONAL CHARACTERISTICS:	
	1	Radiates enthusiasm	5 4 3 2 1
	2	Uses sound judgment	5 4 3 2 1
	3	Dresses and grooms appropriately	5 4 3 2 1
	4	Demonstrates integrity	5 4 3 2 1
	5	Meets physical demands	5 4 3 2 1
	6	Demonstrates leadership	5 4 3 2 1
	7	Shows a sense of humor	5 4 3 2 1
	8	Exercises emotional stability	5 4 3 2 1

FIGURE 11-2
Teacher evaluation form (Example B)

_____Self _____Peer evaluation

Please rate each item and determine total score:

		Poor	Fair	Good	Very Good	Outstanding
		1	2	3	4	5
1.	Lesson planning					
2.	Lesson purpose					
3.	Lesson presentation					
4.	Classroom organization					
5.	Pupil involvement					
6.	Teacher-pupil rapport					
7.	Classroom management					
8.	Questioning skill and technique					
9.	Student response to questions					
10.	Acceptance of students' answers					
11.	Teacher enthusiasm					
12.	Degree to which lesson is student-centered					
13.	Mastery of subject material					
14.	Appropriateness of material					
15.	Teacher appearance					

FIGURE 11-3
Teacher evaluation form (Example C)

Administration guidelines: Please read each item to students and ask them to place an "X" on the picture that best answers the question.

1. My teacher usually looks like:

2. My teacher is nice to me:

   Yes   Sometimes   No

3. My teacher helps me:

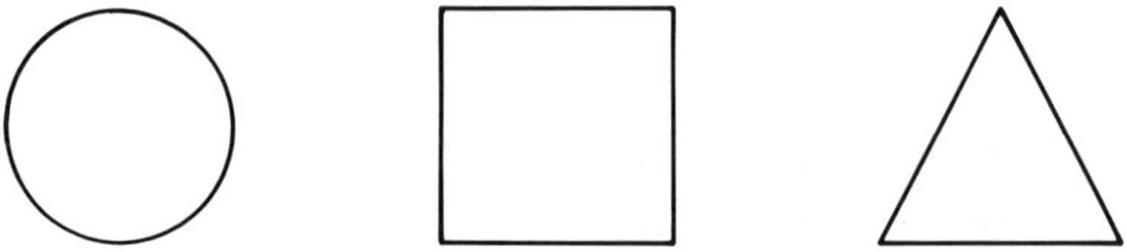

   Yes   Sometimes   No

4. When I ask my teacher for help, she feels:

FIGURE 11-4
Stanford teacher competence appraisal guide

			Unable to observe	Weak	Below Average	Average	Strong	Superior
PLANNING	1 Clarity of aims	The purposes of the lesson are clear.	0	1	2	3	4	5
	2 Appropriateness of aims	The aims are neither too easy nor too difficult for the pupils, they are appropriate, and are accepted by the pupils.	0	1	2	3	4	5
	3 Organization of the lesson	The individual parts of the lesson are clearly related to each other in an appropriate way. The total organization facilitates what is to be learned.	0	1	2	3	4	5
	4 Selection of content	The content is appropriate for the aims of the lesson, the level of the class, and the teaching method.	0	1	2	3	4	5
	5 Selection of materials	The specific instructional materials and human resources used are clearly related to the content of the lesson and complement the selected method of instruction.	0	1	2	3	4	5
PERFORMANCE	6 Beginning the lesson	Pupils come quickly to attention. They direct themselves to the tasks to be accomplished.	0	1	2	3	4	5
	7 Clarity of presentation	The content of the lesson is presented so that it is understandable to the pupils. Different points of view and specific illustrations are used when appropriate.	0	1	2	3	4	5
	8 Pacing of the lesson	The movement from one part of the lesson to the next is governed by the pupils' achievement. The teacher "stays with the class" and adjusts the tempo accordingly.	0	1	2	3	4	5
	9 Pupil participation and attention	The class is attentive. When appropriate, the pupils actively participate in the lesson.	0	1	2	3	4	5
	10 Ending the lesson	The lesson is ended when the pupils have achieved the aims of instruction. There is a deliberate attempt to tie together the planned and chance events of the lesson and relate them to the immediate and long-range aims of instruction.	0	1	2	3	4	5
	11 Teacher-pupil rapport	The personal relationships between pupils and the teacher are harmonious.	0	1	2	3	4	5

11-4, the Stanford Teacher Competence Appraisal Guide. The Stanford guide can be adapted in language for use at grade levels 4-8. It can also be used as principal, self, or peer evaluation. We suggest that a format of the happy, neutral, sad face evaluation scheme be used for student evaluation, grades 1-3, as shown in Figure 11-3.

THE AUBURN (ALA.) PERSONNEL PERFORMANCE APPRAISAL SYSTEM

The Auburn City Schools' Personnel Performance Appraisal System is designed for performance appraisal and staff development-needs assessment. The system emphasizes self-appraisal and continuing professional development. The system, designed by Auburn school personnel over a two-year period (1976-1978), is used for all professional personnel through the assistant superintendent. It undergoes continual evaluation and revision. We will describe it as used with teachers.

SYSTEM CHARACTERISTICS

1. Requires a clear definition of the role and scope of the teacher's job responsibility—that is, a complete position description.
2. Requires the development and adoption of standards of personnel performance as criteria by which the teacher's performance will be judged.

3   Requires the delineation of specific and observable behaviors to serve as evidence of quality of performance by the teacher.
4   Requires the determination of specific performance objectives that are relevant to the teacher's day-to-day performance and toward which the teacher is committed to strive.
5   Stresses close, cooperative, continuous working relationships between the teacher being evaluated and the principal performing the evaluation.
6   Requires in-depth analysis of performance achievement, including the "whys" of success and the revalidation of specific objectives.
7   Stresses independent self-evaluation by each teacher evaluated.
8   Requires a sincere and dedicated organizational commitment to continuing personnel improvement.
9   Requires systematic, on-going monitoring of progress toward accomplishment of objectives, including the collection of objective data as evidential indicators of performance progress.
10 Requires a series of face-to-face conferences between the teacher evaluated and the principal.
11 Is individually and situationally oriented in its specific application.

IMPLEMENTATION

Operationally, the Personnel Performance Appraisal System follows these steps:

1   Working independently, the teacher completes a self-appraisal, and the principal completes an appraisal, using identical forms.
2   A performance counseling conference is held, during which the two appraisals are discussed and any differences are reconciled.
3   At the conclusion of the conference, the agreed-upon appraisal is recorded on a summary form and both parties sign the form. The form is placed in the teacher's personnel file, and the teacher and principal retain their copies.
4   In the event the parties cannot reconcile differences, an appeal may be made according to established procedures.
5   Based on the agreed-upon appraisal, from 3 to 5 growth target objectives are determined mutually to become the teacher's professional growth plan for the subsequent year. These are recorded in triplicate on a worksheet, one copy of which is retained by each party and one copy is forwarded to the district office for professional-development program planning.
6   Periodic conferences occur during the year to discuss progress toward the identified growth targets and make amendments as desired.
7   Cycle is repeated.

The appraisal process occurs annually at a minimum for all professional personnel, and probationary personnel may have more frequent appraisal confer-

FIGURE 11-5

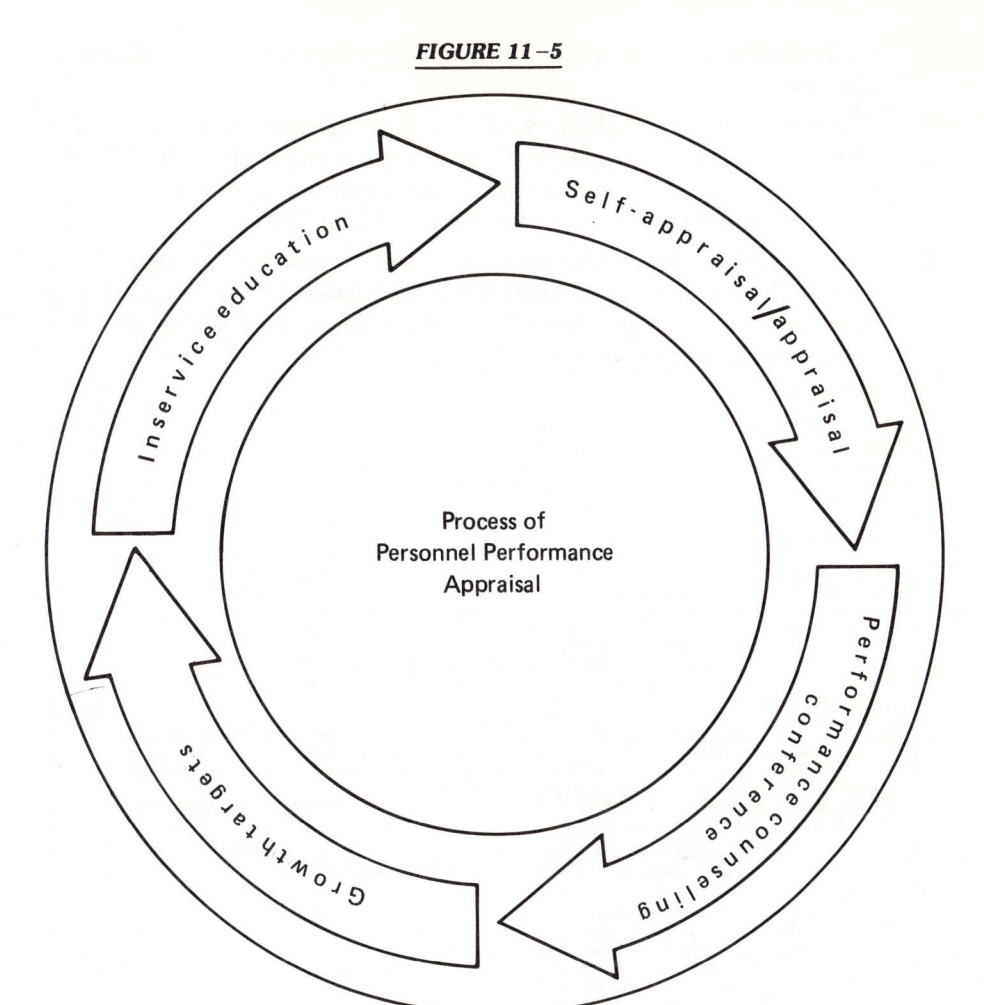

Process of Personnel Performance Appraisal (cycle: Self-appraisal/appraisal → Performance conference counseling → Growth targets → Inservice education)

ences. In most cases, the annual appraisal is on a spring-to-spring schedule, but in a few cases the cycle may be fall-to-fall or winter-to-winter. The latter schedule may be necessary to accommodate a large faculty.

Implementation of the Personnel Performance Appraisal is summarized by Figure 11-5.

TIME SCHEDULE

1. Teachers new to the school district have an orientation to the personnel performance appraisal system during the preschool activities.
2. Growth target objectives formulated during the final appraisal conference of the previous year are confirmed by October 15th of the current school year. Appraisees new to the school district must have growth target objectives

established by that date, either by mutual agreement with the appraiser or by prescription.

3 The summative appraisal conference for all probationary teachers is held by March 15th, and growth target objectives are formulated for the following year. Summary forms and growth target objectives report forms are forwarded to the superintendent of schools by March 30th.

4 The annual appraisal conferences for all tenured teachers are held by May 15th, and growth target objectives are formulated for the following year. Summary forms and growth target objective report forms are forwarded to the superintendent of schools by May 30th.

Auburn City Schools,
Revised, January 1980

AUBURN CITY SCHOOLS
PERSONNEL PERFORMANCE APPRAISAL SYSTEM

Introduction

Of all the factors which impinge on the quality of educational services for students, the factor of paramount importance is the quality of personnel performance. In the Auburn City Schools, we subscribe to the continuous improvement of educational services through a professional growth and development program. If professional growth is to relate directly to personnel performance, then the status of that performance must be appraised systematically. Thus, performance appraisal is a means to an end rather than an end in itself. The Personnel Performance Appraisal System, as a means, should be viewed as a diagnostic tool designed to assist individuals in identifying specific areas in which improvements are needed.

Self-appraisal of one's professional performance is an antecedent to appropriate professional development and is the cornerstone on which the Personnel Performance Appraisal System is based. The teacher is encouraged to look at himself/herself with objectivity and candor as he/she performs this self-appraisal.

Instructions

1. Working independently, complete the self-appraisal. Each Standard of Performance is followed by several indicators which give evidence of the degree to which the standard is being met. If an indicator is true most of the time, mark the indicator with a ✓; if the indicator is not true most of the time, make no mark.
2. On the nine-point appraisal line following the standard, circle the number representing the degree to which the standard is met.

```
       Unsatisfactory / Satisfactory / Outstanding
        Performance     Performance    Performance
        1      2     3    4    5    6    7    8    9
```

3. Schedule a performance counseling conference with the principal.
4. At the conclusion of the conference, record the agreed upon appraisal on the summary form; both teacher and principal should sign the summary form.
5. In consultation with the principal, identify growth targets for the coming year. Within five days, return the completed Growth Target Form to the principal.

*   *   *   *   *   *

I. PERSONAL RESPONSIBILITIES
A. Possesses acceptable degree of good physical and mental health
App. ___
   1 2 3 4 5 6 7 8 9
___ Demonstrates emotional maturity
___ Manifests acceptable degree of physical fitness
___ Accepts constructive criticism and suggestions
___ Other _____

C. DEMONSTRATES SENSITIVITY TO STUDENT NEEDS
App. ___
   1 2 3 4 5 6 7 8 9
___ Makes an effort to see that students have a positive feeling of success about school
___ Listens to and assists students with problems
___ Is observant of and responsive to behavioral changes in students
___ Other _____

B. DEMONSTRATES COURTESY AND RESPECT FOR OTHERS
App. ___
   1 2 3 4 5 6 7 8 9
___ Meets people with ease and assurance
___ Utilizes methods of encouragement and praise
___ Seeks harmonious relationships within and among staff and students
___ Demonstrates respect for the opinions of others
___ Other _____

D. DISPLAYS A COMMITMENT TO A PERSONAL CODE OF ETHICS
App. ___
   1 2 3 4 5 6 7 8 9
___ Displays pride and commitment to the teaching profession
___ Exhibits a belief in the worth and dignity of all people
___ Exhibits integrity in dealing with others
___ Demonstrates an acceptable degree of enthusiasm about his/her work
___ Is willing to assist colleagues when needed
___ Other _____

E. EXEMPLIFIES GOOD PERSONAL HYGIENE
   AND APPEARANCE
   App. _____
   ___ 1 2 3 4 5 6 7 8 9
   ___ Is neat in appearance
   ___ Maintains cleanliness
   ___ Dresses in an acceptable manner
   ___ Corrects mannerisms which detract
       from effective teaching
   ___ Other _____

F. DEMONSTRATES ACCEPTABLE USE OF THE
   ENGLISH LANGUAGE
   App. _____
   1 2 3 4 5 6 7 8 9
   ___ Orally expresses ideas clearly and
       in grammatically correct form
   ___ Uses grammatically correct form in
       all written communications
   ___ Other _____

II. CLASSROOM PERFORMANCE RESPONSIBILITIES
A. PLANNING AND INSTRUCTION

1. Demonstrates evidence of planning
   App. _____
   1 2 3 4 5 6 7 8 9
   ___ Plans and supervises assignments for
       classroom assistants where applicable
   ___ Relates subject matter to life
       experiences
   ___ Uses lesson plans
   ___ Organizes instruction to meet varied
       learning needs of the students
   ___ Utilizes clearly defined instructional
       objectives
   ___ Can clearly communicate the relationship
       of classroom activities to
       instructional goals
   ___ Other _____

2. Demonstrates knowledge of subject
   matter
   App. _____
   1 2 3 4 5 6 7 8 9
   ___ Exhibits required quantity of course
       work in teaching field with acceptable
       grades
   ___ Can explain and discuss basic concepts
       of subject matter
   ___ Develops teacher-made tests which are
       consistent with instruction to
       determine students' needs and progress
   ___ Other _____

3. Varies teaching methods
   App. _____
   1 2 3 4 5 6 7 8 9
   ___ Demonstrates creativity and resource-
       fulness in teaching
   ___ Involves students in a variety of
       classroom activities
   ___ Selects methods that capitalize on
       students' interest and experiences
   ___ Other _____

4. Exhibits effective use of
   instructional aids and resources
   App. _____
   1 2 3 4 5 6 7 8 9
   ___ Exhibits skills in use and care of
       equipment and materials
   ___ Demonstrates knowledge of available
       resources which enrich the
       instructional program
   ___ Other _____

5. Encourages desirable study habits
   App. _____
   1 2 3 4 5 6 7 8 9
   ___ Establishes study habit objectives
   ___ Provides instruction in specific study
       habits when appropriate
   ___ Provides opportunities to practice
       desirable study habits
   ___ Other _____

6. Demonstrates awareness of character-
   istics of students' exceptionalities
   and teaches accordingly
   App. _____
   1 2 3 4 5 6 7 8 9
   ___ Accommodates various learning styles
       and needs
   ___ Shows evidence of having identified
       instructional strengths and
       weaknesses of students
   ___ Identifies pupil needs and cooperates
       with professional staff members in
       the community
   ___ Shows willingness to accept and
       integrate all students into the
       instructional program
   ___ Other _____

7. Attempts to develop critical thinking skills in students
App._____
1 2 3 4 5 6 7 8 9
____Involves students in decision making
____Exposes students to varying points of view
____Demonstrates the art of questioning
____Other_____

8. Instructs pupils in citizenship
App._____
1 2 3 4 5 6 7 8 9
____Attempts to prepare students to live and function as responsible citizens
____Serves as a desirable role model for good citizenship
____Provides opportunities which facilitates self-concept, good citizenship, respect for rights of others
____Other_____

B. MANAGEMENT
1. Demonstrates effective classroom management
App._____
1 2 3 4 5 6 7 8 9
____Requests input from parents when necessary
____Explains classroom policies and procedures
____Seeks assistance for special problems from peers and /or administration
____Works with students as a total unit, small groups and /or individually
____Assists students to develop self-discipline and an awareness of the consequences of their behavior
____Selects and requisitions books and instructional aids
____Rewards and encourages student by use of positive statements and actions whenever possible
____Other_____

2. Maintains adequate and accurate records
App._____
1 2 3 4 5 6 7 8 9
____Maintains pupil performance records so that information can be interpreted to others
____Reports routine information accurately and on time
____Maintains required records necessary for proper administration of school
____Other_____

3. Maintains attractive and effective classroom learning environment
App._____
1 2 3 4 5 6 7 8 9
____Maintains safe and effective use of space
____Maintains clean and orderly room
____Maintains attractive physical room appearance conducive to learning
____Other_____

4. Maintains classroom control
App._____
1 2 3 4 5 6 7 8 9
____Maintains classroom discipline
____Emphasizes adherence to classroom rules and school standards
____Seeks to be firm, fair and consistent with discipline
____Handles classroom incidents and emergencies effectively
____Other_____

C. EVALUATION
1. Uses a variety of evaluation methods
App._____
1 2 3 4 5 6 7 8 9
____Uses informal as well as formal evaluation to determine degree of achievement of learning objectives
____Demonstrates ability to diagnose students' strengths and weaknesses
____Evaluates constructively and reteaches when necessary
____Other_____

2. Communicates with parents concerning student progress
App._____
1 2 3 4 5 6 7 8 9
____Notifies parents of special problems between reporting periods.
____Responds to requests for conferences
____Prepares student progress report each grading period
____Other_____

3. Demonstrates knowledge of growth and
   development in students
   App._____
   1 2 3 4 5 6 7 8 9
   ___Has reasonable expectations for each
      student's performance
   ___Other_____

III. STAFF PERFORMANCE RESPONSIBILITIES
A. DEMONSTRATES PROFESSIONAL BEHAVIOR
App._____
1 2 3 4 5 6 7 8 9
___Seeks adequate information before
   formulating opinions
___Strives to eliminate idle gossip
   regarding students, colleagues and
   and school
___Maintains students' and colleagues'
   confidences in personal matters
___Treats confidential information about
   students, teachers and school affairs
   as such
___Demonstrates punctuality
___Exhibits cooperation in group decision
   making
___Shows willingness to share equipment
   and materials with colleagues
___Other_____

B. DEMONSTRATES AWARENESS OF LOCAL
   SCHOOL POLICIES, PROCEDURES AND
   EDUCATIONAL GOALS
App._____
1 2 3 4 5 6 7 8 9
___Applies information contained in
   handbooks, accreditation reports
   and cirriculum guides
___Administers group standardized tests
   in accordance with the local testing
   program
___Observes the spirit and intent of
   rules and regulations of the school
   and school system
___Other_____

C. ACCEPTS FAIR SHARE OF STAFF RESPONSIBILITIES
App._____
1 2 3 4 5 6 7 8 9
___Participates on school committees
___Supports and attends school activities
   as are required or appropriate
___Participates in school-wide discipline
___Other_____

IV. PROFESSIONAL GROWTH RESPONSIBILITIES
A. DEMONSTRATES A PERSONAL RESPONSIBILITY
   FOR INDIVIDUAL PROFESSIONAL GROWTH
App._____
1 2 3 4 5 6 7 8 9
___Demonstrates awareness of updated
   materials and methods
___Demonstrates cooperative attitude
   towards evaluation in self-improvement
___Maintains an interest in in-service
   training and demonstrates a personal
   responsibility for individual
   professional growth
___Other_____

V. SCHOOL/COMMUNITY RESPONSIBILITIES
A. ESTABLISHES GOOD SCHOOL/COMMUNITY
   RELATIONS
App._____
1 2 3 4 5 6 7 8 9
___Utilizes community resources and/or
   personnel
___Strives to develop a community-wide
   awareness of school programs
___Cooperates with community agencies
   in education-related activities
___Participates in civic and community
   interest groups if appropriate
___Publicizes classroom/school activities
   when appropriate
___Other_____

_____
Teacher

_____
Principal

PERSONNEL PERFORMANCE APPRAISAL SYSTEM
SUMMARY FORM

I. PERSONAL RESPONSIBILITIES

A. POSSESSES ACCEPTABLE DEGREE OF GOOD PHYSICAL AND MENTAL HEALTH

App. _____
     1 2 3 4 5 6 7 8 9

B. DEMONSTRATES COURTESY AND RESPECT FOR OTHERS

App. _____
     1 2 3 4 5 6 7 8 9

C. DEMONSTRATES SENSITIVITY TO STUDENT NEEDS

App. _____
     1 2 3 4 5 6 7 8 9

D. DISPLAYS A COMMITMENT TO A PERSONAL CODE OF ETHICS

App. _____
     1 2 3 4 5 6 7 8 9

E. EXEMPLIFIES GOOD PERSONAL HYGIENE AND APPEARANCE

App. _____
     1 2 3 4 5 6 7 8 9

F. DEMONSTRATES ACCEPTABLE USE OF THE ENGLISH LANGUAGE

App. _____
     1 2 3 4 5 6 7 8 9

II. CLASSROOM PERFORMANCE RESPONSIBILITIES

A. PLANNING AND INSTRUCTION

1. DEMONSTRATES EVIDENCE OF PLANNING

App. _____
     1 2 3 4 5 6 7 8 9

2. DEMONSTRATES KNOWLEDGE OF SUBJECT MATTER

App. _____
     1 2 3 4 5 6 7 8 9

3. VARIES TEACHING METHODS

App. _____
     1 2 3 4 5 6 7 8 9

4. EXHIBITS EFFECTIVE USE OF INSTRUCTIONAL AIDS AND RESOURCES

App. _____
     1 2 3 4 5 6 7 8 9

5. ENCOURAGES DESIRABLE STUDY HABITS

App. _____
     1 2 3 4 5 6 7 8 9

6. DEMONSTRATES AWARENESS OF CHARACTERISTICS OF STUDENTS' EXCEPTIONALITIES AND TEACHES ACCORDINGLY

App. _____
     1 2 3 4 5 6 7 8 9

7. ATTEMPTS TO DEVELOP CRITICAL THINKING SKILLS IN STUDENTS

App. _____
     1 2 3 4 5 6 7 8 9

8. INSTRUCTS PUPILS IN CITIZENSHIP

App. _____
     1 2 3 4 5 6 7 8 9

B. MANAGEMENT

1. DEMONSTRATES EFFECTIVE CLASSROOM MANAGEMENT

App. _____
     1 2 3 4 5 6 7 8 9

2. MAINTAINS ADEQUATE AND ACCURATE RECORDS

App. ___1___2___3___4___5___6___7___8___9___

3. MAINTAINS ATTRACTIVE AND EFFECTIVE CLASSROOM ENVIRONMENT

App. ___1___2___3___4___5___6___7___8___9___

4. MAINTAINS CLASSROOM CONTROL

App. ___1___2___3___4___5___6___7___8___9___

C. EVALUATION

1. USES A VARIETY OF EVALUATION METHODS

App. ___1___2___3___4___5___6___7___8___9___

2. COMMUNICATES WITH PARENTS CONCERNING STUDENT PROGRESS

App. ___1___2___3___4___5___6___7___8___9___

3. DEMONSTRATES KNOWLEDGE OF CHILD GROWTH AND DEVELOPMENT

App. ___1___2___3___4___5___6___7___8___9___

III. STAFF PERFORMANCE RESPONSIBILITIES

A. DEMONSTRATES PROFESSIONAL BEHAVIOR

App. ___1___2___3___4___5___6___7___8___9___

B. DEMONSTRATES AWARENESS OF LOCAL SCHOOL POLICIES, PROCEDURES AND EDUCATIONAL GOALS

App. ___1___2___3___4___5___6___7___8___9___

C. ACCEPTS FAIR SHARE OF STAFF RESPONSIBILITIES

App. ___1___2___3___4___5___6___7___8___9___

IV. PROFESSIONAL GROWTH RESPONSIBILITIES

1. DEMONSTRATES A PERSONAL RESPONSIBILITY FOR INDIVIDUAL PROFESSIONAL GROWTH

App. ___1___2___3___4___5___6___7___8___9___

V. SCHOOL/COMMUNITY RESPONSIBILITIES

A. ESTABLISHES GOOD SCHOOL/COMMUNITY RELATIONS

App. ___1___2___3___4___5___6___7___8___9___

_____
Teacher

_____
Principal

_____
Date

APPENDIX D
GROWTH TARGET OBJECTIVE WORKSHEET

1. Statement of growth target mutually agreed upon by appraiser and appraisee. (What?)

2. Statement of specific means by which the growth target will be achieved. (How?)

3. Statement indicating acceptable evidence for determining successful completion of growth target. (How measured?)

4. Proposed completion date: _____

Appraisee: _____   Date: _____

SUGGESTED READINGS

Biddle, Bruce J., and Ellena, William J., Eds. *Contemporary Research on Teacher Effectiveness.* New York: Holt, Rinehart and Winston, 1964.

Bishop, Leslie J. *Staff Development and Instructional Improvement: Plans and Procedures.* Boston: Allyn and Bacon, 1976.

Bland, Carole J. *Faculty Development through Workshops.* Springfield, Ill.: Charles C Thomas, 1980.

Harris, Ben M. *Improving Staff Performance Through In-Service Education.* Boston: Allyn and Bacon, 1980.
Klopf, Gordon J. *The Principal and Staff Development in the Elementary School.* New York: Bank Street College of Education, 1974.
Sergiovanni, Thomas J., and Starratt, Robert J. *Supervision: Human Perspectives.* New York: McGraw-Hill, 1979.
Thomas, M. Donald. *Performance Evaluation of Educational Personnel,* Fastback 135. Bloomington, Ind.: Phi Delta Kappa Educational Foundation, 1979.
Warthen, B.R., and Sanders, J.R. *Educational Evaluation Theory and Practice.* Worthington, Ohio: Charles A. Jones, 1973.

CHAPTER 12

PROVIDING FOR PERFORMANCE EVALUATION

Introduction
Guarding against wrong decisions
Documenting facts
Appealing principals' decisions
Providing due process
Developing a performance evaluation system
Looking to the future
Case study—the letter writer

It is axiomatic that personnel administration is the most important task of the elementary school principal. Key aspects of that task are evaluating performance and determining when and how to recommend that a person should be terminated. This chapter will be focused on these functions of personnel administration.

INTRODUCTION

Evaluating performance is a difficult task and, as every elementary-school principal will attest, the decision to terminate a teacher's employment is even more difficult. There is no royal road to geometry and, similarly, the path to discontinuing the services of an employee is strewn with rocks and fallen trees. Principals need to check their road maps carefully and make certain they know their way if they are to avoid being tripped up by one obstacle or another.

The decision to terminate obviously involves a number of considerations. Basically, the decision is founded on an evaluation of a person's job performance, a topic that will be discussed later in this chapter. It also involves documenting evidence that would support the decision, knowing on what basis an employee might appeal the decision, and making certain that every employee receives every right guaranteed by law. Finally, and just as importantly, principals have the responsibility to guard against dismissing people who do not deserve such a fate.

GUARDING AGAINST WRONG DECISIONS

Not every teacher who makes a mistake or who temporarily is performing below expectancies deserves a pink slip. Nor should a teacher be terminated solely because someone has lodged a complaint. Principals have a responsibility to eliminate from employment personnel who do not, and cannot, measure up to standards of performance. At the same time principals also must make certain that they do not purge the competent with the incompetent. Principals, as leaders of an enterprise dedicated to truth and learning, have the professional obligation to protect their colleagues from unwarranted accusations.

During the course of a career nearly every teacher will be the object of some complaint. Given the nature of the task it is virtually impossible for a teacher to avoid entirely some objection to his or her behavior or judgment in a given situation. By the nature of their jobs principals will have to deal with those complaints. They will have to separate the real from the fancied and determine what course of action is required. The task is never very easy and it is often difficult.

Assume that a parent brings a complaint regarding a teacher's behavior toward his or her child. The complaint may be regarding the teacher's methodology of teaching or it may be in the nature of criticism of the way the teacher disciplined the parent's youngster. The parent may be reasoned in his or her complaint or may be emotional. In either case, the principal must strive to respond without giving way to emotion or defensiveness.

If a complainant is angry or emotional, frequently it is best to permit him or her to "let off steam." Allow the parent to state his or her complaint in whatever terms may be satisfactory to him or her. There is a tendency in such situations to want to respond in kind; to put the person in his or her place. This may satisfy the principal's ego needs, but rarely is it the best means for dealing with the situation. Usually it is good strategy to allow the parent to expend his or her emotions, responding unemotionally. This is not an act of disloyalty to the teacher who is the object of the complaint. Nor is it disloyalty to the school district. It is simply good strategy to permit emotions to run their course before attempting to discuss the allegation rationally. (It might be noted that more often than not the school secretaries catch more emotional outbursts than do their bosses. Once the parent has filled the secretary's ear with his or her anger, the emotion is spent and the principal has a more rational person with whom to deal.)

Once emotion is reduced, if that is the case, then the principal must atttempt to determine the exact nature of the complaint or allegation. The parent should be requested to state precisely what occurred and when. The principal can take notes and read them back to the parent to make certain the complaint is accurately recorded. This also impresses upon the parent that accuracy is important. In addition, sometimes allegations begin to be less severe when a written record is being made.

The parent should be informed, unless the allegation is quite unusual, that the teacher will be informed of the complaint and be provided the opportunity to respond. In a democratic society no one should be accused without having the chance to answer the accusation. If at all possible, suggest that the parent meet with the teacher to discuss the situation. Frequently parents do not wish to do so, but such a meeting, conducted properly, can be beneficial to all parties. In the right atmosphere, focusing on the child and not attempting to "save face," animosities often can disappear and large problems can turn into small ones. Furthermore, when people are face-to-face, problems often seem less severe.

Whenever an allegation is made against a teacher, the principal must resolve it in some manner. The complaint may be false on its face and dismissed immediately, with the principal so informing the complainant. The allegation may be handled through a parent–teacher conference or through a parent–teacher–principal meeting. Whatever the nature of the complaint, both teacher and parent should know its specific nature and what action the principal has taken with respect to the complaint. If the allegation, upon investigation, is, in the judgment of the principal, without foundation, then the parent should be informed. A teacher should never bear guilt when it is unjustified. Principals have the responsibility of protecting teachers from false accusations and of not permitting those kinds of charges to remain unanswered.

On the other hand, if a teacher has made an error, then it should be corrected. Everyone makes mistakes from time to time. Teachers (and principals, for that matter) are human. Inform the teacher and the parent. To admit error is not weakness. To attempt to bluff in the face of a mistake is foolhardy. Good public relations are built on a foundation of trust. When a mistake is made, admit it, rectify it if possible, and go forward. Cover-ups are a waste of energy and generally lead to greater problems later.

Occasionally a teacher, or the school, is accused of interjecting material into the curriculum that is unsuitable for young children. Materials or books are claimed to contain language or ideas to which elementary school children should not be exposed. Schools and school districts that have been involved in such allegations know that this area is one of the most emotionally laden with which to deal. Generally, there are no simple solutions to such problems and often, despite all attempts to achieve a logical, rational solution, emotions cannot be tempered. Nevertheless, principals have the responsibility of protecting teachers from zealots who would have their way at the expense of others.

School districts should have policies to deal with complaints about books and materials. If the school district does not have a policy, then the principal would be well advised to develop one and seek district approval of its use. A number of organizations have developed model policy statements for this kind of situation. The policy statement should require that anyone who has an objection to any materials used by the school make the complaint in writing. (A form could be used for this purpose.) The complainant should be required to state his or her objections explicitly, citing passages or pages to which there are objections and why. A procedure should be developed for handling such complaints. A standing committee of professional personnel (perhaps including some lay people) should be formed to receive complaints, evaluate them, and make recommendations to the board of education.

A process of dealing with objections to curricular materials or books can protect teachers' academic freedom. Academic freedom is difficult to define. Moreover, only in the twentieth century have courts begun to extend historical concepts of academic freedom from higher education to elementary and secondary schools.[1] The National School Boards Association has taken the position that all school boards need policies on academic freedom. Policies are needed to protect teachers from irresponsible attacks and to guarantee responsible teachers.[2] A teacher's rights should include ample latitude to make professional decisions about how a class or individual should be taught. The selection and use of instructional materials is a natural extension of the teacher's right to academic freedom.[3]

One public school district's policy, which also provides a definition of the concept, is as follows:

> Academic freedom may be defined as the right of a qualified scholar to pursue the search for truth in its many forms and to make public his methods and findings. It is the right of a qualified teacher to encourage freedom of discussion of controversial questions in the classroom and to develop in his students a love of knowledge and a desire to search for truth. The teachers should keep in mind that academic freedom is not a political right guaranteed in the Constitution, but rather a necessary condition for the successful practice of the academic profession in a free society. It is recognized that the application of the principles of academic freedom at the common school level involves considerations which are not equally present in college or university. The teachers should take into account the relative immaturity of their students and the need for guidance and help in studying the issues and arriving at balanced views.[4]

This policy statement recognizes that academic freedom must be defined in part within the context of the school, giving consideration to the age and maturity of the students.

Most individual complaints regarding books or curriculum materials come about when a parent is concerned that the material is unsuitable for his or her child. In recent years, for example, many parents have complained about schools' sex education programs. The courts have upheld the right of school districts to include sex education in the curriculum. At the same time courts have concluded that sex education cannot be required of a youngster if a parent objects. Such a requirement might bring the school into conflict with the student's (and parents') religious freedom as guaranteed by the First Amendment to the U.S. Constitution. The point to be remembered by the principal is that where a school requirement and freedom

---

[1] Lee E. Hartsell, "An Analysis of Judicial Decisions Regarding Academic Freedom in Public and Private Elementary and Secondary Schools and Institutions of Higher Education 1960–1975" (unpublished doctoral dissertation, Auburn University, 1977), p. 30.

[2] *Ibid.*, p. 51.

[3] *Ibid.*, p. 52.

[4] National School Boards Association, *School Board Policies on Academic Freedom* (Bethesda, Md.: Eric Document Reproductions Service, ED 078 558, 1973), p. 7, as quoted in Hartsell, *op. cit.*, p. 53.

of religion conflict, the school must give way unless the public peace, safety, or health is threatened.

Principals should advise teachers of that point and, also, that whatever materials are used in their classrooms must be suitable for the age of the children they are teaching. There is no absolute standard for determining what is suitable for which age youngster. Courts have wrestled with this question and will continue to struggle with it, because there is no simple answer. Principals and teachers must exercise their professional judgment in determining what is appropriate.

Principals, then, have the responsibility to protect teachers by providing a setting in which teachers have the freedom to teach. Parental complaints about a teacher should be handled judiciously. Not every complaint is legitimate and the principal must attempt to separate the wheat from the chaff. Teachers have a right to expect support if they are unfairly accused. At the same time parents have the right to expect that errors be corrected. It is the principal's duty to provide the mechanism for both.

DOCUMENTING FACTS

No person under contract may have the contract terminated at any point without due process of law. This is guaranteed by the U.S. Constitution and is applicable to teachers, principals, and any other person who has a valid contract with any agency or institution. Due process of law as required in teacher contract cases is discussed in a later section of this chapter. One aspect of providing due process is documenting the facts on which to base a recommendation that a teacher's contract is terminated. Without evidence to support a recommendation, a principal may as well not make the recommendation. A court will give short shrift to any case brought against a teacher that is not solidly based on factual data.

Before proceeding further in this discussion it should be pointed out that in the context of this chapter termination of contract means dismissing from employment a person who has a legally binding contract for a stated period of time. That is, the intent of the employer is to end the person's employment before the termination of the contract period. No person, regardless of tenure status, may have his or her employment status terminated during the contract period without documented evidence and due process of law.

Documenting an employee's performance on the job need not be viewed as negative. If a school has a sound staff development and evaluation system, then inexorably there will be evidence that many teachers are performing at superior levels. In short, consistently following sound principles of staff evaluation will produce more positive than negative data.

An essential purpose for gathering data that later may be used in a hearing before the board of education or a court of law is to demonstrate that the person being charged with failure to meet acceptable standards of performance has been given ample warning of deficiencies and has been provided with assistance in overcoming shortcomings. Fundamental to due process of law are that the employee be notified of any problems concerning his or her performance and that the employee be given direction on how to overcome such problems. Both of these points are of critical importance to school principals. In a termination case a principal must be able to present evidence that the principal has notified the teacher that he or she has specific deficiencies and that the principal has offered counsel on how to overcome them.

The foregoing suggests that principals should maintain written records on all phases of a teacher's evaluation program. The key point in a court action is whether or not the employee has been notified, not whether the notification is in writing. However, it is far easier to support a case with written records than with oral testimony. Therefore, principals are advised to keep a written record of all employees' performance. Again, such records will protect the exemplary teachers as well as provide documentation when it may become necessary to recommend dismissal.

Records should be specific. They should include dates and what behavior took place. Included should be dates and times of classroom observation and the results, reports of principal–teacher conferences, observations of nonclassroom behavior (if important), suggestions to the teacher concerning means of improvement, and so forth. This list could be almost endless, but the important point to be remembered is that the data must be specific.

All of the data should be provided to the teacher immediately upon its becoming a part of the teacher's record. If a fundamental objective of evaluation is to improve performance, then there is no purpose in having hidden records. Moreover, it is essential to any case brought against an employee that it be demonstrated that the employee has had prior notice. That cannot be shown if the teacher has not been provided with materials placed in his or her file on a regular basis. To put it otherwise, whenever a principal has occasion to place a report in a teacher's file, then the teacher should have a copy.

In summary, written records are essential in documenting cases regarding teacher evaluation. There is no acceptable substitute for a systematic performance evaluation program, one in which the teacher is informed at every step.

APPEALING PRINCIPALS' DECISIONS

In a sense any employment decision made by a principal may be questioned and appealed to a higher level or to a court of law. The question is: Under what conditions can a teacher successfully appeal an employment decision to a court?

In examining this question, one must differentiate between teachers who have tenure status and those teachers who do not. In addition, one must distinguish between termination of contract and nonrenewal of contract. The chances of a teacher mounting a successful appeal of an employment decision differ according to the teacher's tenure status and according to the teacher's contract status when the decision is made.

As was pointed out earlier in this chapter, no one under contract may have his or her employment terminated during the life of the contract without due process of law. This means that the person is entitled to a hearing and there must be evidence to support the charges that led to the decision to terminate the contract before the date specified in the contract. The employee's status with respect to tenure is only marginally relevant to this kind of situation. A first-year teacher and a person who has been teaching ten years have the same rights when they are under contract. That is, they may expect to complete the contract unless they violate its terms or the employer can demonstrate that the employer has valid reasons for breaking the contract.

Tenure status of the teacher is relevant in the sense that when a person has tenure, a contract may be terminated only for the specific reasons stated in the state tenure statute. If a teacher does not have tenure then, theoretically, a board of education might have a broader range of reasons on which to base a termination decision. Practically speaking, however, the causes for dismissal stated in most tenure laws generally are so inclusive that a school district would be hard put to generate a charge against a nontenured teacher that would not also apply in a case with a tenured teacher.

Tenure status is also relevant when considering the date on which a contract ends. Generally, under most states' tenure laws a teacher with tenure status is considered to have a continuing contract, automatically renewed each year unless the teacher is notified otherwise. By contrast, a nontenured teacher's contract has an ending date and is not automatically renewed. The nontenured teacher has to be offered another contract in order to be reemployed, whereas the tenured teacher is reemployed each year under the terms of the continuing contract. Therefore, in a real sense any time a tenured teacher's employment is to be discontinued, it is a case of contract termination. A tenured teacher always has a contract and it can be changed only for the reasons and by the procedures spelled out in law.

When a nontenured teacher's contract period comes to a close, there is no guarantee implied that the contract will be continued. The contract simply may not be renewed. This is in contrast with a tenured teacher whose contract continues unless terminated. If a school district does not desire to reemploy a nontenured teacher, the district simply does not offer the teacher another contract and the relationship between the school district and the teacher, under normal circumstances, is ended. No charges need be brought against the teacher and the teacher normally is not entitled to a hearing before the board of education or in a court. In a landmark case decided in 1972 the U.S. Supreme Court held that teachers who do not enjoy tenure status are not entitled to a formal statement of reasons if their contracts are not renewed, nor are they entitled to hearings on the merits of their case.[5] To a principal or school board, this means that if it is necessary to discontinue the employment of a nontenured teacher at the conclusion of the contract period, it can be accomplished simply by not offering the teacher another contract.

The foregoing sounds so simple that one wonders why so many problems develop for administrators when a nontenured teacher's employment with a school district is ended. Most of the problems develop because many school boards do not

[5]*Board of Regents v. Roth,* 408 U.S. 564 (Wisconsin, 1972).

understand the law governing teacher contracts in their state and, thus, violate some procedural aspect of the law. For example, most state statutes require that any teacher, regardless of tenure status, be given notification regarding employment for the next school year prior to the close of their contract period. The date on which notification is required varies from state to state. School boards sometimes fail to notify teachers by the date required by law and, thus find that teachers have been reemployed by default. In other states nontenured teachers do enjoy certain procedural rights provided by state law or by collective bargaining agreements. Administrators need to be cognizant of such rights; otherwise they will find themselves losing reemployment cases to nontenured teachers. The fundamental point to be remembered is that nontenured teachers do not, except where specifically stated in law or by agreement, have the same rights with respect to reemployment as do tenured teachers. Nontenured teachers, then, generally can have their employment ended by not renewing their contracts at the close of the school year.

The case of the nontenured teacher often presents professional and moral dilemma problems for principals. Principals understand that when formally notifying a teacher that he or she will not be offered a contract for the following school year, a reason need not be stated in writing. Indeed, school boards usually are advised that a nontenured teacher should never be given reasons for nonrenewal in writing. Principals then can wonder what information they can give a nontenured teacher regarding future employment and at the same time avoid legal problems.

Boards of education are advised not to state reasons for nonrenewal of contract in writing in order that boards can avoid possible court suits by teachers challenging the reasons. That advice, however, should not be interpreted as meaning that principals cannot, through the usual performance-evaluation process, inform a nontenured teacher of his or her deficiencies. The principal need not shirk his or her professional responsibilities in working with all teachers and attempting to assist them to become successful in the classroom. There should be no professional or moral dilemmas with respect to being open and candid with nontenured teachers. However, in a formal notification letter it is better to not state the reasons for nonrenewal that the principal probably has given the teacher in private conference. This is simply to reduce the possibility of lawsuit and does not preclude principals from carrying out their normal professional responsibilities.

As discussed in the preceding paragraphs, teachers may mount successful appeals of terminations or nonrenewals of their contracts only under certain contract and tenure conditions. In addition, teachers may successfully appeal such employment decisions if administrators and school boards have made those decisions for constitutionally impermissible reasons. That is, principals cannot violate teachers' civil rights in making employment decisions. Teachers, like all Americans, are entitled to certain rights guaranteed by the U.S. Constitution. To dismiss (or nonrenew) a teacher for behavior protected by the Constitution is to risk a lawsuit and probably a reversal of the decision. Principals should be conscious of the rights guaranteed all citizens and make certain that employment decisions are not in any way violative of those rights.

It is beyond the scope of this book to examine in detail all the nuances and possible situations with respect to violations of teachers' constitutional rights. However, the following points might be kept in mind by principals as they view teachers' behavior:

1. Teachers have the right to be politically active, to speak out on issues as citizens. At the same time teachers may not attempt to promote their private views to their students. Nor may teachers represent themselves as speaking on behalf of the school or school district.

2. Teachers have the right to practice a religious faith or choose not to do so. The right to practice one's religious faith does not extend to imposing that faith on students, however. A kindergarten teacher who informed her principal that because of her religion she would be unable to teach any subjects having to do with love of country, the flag, or other patriotic matters in the prescribed curriculum, was discharged. The court upheld the dismissal, remarking that the teacher had no constitutional right to require others to submit to her views and to forego a portion of their education they would otherwise be entitled to enjoy.[6]

3. Teachers have the right to live a private life so long as their lifestyle does not interfere with their ability to function in the classroom. This is a critical point. No longer can teachers be expected to live saintly lives. At the same time teachers cannot escape the fact that they are still role models for their students. Where a teacher's behavior causes students to lose respect for the teacher so that the teacher can no longer perform effectively, then the board of education may take action to discharge the teacher.

4. Teachers have the right to pursue truth in their discipline and to encourage students to do so as well. In exercising academic freedom, however, teachers must be conscious of the age and maturity of their students.

In summary, any employment decision made by a principal may be appealed to a higher authority. The chances of an appeal being successful are dependent to an extent on the contract status of the employee at the time the decision is made, the employee's tenure status, and the validity of the data on which the decision is made. The chances of an appeal being successful are greatly enhanced if the employee's civil rights have been violated.

PROVIDING DUE PROCESS

Due process of law, as discussed in another chapter of this book (Chapter 9), fundamentally means fairness. Whenever a teacher's contract is terminated under specific conditions noted in preceding sections of this chapter, due process is required.

Most states' education laws state precisely the steps that must be followed by administrators and school boards in dealing with teachers' contracts. Where state

---

[6]*Palmer v. Board of Education of the City of Chicago*, 603 F. 2d 1271 (7th Cir., 1979).

statutes spell out specific procedures, such laws must be strictly followed. Courts generally interpret such laws as intended to protect employees. Thus, when principals, superintendents, or boards of education fail to carry out each step required by law, the case against the teacher can be lost on procedural grounds.

Although state laws and local school district policies vary somewhat in the specific details required to satisfy due process of law, the following procedures generally are recognized as fundamental.

First, the teacher must know what is expected in terms of behavior and performance. A person cannot be expected to meet a standard of performance or to change his or her behavior if not properly informed by the principal of what is required. This point cannot be overemphasized. It is essential that principals inform teachers of requirements and of possible deficiencies. Otherwise, the case is lost before it is begun.

Second, where a teacher's contract is to be terminated, the teacher must be properly notified of the board of education's intent to consider cancelling the contract. Usually such notice must be given in writing and sent by registered or certified mail.

The notice generally must include several items. The charges against the teacher (the reasons for the termination) must be stated in sufficient detail for the teacher to be able to respond to them. Names of witnesses and the general nature of their testimony should be listed in the notice. The teacher's rights should also be outlined. Such rights would include the teacher's right to contest the cancellation at a hearing, the right to counsel, and the right to present witnesses and evidence on his or her behalf. Finally, the notice should include the date, time, and place the teacher may appear before the board of education to be heard.

The third step in the process is a hearing before the board of education. Courts recognize that a school board hearing is not a court of law and, therefore, courtroom procedures generally are not required. The essential elements are that the hearing be fair and that the board of education's decision be based on the evidence presented at the hearing. Practically speaking, however, in order to ensure absolute fairness in employment decisions school board hearings in recent years are more and more taking on the appearance of courtrooms.

The hearing before the board of education often is the time when the principal either shines or is tarnished. The principal's testimony and the data he or she provides generally are the keys to the case against a teacher. Boards, and courts, generally respect a principal's professional judgment, but that judgment should be buttressed with solid data.

After the board of education has rendered a judgment in the case, the final step in the process for a teacher is a court of law. That court generally will be a state court, unless the teacher alleges that a constitutional right has been violated. Then the action can be taken to a federal court.

DEVELOPING A PERFORMANCE EVALUATION SYSTEM

Evaluating performance means determining whether a person is adequately carrying out the functions of his or her job. It does not mean deciding whether the person is likeable, dresses nicely, or holds the same beliefs as other teachers or administrators, except as those traits may bear directly on the person's ability to perform. In other words, performance evaluation is focused directly on behaviors that indicate adequacy on the job.

Literally volumes have been written about evaluating performance. Further, since the dawn of the "age of accountability" in education the amount of literature dealing with this topic has increased in geometric proportions. It is beyond the scope of this book to review all the literature dealing with evaluating teachers or to describe a program that could be implemented in all schools. For that matter there is no single evaluation program that is appropriate for all schools or school districts. Persons seeking *the* evaluation program or *the* evaluation form might better spend their time searching for the pot of gold at the end of the rainbow. Their chances for success are about equally good in either venture.

Although no single evaluation system is appropriate for all situations, there are generally accepted guidelines for developing a performance evaluation system; guidelines that principals, teachers, and school districts can employ in their own settings.

At the outset it must be recognized that performance evaluation will take place. By some means, formally or informally, everyone's performance is evaluated. There is no avoiding the issue. Therefore, administrators, particularly principals, who inevitably must be at the core of the issue, must exert leadership in the direction of developing the best possible evaluation system. Principals must make recommendations concerning personnel. Those recommendations will only be as good as the evaluation system on which they are based. (The focus in this chapter is on an evaluation system. For a discussion of evaluation of teaching, see Chapter 11.)

School-district policies regarding performance evaluation are basic to a sound system. Most school districts have policies. Some school districts, even at this late date, do not. Many other school districts should examine their policies to determine if they should be revised and updated. Principals, who must administer such policies, should be in the forefront in this process. School districts who do not have sound, updated policies in this area are inviting disaster.

Those persons who are to be evaluated should play a part in the development of the system. Teachers, for example, can provide valuable assistance in determining the criteria to be used for evaluating their performance, the standards of performance to be expected, and the procedures to be used. Teacher–principal committees, formed in such a manner as to be broadly representative of the professional staff, are an excellent vehicle for developing the system. Without teacher involvement in the process, inevitably the system will be perceived by teachers as being imposed from above and thus be subject to failure before the system has been implemented.

Policies should be clear and complete. Everyone should know who is to be evaluated, when, by whom, and on what criteria. The following questions need to be addressed: Who is to be evaluated? Does the principal have the sole responsibility of evaluating teachers? Should self-evaluation be a part of the process? Should evaluation take place once per year? Twice? Should tenured and nontenured personnel be evaluated with the same frequency and against the same criteria? How does classroom visitation fit into the process? Should student evaluations be used with teachers? What written documentation should be used in the process? How can teachers appeal evaluations that they believe are inaccurate or unfair?

The foregoing list of questions is not intended to be exhaustive. It should suggest, however, the questions that should be addressed in developing a performance evaluation system. The point, again, is that the final policy statement and administrative procedures developed to implement the policy should show that such questions have been given consideration.

As pointed out above, the criteria on which a person is to be evaluated should be denoted. The criteria should be stated as specifically as possible. In addition, for every criterion of performance, there should be stated, again as specifically as possible, the behavioral indicators that are evidence that the criterion has or has not been met. It is not being suggested here that every performance criterion and every indicator of that performance be stated in behavioralistic terms. It is unlikely that this is possible or, perhaps, even desirable. It is being suggested, however, that every effort be made to select criteria that are critical to performance and that those criteria be stated as clearly and unambiguously as practicable. For example, assume that for a teacher it has been agreed that one criterion of performance is: "The teacher shall provide for individual differences within the classroom." For that criterion, indicators of performance could be: "(1) The teacher maintains a written record of students' levels of achievement in subject areas for which the teacher is responsible; (2) The teacher makes differentiated assignments for students based on their levels of achievement; (3) The teacher is able to demonstrate that his or her methods of instruction are related to learning styles of students, and so forth." There are a number of indicators that a teacher is providing for students' individual differences. Those indicators that have been determined to be valid should be listed. This provides the person being evaluated and the evaluator with something concrete on which to base judgments. Without specificity, judgments frequently vary from teacher to teacher and, in the final analysis, have little basis in fact.

Specificity, as noted above, can provide a good basis for a person's self-evaluation. One of the hallmarks of a profession is that professionals assume more than a modicum of responsibility for their own performance. Specific performance criteria provide a basis for continuous self-evaluation, an important aspect of many of today's performance evaluation systems.

Finally, given an evaluation system that is specific in nature, there probably will be little or no need to review each teacher's performance on every criterion every year. Often evaluation conferences between principals and teachers become bogged down in details in the attempt to cover every single point. As a result professional-development aspects of evaluation are lost. If a teacher is acknowledged to be doing a good job in a number of areas, why spend a great deal of time reviewing the obvious? It is well to recognize outstanding performance, of course, but why not also spend some time reviewing those areas in which the teacher believes performance could be improved? The teacher could be encouraged to suggest ways he or she can work to improve performance in specific areas during the subsequent year. This is a tricky point because the impression could be left that evaluation should be focused on the negative. Such is not the case. Indeed, the opposite is true. However, in the effort to emphasize the positive, sometimes opportunities for improvement are neglected. There is no need to be negative in approaching professional development among professionals.

Suggestions for developing a performance evaluation system, then, may be outlined as follows:

1. Develop a policy statement (or statements) regarding performance evaluation. The policy should indicate the purposes for evaluation.
2. Determine the criteria to be used in evaluating a person's performance. The criteria should be job-related.
3. Select the measures, or indicators, that can be used in determining whether a criterion has been met.
4. Determine the standard or standards that will indicate adequacy of performance.
5. Determine the procedures that will be used in the process, such as classroom observations, self-reporting, peer reporting, student reporting, or conferences.
6. Determine the written records that will be required.
7. Train each person who will be a part of the process. This may require training people in classroom observation techniques, in conducting administrator–teacher conferences, in completing written records, and so forth.

In summary, decisions to recommend termination of personnel are among the most difficult a principal must make. Such decisions must have a solid foundation in evidence that performance has been unsatisfactory. Evidence to reward good teachers as well as to determine who should not be retained stems from a well-developed system of performance evaluation.

LOOKING TO THE FUTURE

There is little question that high standards of performance will be required of all educators in the foreseeable future. This applies to principals as well as to teachers, counselors, and other personnel. To ensure high standards, more pressure will be applied to develop sounder means of evaluating performance of all personnel. Principals will be at the focal point of this pressure. While collegial means of evaluating performance appear to be gaining some favor, the principal will continue to play a decisive role in making employment recommendations. Self-evaluation and peer-evaluation techniques will have their place in the evaluation process, but in the final analysis, the principal will be expected to recommend reemployment, nonrenewal, or termination.

All of this suggests that principals need to continue to sharpen their skills in the area of performance evaluation. Increasingly those skills will be critical to the evaluation of principals themselves.

CASE STUDY—THE LETTER WRITER

Mary Fernald, Principal of Granada Hills Elementary School, is not surprised when her secretary tells her that the Superintendent is on the telephone. Mary, like most residents of the city, was a regular reader of the city's evening newspaper. She had read the letter published in last night's "letters to the editor" section of the newspaper. The letter read:

Editor, Evening Bulletin:
> The Board of Education recently has seen fit to ask the citizens of this city to vote for a substantial tax increase for the public schools. This is the second increase asked for by the Board within three years. That the schools need more money probably can't be questioned. But whether the administration of this school district and the Board of Education will spend the money wisely is a totally different question. The money from the last tax increase went mostly for buildings, special projects desired by the top administration and to increase the number of central office personnel. The crying need in the schools is increased monies for instructional materials and for libraries. Unless the Board can assure taxpayers that the tax increase will be spent for such purposes, I would urge the voters to vote "NO" on May 8.
>
> Sincerely,
> Joseph Wagnall

Sighing to herself, Mary picks up the telephone. Joe Wagnall is a fifth-grade teacher at Granada Hills and she is certain the Superintendent will not be in a pleasant mood.

Mary's suspicions are correct. The Superintendent is all but livid. "Did you read Wagnall's letter in last night's paper?" he begins. Hardly waiting for Mary's reply, the Superintendent launches into a tirade: "Two Board members called me before eight-thirty this morning. They were in a rage. One suggested bringing Wagnall before the Board on charges of insubordination. He said Wagnall ought to be fired. Everyone knows Wagnall is a teacher and here he is undercutting our campaign to get needed money for the schools. More than that, he misrepresented the facts. The last increase did not go for more administrators, buildings, and whatever else he said. We actually spent more money for instruction as a result of the last increase. You know that, Mary. Well, I want you to talk to Wagnall. Set him straight. I don't know whether I can save his job or not."

How should Mary respond to the Superintendent? Can the Board fire Joe Wagnall? Why? Why not? Assume that Mary talks to Joe. What should she say?

SUGGESTED READINGS

Alexander, Kern. *School Law.* St. Paul, Minn.: West, 1980, Chapter 10.
American Association of School Administrators. *Teacher Tenure Ain't the Problem.* Arlington, Va.: The Association, 1973.
Gorton, Richard A. *School Administration.* Dubuque, Iowa: Brown, 1976, Chapter 10.
Landers, Thomas J., and Myers, Judith G. *Essentials of School Management.* Philadelphia: Saunders, 1977, Chapter 9.

CHAPTER

13

DEVELOPING DESIRABLE COMMUNITY RELATIONS

Introduction
Establishing links with the community
Understanding the power structure
Working with pressure groups
Dealing with the news media
Developing a community school program
Organizing parents
Organizing a volunteer program
Steps in organizing a volunteer program

Keys to desirable relationships with the community
The future
Case study—a grim delegation

INTRODUCTION

During the 1978–1979 televised football games of the National Football League, Dave Jennings of the New York Giants asked television viewers throughout the country to call their local schools and find out how they might get involved as part of an educational team. This national effort to improve school–community relations, promoted by the American Association of School Administrators and paid for by the NFL and broadcasting networks, was one approach to meeting one of the most crucial problems facing schools today—how to develop desirable community relations.

Desirable relations with the community are necessary if many other desirable things are to happen in the schools. Of course, one of those is adequate financial support. However, good community relations pay dividends that exceed financial returns. Faculty and staff morale, pupil discipline, the curriculum, and even a principal's job are related to community relations. Developing desirable community relations requires some knowledge and skills that can only be obtained in an actual community as a school principal. There are, however, some basic requisites for development of desirable community relations. In this chapter we will consider briefly how to develop links between the school and the community power structure, pressure groups, news media, and community school programs, through such processes as organizing parents and developing a leadership team.

ESTABLISHING LINKS WITH THE COMMUNITY

Establishing links between the school and the community is extremely difficult for some schools. The desegregation of schools throughout the nation has required that pupil populations represent a variety of "communities." Since desegregation of residential areas has not kept pace with school desegregation in many localities, the federal courts have required busing in some districts and local school boards have required it in others. The "neighborhood school" of a few years ago is rare today. The school may serve many "communities" that do not associate with one another except through activities or programs in the schools. In such situations, the elementary school becomes a link among communities, and the problems of developing and maintaining desirable community relations are many and complex. At times the principal must be diplomat, arbitrator, promoter, judge, and statesman. Principals assume many roles they never dreamed they would play in order to develop and maintain community support.

Identify organizations and individuals that can link the school to the communities it serves. There are many links. Make a written list and put at the top of it "Pupils." They are the best public relations people available to principals. Usually if the pupils are happy at school, parents are satisfied, and few community relationship problems exist except those of complacency and parental apathy. Then add other links to the list.

Thus a typical partial listing might look something like this:

1   The pupils;
2   Teachers;
3   Bus drivers;
4   Chamber of Commerce;
5   Urban League;
6   The Rev. Sam Pickens;
7   Luella Jones;
8   Coach Rayberne;
9   Parent–teacher organization.

For each organization or individual listed define how the link might provide desirable community relations and the purpose the link might serve in developing and maintaining desirable public relationships. Your list will then grow into a chart that might look something like Figure 13–1 in its incomplete initial stages.

Figure 13–1
Illustration of school–community linkages

Link	Purpose	Potential Link Support
1. Pupils	Inform parents of programs. Inform parents of needs. Inform community of school accomplishments.	Take classwork home. Take notices home. Report cards; invite parents to school.
2. Teachers	Report pupil progress and problems.	Notes, report cards, conferences.
3. Bus drivers	Transport safely; remind parents of their responsibility.	Invite parents to ride buses sometimes, observe safety rules.
4. Chamber of Commerce	Relate businesses to school.	List of vendors for school services. Publish school budget and expenditure. Promote residential areas.
5. Urban League	Racial relations.	Communicate needs and intentions. Identify influential leaders.
6. Sam Pickens—Minister, local church	Communication and good will.	Words of support in Sunday sermon.
7. Luella Jones—women's club president	Communication and good will.	Devote one women's club program to school.

Of course, a chart is only one way to plan. It does, however, identify areas of overlapping functions and will force you to think about how and why individuals and groups might serve to develop desirable relationships between the school and the communities it serves.

Plan your principal role as a community relations link. Principals establish relationships between the school and the community through their personal as well as their professional activities. When the school serves many communities it is unwise to establish personal allegiance with only one of them through civic and community activities. If church membership, civic club affiliations, and recreational activities occur in only one community served by the school, pains should be taken to participate in one or more significant activities in other communities. These may be traditional community suppers, annual drama productions, athletic games, or a variety of events that have a special meaning to the residents of the community and to the pupils that reside in those communities.

Planning a personal schedule that is to be a meaningful link between the school and all communities represented may be impossible. However, to be recognized as a significant and important community leader ought to be a desirable professional goal of every school principal.

Organize key community links into a positive school communications network. More than 200 school districts nationwide have "key communicator" programs. Key communicators are trusted, credible residents or business personnel in the community who are interested in education and who talk to (and are listened to by) many people in the community. The key communicators should be one of maybe a half-dozen feedback techniques the school district has. But they should be the hub of the face-to-face public relations program of your school.

Invite your identified community links to have lunch in the school cafeteria—but keep each group limited to less than 10 members. Ask each if they would be willing to serve as community links and then discuss the objectives of the key communicator program and ask who would be willing to serve as key communicators. From this initiative, you will obtain an integral group made up of both community link personnel and others they have suggested. Keep the key communicators well informed. Hold informal meetings regularly. Develop a telephone chain for dissemination of facts. Always allow key communicators to have access to you. The communication network thus formed will prove invaluable in spreading the "true facts" about the school and hold "rumors" to a minimum.

Identify and eliminate if possible the undesirable links between the community and the school. Some organizations and individuals attempt to use the schools to further their own purposes rather than those of the school. One of the most common problems facing a principal, for example, is who may use the school for meetings, programs, and so forth. Usually the guidelines for making this decision are contained in the form of a board of education policy. (If they are not, they should be. The principal might consider recommending a desirable written policy to the superintendent and the local board.) However, written policies and regulations may leave a great deal to the judgment of the principal, and one undesirable or disturbing incident could remove the use of the school building as a means for involving the community. A good rule of thumb is to refuse permission if a principal has questions about the desirability of persons or groups requesting use of the school building. Principals should assist the superintendent and the school board in developing effective policies.

Although the school "belongs to the public" there are certain types of activities that should not take place in the school building. For example: Rallies or demonstrations that might cause harm to the facility; events favoring only one candidate for political office; groups advocating violence; and others. To determine suitability, ask questions as: Does the group serve community interests? Are the activities educationally related?

Keep paramount the purposes and goals of the school and the welfare of the pupils. There are ties established between the school and business concerns in the community because the schools are "big business." Salesmen and vendors of all kinds can plague the life of principals, interfere with their instructional leadership role, and keep them from accomplishing their job. It is the opinion of the authors that salesmen and vendors should never interfere with the responsibilities of principals or teachers during school hours. Hopefully, the school board would develop a policy that would require all salesmen and vendors to contact an appropriate administrator or purchasing agent in the central office rather than the school principal. However, business concerns are links in a community. The school needs them as much as they need the school, but business affairs should never interfere with the operation of the school, and the principal has a responsibility to make sure that they do not.

Businesses seeking to sell to the schools want to be perceived favorably by the school, and they usually take their cue from the actions of the administrator. For example, if they think a steak dinner will gain attention and approval, the principal will be issued an invitation after an initial contact. Gifts "in appreciation" may appear at Christmas or at any time and in various forms. In some instances they are in the form of gift certificates or checks.

Needless to say, high ethical standards should never be compromised, regardless of the temptations or pressures. Such action is not worthy of the professional leader and will inevitably lead to professional and personal harm as well as injure the school and desirable school–community relations. Surely there is no need to belabor the point further. Every practicing school administrator has faced the temptation to forget the school and establish a personal but temporary link with a business concern. *Make your ethical standards known in no uncertain terms.* This will eliminate many future problems and make relationships with the business community pleasant, productive, and in the best interest of all concerned. This may be done by simply writing a code of ethics to give to salesmen, vendors, etc. It may be done as one member of a group of principals, or alone, provided the action is within the framework of Board policy and regulations. An illustration of such a code follows:[1]

Principals' Code of Ethics Relating to the Business Community

As an ethical business administrator the principal's relationship with the community will be characterized by:

1   Cordial and frank relations with representatives of the business community;
2   Written standards for business efficiency in the school that strive to obtain maximum value for each dollar expended;
3   Systematic and accurate accounting of all funds and properties placed in trust with the principal;
4   Adherence to the policies and operational procedures of the local Board of Education and existing laws;
5   Decisions based first on concern for the educational welfare of pupils rather than personal benefit.

The following sections of this chapter deal with other ways to develop significant and influential links to the community.

UNDERSTANDING THE POWER STRUCTURE

Principals should keep in mind the fact that power and authority are two different things. School secretaries, for example, may not have the authority to make

---

[1] Derived from a code of ethics developed by the Association of School Business Officials of the United States and Canada.

decisions regarding the operation of a school, but in some schools they sometimes appear to be the most powerful members of the school staff. A principal may have the authority to assign responsibilities to teachers, but (in actuality) the power may reside in the hands of the union. It is quite frustrating when principals realize that having authority to do something does not mean having the power to do it. Throughout the school and the community are individuals and groups that can provide the necessary power to get done those things that should be done.

Identify the sources of power in the community. Who gets things done? Who do people turn to for leadership in resolving an issue? To whom do the politicians go to influence and win votes? Observing and listening will usually reveal the answers to these questions. News media do not always identify influential people, but your local newspaper is a good place to look for some clues to power sources. Again, it is a good idea to make a list. Keep in mind that power has a tendency to flow from one person to another. It is not stationary. A listing from time to time will help identify trends in power and power structure in the community. Also look for those powerful people behind the scenes.

Involve desirable power structures in the life of the school. People do not usually oppose those organizations to which they belong. If the community power structures do not perceive of the school as belonging to them, it is unlikely that community support for the school will occur.

Some groups and individuals have both power and authority. This is usually true of school board members. Work with the superintendent to involve the board as a body and as individual members in the life of the school. Ask for their advice.

Ask for help. Use the supporting power available to get done those things that are for the benefit of the pupils. However, make certain that requests for involvement and assistance are legitimate and honest requests—not requests to manipulate people or "con" them. People who have power can see through dishonesty and insincerity very quickly. Keep everything "up front."

WORKING WITH PRESSURE GROUPS

Pressure groups are links to the community. They can be harmful or beneficial. Principals usually resist them, but they can be influential and beneficial in helping the school to accomplish desirable ends. Theoretically, pressure groups are formed to force an individual or an organization to comply with the wishes of the group. They were used extensively during the 1960s to force school desegregation, to prevent school desegregation, and to accomplish any number of purposes considered desirable by the group. Although most pressure groups are formed when an impasse is reached in communication, this is not always the case. Influential people who want publicity or who wish to make themselves known for political purposes sometimes form pressure groups to achieve their personal desires.

Identify the true reason pressure groups form in your community. Pressure groups may help the school reach its desirable goals. They may be detrimental to the school. Whatever the case, they cannot be ignored. They are a link to the community and may indicate a weakness in communication between the school and community if they are "pressuring" the school.

Keep lines of communication open so that groups will use more desirable means than that of pressure to accomplish their school-related goals. Some people would argue that pressure groups do not form when there are open channels of communication between the schools and the communities they serve. However, this is not necessarily the case when people use their overt actions to influence others. It is not unusual for political aspirants in the community to use a parent–teacher meeting or a school board meeting where important plans are being made to demonstrate or "grandstand."

Recognize pressure tactics for what they are and do not panic. Some groups do not want issues and problems solved, although they may be literally screaming for a solution. If the problem did not exist they would not have an audience to listen to them. These groups are easy to identify. Their leaders attend public meetings regularly and are skilled performers. The legitimate pressure group usually dissolves when some solution is reached regarding the issue of concern.

DEALING WITH THE NEWS MEDIA

Newspapers, television, radio, and other forms of mass communication can assist greatly in the development of good community relations. Sometimes they warp the facts because they do not fully understand or because they are biased or prejudiced. For the most part, however, the media are anxious to report news; especially the news that will cause the public to buy the newspaper, turn on the radio, or watch their local television channel. There are several tried and true principles regarding dealing with the media. Most of the time they are very effective in developing good relationships with the community. They are worth remembering.

Make it possible for the media to get their story. The news media are going to get their story in one way or another. It might be a story that everyone connected with schools would rather not be told, but if the media are interested, help them get the true story.

The late Mayor Hartsfield of Atlanta, Georgia, pioneered effective principles for working with the press. Some of them were demonstrated when Atlanta Public Schools were desegregated in the 1960s. Atlanta led the way in the deep south toward racial desegregation, and news media from throughout the world descended on the city to get the story of the first black student to attend an all-white school in Atlanta. Mayor Hartsfield set up a "press room" complete with typewriters and telephones in the City Hall, and with the assistance of Dr. J. W. Letson, Superintendent of Schools at that time, a direct phone line was established between the school principal's office and the press room and was connected to a loud speaker so that all could hear the conversations at the same time. Every hour Dr. Letson would talk to the principal about what was going on in the school or what the pupil was doing at the time. Representatives of the press were barred from the school, but they got their story, enjoyed a cocktail party given them by the Mayor, toured the city with the Mayor as their guide, and everybody had a chance to make their "deadlines." This kind of respect for the press, the assistance given them in reporting the story, caused Atlanta to get worldwide favorable publicity and set the stage for favorable community relations in a situation that could have been disastrous. Dr. Letson and Mayor Hartsfield set an example followed by schools and school districts throughout the country when they were confronted by news media during a crucial time. Principals may be fortunate enough to have the burden of press relations assumed by the central office. If this is the case, the principal also has opportunity to select those newsworthy items to bring to the attention of the press.

Protect the rights of pupils and others. Although getting the true story is important, pupils and others have a right to privacy and some information is confidential. Principals should be very much aware of their ethical and legal responsibilities regarding what they tell the press. The public does not have a right to know about things that might harm others, and every school principal must be trusted to keep confidential matters that are confidential. Usually reporters understand and will be sympathetic when a "no comment" is given in response to a question. Reminding them of their responsibility to protect the confidentiality of some of their news sources usually slows up the ardent "crusaders" but seldom stops their attempt to get a story. Help them find another point of access.

Never tell a reporter something you do not want the public to know. There is no such thing as "off the record" comments. Just do not say it if you do not want it published. Violate this principle and you will regret it, regardless of how trustworthy the reporter may seem or how much they assure you it is "off the record." Nothing is "off the record" regarding the actions of a public servant.

Toot your own horn. The public has a right to know about the school and what is happening there whether the events are desirable or undesirable. There are thousands of stories at a school during a school year and some will greatly benefit school–community relations. However, the very fact that the principal attempts to keep the public informed in an honest manner will, in the long run, pay great dividends in desirable relations. Of course, principals should abide by the policies of the local board of education regarding the release of news and the admittance of media representatives on school property during school hours.

Although prepared written press releases are sometimes advisable, the media usually like to write their own. Simply asking the editor will provide a principal with practical guidelines for ways to get the news to the media.

Let errors in news stories stand. Reporters and editors will erroneously report the facts sometime, or will not report all of the facts and "twist" the story. Usually it is better to let the errors stand rather than try to correct them, but of course there are circumstances when it may be essential that the error be corrected. Reporters and editors, like most people, do not like to be corrected. Most ethical, professional news people take pride in the accuracy of their insight into a situation, but not everyone is perfect. In most cases, correcting the error will not correct the message received by the public and may cause more misunderstanding.

Keep the characteristics of the media in mind when using it to communicate with the general public. The general public will miss "details" of an announcement or story over radio or television, especially if it is of any length. Newspapers are much better media for relatively long or detailed communication. Radio and television have the advantage of immediacy, but newspapers are printed records that can be studied, referred to later, and stored for retrieval when needed. For example, announcing that school will be unexpectedly closed for the day because of a snowstorm is a story to go to radio and possibly to television. Newspapers may not even be interested. However, changing of attendance zones in a community is a newspaper story. The public will need to have that in writing. The two keys then to good media relations are honesty and candor. Specific techniques of note for principals are:

1. Know the school-district approved public information policy in dealing with the media.
2. Know what is and what is not newsworthy; that knowledge, together with the interest of the reporter, can help you make decisions.
3. Know the basic elements of a news story.
4. Know the individuals you are dealing with.
5. Know media deadlines in your town.
6. Be patient with reporters.
7. Be equitable in dealing with news in a multinewspaper town.

DEVELOPING A COMMUNITY SCHOOL PROGRAM

Flint, Michigan, is famous for its community school program. In brief, the schools in Flint, because of the Mott Foundation, are open to the public for all kinds of instructional and recreational activities in the late afternoons and evenings. When as many as 12 people want instruction on any subject, provision is made for teaching that subject at the local schools. Gymnasiums are kept open for community groups of all ages; and most schools have indoor pools that serve as public recreational facilities as well as in-school instructional facilities.

Not all school systems and local schools can establish a program like Flint's, but involvement of the public in activities at the school can be accomplished in almost all instances. Simply making the playground available after school for recreational activities (both supervised and unsupervised) is a step toward community involvement. Why not invite mothers to a coffee klatch with the principal during school hours? Why not use the school (board policy permitting) for community educational programs and classes? The cardinal rule in helping a community feel that the school is truly a community school is to *involve* people at the school building in school-related activities. It is highly unlikely that any school has ever received good public support or enjoyed good public relations unless people in the local community come to the school to accomplish some purpose they consider important or desirable.

There is evidence that when the school is "open" to the public and facilities are available to school-age children, vandalism is less and school–community relations are improved.

Design programs at the school for the community. Planning is important. In some neighborhoods, especially in certain areas, precautions must be taken for night activities. Also, in some cases an overt attempt to use the school by the community for other than formal instruction may be so novel as to constitute a rather traumatic change in public perception of the school. Care must be taken to anticipate problems and provide acceptable remedies. Even in the worst ghetto, urban blight, or isolated rural community, the school can become a symbol of community pride.[2] It is the only institution or agency that represents every segment of a community.

ORGANIZING PARENTS

Parents of pupils attending the school can provide an invaluable link between the school and community. Principals probably accept the idea of parental involvement in school but may have had problems of such magnitude with parents "trying to run the school" that any thought of parental involvement is distasteful. Others may consider a parent–teacher organization as fulfilling the total role of parental involvement. Some principals may be searching for constructive ways to involve parents in the school. In any of the cases mentioned above, some principles of how best to organize parents as a valuable resource to the school may be helpful.

Provide for involvement of more than one type of parent group. Pupils in almost every public elementary school represent families from a wide variety of socioeconomic conditions. There may be groups of parents who do not wish to join a parent–teacher organization or cannot find the time to participate in formal organizational activities no matter how desirable participation may seem to them. Some parents may have had past experiences that cause them to reject any contact or involvement with a school. Regardless of the reason, parents can be valuable assets to the school but they require ways for involvement that differ from most traditional practices. It is these parents that do not feel a part of the school-community, and are torn between lack of support of their children in school and the formally organized parent groups. Find some ways to involve them. Provide some acceptable alternatives. They are a valuable link that can supplement and complement formally organized groups.

Relate all parent activities to the instructional programs of the school in which their child is involved. In this sense the term "instructional program" includes all school-directed activities in which the child participates. Parents are not usually interested in organizations or activities for the purpose of the organization or activity per se. The involvement is because parents might benefit their child. For example, most parents will not join the PTO or PTA just for the sake of joining. They will

---

[2]Kenneth A. Schumack. "The Principal and the Community." Paper at annual meeting of National Association of Elementary School Principals, Atlantic City, New Jersey, April 24–28, 1976.

not attend programs unless they see the relationship between the programs and their child's work in school.

One elementary school recently invited all parents of pupils in grades 1 through 3 to come to the school for two hours one evening to help teachers make teaching materials to use in teaching their children reading and mathematics. Parent participation was almost 100 percent. It was considered the most valuable activity of the school year by the school principal and most teachers. That one evening (followed by some other similar sessions at the request of parents) established a bond between the school and the community and was of great assistance to teachers.

The number of parents attending any school function is directly proportional to the number of pupils directly involved in the function.

Identify parent leaders who will involve others. One of the quickest ways to kill any parent organization or activity, no matter how potentially desirable it is, is to fill status positions or PTO "offices" with only the enthusiastic, driving, intelligent, domineering people who must have everything done only their way. There is always the "in group." Usually they cannot understand why other parents are so apathetic about the school. Also, probably just as inhibiting are parental and professional leaders that insist on doing everything "the way we've always done it." People like to be asked to do things and to be recognized for their participation and accomplishments. Invite participation by asking parents to do meaningful jobs.

Put parents to work in the school. In some elementary schools parents serve as volunteer aides for brief periods of time during the school week. Of course many parents are employed on jobs and cannot work at the school during the school day, but a great many can help out and are delighted to find a positive and meaningful way to assist. Library aides, office assistants, lunchroom and playground aides are some of the many roles parent volunteers can fill.

Any parent volunteer role must be carefully planned and explicitly spelled out before it is assumed. The work should be meaningful and produce tangible, short-range results that fill a recognized need. If the school library is already well staffed with professional and paraprofessional personnel, for example, there may be no need for parent volunteers in the library. To assign a parental volunteer who sits all day may be more harmful to school–community relations than having no parental involvement at all.

Provide and publicize ways parents can communicate with the school. The very best communication system is worthless unless it is used. Parents should know who to call at the school regarding:

1   Teacher conferences;
2   Grades of pupils;
3   Schedules;
4   Courses of study;
5   Absences;
6   General complaints;

7 Report cards;
8 Textbooks;
9 Fees and school club dues;
10 Transportation;
11 Volunteer work;
12 Substitute teaching.

Providing parents a list of topics like those above with telephone numbers and appropriate names at the beginning of the school year is a small but important act that can pay real dividends in community relations. It is especially important that parents who have children in school for the first time have such a list. Also, making assignments to the faculty to be a contact person for one or more topics involves them in understanding more about pupils' backgrounds and needs. Open lines of communication do not occur without work and planning. Regardless of how it is done, parents need to know that they can get direct answers to their questions, that someone in the school is concerned about their chilldren and that they can make a difference in the school.

ORGANIZING A VOLUNTEER PROGRAM

While it is true that parents form an important source of volunteer workers for the elementary school, principals should realize that there are other potential sources for volunteer programs:

1. Tuscaloosa, Alabama, has organized a Voluntary Action Center. Affiliated with the United Way, it has a President, Executive Director, and Board of Directors. It publishes regular newsletters, provides training, and has a yearly financial statement. One of its major components is *Volunteers in Education,* which has a full-time coordinator to implement the program in city and county schools. During the first operational year 314 volunteers provided over 45,000 volunteer service hours to the schools. A Human Resource Directory was compiled and distributed to all schools. For more information contact

Volunteer Action Center
1904 University Boulevard
Tuscaloosa, Alabama 35401

2. Utilization of retired teacher volunteers is becoming popular. Retired teachers bring vast wisdom and expertise to the school volunteer program. Many possess highly specialized skills in disciplines crucial to the development of challenging programs and are willing to contribute their services. Depending on the size of your community, you can contact local chapters of Senior Citizens' organizations, NEA, and Retired Teachers Associations.

3. High school and college students may also be available for volunteer work. Various programs for Future Teachers of America and preservice requirements for education students can benefit the local elementary school.

STEPS IN ORGANIZING A VOLUNTEER PROGRAM

1. Determine needs—of school, teachers, and students. Then prioritize and set realistic goals.
2. Develop plans. Prepare objectives, procedures, and activities.
3. Recruit volunteers. Investigate every possible source—parents, retirees, students from high schools and colleges, working personnel, and interested lay citizens. Send letter of invitation (including the 5 Ws, the qualifications, training involved, and rewards) through students and others. From completed applications determine volunteers' abilities, needs, and interests.
4. Implement the program. Select volunteers. Match skills of volunteers with needs of teachers and students. Place volunteers. Successful implementation is dependent on
   - An effective training program and
   - Proper supervision and coordination of volunteers' work.

   A coordinator of the program should be selected at an early stage of the program. All policies, procedures, and communications should be effected through the coordinator, with the principal assuming final responsibility. Orientation sessions should be provided for all volunteers, during which time volunteers are presented the objectives and all procedural guidelines for the program. *Communication is vital. All procedures must be understood and accepted by volunteers.*
5. Reward and recognize volunteers. Recognition is not so much something *you do* as it is for something *you are*. It is a sensitivity and feeling for others as persons—a smile, a "thank you," a cup of coffee, a letter of thanks, a lunch—a genuine concern. Without it, your volunteer program will not have achieved its full success potential.

KEYS TO DESIRABLE RELATIONSHIPS WITH THE COMMUNITY

There are several tried and basic conditions at all schools that establish quickly a climate that supports desirable community relationships.[3] They are important keys to desirable school–community relations, and yet are so simple that they are often taken for granted. It is probably safe to say, however, that without these keys, none of the other desirable practices identified in this chapter will be effective.

An attractive and clean school building. Citizens will judge a school by its physical appearance. If the school is physically orderly and clean, it usually follows that the principal, faculty, staff, and students take pride in their work and their accomplishments. Although there are many reasons why at times there may be paper on the grounds, peeling paint, or smelly rest rooms, there is really no excuse

---

[3] Paul Meigs, "Public Relations—A School Function," *The Bulletin* 16(1) (Fall–Winter, 1979), pp. 12–13, Alabama Association of Secondary School Principals, Montgomery, Alabama.

for clutter, dirt, bad odors, and a generally unsightly school plant. Very old buildings and grounds can be kept neat and reasonably clean. Although there is some wisdom to the caution "don't judge a book by its cover," it should be remembered that a school is not a book and it, as well as its principal, are judged by their appearance.

The first day of school. First impressions are lasting ones, and every parent asks the elementary child what happened during the first days of the school year. This is a time to set the stage for a good year and desirable school–community relationships. Every detail of the first few days of school should be planned by principals and teachers before the first class begins in the fall. There is never too much planning. Every effort should be made to anticipate events, have the day organized, and convey to all concerned what will happen in the next few days. Also, despite the fact that there may be many reasons not to distribute materials and textbooks the first school day, parents and pupils should either know when "free" materials are to be distributed or have them in hand the first day. Instruct every pupil in some subject the first day. This one thing probably has more to do with saying how organized and well run the school is than anything else. It also indicates that instruction is the major function of the school. Nothing is worse than a confused, disoriented student body and faculty. The principal makes the difference.

The telephone. For most of the community, the first contact with the school is by telephone. Whoever is responsible for answering the school phone should be trained in how to answer politely, answer common questions, and to whom to refer the call for appropriate action. Even though parents may wish to talk to children or teachers "immediately," most respect and understand the fact that the instructional process cannot be interrupted except in an emergency. However, what to do in case of emergencies should be clearly understood, and where there is an emergency, the welfare of all concerned should be considered.

Thank you letter. It takes a little time, but a simple "Thank you" to someone who does something for the school or a child pays great dividends in community relationships. This extends to pupils, teachers, and staff.

Activity calendars. Send a copy of the activity calendar of the school home with each pupil. Some will not get there, of course, but a lot of them will, and there is really no substitute for knowing what will be happening in the school.

Handbooks. Parent and student handbooks are helpful in most schools. However, there are circumstances where handbooks are not appropriate. They should be friendly and informative, not a list of "don'ts."

Parent coffees and open houses. In addition to attending activities in which their children participate, coffees and open houses (or similar activities) provide a time for parents and pupils to talk to the principal, other parents, faculty and staff, and administrators. Such affairs held periodically may be what is needed to organize parents for community–school activities.

Classwork and homework. Probably more poor relationships have been created over "how much homework" than almost any other school factor. The development of sound operational policies regarding these exercises is most important and all parents should understand the policies. If your board of education does not have such a policy, recommend one to the superintendent for consideration.

Many schools report to parents through parent–teacher conferences as well as by report cards regarding the academic progress of pupils. Conferences are by far the more desirable of the two methods, but use of both methods is better than use of either one of them. Of course, the best reporting is done by letting pupils take their work home to show to parents. Encourage this practice. It is a very important key to good relations.

The principal. The most important single key to good school–community relations is a good school principal who is concerned about what is happening to children at school and what parents think about it. Thomas Baker offers the following sure-fire tips to principals who wish to "sell" their school to the public:

1. Recruit parents early;
2. Welcome visitors;
3. Give visitors something to take home with them;
4. Try something new on open-house day;
5. Recognize your potential allies;
6. Show off what's right with education;
7. Make your pitch on Monday;
8. Practice preventive communication;
9. Read the literature;
10. Evaluate your PR progress;
11. Make the most of kids' artistic talents;
12. Write a letter to the editor;
13. Remember, the best PR is more PR.[4]

When such concern is present in the school's leadership, desirable school–community relationships will exist.

THE FUTURE

Trends in the nature of schools and communities suggest that achieving good school–community relations will become an increasingly difficult task. Principals increasingly will find themselves reacting to pressure groups and environmental influences who are looking to them to make decisions or provide leadership in solving problems over which neither the principal nor the school has any direct control. The geographic relationship of parents' residences and the school building has much to do with parental involvement and interrelationships of the school to

---

[4]Thomas A. Baker, "How to Sell Your School to the Public: Thirteen Sure Fire Tips," *The National Elementary Principal 59* (March 1980), pp. 44–47.

the community it serves. Busing, population shifts, consolidation, and increasingly undesirable sites for potential school buildings are but some of the more obvious reasons why physical distance between the school and the community is likely to increase in the near future.

There is a limit to what the school can be expected to do, and in self-defense it is possible that buffering devices "to screen (reject, delay, prioritize) issues"[5] will be erected between the school and the community. These devices may be designated authority centers such as laws, commissions, boards, and committees. The problem of governance in education is going to continue to be a major issue, with perhaps less and less authority residing in the local school to solve problems that overlap the jurisdiction of the school and the community.

Regardless of the future, the principal is currently considered by most communities to be responsible for what happens at school. Better ways must be found to establish desirable school—community relations or the decline and fall of public school principals will be sooner than we think.

CASE STUDY—A GRIM DELEGATION

Evelyn Merritt was surprised to find the outer office filled with silent and grim-faced parents when she returned from a check of the leaking pipe in the "Boys' Room." She recognized Sam Porter as the probable spokesman since he was standing slightly in front of the group.

"Good morning, Sam. My, what a distinguished looking group of visitors we have this morning. Can I help you?"

"Morning, Evelyn. We want to talk with you."

"Certainly, Sam. Will you all please follow me to the library where we will have room to sit down?"

As the group marched quickly down the hall toward the library, Evelyn could feel anxiety and fear welling up inside. This was the largest delegation she had ever faced since becoming principal of Fair Oaks Elementary. Also, it appeared to be a group of only the more economically affluent parents; most of the neighbors of Sam Porter, a prominent CPA in Rolling Hills. What was the problem? She had no idea what the group wanted, but from the expressions on their faces it wasn't going to be good.

They entered the library, and after a brief explanation to the librarian and dispersal of a group of sixth-graders from one of the larger tables, Evelyn asked the group to sit down. There was no comment as they took their seats.

"Well, I'm glad to see you this morning. What can I do for you?" Better take the initiative and break the ice, Evelyn thought.

Sam addressed her very formally.

"Mrs. Merritt, we are very much disturbed about two serious problems here at Fair Oaks. They are related. First, several of our kids were caught smoking pot at the recreation center last night and they said they got it here at school. Second, the kids report that the grass is being brought in by people from the Red Ridge area. Now we know that group was bused in after the new attendance zones went into effect and you had little to do with that.

[5]E. Mark Hanson, *Educational Administration and Organizational Behavior* (Boston: Allyn and Bacon, 1979), p. 190.

However, you are the principal and you are responsible for what goes on here. We want to know what you are going to do about these problems. We just do not want our children going to school with pushers and Lord knows what else! Something has to be done!"

If you were Evelyn what would your response be? What are the obvious links to the community? Is the pressure group part of a power structure? What could have been done to prevent the need for the delegation to come to the school? What are the possible causes of the symptoms of poor school–community relationships?

SUGGESTED READINGS

Carter, David G., and Harris, J. John, III. "The Socio-Political System of the School: Revisited." *Planning and Changing* 6(2), Summer 1975, pp. 112–119.

Davies, Don. *Schools Where Parents Make a Difference.* Boston, Mass.: Institute for Responsive Education, 1976.

De Lellis, Anthony J. *NASSP Bulletin* 63(426), April 1979, pp. 53–59.

Fleming, Charles, and Olsen, Mary. "Communication for the Times of Crisis." *NASSP Bulletin* 58(378), January 1974, pp. 38–41.

Gold, Barry A., and Miles, Mathew B. *Project or Social Architecture in Education. Final Report: Part III: Case Studies.* New York: Center for Policy Research, December 1978, Chapter 7: "Change and Conflict. Educational Innovation in Community Context."

Jenkins, Kenneth A. "Community Participation and the Principal." *NASSP Bulletin* 60(403), November 1976, pp. 70–72.

Moss, Otis. "The Role of the Church and Clergy." *Phi Delta Kappan* 60(3), November 1978, p. 2245.

North Carolina State Department of Public Instruction, Division of Human Relations. *The Principal and Human Relations.* Raleigh, 1972.

Oregon University, Eugene. ERIC Clearinghouse on Educational Management, Advisory Committee. Chapter 1 of "The Best of the Best of ERIC." 2 (EA 011 100). Washington, D.C.: National Institute of Education (DHEW), 1979.

Schumack, Kenneth A. "The Principal and the Community." Paper presented at the annual meeting of the National Association of Elementary School Principals, Atlantic City, New Jersey, April 24–28, 1976.

Sills, James H., Jr. "The School Principal and Parent Involvement." *Contemporary Education* 50(1) Fall 1978, pp. 45–48.

CHAPTER

14

MANAGING THE SCHOOL PLANT

Establishing a good learning environment
Developing pride in the school
Planning thoroughly and creatively for care of the plant
Protecting the capital investment
Preventing vandalism
Conserving energy
Showing the school off to the public
Looking to the future

While elementary principals are expected to be instructional leaders, they are also responsible for supervising the maintenance of the school building and grounds. Although these two roles seem to be on opposite ends of the continuum, they are not—or at least they should not be. Principals who serve as instructional leaders extend this responsibility to include establishing and maintaining a wholesome physical environment that facilitates learning.

ESTABLISHING A GOOD LEARNING ENVIRONMENT

The school's environment includes much more than physical facilities and the school grounds. Its nature depends on attitudes and activities of the staff and students, as well as other factors, some of which seem almost to defy objective identification. Happiness, fear, anger, and frustration are not always obvious emotions, but they can sometimes be "felt" in a school. A casual walk past open classroom doors might reveal purposeful instructional activity, organized chaos, or even apathy. In addition, other environmental signs can be perceived through the senses of sight, smell, touch, taste, and hearing. The principal's success in managing the school plant may be judged by use of all five senses as well as subjective impressions of staff and student attitudes. Walter McQuade comments as follows:

> Some of the ways it (the environment) affects him [the student] are quite easy to see. If it is bad, it can impede the teaching process itself, concretely and specifically; if he can't hear the teacher when a truck goes by outside; if he is too hot or too cold; if he can't see the blackboard for the glare; if his chair is uncomfortable. And if the class is too big—or even if the room is simply overcrowded—you will find the children become more restless and aggressive.
> So a bad environment can impede learning. But a good environment is not just neutral. Children react to it. They do this through their senses, particularly eyes, ears, and touch; but also in more complicated ways—ways involving physical motion and muscular coordination; social ways; emotional ways.[1]

Establishing an environment conducive to learning is not a simple task. So many variables are involved that it is often difficult to determine which have the most influence. As might be expected, numerous studies have been conducted to determine what effect the environment has on the learning process.[2] The results vary, some showing positive environmental effects on learning and others showing negative. Overall, the research is inconclusive.

Perhaps the most important requisite for establishing an environment conducive to learning is to be aware of the environmental conditions both inside and surrounding the school building. Few people notice the absence of litter, the lack of offensive odors, the absence of glare, or the cleanliness of the windows; these things are taken for granted. Children especially do not notice hazards to learning unless they are made aware of them. Principals, teachers, and students can become accustomed to environmental conditions—both good and bad. Establishing a good learning environment requires efforts of all persons who directly affect that environment, especially the principal.

Richard Gorton lists the following general responsibilities of principals regarding maintenance of the school building and grounds.[3]

1 Keep informed about the work schedule and specific responsibilities of the custodial staff.

2 Tour the school building and grounds regularly to observe the extent to which they are being kept clean, neat, and in good repair.

3 Design some method or procedure for teachers, students, or others to inform the principal or custodian of any problems in plant and grounds maintenance or appearance.

---

[1] Walter McQuade, Ed., *Schoolhouse* (New York: Simon and Schuster, 1958), p. 20.
[2] Research is conducted at the Architectural Research Laboratory of the University of Michigan in Ann Arbor; The Education Facilities Laboratory, Inc., New York; The School Environments Research Project, The University of Michigan; The Educational Facilities Laboratory, The University of Tennessee, Knoxville; and elsewhere.
[3] Richard A. Gorton, *School Administration: Challenge and Opportunity for Leadership* (Dubuque, Iowa: Wm. C. Brown, 1976), pp. 138–139.

4   Develop a good working relationship with all members of the custodial staff, particularly the head custodian.

Can principals be both building managers and instructional leaders? They can—and they should. In fact, the roles are complementary. There is general agreement regarding the principal's role in school plant maintenance. In brief, the principal is expected to coordinate the various staff roles including custodial services, but is not realistically expected to possess a high level of expertise in custodial programs.[4]

There is no doubt that the appearance and maintenance of school grounds and physical facilities will affect the instructional program—either positively or negatively. With that in mind the following general responsibilities for principals may serve as a guide toward influencing teaching and learning positively in the school. All are discussed in subsequent sections of this chapter.

1. *Keeping the school clean and orderly.* The instructional and public relations value of good housekeeping cannot be overemphasized. This requires cooperative efforts of everyone in the school, but also means systematic mopping, dusting, sweeping, vacuuming the carpets, polishing, scrubbing, trimming the lawn, washing the windows, and keeping supplies and equipment properly stored.

2. *Conserving energy.* Energy conservation programs in which pupils, teachers, administrators, and staff members may participate are important. Keeping thermostats at 68° F. is only one of many ways to accomplish this. There may be very few things more important to teach elementary pupils than energy conservation; it has taken top priority in recent years.

3. *Preserving property.* Taxpayers have made a sizable capital investment in the school building and grounds, which, in effect, they place in trust with the principal. Vandalism, theft, fire, weather damage, and misuse are but some of the major factors that cause destruction of the environment.

4. *Protecting health and promoting safety.* Many factors create health and safety hazards, ranging from poor temperature and humidity control in buildings to damaged or poorly constructed playground equipment. Recent laws have concentrated on provision of facilities for special-education services in the school. Complying with these may help eliminate some previously unnoticed hazards.

5. *Operating efficiently.* Efficiency in this context means developing and maintaining operational measures that produce the most effective learning possible for the expenditure of money, time, and energy. Most operations or activities in the school and on the school grounds require supervision and effort to assure that appropriate facilities and equipment are effectively and efficiently utilized. Cleaning classroom floors during school hours, for example, is obviously inefficient operational practice.

6. *Planning thoroughly and creatively.* Attention to detail is necessary. A loose roof tile or missing window caulking may mean eventually the loss of instructional space because of bad weather. Careful planning for continuous

---

[4]See K. Forbis Jordan, *School Business Administration* (New York: Ronald, 1969), pp. 216–220.

maintenance and utilization of facilities is important; thus the need for custodial checklists that help prevent essential details from being overlooked.

Creative planning in an era of shifting school populations and changing programs is essential. In the sixties, overcrowded elementary schools were a problem; in the eighties there may be a surplus of classroom space.[5] Demands for different or changing programs may require changes in the use of facilities. Almost every elementary-school principal has already been faced with the need to plan creatively for programs for exceptional pupils. Even an outmoded physical plant can facilitate instruction in new programs if use is adequately planned.

7. *Developing pride in the school.* The school plant is a vitally important place in the lives of hundreds of people who literally live there a large portion of their waking hours. No one wishes to be in a place they are ashamed of. Principals help foster school pride within parents, teachers, pupils, and staff through their management and leadership skills.

Perhaps some of the seven functions outlined above are more important than others; their relative importance is a matter of opinion because they are interrelated and all contribute to the total process of developing attitudes toward the school on the part of all people concerned.

DEVELOPING PRIDE IN THE SCHOOL

Pride is taught best through example. People are proud of those objects, behaviors, or traits that others admire and that they feel they were somewhat responsible for creating. Pride may be neither rationally nor logically created, but its development in an individual requires that the person participate in or be a part (even vicariously) of whatever the source of pride may be. Even though some parents may be totally unaware of what goes on in the school, they may be proud of the school.

When elementary pupils are asked what they like most about school, they usually respond with "My teacher." That is as it should be. It is the people—teachers, staff, and principal—who make a difference in their lives; they interact with these people; they react to their environment. People learn to affect their environment by interacting with it. Students must learn to help produce a better school environment and thereby develop pride in the the school they attend.

A very obvious but often overlooked point is that people are not proud of something with which they disagree. Acceptance precedes pride. Probably most students accept the school plant as it is simply because they have little or no concept of what it means to alter the school environment. They usually have no choice about where they are or the conditions they live in. A favorable, pleasing school environment helps foster positive acceptance.

Assuming the validity of the conditions outlined above as prerequisites for pride, some characteristics of a program to develop pride in the school can now be identified.

[5]For some creative suggestions on use of surplus space see *Fewer Pupils/Surplus Space* (New York: Educational Facilities Laboratories, Inc., 477 Madison Ave., New York, N.Y., 10022).

1. The school must be doing something (hopefully many things) perceived as worthwhile—at least one or more acceptable activities. For example, lay citizens with no children in a school may develop pride in a school with a winning athletic team even though they may have neither seen the school building nor met any member of the faculty.

Pride in the school plant is only possible when the plant is "acceptable." Acceptable standards must be maintained if pride is to result, just as a team must keep winning if people are to be proud of it. What is considered acceptable depends on the expectations and values of the people in the school community.

2. People must participate in the school in some manner; they must feel a part of it; have an awareness of common ownership.

Pupils (along with teachers, staff, and administrators) are by definition a part of the school. Parents are a part because they have children attending, and businesses may be a part because they sell to the school or provide a service to it.

If pupils are to be proud of the cleanliness of a school building, involve them in developing ways for keeping the school clean. If parents are to be proud of the school, find some way to involve them. Seldom are people proud of something they know nothing about or are not involved in..

3. Teachers must teach by example. Teaches who dislike (or even hate) the school cannot possibly teach children to like it. Principals who do not keep their office orderly and clean face a difficult, if not impossible, task when they try to teach orderliness and cleanliness to others.

Unless teachers and administrators demonstrate a concern for the school plant and its operation, the pupils will care little about protecting physical facilities.

PLANNING THOROUGHLY AND CREATIVELY FOR CARE OF THE PLANT

Managing the school plant effectively and efficiently requires careful planning on the part of the principal. For example, simultaneous operation of a number of complex activities within one building or a limited space makes scheduling a necessity. Schedules are one type of plan. Like most good plans they should be capable of change without destroying their total effectiveness. Scheduling the instructional program was discussed in Chapter 3, but in terms of operation of the school plant, scheduling the work of the custodial staff is just as essential as planning a good instructional schedule.

Development of an effective custodial operation schedule requires careful planning, but in the long run it will save time and money in school plant operation and maintenance. It will aid the principal by helping to[6]

1   Serve as a training aid for the custodial staff;
2   Inventory all jobs to be done by the staff;

[6]Adapted from Georgia Department of Education, *School Plant Service; School Plant Operation Scheduling System* (Atlanta, Ga.: 1970).

3 Remove uncertainties concerning scope of the custodial job;
4 Reduce the time the principal has to spend in supervising and monitoring custodial service;
5 Indicate when jobs must be done;
6 Keep building and grounds in good condition at all times.

Developing a scheduling system is an excellent planning opportunity and inservice educational experience. The Georgia State Department of Education[7] developed a system that provides the benefits listed above, is uncomplicated, and can be implemented by any school or school district. The system operates by a job-order control method using job-order cards for every housekeeping task necessary for efficient school plant cleanliness and maintenance. Required tasks are printed or typed on about 150 index cards. Identification of those jobs should be a joint effort of the principal and custodial staff. Divide the school plant into eight areas and assign each area a color. For example:

Area 1 Grounds—Green
Area 2 Corridors and stairs—Buff
Area 3 Classrooms, offices, library—Blue
Area 4 Toilet rooms—Orange
Area 5 Gymnasium and auditorium—Gray
Area 6 Custodial supply closets—Pink
Area 7 Cafeteria, kitchen—White
Area 8 Mechanical rooms, boiler room—Brown

Job cards in the appropriate color should contain all information necesssary for the performance of the job—location, time allowed, materials required, and procedural instructions. Preparing these cards initially requires time but probably will save much valuable time during the school year.

Place the colored job cards on a scheduling board (approximately 40"× 48") divided into vertical columns. Label the columns: weekly, biweekly, monthly, three, six, and twelve months. Then place the cards in the appropriate column based on the frequency assigned the particular job listed on the card.

Divide the board horizontally near the center into working sections, each of which has individual pockets to hold job cards by area (color coded) and by frequency. Use the upper section for jobs waiting to be done and the lower section for jobs that have been completed or for jobs held in reserve for future scheduling. The custodial personnel take cards from the upper section, complete the work, date and initial the card on the back, and then return the card to the job-completed pocket. The principal (or person assigned) checks the cards in the job-completed section, making sure that the work has been performed and that the cards are dated and initialed. If everything is okay, return the card to the jobs in the reserve section.

[7]*Ibid.*

When the work is scheduled to be done again, move the cards from below the line to their appropriate pocket above the line.

A daily task chart should be made for each area (color coded) and kept by the scheduling board. The daily task chart may also include a time schedule. It usually takes only a few days before the custodial staff no longer needs to refer to the daily schedule.

Job assignments should be made by the chief custodian, subject to the principal's approval. Delegate that responsibility as the situation warrants.

Planning is a prerequisite to efficient and effective school operation; effective maintenance of the school plant is basic to all operations in the school. Scheduling is one of the principal's responsibilities. Developing an overall school operational schedule is probably best accomplished when those participating in the schedule have some voice in making decisions regarding its structure and how it is to be attained as conditions and circumstance require. Other concerns of the total staff and faculty, related to efficient operation, require careful planning. Some of them are:

1   School year calendar of events;
2   Assignments of staff for various extracurricular duties;
3   Deadlines for required reports;
4   Emergency operational procedures;
5   Reporting maintenance needs;
6   Plant use by nonschool groups;
7   Time for planning.

All seven items are important for school plant maintenance, but the last item, time for planning, deserves special mention because it is so often overlooked. Because planning is so important, it should receive high priority in terms of time; furthermore, it needs to be scheduled. However, do not confuse high priority with amount of time required. Some important planning may take relatively little time; other planning requires an extensive time commitment. Put announcements and directions in writing. Use valuable staff and faculty time for planning rather than for announcements or giving directions. A faculty and staff may do enough planning together, but it is doubtful that they will ever do too much. Use planning as an inservice activity for the entire faculty and staff—for a minimum of one hour each week (or equivalent) during the school year and for several days both before the school year begins and after the school year is completed (see Chapter 3). Care of the school plant should be on the agenda of each of the planning sessions as deemed necessary.

PROTECTING THE CAPITAL INVESTMENT

School plants are usually built to last approximately 30 to 50 years. Some buildings are used much longer. Such practice creates operational and management problems, no matter how well the facility was planned. When programs and operations change, school buildings may become functionally obsolete. Planning and utilizing a building effectively as well as keeping it physically well maintained are means of protecting the citizens' investment. Principals have a responsibility to protect the capital investment placed in their trust and care. That challenge perhaps can be best described by the phrase "protection against obsolescence."

> School buildings are called obsolete for a number of reasons. Some of the most common are the "toos"—too old, too small, too large, too far from the new center of population, too expensive to maintain, too hard to heat, too hot, and too inflexible to meet the needs of new teaching techniques.
>
> Some of the "not enoughs" are not enough electric outlets to accommodate the proliferating electronic teaching aids, not enough wet work areas . . . not enough storage space.
>
> More difficult to correct are malfunctions like perennially leaking roofs, cracking walls occasioned by settling foundations, partitions left hanging in the air by subterranean bound floor slabs . . .
>
> Many of the older schools were designed without much consideration for accommodating the custodial process. In some cases, the resultant inefficiency is a costly item and justly is considered a factor in the obsolescence index of the school.[8]

Principals cannot do all that needs to be done to prevent obsolescence, but they should make efforts to recognize it and work with the superintendent and other central office personnel to correct the real problems that exist. Most important of these is deciding when and how to recommend building structural changes. Much of the obsolescence is real, some is not. Some is just faddism, and some is just a misrepresentation brought about by the constantly accelerating rate of change.[9] Some thoughts to consider about change:

- Don't jump on the fad bandwagon;
- Examine change carefully;
- Don't change just for change's sake.

Sometimes a change for the better may create temporary obsolescence. For example, many schools have attempted team teaching. The idea sounded so good the principal or other leaders supported renovations that included removing partitions to open the classroom space. When some teachers could not work effectively in such open arrangements, the partitions were replaced. Some of these experiments were quite costly and they failed. In other cases the changes proved to be functional and efficient. Team teaching per se can and is an effective method for some teachers; it is instructional disaster for others. The lesson to remember is to make sure the instructional techniques and methods suit the facility and vice versa.

[8] American Association of School Administrators, *To Re-Create a School Building* (Arlington, Va.: American Association of School Administrators, 1976), pp. 48–49.
[9] *Ibid.*, p. 48.

Otherwise the capital investment is not accomplishing its purpose—the facilitation of learning.

Teaching technology, teaching methods, furniture, and programs are changing and creating a need for redesigning or replacing instructional space. Some examples are individual wet carrels for students, stackable chairs and desks, adult education classes in the building, and special education programs.

Principals should recommend space studies and be constantly alert to needed space change. It is a good idea to involve specialists before making changes such as removing walls or redesigning an area. Keep in touch with those responsible for such planning in the school district. If the responsibility is yours, seek help and involve others in the planning.

PREVENTING VANDALISM

Vandalism occurs at almost all schools at some time. One basic problem in controlling or minimizing vandalism is deciding how effectively to teach pupils respect for others' property. Pupil involvement in activities designed to care for school property, to establish pride in the school, and to share responsibility for the upkeep and cleanliness of the school plant can help solve this problem. But vandalism is not limited only to students. People other than students cause damage or destruction to school property. In recent years, vandalism has become a multimillion-dollar problem.

The American Association of School Administrators made the following suggestions regarding ways to stop vandalism, summarizing practices from school districts in all parts of the country.[10]

- Upgrade the exterior. Use a minimum of fences and "Don't" signs, letting landscaping, seating, and other friendly barriers direct traffic lanes.
- Enlist the community, including pupils, in landscaping plans. A person hesitates to destroy something that person helped create.
- Extend school hours by community use. An active building discourages vandalism. One school district turned two classrooms into a satellite police post. Result: vandalism down; pupil–police communication up.
- Consider reorienting the entrance. The community sometimes grows away from the front door.
- Eliminate hidden or dead-end corridors or passageways. Vandals do not like to be seen.
- Consider live-on-site custodians. A district in Florida has retired couples living on site in mobile homes. Result: decreased vandalism.
- Don't hesitate to rename a school. Honor a more relevant hero.
- Make creative use of "vandalism funds." Encourage pupils to let the students

[10]*Ibid.*, p. 42.

know that certain funds will be used in the school in any way they vote if it is not needed for vandalism repairs.
- Above all, involve the community in the planning. Let them know the school belongs to them.

Keeping the area well lighted at night is a known deterrent of vandalism. It is also a known way to use much electrical energy, and electricity is expensive. Installing a switch that will automatically cut the lights off in daylight and on at night will save electricity. Also using fewer bulbs with lower wattage may provide enough light to accomplish the purpose. Energy conservation is a must. It is an economic problem that cannot be overlooked in managing today's school plant.

CONSERVING ENERGY

Educational Facilities Laboratories has developed a computer-based technical service designed to help schools help themselves in conserving energy.[11]

The California Association of School Administrators offers these suggestions for energy conservation practices in the elementary schools:[12]

- *Interior lighting.* Turn off lights when they are not needed. Reduce lighting levels in corridors by cutting off half of them or one where two now exist.
  Use fluorescent lamps.
  Use light-colored walls and ceilings.
  Keep light fixtures clean.
  Use multiple switches for large areas so all lights do not come on if not needed.
  Utilize natural light where possible. Turn off business machines and equipment when not in use.
- *Exterior lighting.* Use photoelectric switches.
  Use efficient lamps—mercury and sodium vapor.
  Reduce or eliminate decorative lighting.
  Avoid night sports activities.
- *Heating, ventilating, and air conditioning.*
  Keep thermostats at 68° F. in winter and 78° F. in summer.
  Do not heat or cool large areas when not in use, if possible.
  Improve insulation. Shut off air-conditioning systems when buildings are not occupied.
  Activate systems later in the morning and close them off earlier at the end of the day.
  Avoid systems that involve simultaneous cooling and heating.
  Maintain mechanical equipment.

[11]For use of the service contact Educational Facilities Laboratories and ask for "Information about the Public Schools Energy Conservation Service" (PSECS) (New York: The Laboratories, 1975).
[12]*Op. cit.,* AASA, *To Re-Create a School Building,* pp. 28–31.

Turn off heating, ventilating, and air conditioning in moderate weather.
Put window shades or curtains on sunny sides of buildings to regulate light and heat through their use.
- *Water Heating.* Reset heaters at 100°F. and use boosters in the kitchen.
Repair leaks.
Insulate pipes.
- *Scheduling.* Recommend decreasing length of school day by opening one-half hour later in winter and closing one-half hour earlier in summer.
Consider a four-day week.
Close when weather is excessively cold.
Fully utilize buildings.
Stress outdoor sports and play rather than indoor activities.

These are only a few of the many ways to conserve energy. Principals must take the leadership in developing an energy conservation program. Make energy conservation a habit, not a fad.

SHOWING THE SCHOOL OFF TO THE PUBLIC

Community involvement, parental involvement, and pupil participation have been stressed in previous sections as a strategy for cooperative, supportive action essential to effective and efficient programs and operations. There are many ways to involve these groups, ranging from informal suppers to volunteer programs. However, there are other ways of showing the school off to the public and developing pride in co-ownership of the school operation. Consider the following:

1. Keep the school looking neat. Too often the quality of the school program is judged by the appearance of the grounds. This is especially true if school is closed for the summer and no one is there to cut the grass. Everyone can see the school grounds.

2. Invite parents to come to school as "guests of honor" and treat them that way. This may be a new and unique experience to some parents. Some may decline if invited. Most parents will come, however, and will, therefore, become a part of the school.

3. If policy permits, use the building after school hours for community and adult-educational programs.

4. Keep parents informed. Use every available means, but especially let the pupils take communications and class work home with them when possible.

LOOKING TO THE FUTURE

Managing the school plant is a responsibility that is not likely to diminish much in the years ahead. Some people argue that each school needs both a full-time manager and a full-time instructional leader and supervisor. We maintain that a good instructional leader must be a good manager of the school plant and also be a good supervisor, but the principal does not have to do all of these jobs alone. A good manager will delegate tasks to others. The roles of manager and instructional leader are not discrete.

As energy problems, economic conditions, shifting populations, and program changes occur, good management of the school plant will become an even greater challenge. Planning will become even more important and effective use of human and material resources will call for innovations that are carefully controlled or evaluated. The 1980s promise to be a decade of change.

SUGGESTED READINGS

Abend, Allen C., Bednor, Michael J., Froehlinger, Vica J., and Stengler, Yale. *Facilities for Special Education Services*. Reston, Va.: The Council for Exceptional Children, 1979.

American Association of School Administrators. *To Re-Create a School Building—"Surplus" Space, Energy and Other Challenges*. Arlington, Va.: The Association, 1976.

American Association of School Administrators. *Vandalism*. Arlington, Va.: The Association, 1976.

Association of School Business Officials. *Educational Resources Management System*. Chicago: Research Corporation of the Association of School Business Officials, 1971.

Davis, J. Clark. *The Principal's Guide to Educational Facilities*. Columbus, Ohio: Charles E. Merrill, 1973.

Ewald, William R., Jr. *Environment for Man the Next Fifty Years*. Bloomington: Indiana University Press, 1971.

Tonigan, Richard. "Do-It-Yourself Ideas for Principals Facing Plant Management Problems." *School Management 15* (June 1972), p. 35.

Wheeler, David L. *The Human Habitat*. New York: Van Nostrand Reinhold, 1971.

CHAPTER

15

MANAGING THE MONEY

Introduction
Identifying areas of accountability
Accounting for funds
Raising money for the school
Developing a budget
Cutting costs while maintaining quality
Legally administering the funds
The future

INTRODUCTION

The economic welfare of schools generally follows the economic peaks and valleys experienced throughout the nation. In the early 1980s schools are in the valley of the shadows of recession. For many administrators this means that decisions must be made on which expenditures to cut from an already lean program. Like most American families who are reducing their standard of living, school principals and faculties must reduce some services and programs to cut costs that rise more rapidly than income.

It is difficult to predict how much the schools will have to change because of uncertain or poor economic conditions or how bad the economic situation will become throughout the country before it improves. However, we may safely assume that conditions will improve, and furthermore, that in this period of economic woes competent, fiscal management can help produce programs of higher quality than is currently the case. The challenge to exemplify creative economic and educational leadership despite such a situation confronts every school administrator. This chapter suggests possible ways of answering that challenge. The methods are based on several important assumptions.

1   Principals have limited control over school expenditures and revenues.

2   Principals can influence positively the quality and quantity of instructional programs in the school.
3   Principals are held accountable for expenditure of funds allocated to their school.
4   Administering funds requires that decisions be made regarding which programs and activities of the schools are the most important.
5   During the 1980s public schools will be forced to reduce operational costs in the face of demands for increased expenditures.
6   Creative and innovative leadership on the part of the principal is more necessary during periods of economic decline than during periods of growth.
7   Maintaining and improving quality of instruction is more important than maintaining or expanding quantity of services and programs.

The first commandment for principals in this decade is "Thou shalt survive." In order to obey that commandment, principals must be both very competent fiscal managers and creative instructional leaders. Nobody ever said the job was going to be easy, but it will be satisfying and rewarding for those who meet the challenge. Hopefully, the advice given in this chapter will be of help.

A distinctive characteristic of public education in the United States is its diversity. Consequently, it is very difficult to make helpful generalizations. They usually fit no single situation exactly and consequently provide a somewhat valid excuse for disregarding them. However, the following principles hold promise for almost any situation. Consider them carefully and determine how they might serve to improve the economic situation at your school.

IDENTIFYING AREAS OF ACCOUNTABILITY

Identify what is expected of you as a fiscal manager. Reasonably you can only be held accountable for what you are responsible for controlling. That does not mean that some people may not attempt to hold principals accountable for things beyond their control. Some people are not reasonable, especially where money is concerned. A problem in some schools is the difference of opinion among influential people regarding the principal's fiscal responsibilities. The board of education or the superintendent may not have expressed expectations regarding fiscal responsibilities of principals. Also, a principal's perception of responsibilities may differ from those of parents, students, faculty, and superintendent. What are your fiscal responsibilities as principal? For example, can you influence the amount of revenue available to the school? How? Perhaps you are expected to raise funds, influence tax laws, or make investments. Perhaps your success will be judged largely in terms of the amount of money you bring into your school. On the other hand, raising funds is considered an undesirable role for principals in some school districts.

Are you expected to keep financial accounts for all expenditures and receipts, or are some accounted for at the central office and some in the local schools? What financial reports do you have to make? Are you required to prepare a school budget? If not, should you make one anyway? Are some programs controlled through the central office, the state Department of Education, or the federal government? Which ones do you alone control? What is your responsibility when fiscal control is shared? What is the policy regarding acceptance and accountability of gifts? Is it legal for the school to have its own fiscal fund or make investments? Do you purchase everything through the district office? What kinds of things do you have authority to purchase? What about petty cash? What are the regulations regarding bids? Are you permitted to see salesmen and vendors? What are the regulations regarding vending machines, athletic events, extracurricular activities? The list can go on and on, and none of the questions is unimportant. Unless you know the answers to those listed above, as well as others you have thought of while reading this, you should initiate an immediate search for an authoritative reply to each.

The first place to seek advice is your local school district's written policies and administrative regulations. Maybe a phone call to your immediate supervisor will be sufficient. Find out what is expected of you because regardless of whether you agree or disagree, evaluation of you as an elementary principal is going to be based to a great extent on judgments made regarding your performance as a fiscal manager. Hopefully you will use that role to be an effective instructional leader.

ACCOUNTING FOR FUNDS

There are certain practices that have proven to be sound fiscal accountability measures. They are identified here with the reminder that exactly how you might best accomplish them will depend on the sources and knowledge available to you. All of those listed are essential practices. Establish sound bookkeeping and business practices for all receipts and expenditures regardless of source of funds.

Some principals make the error of considering "local school funds" such as gifts from booster's clubs, PTA's, and those raised by the school as belonging to their school alone, and consequently not subject to public accountability. "I raised this money and it's mine to spend as I wish" is a naive expression, to say the least. That kind of thinking can be disastrous. Regardless of the source of funds coming into the school, they are public monies. Yes, even if the school is a "private school." A good administrator accounts for all receipts and expenditures accurately no matter which receipts and expenditures must be reported to meet express legal requirements. Every penny must be accounted for. There can be no compromise of this principle if the principal is to avoid possible trouble and if effective leadership is to exist, because regardless of the source of funds the money belongs to the public. It may be in the form of a student fee, an appropriation from tax revenues, receipts from a school play, or a gift from an individual or a group. Regardless of the source, funds are placed in the trust of the school administrator to be used for the benefit of the school. They are public monies.

Every principal should strictly adhere to the following generally accepted bookkeeping procedures:

1. *Receipts should be issued when funds are received from any source and a record of that receipt maintained.* If your accounts are "centralized," you are notified in some manner of the amount of money available to the school. Notification may be given in a variety of ways; but even if you receive funds from a central source, some record of receipt should be at the school. Sometimes the transaction is by computer record at the central office when allocations are made centrally, and the school does not receive the money but rather a letter receipt of allocation of funds from the superintendent. Funds continuously coming into a school also include items such as locker rentals, club dues, ticket sales, vending machine sales, picture sales, donations, lunch money, and many others. Issue a receipt for each immediately, post the receipt in the books, and maintain a record. The record should show where the funds came from, the amount, date received, and the disposition. A simple receipt form in duplicate is generally used for funds received through transactions within the school. For funds from intraschool organizations, two sets of records should be kept, one by the organization and one by the principal's office. The principal is responsible for proper accounting of funds by organizations sponsored by the school, and he or she usually deposits funds collected by school organizations in order to ensure that proper records are maintained, even if each school group has its own bank account separate from the school account.

2. *Deposits should be made daily.* There are many ways to arrange this. Some large school districts contract with armored trucks or armored guards to pick up daily bank deposits. Sometimes the principal takes the money to the bank. However the deposit is made, make it daily with proper deposit slips prepared to check against the monthly bank statements. Banks will be glad to cooperate in making arrangements, but check with the central office first. (In fact, most principals new to the school district usually find the procedures explicitly expressed in writing through the central office. However, every school system is different.)

3. *Purchases should be made only on an authorized purchase order approved by the school.* The purchase order is very important. Forms may differ, but the information on them is rather standard. It takes a little time to fill out a purchase order but it is really time saved. Unless principals can account for *all* purchases, they are subject to accusations of misuse of funds. You have a right to expect and to insist on adherence to proper purchasing procedures on the part of everyone in the school.

4. *All payments should be made by check.* There is only one exception to this: petty cash purchases of a small amount (usually $5.00 or less). Even then, abide by the practice stated next.

5. *Petty cash funds should be minimal and receipts must verify each expenditure regardless of how small.* Exactly what can be purchased and the maximum amount to be purchased through petty cash should be determined and communicated to the staff and faculty. The cost of processing checks, purchase orders, and so on should be a factor in determining the maximum amount of a petty cash purchase, but to keep it as small as possible is a sound rule of thumb. Individuals taking money from petty cash should sign a receipt that indicates the purpose for the money, how much was received, and the date. These receipts should be kept on file to protect everyone concerned and for audit purposes.

6. *Two persons should take part in all transactions.* This is most important. No individual should originate a purchase order or issue payment without written verification of the transaction by another person. The verification is usually a signature on the appropriate form or check. All checks *must* have two signatures.

7. *Ticket accounting procedures should be implemented in all activities where admission is charged.* More principals get into difficulty over school ticket sales than almost any other activity. Whatever the practice may have been at your school, make sure that prenumbered tickets are printed that will identify the school and the type of event (various colors for types of events may be used). Records of ticket numbers issued to sellers should be made before tickets are issued. Appropriate ticket tally sheets should be maintained and retained for audit (see Figure 15–1). Records must be maintained to show free admissions. Season tickets

FIGURE 15–1

```
                        Ticket Sales Form

    Name of school: _____
    Date: _____
    Visiting school: _____
    Ticket seller(s): _____

                        _____
                            Ticket Tally

    General admission tickets
        Beginning number: _____
        Ending number:    _____
        Total tickets sold: _____
        Total tickets sold _____X_____ =$ _____
                                 price
                                 per
                                 ticket
    Number of visitors admitted at no charge: _____
                                APPROVED: _____
                                          (Signature of Principal)

                                          _____
                                          (Signature of Ticket
                                           seller(s)

                                          _____
                                          (Signature of Ticket
                                           seller(s)
```

must also be properly numbered and accounted for, and they should be distinguishable from single-event tickets.

8. *Monthly financial reports should be prepared.* You may not be required to make formal financial reports monthly, but your school board should require a periodic report of all financial transactions at the school. Unless you are in a school district in which financial accounting is totally automated, you may spend a great deal of your time making reports to a large variety of groups and agencies. Ways to reduce the number of required reports should be sought. Probably you are reporting the same data but in several different forms. However, a monthly financial report can help you keep up with what is happening. Make the monthly report for your benefit as well as to comply with regulations. The report should show as a minimum: the balance brought forward, amount of funds received, total cash available, expenditures for the period, all obligations (including time payments), and cash balance.

9. *Internal and external audits of all accounts should be made periodically.* Routine internal audits may be conducted by personnel employed by the school board. These audits are important to prepare for annual external audits and to make sure everything is as it should be regarding fiscal accountability. Audits are a protection for the principal, and there should always be an external audit when there is a change in administration of the school central office or a change in the administration of the school.

During the course of an audit the following records should be available:[1]

- The ledger;
- Bank statements and/or savings account book;
- Cancelled checks;
- Receipt books;
- Checkbook;
- Purchase orders and invoices;
- Reconciliation report on ticket sales;
- Schedule of accounts receivable;
- Schedule of accounts payable;
- Monthly financial reports;
- Monthly claims for reimbursement.

Although there may be other objectives, audits usually are made to determine the following:

- Whether financial operations are properly conducted;

---

[1] Alabama State Department of Education, "Audit Guide for Local School Accounting," Bulletin 1978, No. 20, May 1978, p. 4.

- Whether financial reports are presented fairly and accurately;
- Whether the school has complied with applicable laws and regulations.

10. *Assume responsibility for financial planning as well as protecting school funds.* Every school principal should prepare a budget whether it is required or not. A budget is a plan, and its development may serve as a process for making practical improvements in the school program as well as anticipating revenues and expenditures. (See the later section on Developing a Budget.)

Protecting monies placed in the trust of the principal is partially accomplished by making certain that all employees who handle funds are bonded. See your superintendent or the appropriate central office employee about who is bonded or how a bond may be obtained. Most state laws require such bonds, but again, protect yourself by making certain that you are bonded. Chances are you are covered in a "blanket bond" that covers all administrators in the school district. However, if you do not know, check it out.

The ten safeguards listed above should be considered basic for good business practices relating to accountability of funds. Obtaining enough money is another problem that the principal may be expected to solve.

RAISING MONEY FOR THE SCHOOL

Ideally the school is totally supported by funds made available to the school district through the levying of certain taxes and through rentals, investments, fees, donations, and so on. Probably there will not be enough money to do all that the principal thinks should be done at the school. Generally, money will be in short supply for education, and chances are the situation will worsen during the 1980s. You may have to raise money, and perhaps you already take great pride in your money-raising ability. Whatever the case may be, principals probably have no business raising money to carry on the school program. Most principals are capable of being good fund raisers, but they should be spending their time working with students, faculty, staff, and parents in tasks directly related to the instructional program and not assuming the responsibility for adequately funding the school's programs. Consequently you will find little in this chapter regarding how to raise money. Nevertheless, it should be helpful to you if you will keep the following principles in mind as guides to decisions regarding fund raising.

1. Time scheduled for instruction should never be used for fund-raising activities no matter how important the funds. Hold such activities on weekends, at night, or after school is dismissed. Activities that interfere with instruction are always eagerly encouraged by some people, and official sanction of one will open the way for other opportunities to make noninstructional activities a priority objective. Parents and the general public feel that they pay enough taxes and fees not to be bothered with fund-raising activities.

2. Raise money only for those items that contribute to the educational welfare of pupils and are not included in the school budget because of lack of funds.

If the items or activities are worthy, why not budget for them as a part of the regular program?

3. Never use pupils to solicit money for the school. This is exploitation in its worse form. You expose pupils to abuse, raise temptations for those who need money, and in general, teach them how humiliating it is to beg. Frankly, no school program is worth the cost of using pupils to solicit funds. A pancake breakfast, Halloween carnival, book fair, or similar activity can involve parents and others in wholesome and profitable activities. They would be more beneficial, however, if they were held for purposes other than raising funds. (See Chapter 13 on School–Community Relations.)

Door-to-door sales by pupils, however, are usually more harmful than they are beneficial. Citizens resent the door bell ringing and the solicitation, and yet feel guilty if they do not buy something. (After all, they want to be friendly with the neighbor's children.) Children are good salespersons. Most have an honest appeal that wins hearts and dollars. But even in its best light, a sale exploits pupils, and in some places exposes them to real physical danger. There really seems to be little educational justification for such practices.

4. Never sponsor raffles or lotteries of any kind regardless of how well they conform to state or local laws. We know of at least five principals in a nearby state who learned this the hard way during the 1979–1980 school year. The practice of selling chances, even for a good cause, is suspect in many communities and principals may find themselves on the wrong side of public opinion, board policies, and possibly state laws. The money raised is usually not worth the cost.

Although sounding harsh on the surface, it seems reasonable to assume that if the public wants an educational program or activity badly enough, it will find a way to pay for it through acceptable revenue-raising methods that do not exploit pupils, teachers, and administrators. Fewer programs of higher quality are much more desirable than many programs or activities that depend on the fickle charity of the public or the exploitation of elementary-age children.

DEVELOPING A BUDGET

A local school budget is important and the role that the principal may play in its development depends to a large extent on the degree to which the budget-making process in the school district is centralized.[2] School district budgets are usually prepared using predetermined formulas for making allocations to local schools.[3] For example, a certain dollar amount per teacher unit for instructional supplies may be allocated to the school. The principal in such a situation may provide data for the development and utilization of districtwide allocations. Administration of such funds is controlled through guidelines and regulations. Principals may or may not participate in developing these regulations.

The principal is responsible for some particular funds. Identifying those funds

---

[2]Richard A. Gorton, *School Administration Challenge and Opportunity for Leadership* (Dubuque, Iowa: William C. Brown, 1976), p. 123.
[3]*Ibid.*

or expenditures that the principal can plan for is a prerequisite to budget development at the local school level. For example, in local schools the salaries of personnel are determined by the local board of education. The principal probably has little voice in personnel salary determination and does not formulate the payroll each month. Salaries usually account for well over 70 percent of the operating funds spent for education. Consequently, the amount to be planned for expenditure is relatively small when viewed in light of the total amount of funds available for education in a district, but careful planning is essential if sound support of the instructional program is to occur. On the other hand, the principal may have discretion regarding how instructional supply monies are to be spent.

Ideally, the educational program is identified first and estimates are made regarding how much it will cost. Then the amount of money available for the coming fiscal year is estimated. A decision is then made to raise funds, to expand programs, to cut programs, or to reduce expenditures. Realistically the process is not that simple. This is especially true during a period of economic crisis. There are no simple answers. One solution to a financial problem may cause several other problems that are more costly in the long run. For example, to discontinue transportation of pupils by school bus may make thousands of dollars available for other purposes more directly related to instruction. However, the cost of getting pupils to and from school for the average taxpayer would probably increase because buses cost less per pupil to operate than private automobiles. The taxpayer recognizes what comes from his own pocketbook whether it goes to the school before it is dispersed or goes directly from his pocket to the gas station attendant.

Budgets are made for the purpose of planning wisely for revenues and expenditures over a given period of time, usually 12 months. The period may be a calendar year, January 1 to December 31, or a fiscal year as determined by the state legislature.[4] There may be several levels of budget development (state board of education, local board of education, local school, classroom). All levels are interrelated and budgets made at each level should reflect the best educational and fiscal planning possible for the wise use of available resources. Obtaining the most education possible from every dollar spent should be a goal common to all organizational levels.

The following general principles should guide the budget-making process.[5]

1. Budgets should be considered in terms of their long-range consequences as well as plans for the current year.

For example, if the cost of duplicating continues to rise, should the current duplicating methods be retained, or should a five-year plan be developed with the teachers?

2. All of those people directly affected by the budget should have some voice in making budget decisions if they are capable of providing relevant information that will affect the decisions made.

Pupils may or may not provide needed data. Chances are they would not know how to respond to a direct question regarding budgetary need. They may

---

[4] K. Forbis Jordan, *School Business Administration* (New York: Ronald, 1969), p. 110.
[5] *Ibid.* These principles were derived from those stated by Jordan but have been revised somewhat to apply more to the local school level.

express needs, however, without knowing a budget is in the making. For example, they may informally indicate the need for another water fountain on or near the playground. Data may be generated in a number of ways, but some organized means for involving faculty and staff in resolution of budget issues at the school should exist.

3. Decisions relating to the budget should be based on true assessments of educational program needs, fiscal resources, and pertinent statutory limitations.

Sometimes these three factors conflict. For example, there may be a great need for parent-education classes at the school but no money to pay for janitorial service at night. Policies may restrict the use of schools. How important is the program in relation to other programs and activities? What takes priority? What is realistic?

4. Sound business practices should be observed throughout the formulations and administration of the budget.

See the ten recommended business practices on preceding pages. Pay special attention to time-payment accountability to make certain the law is not violated. For example, in some places it is illegal to carry a debt into the next fiscal year.

5. The budget should be viewed as a guide to permit operational flexibility and not as a straitjacket to educationally sound utilization of resources.

Planning is an academic exercise if the decisions made are constantly changed. Nevertheless, no one can foresee conditions and circumstances to the extent that planned expenditures will coincide exactly with actual expenditures. Also, changes always occur in the program as the school year progresses. Do not be guilty of letting the "tail (budget) wag the dog (program)."

6. Determine the leeway you have as a principal in administering the budget.

There are some aspects of administration that principals are usually glad to leave to the central office, and others that require local school decisions. Traditions, policies, and regulations differ among school systems. Check with your superintendent. Do not assume that "they won't let us" when an unusual but needed expenditure arises. You may be surprised at how much leeway you do have in administration of fiscal resources.

7. Budget appraisal or evaluation is a shared responsibility of the school board, central office staff, principals, faculty, staff members, and interested lay citizens.

An attitude of "we're all in this together" will pay dividends in ideas, better public relations, and professional understanding. The budget is not a private document; it is public information. Welcome and even invite appraisal as the year progresses as well as immediately before the final budget is adopted.

More careful financial planning is essential when funds are in short supply while needs remain the same or have increased. In such periods it may be practical to make program determinations after the amount of revenue has been decided. This order of decision making is contrary to sound administrative budget making in a period of economic growth, but is probably a more realistic way to establish necessary priorities. In brief, the budget-making process may begin with a detailed study of the current fiscal year budget and actual expenditures. The objective would be to cut current expenditures without doing harm to the instructional program.

Regardless of where the cutting process starts, decisions regarding program costs and quality are going to have to be made.

Sound budget development is difficult, if not impossible, to achieve without a reasonably accurate estimate of program costs. Most school districts are developing program budgets rather than traditional line-item budgets in order to relate expenditures to programs. Line-item budgets identify expenditure estimation in terms of functions rather than programs. For example, transportation, current operating expense, capital outlay, and instruction are functions and are some of the acceptable budget categories more or less standardized throughout the United States.[6]

Recently school districts have moved to program analysis for estimating expenditures. These program-based plans and estimates are called by many names, but the most commonly used term is the acronym, PPBS; Planning, Programming, Budgeting System. Other terms are ERMS, Educational Resources Management System; PPBES, Planning, Programming, Budgeting, Evaluating System; and EPMBS, Educational Program Management and Budgeting System. Richard Gorton has summed up the differences between the two approaches to budget development as follows:[7]

PPBS		The traditional approach
Stages:		Stages:
1 Assess educational needs.	1	Ascertain teacher needs in the area of supplies, books, and so on.
2 Define educational objectives and the criteria and methods to be used in evaluating the objectives.	2	Determine the merits of teachers' budget requests on the basis of perceived need.
3 Determine programs and priorities to achieve objectives.	3	Estimate the cost of teacher requests.
4 Ascertain and cost-estimate the resources needed to carry out programs.	4	Organize the budget around categories of needs, such as instructional supplies, and books.
5 Organize the budget around program areas and objectives.		

Program budgeting is based on an ability to identify program objectives and to make estimates of what the costs would be to achieve adequately those objectives. Effectively developing a program budget is a time-consuming process requiring the total school faculty and staff. Salary and nonsalary items spent on each program must be determined. Figure 15–2 shows instructions and forms for

---

[6]The U.S. Office of Education and state department of education make variations in the categories frequently. The problem is having the same meaning for terms so financial reports across organizational levels communicate accurately.

[7]Gorton, op. cit., p. 125.

FIGURE 15-2

Allocation of Assigned Time for Administrators - Support Services

A. The administrator completes the following:

1. Enter name and name of building where office is located.

2. Determine the percentage of time devoted to each job area and enter same in "Percent of Time" Column. Add additional job area(s) as required.

   Note: In determining the percentage of time for each job area, it is recommended that such allocation be based upon the assigned time - the length of time that an administrator is required to be on duty. If an administrator is not employed on a full-time basis, the business office will prorate the salary. If part of the assigned duties involve teaching on a part-time basis, Form 1 should be completed for that portion.

3. Total the percent of time column - result should be 100.0%.

4. Enter goal(s) for each job area according to the activities completed.

   Note: If the instructional program design is changed later, it may be necessary to change the goal(s) for one or more job areas.

B. The business manager completes the following:

1. Enter salary, cost of fringe benefits and the total of same. If part of the individual's compensation is for non-administrative duties, prorate the salary according to the assignment.

2. Compute cost for each job area utilizing the figures in the percent column.

3. Total the cost column to determine if the total equals the cost of the salary and fringe benefits.

FIGURE 15-2 (continued)

ALLOCATION OF ASSIGNED TIME
(ADMINISTRATORS -- SUPPORT SERVICES)

Name: _____ Building: _____

Salary: _____ Fringe Benefits: _____ Total: _____

CODE	GOALS	JOB AREA	#students served	PERCENT OF TIME	COST
		Curriculum Development			
		Staff Training			
		Media Services			
		Other ( )			
		Other ( )			
		Community Relations			
		Negotiation Services			
		Staff Relations			
		State and Federal Relations			
		Other ( )			
		Other ( )			
		Fiscal Services			
		Other ( )			
		Other ( )			
		Facilities Acquisition and Construction Services			
		Other ( )			
		Other ( )			
		Operation and Maintenance of Plant Services			
		Other ( )			
		Other ( )			
		Pupil Transportation Services			
		Other ( )			
		Other ( )			
		Food Services			
		Other ( )			
		Planning, Research, Development and Evaluation Services			
		Informational Services			
		Other( )			
		Staff Services			
		Other( )			
		Data Processing			
		Other( )			
		Community Services			
		Other( )			

FIGURE 15-2 (continued)

TEACHER/TIME ALLOCATION
(TWO-WEEK WORKSHEET)

TEACHER _____
TEACHER NO. _____
GRADE _____
COST CENTER _____ (School)

PROGRAM	PROGRAM CODE	DATE / Indicate Time in Minutes	Total Time by Program	Remarks

Daily Total

FIGURE 15-2 (continued)

Individual School Summary of Salaries and Fringe Benefits by Job Areas (Teachers and Instructional Aides)

Name of School: _____

Name of Teacher or Aide	Language Arts	Reading	Career Education	Dramatics	Foreign Language	Mathematics	Music	Science	Social Science	Arts - Crafts	Health and Sports

FIGURE 15-2 (continued)

			Elementary School		Middle or High School		High School		Other	
ALLOCATION OF ASSIGNED TIME TEACHER OR INSTRUCTIONAL AIDE			Grades ___ to ___		Grades ___ to ___		Grades ___ to ___		Grades ___ to ___	
CODE(S)	GOAL(S)	JOB AREA	PERCENT OF TIME	COST	PERCENT OF TIME	COST	PERCENT OF TIME	COST	PERCENT OF TIME	COST
		Language Arts								
		Reading								
		Business								
		Career Education								
		Dramatics								
		Foreign Language								
		Mathematics								
		Music								
		Science								
		Social Science								
		Arts-Crafts								
		Health & Safety								
		Home Economics								
		Physical Education								
		Vocational Education								
		Other( )								
		Other( )								
		Other( )								
		Gifted & Talented								

Name ___ School ___ Grade(s) Taught or assignment ___ Or Ages Taught or assignment ___ Or Subject(s) Taught or assignment ___ Salary or wages ___ Fringe Benefits ___ Total ___

costing salaries by programs.[8] Personnel must complete a time study. Line-item budgeting is easier to accomplish, but it tells little, if anything, regarding specific instructional programs. Despite the difficulty, it is highly probable that a type of program budgeting will become commonly accepted practice throughout the country before the end of this decade. Public demands for educational accountability based on program results and the mass production of the minicomputer are but two of the developments that will contribute to this development.

In practice it is desirable to develop budgets that indicate both program and line items. Forms used in such planning are sometimes called crosswalks because they combine two types of accounting systems: line-item and program accounting.

Figure 15-3 is an example of a crosswalk based on a State Accounting Code for line items and a Program Account Code.[9] Under the column "Account Code (State)" the numbers refer to functional categories or line items on the state budget and financial report forms. Totals in the extreme right hand column will be line-item totals as used in a traditional budget. Totals at the bottom of the form will be estimated expenditures of programs.

Regardless of many claims to the contrary, both traditional line-item budget categories and program categories are desirable. There are times when reports and appraisals by program are essential. At other times the traditional categories are desired. Use both. A crosswalk helps.

---

[8] Alabama Education Study Commission, "A Manual for Development of a Program Management and Budgeting System," Montgomery, Ala., July 1977, p. 65.
[9] *Ibid.*

FIGURE 15-3

Crosswalk Example

Program Expenditure Budget-Work Sheet-1

System

INSTRUCTIONAL DETAIL	Account Code (State)	PROGRAM									Total
		Comm.	Math	Sci.	So.Sci.	Arts	V-C Ed	H,S&PE	SP Ed	ROTC	Other	

Day Sch./Basic Ed.:

Salaries
Kind. Teachers
Elem. Teachers
H.S. Teachers
H.S.Voc. Teachers
Voc. Rehab.
Exceptional Pre-School
Other

Materials
School Library Resources
Sch. Supp. & Other Exp.
Sch. Mat. & Other Exp.
Other Instruc. Mat.
Free Textbooks
Voc. Supp. & Other Exp.
Exceptional Pre-School

TOTAL:

Summer School:

TOTAL:

CUTTING COSTS WHILE MAINTAINING QUALITY

Cutting costs while maintaining quality instructional programs in periods of rising inflation and sinking recession appears impossible; and although you may receive "pep talks" from time to time from politicians and others, it is at best a most difficult objective to accomplish. Several articles and references are listed at the end of this chapter that will provide some useful hints and good ideas. Your staff and faculty can usually come up with others also. In this period of economic down-turns and the decline of public support for education you probably need all the help you can get, for chances are your school will not escape the "crunch."

Although there are no simple solutions, the following steps may help in your efforts to cut costs while maintaining quality:

1. *Identify those fiscal resources over which you have some control.* This may take a little time, and you will probably be surprised at how much you do control at the school. A large amount of money is "in and out," that is, collected for a purpose and spent for that purpose. In some cases, considerable cash accumulates from time to time.

It should be noted that the suggestion is made to look at revenue first before considering cuts in spending. You must know what you can exercise control over.

2. *Identify costs of programs, activities, and functional line items that you*

influence as principal or as a member of the school staff and faculty. There is probably little you can do about wages and salaries, but you may be able to cut the electric bill. Make a list of those items and programs where you, the faculty and staff of the school, and pupils, can make a difference.

3. *Collect practical ideas for cutting costs of specific items and programs.* You have a lot of creative people working with you. Gather their ideas. Make the cost-cutting an educational experience for pupils. They need to learn values like thrift, and involving them can provide great benefits in public relations.

4. *Keep the purposes of the expenditures in mind.* Cutting costs is a great idea, but remember that the objectives of the school must be reached. For example, do not cut out teaching supplies and materials. Some teachers may waste such materials and that should be stopped, but do not hinder the instructional process. Remember your goals and objectives.

5. *Prioritize the strategies for cutting costs.* Pick a few places to start that appear to be most beneficial to all concerned. Maybe energy conservation, which will possibly not harm the quality of the school programs, is a good idea to try first. Such projects have proven to be valuable instructional programs in some schools. Consequently, the benefits come from two sources: reduced expenditure and improved curricula.

6. *Give the ideas an enthusiastic trial over a period of time.* Usually reducing costs means the school "family" has to change its behavior and perhaps some traditions. This is difficult and probably will not take place without complaints and possibly some arguments on the part of a few people, even if they agree to give it a try. Time is required for new habits and traditions to become accepted. For example, one strategy to cut duplication and paper costs for classroom materials is increasing the use of transparencies and overhead projectors rather than using so many handouts and worksheets. This calls for changed teaching techniques. There will be some who will try it once and say "See, I told you it wouldn't work." Be patient. Who knows, maybe they will be right.

7. *Keep accurate records of costs before, during, and after trying a cost-cutting strategy.* These records need not be elaborate, but they do need to show whether greater cost-effectiveness has occurred or not. They may or may not correspond to existing accounting forms and procedures used in the school system.

8. *Publicize your efforts.* Success has a tendency to create more success, or at least more effort, but the failures are as important as successes. They provide sound evidence of justification for continued levels of expenditure if they truly show that quality will suffer when cost is cut.

Another useful tip is to refrain from talking about savings unless you can demonstrate some cut in expenditures. Changes and the cuts will not reduce the number of dollars in a period of inflation. Just to refrain from increasing the dollar amount in a period of high inflation means reduction in costs somewhere.

LEGALLY ADMINISTERING THE FUNDS

The principal is usually responsible for making sure that the school operates within the budget allocations authorized by the school board. Monthly financial reports generally are required by the central office as evidence that the financial planning reflected in the budget document is accurate or in error.

Most school boards are very specific about principals' fiscal responsibilities and the quantity and nature of financial reporting to local, state, and federal levels. The amount of money coming into and out of the local school in any one year can be very large indeed. Student and extracurricular activities include admission to plays, concerts, athletic events, school fairs and carnivals, gifts, and commissions for sales of such things as school pictures, student newspaper, and other items. As has been mentioned earlier, the principal should be aware of the fact that regardless of source, the monies collected and distributed at the school are *public* monies and must be accounted for in the same manner used to account for other funds in the school district.[10]

It should be remembered that an appropriation from school funds is void if it was made to cover an illegal expenditure. Appropriations "may be made only for purposes expressly authorized or necessarily implied by the statutes."[11] For example, if a principal makes an unauthorized or illegal purchase the school district is not legally obligated to cover the cost.

Make certain you are knowledgeable about the status regarding the administration of school funds. Almost all principals are very honest persons and would not intentionally misuse school funds. However, ignorance of the law is no excuse if illegal acts are committed. Some other specific legal points regarding collection and administration of local school funds are as follows:[12]

1   Pupils may be charged incidental fees for expendable materials, locker rental, and so on, but a tuition fee for general support of the school program is violation of the constitutional guarantee of free public schooling.

2   School funds may be expended only for purposes authorized expressly or by implication by the statutes.

3   Money collected for one fund cannot be diverted to another unless the statutes so provide.

4   Unless a statute specifically prohibits it, a board of education may transfer funds from one budget category to another provided the total appropriation is not exceeded.

5   A board of education is not bound by purchases made by a school superintendent or a school principal and can refuse to ratify an administrator's purchase.

---

[10]There have been a number of court decisions on this, but for a very clear statement of legal responsibilities as interpreted by the courts, see *The Law and Public School Operation*, 2d ed., by Leroy J. Peterson, Richard A. Rossmiller, and Marlin M. Volz (New York: Harper & Row, 1978), pp. 172–178.
[11]*Ibid.*
[12]*Ibid.*

THE FUTURE

Judging from past experience it is likely that controls, restraints, reports, audits, public hearings, and accounting methods and forms will increase in importance and demand increasing attention of school principals. Automation and the use of minicomputers will become common throughout the country as hardware costs continue to decline and software computer programs become more prevalent. Wise administrators will begin to use the computer whenever possible to provide data for financial planning and to account for funds more accurately and efficiently.

Changes are already underway to revise the ways states distribute state funds for use by local school districts. These new disbursement formulas will be accompanied by new accounting and reporting procedures as well as new requirements for the budget-development process. The trend toward consolidation of fiscal affairs in the central office of local school districts will continue. At the same time local school principals will be increasingly involved in establishing priorities for programs and expenditures.

The instructional practices, roles, and functions of the schools will continue to change as resources become scarce. There may be a return to the neighborhood school concept, rearrangement of the school year, and increasing specialization of roles of staff and faculty. Opportunities for creative leadership in administering and accounting for funds will continue to increase. As these things happen, principals' roles will become more important than ever before. They will remain the key to the efficient and effective use of fiscal resources.

SUGGESTED READINGS

Brown, Oliver S., et al. "All Kinds of Ways to Cut Costs." *American School Board Journal*, May 1959, pp. 17–25.

Hirsch, Harvey D. "Are You Really Serious About Cutting Costs?" *Nation's Schools* 88(1), July 1971, pp. 37–38.

McNeill, John D. "Think Shrink: Four Approaches to Reducing School Costs." *Phi Delta Kappan* 57(3), November 1975, pp. 191–192.

Willey, Darrel S., and Hander, H. Wesley. "Program Budgeting—A Kindergarten Approach." *School Business Affairs*, June 1970, pp. 143–145.

CHAPTER 16

LIVING WITH A UNION

Introduction
A growing phenomenon
Understanding the territory
The principal as manager
Administering the contract
Coping with a walkout
Future trends
Case study—a special request

Unions have become part of the everyday life of principals in the majority of states. A portion, sometimes a significant portion, of many principals' time is spent on labor relations. This chapter contains material that should be of assistance to principals in this aspect of their jobs.

INTRODUCTION

Although relatively new to public education, the union movement has had a profound impact on school management. In the not too distant past, policy making for schools was largely in the hands of boards of education and school administrators. Where teachers played a part in the policy-making process, the role generally was advisory and minor in nature. That picture has changed. Teachers, indeed employees in general, now play a significant role in school district decision making. School boards and administrators at all levels often must modify their decisions to accommodate to teachers' demands. This is not an altogether negative development, as will be noted later. However, at the same time, contracts with teacher unions frequently contain provisions that severely limit administrators, especially principals, in their management of schools. Sometimes management is so restricted that there is a real question as to whether the beneficiaries of the educational system, the students, are indeed benefited.

Principals need to understand, then, the growth of the union movement in education, the issues at the bargaining table, how to live with a union contract, and how to deal with a work stoppage. These are the subjects of this chapter.

A GROWING PHENOMENON

Trade unions have a long history in the United States. Teacher unions also have existed for many years, although it was not until the early 1960s that the union movement began to have a serious impact on education. The issuance of Executive Order 10988 by President John F. Kennedy in 1962 often is cited as a key to opening the door to collective bargaining by public employees.[1] The President's Order gave permission to employees of the federal government to join an employee organization and required the employing agency to recognize and negotiate with the representative organization. Negotiations were confined to personnel policies and practices and to matters affecting working conditions. Limitations, including prohibiting strikes, were placed on the scope of bargaining.

Executive Order 10988 had no legal effect on the states. However, it had a "moral" effect in that the nation's largest employer of public service employees had sanctioned collective bargaining. Wisconsin, in 1959, was the first state to enact a comprehensive public employees bargaining law, but in the 1960s a number of other states followed suit.[2] By 1979 at least 33 states had enacted some kind of bargaining statute.[3] The movement has been nationwide, with only the South as a region generally failing to enact state laws dealing with negotiations (Florida and Tennessee are exceptions to this generalization). The movement had its impetus in the heavily industrialized states where unions were strong and had a long history. These also are the states that generally have provided the most benefits for teachers. Myron Lieberman calls this a paradox, saying, "bargaining has emerged first and foremost in the states where it has the least justification and has yet to emerge in many states where its justification is comparatively greater."[4]

The teacher union movement was spearheaded by the half-million member American Federation of Teachers (AFT), which is affiliated with the AFL-CIO. The National Education Association (NEA) was slower to embrace collective bargaining. The NEA, with approximately two million members, moved somewhat cautiously

---

[1]Myron Lieberman and Michael H. Moskow, *Collective Negotiations for Teachers* (Chicago: Rand McNally, 1966). pp. 83–84.

[2]*Ibid.*, p. 47.

[3]The number of states with bargaining legislation varies slightly, depending on one's definition of "bargaining." Some sources list as many as 35 or 36 states that have "collective bargaining type" statutes. See Judith Esmay, *Collective Bargaining and Teacher Strikes* (Columbia, Md.: The National Committee for Citizens in Education, 1978), pp. 57–74.

[4]Myron Lieberman, "Eggs That I Have Laid: Teacher Bargaining Reconsidered," *Phi Delta Kappan,* 60(6), 1979, p. 419.

into negotiations. However, once the organization made the decision to enter into collective bargaining, it did so with vigor. Today it is difficult to draw distinctions between the AFT and the NEA when the organizations sit across the bargaining table.

A more recent development in the collective bargaining movement has been the growth of principals' organizations formed for the purpose of negotiating with boards of education. There are several reasons for this development. The AFT has always excluded principals from its membership. The NEA has not formally excluded principals from membership in its local affiliates, although local units have that option. However, in practice principals have felt less and less comfortable in an organization that has as its primary concern teacher welfare. At the same time boards of education generally perceive principals as part of overall management, thus providing another reason for principals not to affiliate with the teacher organization. Finally, principals frequently have been bypassed in the collective bargaining process. Teacher organizations and school boards, without consulting principals, sometimes have reached agreements that have adversely affected local school operation. In such cases principals have found themselves in the position of administering a contract that has provisions inimical to sound school management.

For these reasons principals gradually have drawn together in the effort to protect and advance their own specific interests. The development of negotiating units composed of principals has been most noticeable in large cities. The movement, like its counterpart among teachers, can be expected to spread.

Although the union movement in education has bordered on being pervasive, there are still thousands of teachers and administrators who remain outside. Can school districts that currently do not have collective bargaining remain untouched? There is no ready answer to that question. States can by law prohibit collective bargaining by public employees. However, social, economic, and political forces can interact to cause repeal or modifications of such laws. Perhaps another way of approaching an answer to the question is to ask another question: Can school districts in areas where there is no collective bargaining make unions unnecessary?

The teacher bargaining movement has been characterized by two strong thrusts. The first is that teacher unions have focused strongly on issues of economic benefit to teachers. There has been a heavy emphasis on salaries, fringe benefits, and working conditions, such as class size and length of work day. This is not surprising in view of teachers' relative standing economically with other groups in society. It also is not surprising when one is reminded that a union, or any other organization for that matter, is in the business of representing its clients. A union could not remain in business if it did not seek benefits for its members. This, in a real sense, is the organization's raison d'être.

A second thrust in the bargaining movement has been for teachers as a group to demand a greater role in the policy-making process. A number of issues negotiated at the bargaining table have dealt with curricular and other educational policy concerns.

For school districts that do not now bargain collectively with their employees, the answer to the question posed above *may* be to focus their attention on those issues that may galvanize teachers into desiring union representation. School boards might well make certain that their employees' economic needs are being met to the fullest extent possible. Furthermore, school districts and school principals can make certain that teachers participate meaningfully in decisions that affect them. The last two statements probably appear in every school administration textbook published in the last fifty years. They also are statements that frequently are forgotten or are given halfhearted lip service. Administrators need constantly to be asking questions about teachers' needs, both economic and professional.

Perhaps the best people to answer these questions are the teachers themselves. School districts and principals, regardless of whether or not collective bargaining exists, need to establish the kind of working relationship with teachers that permits the free exchange of ideas and concerns. For example, there is no reason why administrators in areas where unions do not exist cannot meet with representative members of employee organizations and discuss matters of mutual concern. There is no reason why administrators cannot share some of their problems, financial or otherwise, that affect teachers. One purpose of such meetings, conducted on a regular basis (and not just as a crisis is developing), is to establish the type of climate in which it is understood that administrators and teachers ultimately do have common goals. Another purpose is to build a basis for understanding the reasons why certain decisions may have to be made. A third purpose is to establish a structure to resolve the conflicts that will inevitably arise between management and employees. Nothing feeds the rumor mill more, or creates distrust faster between administrators and teachers, than misunderstanding concerning the reasons for decisions or the concealment of information.

At the school level principals can involve teachers effectively in decision making. Teachers should be involved in decisions that affect them personally and in which their expertise can enhance the quality of the decision. This does not mean that principals must abdicate their roles as educational leaders. Nor does it mean that faculty must vote on every matter. The principal, working with teachers, can determine on which matters teachers' advice should be sought and on which matters teachers, or their representatives, should make decisions. Many successful principals have faculty councils or advisory groups that meet regularly and keep the lines of communication open between teachers and principal. Some principals structure such meetings rather formally. Others find it better to use an informal setting, providing for freewheeling discussion. Whatever the preferred mode of operation, it is essential that principals make certain that teachers are free to speak their minds without fear of retaliation. It also is vital that when agreements or decisions are reached as a result of such meetings, principals follow through with action.

Operating with teachers in the manner suggested above is not easy. It is time-consuming, and sometimes it is painfully ego-deflating. However, the payoffs can be enormously rewarding.

If schools involve teachers as has been suggested, will unions be unnecessary? Maybe. But that does not mean that unions will not emerge anyway. The movement that spans nearly 80 percent of the states already may have the momentum to encompass the few states that thus far have resisted strong union organization. Nevertheless, sound administrative practices, instituted at once and in good faith, could retard, modify, and, conceivably, make a union truly unnecessary. For school districts who are in this position, however, the clock is about to strike midnight.

In summary, the collective bargaining movement in education, spawned in the early 1960s, already has significantly affected education. While educators may still argue the merits of unions in education, the fact is they are a part of the education scene and there is little likelihood that they will disappear.

UNDERSTANDING THE TERRITORY

Collective bargaining statutes come in a variety of forms. What may be permitted in one state may be unlawful in another. It is important for the principal to understand that collective bargaining laws do vary from state to state. It is essential to understand the law in one's own jurisdiction.

States' collective bargaining laws may be analyzed in terms of which employees are covered, the scope of negotiations, provisions dealing with unfair labor practices, arbitration procedures, and so forth. In an analysis of 30 state statutes dealing with negotiations, Zirkel found that 14 of the laws dealt with teacher organizations only, 13 states' laws covered all municipal employees and 3 of the states studied had laws that covered all public employees.[5] Twenty-nine of the laws protected teachers from unfair labor practices by boards of education, while only 19 contained provisions regarding unfair labor practices on the part of the teachers' organization.

The scope of negotiations is a vital part of any bargaining law. Zirkel found that the majority of states he studied defined the scope of negotiations in terms of the National Labor Relations Act's "wages, hours, and working conditions" or variations thereof.[6] Such a phrase, without modification, obviously can be broadly interpreted. Some 29 of the states in Zirkel's study specified items on which the board and the employee organization had to negotiate. Fourteen states listed items which were permissive to negotiate; that is, it was permissible to bargain on the issue if both sides agree. Where items are "permissive," neither side is legally obligated to negotiate on the issue. In only 16 of the 30 states did the law list items that were excluded from the negotiations process. Thus, in some states the length of the work day can be negotiated; in others it may not. In some states, the school calendar can go to the bargaining table; in other states it cannot.

Three other kinds of provisions in state bargaining laws deserve mention. Eighteen states have provisions dealing with administrator or supervisory negotia-

---

[5]Perry A. Zirkel, "An Analysis of Selected Aspects of State Teacher-Board Negotiations Statutes," *NOLPE School Law Journal* 6(9), 1976, pp. 9–22.

[6]The National Labor Relations Act of 1935 (Wagner Act) is the basic federal act guaranteeing employees the right to organize and bargain collectively. It was amended by the Labor Management Relations Act of 1947 (Taft-Hartley Act) and the Labor-Management Reporting and Disclosure Act of 1959 (Landrum-Griffin Act).

Figure 16-1
Percent of school district–teacher organization contracts with certain key provisions as of 1975. From Lorraine McDonnell and Anthony Pascal, Organized Teachers in American Schools (Santa Monica, Calif.: Rand, 1979), pp. vi, 12.

Provisions	Percent of Districts with Provision
Grievances subject to arbitration	83
Teacher-evaluation procedures	65
Duration of school day specified	58
Teacher can exclude disruptive student	46
Teacher can refuse assignment outside of subject and grade	27
Maximum class size specified	34
Seniority and credentials determine promotion	32
Specific criteria required for transfer	29
Instructional committee in each school	31
Reduction-in-force procedures	37
Minimum number of aides per classroom specified	29

tions; 7 states permit the strike under specified conditions; and 19 states allow binding arbitration of contract disputes.[7]

Thus, there is no single collective bargaining law. While there are commonalities throughout the various states' laws, there also are many differences. Administrators in general, principals in particular, need to familiarize themselves with their own state's negotiations act. Answers should be sought to questions such as these: What items may or may not be negotiated? Is provision made for administrators in the bargaining process? Is the strike permitted? If not, what are the penalties? What is an unfair labor practice? If a dispute cannot be settled, what are the provisions for fact-finding, mediation, and arbitration?

Just as important as understanding state law governing the bargaining process is understanding the trends in issues being negotiated between school boards and teacher organizations.

A study conducted by the Rand Corporation[8] suggests that bargaining by teacher organizations follows a distinct pattern. "Teacher organizations first bargain over and obtain increases in salary and fringe benefits; they then move on to working conditions and job security, and only last to issues of educational policy."[9] This generalization is underscored by the data shown in Figure 16-1, that reveal the percentage of school-district teacher organization contracts containing key noncompensation items as of 1975.[10] It will be noted, as an interesting contrast, that a grievance procedure appeared in 83 percent of the contracts, while provisions for an instructional policy committee in each school appeared in only 31 percent of the contracts.

[7]*Cuebook: State Education Collective Bargaining Laws* (Denver, Colo.: Education Commission of the States, 1978), as noted in *Phi Delta Kappan* 60(6), 1979, p. 473.
[8]Lorraine McDonnell and Anthony Pascal, *Organized Teachers in American Schools* (Santa Monica, Calif.: Rand, 1979).
[9]*Ibid.*, p. vii.
[10]*Ibid.*, pp. vi, 12.

While there has been a pattern to the development of contract provisions, it is clear that as social and economic conditions change, new issues will emerge and old issues will shift in order of priority. For example, reduction-in-force procedures were spelled out in only 11 percent of contracts in 1970, but appeared in 37 percent of contracts five years later, reflecting emerging teacher concerns with declining school enrollment and its effect on their jobs. The Rand study, which should be read carefully, indicates that bread-and-butter issues have been high-priority items with teacher organizations. Secondary issues have been working conditions and job security. Only when these kinds of concerns have been dealt with in some manner do teachers turn to policy issues.

THE PRINCIPAL AS MANAGER

Over time more and more of the items appearing in negotiated contracts have affected the work of the principal. A cursory look at Figure 16-1 will reveal many items that directly affect local school operation. For example, note the provisions on student exclusion and teacher assignment. Collective bargaining has meant less latitude for principals in managing their buildings. At the same time that this has been occurring, principals, especially at the elementary-school level, have experienced considerable anxiety and ambivalence concerning the entire collective bargaining process.

As pointed out earlier, most boards of education and superintendents perceive principals as part of management. In most school districts principals are represented on the management team. Principals advise the district on the potential effect of specific items on local school operations. Where this is the case, principals should study contract proposals carefully, asking such questions as:

1 How will the demand affect the school program?
2 Will a reduction in teachers' work hours affect extracurricular activities?
3 Will teachers' classroom and supervisory duties be reduced?
4 Will the curriculum be affected in any manner?
5 Are there any demands that will limit the principal's ability to make effective decisions?
6 How will the teacher-evaluation procedures affect the school?

This list of questions is not intended to be exhaustive. It is intended to suggest that principals should be keenly aware of contract proposals and be prepared to advise their school boards accordingly.

Although school boards may view principals as part of the management, many principals wonder where they fit into the organization. Principals often have perceived the collective bargaining process as meaning an erosion in their leadership. Boards of education have reached agreements with teacher unions in some instances without consulting principals, then left principals to administer contracts that have seriously impaired the principal's authority. In some school districts, particularly the very large, principals are so removed from top management that it is very difficult for them to feel that they are a part of it. Indeed, they often feel that they have little influence with the central administration. Finally, a significant number of principals, particularly elementary-school principals, believe that being identified as part of management adversely affects their relationships with teachers in their schools with whom they have to work on a day-to-day basis.

This concern may or may not be justified. It certainly is not axiomatic that collective bargaining must drive a hard wedge between teachers and principals. Principals need not retreat to their offices and become "operators by the book" once a union contract is signed. Effective, creative leadership and positive relationships with staff can be maintained and developed. In this connection it should be pointed out that principals who, prior to union contracts, had good working relationships with their teachers, including the use of curriculum or instructional-policy committees, were more successful in managing union contracts than those principals who in a sense already were isolated from their staffs. This suggests that positive working relationships, once established, can be enduring. It also suggests, as was noted in a previous section of this chapter, that principals can do a great deal to build good working relationships with their teachers.

Feelings of ambivalence on the part of many principals may be part of the reason for the growth of unionism among principals, alluded to earlier in this chapter. Although not yet as widespread as teacher unions, over 1000 local administrator union organizations now exist.[11]

Resrarch indicates that, despite possible feelings of ambivalence toward collective bargaining pe se, or their role in the process, principals play a key role in determining whether or not collective bargaining works in the school building.[12] As pointed out earlier in this section, as collective bargaining has developed, more and more of the items in contracts have affected management of local schools. Inevitably, then, the principal has emerged as a key figure in contract administration.

ADMINISTERING THE CONTRACT

In administering a contract, the first step is to study and understand it. There is no substitute for a principal's own personal knowledge of the contract. During the course of the school year, many questions are likely to arise over contract provisions. Contract language is sometimes not precise and honest disagreements will result. There will be persons in the school, particularly the union's building representative, who will be happy to interpret the contract for the principal. Unfortunately, some persons may not be disinterested parties. The principal should call upon the central office for advice on contract interpretation as necessary, but avoid permitting the union or its representatives to do it for him.

It is important, too, for a principal to understand the role of a building

[11]*Ibid.*, p. 49.
[12]*Ibid.*, p. 81.

representative and to establish a reasonable working relationship with that person.[13] The building representative is not the the administrator of the school. That is the principal's role. The representative is there to serve his or her clients, the teachers. This is the function expected of the union's representative. Therefore, the principal should not expect the building representative's values to coincide with those of management.[14] Because of the nature of their positions, the principal and union representative often will reflect different perceptions of the same problem. For a principal to expect the union representative always to share the principal's point of view is to invite disappointment. Principals must bear in mind that union leaders are obligated, despite their personal feelings, to represent their clients. If a teacher brings a grievance, then the representative must attend to it. In such a situation neutrality may be the most a principal can expect from a union representative.

Understanding the roles of the local union leader can be of help to the principal in developing a positive working relationship with that person. It will assist the principal in knowing what to expect when problems emerge. In order to further develop a working relationship with the building representative, it would be well for the principal to schedule regular meetings for the purpose of sharing mutual concerns and discussing any problems or issues that may be of concern to teachers. This can forestall major problems. In these discussions it must be remembered that the principal cannot give more, nor can the union representative accept less, than the contract permits.[15] Both sides are obligated by the terms of the contract.

The heart of the collective bargaining process is the grievance procedure.[16] Grievances may arise over an interpretation, application, or alleged violation of a contract. The procedures for resolving a grievance that are set forth in the contract must be followed. Grievances should be submitted in writing and contain specific details and facts. It is good practice for principals to make their responses short and to the point. If the principal's judgment is appealed, then the principal can be prepared to support the decision in greater detail. Principals should avoid permitting personal feelings to cloud their judgment in responding to grievances. Objectivity must be maintained.

It is occasionally necessary for management to correct employee conduct in some manner. This should be handled judiciously, of course. A written reprimand is strong criticism, so it should be undertaken with discretion. If a reprimand is filed, then both the employee and the union should be notified. "Only that which the union can protest constitutes disciplinary action."[17]

In administering a contract, the principal must first of all understand its provisions. The principal must also understand that he or she should not in any way modify the terms of the contract. If in doubt about the interpretation of a provision

---

[13]Much of this discussion is drawn Harry Kershew, "After You've Signed a Contract, What's Next?" in J. Donald Herring and Joseph A. Sarthory, Eds., *Collective Bargaining Techniques in Education* (Austin, Tex.: Mesa, 1980), pp. 195–201.

[14]*Ibid.*, p. 197.
[15]*Ibid.*
[16]*Ibid.*
[17]*Ibid.*, p. 200.

in the contract, the principal should obtain advice from the central office. The principal must make every effort to understand the role of union representatives and not expect behavior that is antithetical to this role. Finally, if a problem results in confrontation, the principal must try to remain calm when others' tempers are rising. Maintaining self-control when other persons are losing it can be a great asset to a principal who is faced with a confrontation over an employee grievance.

COPING WITH A WALKOUT

Increasingly school districts have had to deal with teacher strikes. Often management personnel have been unprepared to cope with the complex problems associated with either the threat of a walkout or an actual strike. Some of the problems administrators have encountered have been psychological in nature. People behave differently in stressful situations. That very pleasant fourth-grade teacher down the hall who has a cheery "Good morning" for everyone every day may evince dramatic changes in personality on the way to the picket line. It is understandable that principals have been shocked, not only by the fact that teachers walk out, but also by some teachers' behavior just prior to or during the strike. This is to suggest not that all teachers on strike would be guilty of unseemly behavior but that strikes might spawn some actions on the part of teachers with which principals ought to be prepared to deal.

For example, as the possibility of a walkout grows, the principal might find that attendance at faculty meetings declines. Or teachers may attend the meetings, but sit in silence. Teachers may enter or leave buildings en masse. There may be a "slowdown"; that is, teachers will perform only required duties and at minimum levels. There may be efforts on the part of teachers to solicit support from students, telling students the teachers' side of the story. It may be suggested to students that they defy substitute teachers or that substitute teachers' assignments will not be accepted by regular teachers when the strike is over.[18]

Once a strike has begun the principal may expect additional problems. Essential items such as lesson plan books, seating charts, attendance books, and curriculum materials may mysteriously disappear. Desks, cabinets, and lockers may be locked, with keys missing. Rumors will proliferate. Board members and administrators may receive telephone calls at all hours. Communications may be disrupted. There may be harrassment of substitutes or of any person who crosses the picket line. The school's parking lot may be a target for tire slashers and fender benders.[19]

If the decision is made to keep the schools open, then the school district and its administrators ought to be prepared in advance to deal with as many eventualities as possible. The following suggestions for planning have been drawn from A. Bernard Hatch and Judith Esmay.[20]

---

[18]A. Bernard Hatch, "How to Keep Your Schools Open During a Strike," in Herring and Sarthory, *op. cit.*, pp. 223–231.
[19]*Ibid.*
[20]*Ibid.* and Esmay, *op. cit.*, pp. 32–33.

1. Review all pertinent legislation and legal questions with the school board attorney.
2. Review all school board policies.
3. Arrange for substitutes—teachers, food service workers, persons able to transport children. (Make certain volunteers are warned that they may be subject to pressure by strikers.)
4. Encourage parents to arrange car pools in the event bus transportation is halted. (Arrange for appropriate insurance.)
5. Organize a public information center.
6. Establish an internal communication system. Have a back-up telephone system, since strikers have been known to tie up regular systems. Parents can develop a telephone tree so that every parent can be notified quickly of new developments.
7. Arrange for early morning announcements on radio and television stations.
8. Request that morning newspapers have a box on the front page for school information.
9. Develop a comprehensive security plan to include:
    a. Planning with police and fire officials and utilities in order to know what to expect from each;
    b. Employing private security personnel to protect personnel, buildings, and equipment on a 24-hour basis;
    c. Providing keys for principals for immediate access to all parts of their buildings.
10. Determine what all service employees intend to do regarding honoring picket lines.

A strike is never a pleasant prospect. However, some of the trauma can be reduced by careful advance planning. Principals should be a part of that planning. They also need to prepare themselves for dealing with the stress that accompanies a strike.

FUTURE TRENDS

Teacher unions are here to stay, at least for the foreseeable future. In all likelihood the union movement will continue to spread, and in a few years teacher unions will exist in virtually every state. As a result there will be a growth of teacher influence in decision making, particularly in curricular and educational policy matters.

The two major teacher unions, the AFT and NEA, will continue to enroll most of the nation's teachers and to exercise the most influence at the bargaining table. The probability that the AFT and NEA will merge is not high. If economic conditions worsen, the two organizations may from time to time form alliances on specific issues or in selected locations. However, the two organizations will be likely to continue to maintain their separate identities.

Concomitantly administrators, too, will continue to be drawn toward union-type activity. Continued erosion of authority to teachers, inadequate communication with the superintendent and board of education, a lack of impact on decision making, and the desire for salary improvement and additional fringe benefits are some of the factors that will influence principals to move toward unions.[21] It is possible that this trend can be reversed, but significant changes in administrative leadership at the central office level will be required for this to occur.

In the immediate future key issues in collective bargaining will be salaries and fringe benefits, the scope of negotiations, and the teachers' role in educational policy making.[22] Economic conditions will dictate that wages continue as a high-priority item for teachers. The scope of negotiations, what may or may not be negotiated, will continue to be a critical issue. Unions continually press to expand the number of items that can be placed on the bargaining table, exerting pressure on local school boards and on state legislatures. In the view of some union leaders, everything should be negotiated. Educational policies, in the perception of the AFT's Albert Shanker and the NEA's Terry Herndon, fall within the collective bargaining process.[23]

Principals will continue to play a key role in collective bargaining because it will be their responsibility to make the contract work. "The inevitability of collective bargaining implies that principals can best do their jobs by accepting the contract, working with teachers to adapt it to the school, and employing it as a mechanism for better management and teacher participation."[24]

CASE STUDY—A SPECIAL REQUEST

Tom Phillips has been a fifth-grade teacher at Clark Elementary School for eight years. Tom has been one of the school's most respected and well liked teachers.

During the lunch period Tom stops at the office of the Principal, Bettye Williams. He tells Bettye that an emergency has developed and that he would like to leave school at 2:30 P.M., an hour before the time teachers generally are permitted to leave. "My students will be with the music consultant," he explains, "so my classes will be covered, Bettye. I really need to leave."

Bettye Williams ponders only a moment, then nods. "Go ahead, Tom. And I will check on your class, too, to be sure everything is all right."

All goes well and Bettye has almost forgotten the matter, when two weeks later another teacher, Nancy Blackburn, makes a similar request. In contrast to Tom Phillips, Nancy is among the marginal teachers. She has made several "special requests," mostly for rather flimsy reasons. Bettye has denied most of Nancy's requests in the past and she does not hesitate to deny this request as well, especially when Nancy refuses to tell Bettye why she must leave school early.

[21]William P. Knolster, "Administrative Unionization: What Kind of Solution?" in Herring and Sarthory, *op. cit.*, pp. 251–258.
[22]National School Labor Relations Service, 1979, *1*, pp. 2–3.
[23]*Ibid.*, p. 3.
[24]McDonnell and Pascal, *op. cit.*, p. xi.

One day later Nancy Blackburn is threatening to bring a grievance, using the Tom Phillips incident as a basis. Pertinent sections of the teachers' contract with the board of education are as follows:

> The teachers' workday shall consist of not more than 7 hours and 45 minutes (which shall include a duty-free lunch period), exclusive of such other duties as can be required of teachers by law. . . .
> Teachers may leave the building without requesting permission during their scheduled duty-free lunch periods, provided they clock out by hours and minutes when leaving and clock in by hours and minutes when returning.
> Classroom teachers shall have a duty-free lunch period of at least 40 consecutive minutes.
> Teachers may not leave the building at any other times except with permission of the principal or his or her designee and only in the event of an emergency as determined by the principal or his or her designee.

Can Nancy Blackburn sustain a legitimate grievance? Should Bettye Williams have required more explanation from Tom Phillips? Is the last clause in the contract workable? Would you suggest changes? Should Bettye Williams have excused either Tom or Nancy?

SUGGESTED READINGS

Esmay, Judith. *Collective Bargaining and Teacher Strikes.* Columbia, Md.: The National Committee for Citizens in Education, 1978.

Evans, Max, Knox, Donald M., and Weidenman, Charles F. *Trends in Collective Bargaining in Public Education.* Seven Hills, Ohio: American Association of School Personnel Administrators, 1978.

Herring, J. Donald, and Sarthory, Joseph A., Eds. *Collective Bargaining Techniques in Education.* Austin, Tex.: Mesa, 1978.

Lieberman, Myron. "Eggs That I Have Laid: Teacher Bargaining Reconsidered." *Phi Delta Kappan 60,* 1979, pp. 415–419.

McDonnell, Lorraine, and Pascal, Anthony. *Organized Teachers in American Schools.* Santa Monica, Calif.: Rand, 1979.

National School Public Relations Service (published by the National School Boards Association and the American Association of School Administrators, 1620 Eye Street, N.W., Washington, D.C. 20006).

Pisapia, Joseph R. "Trilateral Practices and the Public Sector Bargaining Model." *Phi Delta Kappan, 60,* 1979, pp. 424–427.

INDEX

A

Abbott, Max, 64, 73
Abend, Allen C., 272
Accessing Needs, 76–80
Accountability, 274–275
Accounting for Funds, 275–279
Achievement, 30
Achievement Tests, 157
Administering Funds, 289–290
Administering the Contract, 299–301
Administration, 2, 16
Administrative Leadership, 17–22
Administrators, 2–3
Adviser-Advisee Ratio, 125
Adviser selection, 125
Air Conditioning, 270
Alabama Education Study Committee, 287
Alabama State Department of Education, 278
Alexander, Kern, 172, 243
Allen, Louis, 40–41, 61
American Association of School Administrators, 243, 268–269, 272
American Federation of Teachers (AFT), 293–294, 303
American Personnel and Guidance Association, 128
American School Counselor Association, 131
Analysis, 87
Anderson, Robert H., 79
Armstrong, David, 166
Assigning Students to Advisors, 124–125
Association for Counselor Education and Supervision, 131
Association of School Business Officials, 248, 272
Association for Supervision and Curriculum Development (ASCD), 9, 61, 117, 145
Auburn (Ala.) Personnel Performance Appraisal System, 219–228
Authority, 5

B

Bad school environment, 264
Bailard, V., 164
Baker, S. B., 140
Baker, Thomas, 258
Ballast, Daniel, 140
Bannister v. Paradis, 169
Barbacobi, Don R., 155
Barnes, Melvin W., 73
Beauchamp, George A., 117
Bemis, Warren G., 61
Biddle, Bruce, 228
Bilingual, 151–154
Bilingual Education Act, 153
Bishop, Leslie, 228
Bland, Carole, 228
Board of Regents v. Roth, 236
Bomb Threats, 187–188
Boocock, Sarane, 203
Boy, A.V., 123
Boyce, A.C., 206
Brandt, Ronald S., 166
Brown, Jeanette, 131
Brown, Oliver, 291
Brown v. Board of Education, 146–147
Buckley-Pell Amendment, 142–144
Burnout poll, 6–7
Burns, James, 26

C

Canter, Lee, 203
Capital Investments, 267–269
Censoring, 182
Center for Applied Linguistics, 153
Changing demands, 4–6, 14
Child abuse, 186–187
Civil Rights Act of 1964, 146
Clearing House, 29
Clelland, Richard, 155
Clinical Supervision, 97–100
Clinical Supervision Model, 85, 97
Cohen, J. J., 140
Collective bargaining, 4, 298–300
Collective entity, 75
Combs, Arthur, 29
Commercial, nonsubject-matter tests, 157
Communication network, 137
Communities, 245–246
Community links, 245–247
Community School Programs, 252
Computers, 15

Conference reporting, 162–165
Conserving energy, 263, 270–271
Consulting, 132
Contract negotiation, 28
Controlling demonstrations, 181–182
Coordinating, 132
Counseling, 122–124, 126, 131–132, 144, 146
Counseling with teachers, 80–84
  proactive, 82–83
  reactive, 83–84
Courts, 167–192
Curricula, 2
Curriculum
  definitions of, 105–108
  goals, 104–105, 107–111
  human resources, 113–114
  improvement of, 114–117
  leadership, 102
  materials, 112–113
  methods, 114
  need for instruction, 103–105, 114–117
  principals, 112–115
Custodial operation schedule, 266–267
Cutting costs, 288–289

D
Damon, Parker, 197–198
Data, 235
Davis, J. Clark, 272
Dealing with the news media, 250–252
Declining enrollment, 2, 4
De Jouvenal, Bertrand, 19
Delegation, 5
Determining objectives and identifying activities, 76
Developing a budget, 280–287
Developing a grading system, 158, 159
Developing discipline, 198–201
Developing your own philosophy, 3, 32
Dinkmeyer, Don, 140
Discipline, 192
Dismissing incompetent staff, 28
"Directory information," 143
Diversity, 2–4
Documenting facts, 234
Drake, Thelbert, 147, 155
Dress codes, 182–183
Drucker, Peter F., 33–34, 38–43, 61
Drug abuse, 169, 183–184
Due process, 147–148, 171, 181, 238
Dunn, Finley Peter, 168
Dykes, Archie R., 29

E
Education, 2–3
Educational and Economic Leadership, 274
Educational innovation, 52–54
Educational Leadership, 101
Education for All Handicapped Children Act of 1975, 146
Elementary and Secondary Education Act (ESEA), 128
Elementary counselors, 128, 131
Elementary principals, 1–14, 20–25, 78, 123
  demands, 1–6, 14
  leader behavior, 17–22
  major problems, 3
  management leadership, 24
  negotiations, 3
  peer relationships, 6
  principal is the key, 22–26
  responsibilities, 2–5, 22–25
  role expectations, 2–6, 41–42
Elementary school, 4
Emotional reactions to evaluations, 209
Enforcing attendance, 172–173
English, Fenwick, W., 106
Environmental conditions, 262
Environmental signs, 261–262
Epstein, J., 140
ESEA, 128
Esmay, Judith, 293, 301–304
Establishing good school environment, 261–264
Establishing priorities, 41–43, 211
Establishing purposes, 134, 207
Evaluating, 77–78, 136–137
Evaluating teachers, 205–206
  three fundamental methods, 206–207
Evaluation forms, 214–218
Evaluation policies, 240
Evaluation purposes, 207
Evaluation system, 239–242
Evaluation techniques, 156
Evaluator/Evaluatee understanding, 208
Evans, Max, 304
Exceptions to attendance, 172–173
Executive Order 10988, 293
External audits, 278
Ewald, William R., 272

F
Family Educational Right and Privacy Act, 142–144
Federal support, 128

Feiber, M., 140
Fiedler, Fred, 26, 71
Field trips, 83–84
First Aid, 185–186
Fiscal managing, 273–291
Fiskel, Andrew, 155
Five action models, 40–41
Five federal statutes, 129
Flanders, Ned, 101
Flanders Analysis Category System, 86–92, 94–97, 100
Flanders Interaction Analysis, 86–92
Fund raising, 279–280

G
Gaff, Jerry C., 78
Gay, L. R., 158
George-Barden Act, 128
Georgia State Department of Education, 265–266
Gephart, William, 212
Gersin, Patricia D., 29
Goldhammer, Robert, 101
Good, Carter, 97
Goodlad, John I., 118, 104
Gorton, Richard A., 73, 104, 243, 262–264, 280, 283
Goss v. Lopez, 181
Governing students, 192–203
Grading students, 158–159
  norm-reference grading, 158
  criterion-reference grading, 158
  percent grading, 159
  future-reference grading, 159
Graff, Orin B., 29
Grievances, 300
Griffiths, Daniel E., 73
Grolelueschen, Arden D., 104
Guarding against wrong decisions, 231–234
Guidelines, 45–47
Guidance Council, 135–136
Guidance program, 19, 127–131, 136–137
Gysbers, Norman, 140

H
Haefele, Donald L., 206
Halpin, Andrew W., 13
Hamacheck, Don E., 61
Hammong, Janice, 194
Handicapped, 146–150
Hanson, Mark E., 61, 65, 70, 72–73, 259
Harris, Ben, 68, 78, 229

Hartsell, Lee E., 233
Hatch, Bernard A., 301–302
Havelock, Ronald B., 101
Heating, 270
Herring, Donald J., 304
Hersey, Paul, 14, 26
Hirsch, Harvey D., 290
Hoover, Kenneth H., 166
Houts, Paul, 22, 78
Howe, Harold, 32
Hudgins, H.C., 181, 191

I
I/D/E/A/, 126
IGE proponents, 126
Implementing the program, 76, 135–136
Improvement programs, 3
Incompetent staff, 4
Individualized education plan (IEP), 148–149, 154–155
Informing pupils and parents, 137
Ingraham v. Wright, 178
In loco parentis, 169–170, 180, 185
Instructional improvement, 77–101
Instructional leader, 78–79, 261, 271
Instructional Needs Survey, 85–86
Instructional programs, 2, 78–79, 134
Instructional supervision, 98
Interaction analysis, 88
Interaction matrix, 90–91
Interior lighting, 270
Internal audits, 278–279
Internal Revenue Code, 142
Involving parents, 196–198

J
Jackson, Reverend Jesse, 22
Job assignments, 267
Job cards, 265–267
Job description, 10–13
Job targets, 212
Jones, Frederic, 199, 203
Jordan, K. Forbis, 172, 263, 281
Journal of Research and Development in Education, 9, 101
Journal of Teacher Education, 73
Joyce, Bruce, 78

K
Keat, Donald, 135
Keller, Ed, 22
Kelly, Joan, 194
Kershew, Harry, 300
Kimbrough, Ralph B., 29

King, Martin Luther, Jr., 152
Klausmeier, Herbert J., 69
Klop, Gordon, 229
Knezevich, Stephen J., 26
Knolster, William P., 303
"Knowledge Base," 16
Kohurt, Sylvester, 203
Kossack, Sharon, 152
Kooper, Bob, 82
Krajewski, Robert J., 3, 52–53, 59–60, 79

L
Ladd, Edward, 193, 198, 200–203
Landers, Thomas, 243
Lao-Tzu, 20
Lau v. Nichols, 151–152, 154
Leadership, 75, 83
  function, 2, 18–19
  positions, 2
  skills, 81
Learning climates, 123
Learning environment, 261–264
Liability for defamation of character, 177
Liability for pupil injury, 174–176
Liability for school personnel, 174–177
Liberman, Myron, 293, 304
Lipham, James M., 26, 61
Lip service, 295
"Local school funds," 275
Lowell, James Russell, 28

M
MacKenzie, Alex R., 45–47
Mager, Robert F., 162
Mahoney, Maureen, 194–196, 203
Mallory, Richard, 200–201
Management
  definition, 13, 19
  function, 13
  guidelines, 6–9
Manager
  beliefs, 29–30
  educational philosophy, 30–34
  guidelines, 45
  improvement process, 37–38
  priorities, 38–43
  skills, 14–15
Managing
  school plant, 261–262, 265, 271
  self, 29–40
  time, 44
Marks, Sir James R., 118
McDonnell, Lorraine, 297, 303–304
McNally, Harold, 78
McNeill, John D., 191

McQuade, Walter, 262
Meigs, Paul, 256
Metz, Stafford, 128
Millman, H. L., 140
Mills, Troy, 21
Mills v. Board of Education, 147
Mitchell, Anita, 131
Molnar, Alex, 118
Moni, Linda, 128
Monthly Financial Reports, 278
Muro, James, 140
Myrick, Robert, 128, 130, 135

N
NAESP Study, 2–4
National Academy Press, 157
National Association of Elementary School
    Principals, 2–6
National Clearinghouse for Educational
    Statistics, 128
National Defense Education Act, 128
National Education Association, 293–294,
    302–303
National Elementary Principal, 6, 181
National Labor Relations Act, 296
National School Board Association, 233
National School Labor Relations Service,
    303
National School Public Relations Service,
    304
Negotiations, 3, 294–301
Newport, M. Gene, 61
Novotney, Patricia B., 100

O
Objective Analysis, 86–92
Observing Instruction, 85–100, 211–212
Occupational Outlook Handbook, 128
Ohlsen, Merle, 124
One-Parent Families, 195, 197–198
Organization
  assumptions, 68–69
  challenges, 64
  roles, 64–68
  selecting team for, 62–63, 72
  structure, 68–70
Outlaw, Helen B., 80–81
Owens, Robert G., 26

P
Paddling Pupils, 177–178
Palmer v. Board of Education, 238
Parental Rights, 142–144, 172
Parents, 2, 4–5, 132, 135, 137–138
Parsons, Frank, 127

Payments, 276
Perceiving, Behaving, Becoming, 101
Petty Cash Funds, 276–277
People v. Jackson, 169
Peterson, Leroy J., 290
Pharis, William L., 2, 4, 7, 19
Pine, G.J., 123
Pinnell, Gay, 123
Pisapia, Joseph, 304
Planning
 changing, 132
 communication, 134
 delineating role functions, 134
 selling of ideas, 134
P.L. 94–142, 146, 147, 149–150, 154–155
Positive Evaluation, 208
Pottker, Janice, 155
Powell, John, S.J., 61
Power Structure, 248–249
PPBS, 283
Preobservation Conference, 99
Preserving Property, 263
Preventing Obsolescence, 267–269
Preventing Vandalism, 269–270
Pride in Schools, 264–265
Principal, 2–11, 13–16, 19–26, 78
Principal as Manager, 298–299
Principals' Code of Ethics, 248
Principals' Decisions, 235
Proactive Counseling, 123–126
Proactive Practices, 82–83, 123
Process Critique, 100
Professional Development, 75
Professional Growth, 75
Protecting Health, 263
Public Support, 245–248
Purchase Orders, 276

Q
Qualifications, 12–13, 24–25
Quander, Nellie, 2

R
Racism, 144–146
Raising Money, 279–280
Rand Corporation Study, 297–298
Range, Dale, 203
Rapport, 97–98
Reactive Practices, 83, 123, 127
Recruiting Volunteers, 255–256
Redefining the Family, 194–196
Rehabilitation Act of 1973, 146
Rich, Dorothy, 196–197
Roe, William, 147

Rossmiller, Richard, 191
Rutherford, Robert B., Jr., 166

S
Sarason, Seymour B., 79
Schaefer, Earl S., 75
Scheduling, 271
School Maintenance, 261–271
Schroder, William, 166
Schumack, Kenneth, 253
Searching Youngsters, 179–180
Secondary Teachers, 130
Section 504 Regulations, 146–151
Self-governance, 201–202
Sergiovanni, Tom, 229
Sexism, 144–146
Shender, Karen, 153
Shertzer, Bruce, 128
Simon, Anita, 87, 101
Smith, Vernon, 118
Staff Development, 75–80
Stanford Teacher Competence Appraisal Guide, 95, 219
Stone, Shelly, 128
Stoops, John A., 32–33
Student Advisory Committee, 138
Student Behavior, 4–5, 28
Student Government, 138
Suspending and Expelling, 180–181
Sutton, Dorothea, 80
Systematic Comprehensive Guidance Program, 131–135

T
Tankard, George, 118
Tannenbaum, Robert, 71
Tanner, Daniel and Laurel, 103, 118
Teacher
 advisor program, 125
 colleagueship, 80
 conferences, 241
 Evaluation Process Checklist, 210–211
 principal committees, 240
 Self-Improvement Model, 85–97
 supervision, 3, 28
 support, 83
 union, 293–294
Tenure, 235–237
Theory into Practice, 18, 101
Thomas, Donald, 229
Thomas, George, 162
Ticket Accounting, 277
Title VII Resource Centers, 153
Title IX, 145–146
Tonigan, Richard, 272

Tort, 174
Tortious Act, 175–176
Trachtman v. Anken, 182
Trust, 120–123, 127
Trust Relationship, 121–122

U
Ulcer-producer List, 34–36
Understanding Children, 193–194
Undreamed-of Roles, 6–9
Union Contract, 299–300, 302–303
Union Movement, 293–296
Unwanted Visitors, 189
Updike, John, 44
USOE, 283

V
Vacca, Richard, 181, 191
Video-taping, 29–35, 92–97
Vocational Act, 128
Volunteer Programs, 255–256
Volz, Marlin, 191

W
Walden, John, 176, 178–179, 182, 193, 203
Walkouts, 301, 302
Wallerstein, Judith, 194
Wayson, William, 80, 194
Wheeler, David, 272
Wilhelms, Fred, 49, 87, 101
Willey, Darrel, 291
Wilson, Craig, 106, 108, 118
Winters, K., 140
Witherell, Carol, 79
Woellner, Elizabeth, 23
Wood v. Strickland, 174
Working conditions, 12

Z
Zakariya, Sally Banks, 2, 4, 7, 197
Zintgraff, Paul, 52–53
Zirkel's Study, 152–153, 155, 191, 296